# CONNECTICUT: A New Guide

WILLIAM BIXBY

# Connecticut: A New Guide

CHARLES SCRIBNER'S SONS, NEW YORK

*917.46*
*B624c*

LIBRARY OF CONGRESS CATALOGING IN PUBLICATION DATA

Bixby, William.
Connecticut: A New Guide

  Bibliography: p. 376.
  1. Connecticut—Description and travel—1951—Guide-books.  I. Title.
F92.3.B59               917.46′04′4             73-20261
ISBN 0-684-13787-9

# ACKNOWLEDGMENTS

The preparation and writing of a book such as this involves many people, organizations, government agencies, and state commissions. Without their cooperation this book could not have been written. The mayors, managers, and first selectmen of the 169 towns and cities in the state have been particularly cooperative in supplying material and reading the various town stories critically and constructively. Their reviews and their colleagues' reviews of the material were invaluable in the final checking of factual information for accuracy and completeness. To them all the author extends his thanks.

No less helpful have been the Chambers of Commerce, the historical societies, the Development Commission, the Transportation Commission, and the Historical Commission—all of which were most cooperative.

Dr. Howard T. Oedel, of the History Department of Southern Connecticut State College, in New Haven, read and made many helpful suggestions and corrections to assist in the completion of the chapters on the history of the state and the Connecticut Indians. Dr. Joseph B. Hoyt, Chairman of the Department of Geography at Southern Connecticut State College, read and commented most helpfully on the chapter concerned with the topography and geology of the state. Their time, their help, and their cooperation are deeply appreciated.

There is perhaps no book of this sort that does not have at least one interested party who does more than merely gather material, help organize it, and assist in editing it. Two such people have worked indefatigably with me during the writing of this one: my wife, Susan, whose knowledge of historic and architecturally important buildings in the state proved invaluable, and Miss Beverly Anderson of Guilford, who worked on every aspect of the book, contributing her knowledge and time more than generously. To both of them, my heartfelt thanks.

All of the above is not to excuse the author from any errors found in the book. For them, if they exist, he takes full responsibility.

W. B.

The pictures in this book were supplied by the Connecticut Development Commission, William Bixby and William Bixby Jr.

# HOW TO USE THIS BOOK

The book is divided into three sections. The first deals with overall facts and history of the state as well as its physical characteristics.

The second deals with the towns and cities within the state. There are 169 towns and cities in this New England state that are self-governing. The smaller towns still have town meetings and these meetings pass on legislative matters. Such towns are governed by a Board of Selectmen. The First Selectman is the elected leader of the town. Town managers run larger communities and mayors preside over cities. There is no county government in Connecticut and the chain of governing runs directly from town or city to the state level.

The third section deals with concise information on a wide range of activities and places visitors may enjoy.

In each of the town descriptions there is a section devoted to things to see and do within that town. In many instances the appendices of the third section supply details and give those looking for some special activity a chance to survey the state's resources in his or her field at a glance. Hikers, for example, can see the appendix on hiking; those interested in art or historic houses to visit can refer to the proper appendix without reading all the town stories individually to discover where museums and houses are located.

Places open to the visiting public are listed at the conclusion of each town description (locations, hours, and known charges will be found in an appendix). There are, of course, many places to visit in a town that are not specifically open to the public. Most churches and school and college campuses, for instance, are available for discreet visitation but do not solicit visitors. The town beaches along Long Island Sound require a car sticker issued by the town. Nonresidents may, in some towns, be allowed to use the beach by paying a fee. The same is true of town parks and recreational facilities that are usually maintained for residents, but here, too, in some cases out-of-town visitors may enjoy them. Should you wish to visit or utilize such town facilities and are in doubt about the regulations, check with the town or city hall or inquire of the local police department.

Directions to state parks and forests are included in each town writeup. In the case where patches of forest are scattered about the town, either inquire locally or refer to the Connecticut map issued by the State Department of Transportation. Directions to ponds and lakes outside state parks and forests where you may fish are included in town descriptions, but where intricate directions might prove confusing, you should inquire locally. Hunting is permitted in some state forests and this information is printed in the forest description of the town. Other areas where hunting is permitted are mentioned in the town stories and you are referred to the appendix for directions and places to inquire for permits and licenses.

Inevitably there will be changes in local situations and times and charges for visitors will be altered too. The reader is advised to seek out the town clerk's office in small towns, the town manager's office in larger ones, and the city halls in the cities, for further information.

# CONTENTS

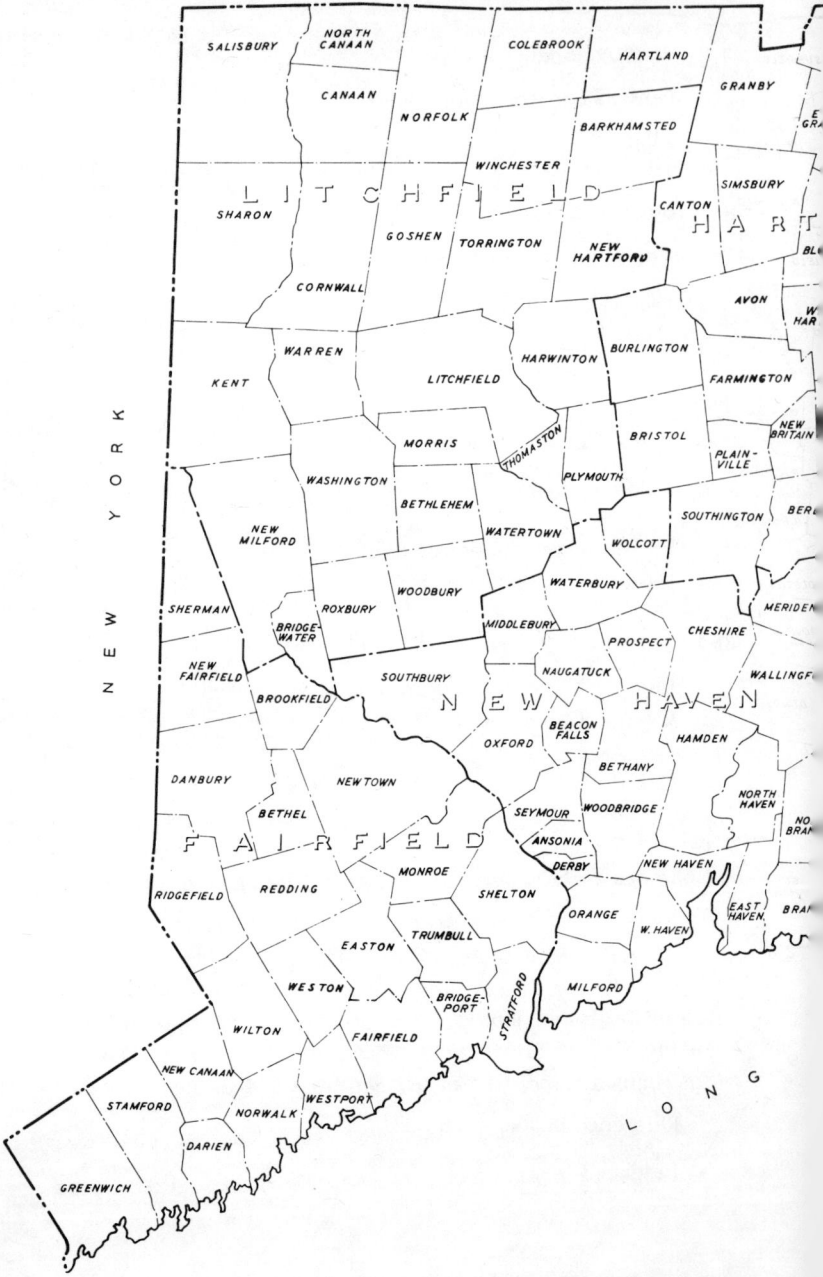

C H U S E T T S

SUFFIELD

SOMERS

STAFFORD

UNION

WOODSTOCK

THOMPSON

ENFIELD

WINDSOR LOCKS

ELLINGTON

E. WINDSOR

TOLLAND

EASTFORD

PUTNAM

WINDSOR

ORD

SO. WINDSOR

VERNON

WILLINGTON

ASHFORD

W I N D H A M

POMFRET

KILLINGLY

TOLLAND

COVENTRY

MANSFIELD

CHAPLIN

HAMPTON

BROOKLYN

EAST HARTFORD

MANCHESTER

BOLTON

ANDOVER

WINDHAM

CANTERBURY

PLAINFIELD

WETHERS-FIELD

GLASTONBURY

COLUMBIA

SCOTLAND

STERLING

ROCKY HILL

MARLBOROUGH

HEBRON

LEBANON

SPRAGUE

FRANKLIN

LISBON

VOLUNTOWN

CROMWELL

PORTLAND

E. HAMPTON

COLCHESTER

NORWICH

GRISWOLD

BOZRAH

PRESTON

M I D D L E S E X

EAST HADDAM

SALEM

MONTVILLE

NORTH STONINGTON

DURHAM

HADDAM

LEDYARD

N E W   L O N D O N

CHESTER

LYME

WATERFORD

KILLINGWORTH

DEEP RIVER

ESSEX

EAST LYME

NEW LON-DON

GROTON

STONINGTON

MADISON

GUILFORD

CLINTON

WESTBROOK

OLD SAYBROOK

OLD LYME

FISHERS ISLAND

R H O D E   I S L A N D

S L A N D   S O U N D

CONNECTICUT

# 1

# The State
# of Connecticut

# 1
# CONNECTICUT TODAY

STATISTICS AND VISITORS' INFORMATION

*Name:* Connecticut from the Algonquian word *quinnehtukqut,*
    meaning: "beside the long tidal river"—which is the Connect-
    icut River itself.
*Size:* Third smallest state (Delaware and Rhode Island are smaller);
    area: 5,009 square miles.
*Population:* 3,032,217 (1970 census); population density: 605 per
    square mile, based on total area.
*Capital:* Hartford.
*Nicknames:* Officially, "The Constitution State," but frequently
    called "The Nutmeg State."
*State Bird:* Robin.
*State Flower:* Mountain Laurel.
*State Tree:* White Oak.

Third smallest of the fifty states, Connecticut ranks number one
in per capita income. The high ranking in per capita income, plus
the fact that it is regarded by many people as the most desirable of
all states to live in, stems from three important facts: the high level
of technological development among major industries (aircraft
engines, space hardware, electronics manufacture, etc.); the location of so many insurance companies in the Hartford region; and

the proximity of the southwestern county (Fairfield) to New York City. The insurance business produces highly paid personnel and executives in all top professions move daily back and forth between Manhattan and the affluent suburbia that is lower Fairfield County. Many artists and writers live in the state and it is a well-chosen place for them, since their major market is New York City and occasional journeys there cause no great hardship. Most people in these professions live in Litchfield and Fairfield counties—the western part of the state.

The population of the state is made up of a healthy mixture of ethnic backgrounds. Italians, Germans, Poles, Swiss, and many middle-European backgrounds are represented. Blacks, however, form a very small percentage of the total population. Most immigrants came in the mid-nineteenth century when the demands for manpower in that burgeoning industrial era could not be met by the existing population. This also was the time, of course, of the great migrations from Europe to New York, the entire Atlantic seaboard, and the Midwest. The communities in Connecticut that attracted these immigrants were on the rivers, since water power drove the machinery of that day. Thus the valley towns along the Naugatuck, Quinnipiac, Quinebaug, Shetucket, and Willimantic rivers received this influx. Towns in the hills and away from manufacturing remained, quite accidentally, composed of people of English ancestry.

**Airports**

The largest airport in Connecticut is Bradley-International, served by major airlines. It is located in Windsor Locks, north of the state capital, Hartford. Limousine service is available to and from Hartford and other cities in central Connecticut. Bridgeport Municipal Airport, Tweed–New Haven Airport, and Trumbull Airport in Groton are served by smaller commercial lines. Light plane airports (some with charter facilities) are located in: Ansonia, Burlington, Chester, Danbury, East Haddam, East Windsor, Ellington, Griswold, Killingly, Madison, Marlborough, Meriden, Monroe, New Milford, Oxford, Plainville, Plymouth, Simsbury, Waterford, Windham (Willimantic), and Woodstock (2). Seaplane facilities are available at East Haddam, East Hampton, and Groton. New York airports are served by limouisine from New Haven and towns in Fairfield County.

## Rail Transportation

This is a touchy subject in Connecticut. For years, the now defunct New York, New Haven, and Hartford Railroad was in and out of financial trouble. When it went under, the Penn Central took over and did an astonishingly bad job. At this writing, the Penn Central (despite monetary injections from Washington) is also teetering on the brink of total failure. There are pressures to keep the line going at all costs. Not the least of these is the daily commuting traffic from Connecticut to New York. And somehow it *does* seem inconceivable that all rail traffic in the state will come to a full and final halt.

That being the case, let us assume that trains are running. Service to towns along the shores of Long Island Sound is reasonably good although lesser stops have been cut out. The small size of Connecticut, however, does not make this lessening of service insupportably inconvenient to the visitor. Service also is available to Hartford and north to Springfield, Massachusetts.

## Bus Transportation

This is somewhat more reliable than the railroads. At least service is more frequent and schedules more or less adhered to. There are interstate carriers, such as Greyhound and Continental Trailways, which travel to major points in the state like Hartford, New Haven, and New London.

There are also interstate carriers connecting the smaller cities within Connecticut and some of the larger towns. Arrow Line, for example, takes passengers from Hartford to northwestern Connecticut—Norfolk and Canaan, and on to Great Barrington and Stockbridge, Massachusetts, and Albany, New York, from which there are connecting lines north and west. One can also reach western Connecticut on the Arrow Line—Waterbury, Torrington, etc. The same company makes weekend trips (Friday and Sunday) between Hartford and the University of Connecticut at Storrs. "Super Service," a subsidiary of Greyhound, is based in Providence and goes to and from New London, Bridgeport, Danbury, and western Connecticut.

## Highways

Roads are extensive and always expanding, allowing access to nearly any point in the state by car. Roadside services are available on most roads and the state is so heavily populated that one is never far from a gas station or telephone. Nearly every settlement of any size at all will have at least one gas pump, if only at the local store, manned a few hours a day.

A very good highway map is available from the Department of Transportation, P.O. Drawer A, Wethersfield. It gives all major highways, state routes, and shows secondary roads, points of interest, and state-owned recreation areas.

On the turnpikes, the signs stating "Food—Phone—Gas— Lodging" in rural areas, and "Travel Services next (3) exits" in urban areas, mean that there is a restaurant within $1\frac{1}{2}$ miles of the exit, a public outdoor pay telephone within $\frac{1}{2}$ mile, gas stations open 24 hours* within 1 mile and those open less than 24 hours within a $\frac{1}{2}$ mile of the exit, plus a motel with at least 10 units within 3 miles of the exit.

## Accommodations

Rates vary widely depending mostly on quality, location, and whether there is a "brand name" involved. The Connecticut Development Commission has published a fairly comprehensive list of hotel and motels, by towns, giving average rates. (Its address is 210 Washington Street, Hartford, Connecticut.) An average minimum rate comes out around $13.50, although there are cheaper and more expensive rooms available.

## Laws

There are, obviously, as many laws as legislators have ideas they've been able to sell. There are even some of the antiquated "Blue

* These hours are subject to change due to the energy crises.

Laws" left over from Connecticut's earliest General Assemblies and never revised or rescinded. Only those of most interest to the visitor are briefly described here. Of course, with annual sessions of the legislature, these are subject to change—and probably to numerical, if not qualitative, increase.

The speed limit is posted on all passable roads. The law in Connecticut specifies that one may not operate a motor vehicle "at a rate of speed greater than a reasonable speed." This means, essentially, to obey the posted speed limit. On turnpikes, maximum speed is 70, although 60 is the posted speed, and anything over this is left to the discretion of the lurking state trooper. On other roads, statutory "absolute maximum speed limit" is 60, and posted limits run from 25 to 50.*

There is no passing on the right in Connecticut; the left lane on four-lane roads is for passing. On secondary roads and state routes, passing zones are shown by a single dashed line or a solid line, and a dashed line on your side. Two continuous double lines means nobody passes anybody. Major difficulties can be encountered by ignoring the 25 mph school-zone limit and by passing a school bus that has its red lights flashing.

Liquor laws are probably even more confusing than traffic laws and more subject to change. An interesting example is the law concerning women and their place at a bar. Prior to 1967, a woman could sit a distance of three feet or more from a bar; in 1967 a law was passed making it legal for her to sit but not stand at a bar; immediately bar stools were removed from many establishments. In 1969 Puritanism was overridden and women were allowed to stand at a bar.

The drinking age was lowered to eighteen in 1972 and many proprietors require that the "younger person" present adequate identification—either a majority card, which has a picture, or two other types of identification. There are no restrictions on what the eighteen-year-olds may drink.

There are, however, restrictions on what is available, depending on what kind of license an establishment has purchased. A cafe can serve liquor, wine, and beer. A tavern can serve only beer. Restaurants have three types of licenses—beer only, beer and wine, or beer, wine, and liquor. Hotels can have either a beer

* Speed limits are subject to change due to the energy crises.

license or a liquor license, allowing them to serve anything. Grocery stores are permitted to sell only packaged beer, no wine or liquor. A drugstore can have a beer license or a complete license allowing liquor and wine, also all packaged. A "package store" has a complete license.

Drinking hours have a hangover flavor from Puritan times, though these too are changing. Establishments serving liquor or beer and wine may be open Monday through Thursday 9:00 A.M. to 1:00 A.M., Friday and Saturday 9:00 A.M. to 2:00 A.M., and Sunday, 12:00 noon to 11:00 P.M., except taverns, which must close on Sunday. Some towns are "dry." These do not allow the sale of liquor at all, packaged or by the glass, although drinking *is* allowed. Some communities have passed an ordinance prohibiting the sale of liquor by the drink on Sunday. Restaurants in these communities are usually closed that day.

Package stores are open Monday through Saturday, 9:00 A.M. to 8:00 P.M. (There is always someone in the legislature who wants the hours extended; hence there is always a bill to that effect in process. But package-store owners recently had the hours reduced to the above schedule and seem happy.) Grocery stores and drugstores, though open later, can sell beer (and liquor) only until 8:00 P.M.

# 2
# HISTORY

The colonization of Connecticut by the English began in 1633. By that time the Plymouth colony (first English settlement in New England) had been established thirteen years. New Netherlands (New York) had been occupied by the Dutch for nine years while the Massachusetts Bay colony was in its third year of existence.

Plymouth, of course, was settled primarily for religious reasons. The motives for the establishment of Massachusetts Bay Colony combined religious discontent with a strong desire for trade. The entire Dutch venture in the New World was based on trade.

So far as is known, the Dutch explorer and navigator Adriaen Block was the first European to see and report on Connecticut. In 1614, he sailed into Long Island Sound from the western end and went as far east as Rhode Island. It is believed that on this voyage he discovered and sailed up the Connecticut River as far as the Enfield Rapids. In the following years, until 1632, Dutch traders developed a lively business along the shores of the Sound and for short distances up the rivers. During this time also, a few hardy English explorers from the Massachusetts Bay colony and the Plymouth Company had penetrated the wilderness, coming overland from Massachusetts or by sea, inspecting Narragansett Bay in Rhode Island, the offshore islands including what now is Block Island, and so along to the mouth of the Connecticut River. They too were hoping to develop trade with the Indians.

In the year 1633, the Dutch bought a strip of land from Indians on the site of what now is Hartford and built a trading post. That same year, a group of men from Plymouth established one upriver from Hartford where the Farmington River empties into the Connecticut. This was to become Windsor.

In this probing for trade, the Dutch bought their land from the warlike Pequots (see Chapter 3) in southeast Connecticut, who claimed to have conquered the river valley territory. The English bought their land from Indians who had lived on that land for generations. This difference of purchase was used later by the English to justify the legitimacy of their claim. In fact, at that time, Massachusetts Bay Colony leaders believed that, under the terms of their charter, they had sovereignty over all English settlements in the Connecticut wilderness. Acting on this supposed authority they attempted to issue orders and rules from Boston.

In September of 1634, another English settlement, under a Captain John Oldham, was founded downriver from the Dutch trading post. It became Wethersfield.

By 1635, what was to be Hartford had been established. Thus there were three English settlements clustered upriver from the sea and, in the middle, the Dutch trading post, called the House of Good Hope. All the towns erected palisades or wooden stockades to protect them in case of Indian attack. They did not fear the local Indians so much as the Pequots, who had warred on the local Indians since their arrival in the late sixteenth century from the western mountain territory of the Mohicans. All three English settlements were acting as independent units at first but their isolation in the wilderness and their worry about Pequot raids brought them to some form of cooperative effort in plans for their defense.

Late in 1635, the entire pattern of western migration from Massachusetts—by sea or land—was upset with the arrival of the ship *Abigail* bearing John Winthrop, Jr., among others, who held a deed from the Earl of Warwick claiming a great swath of land that included Connecticut. Winthrop had been instructed, by the "lords and gentlemen" who were concerned, to sail to New England and set up a relatively lavish outpost for their possible occupation. It also was thought to have been a possible place of refuge for Oliver Cromwell in the event that he had to flee the country. Winthrop's claim through the Earl of Warwick included the existing three towns and it threw into doubt the assumed jurisdiction of Massachusetts over Connecticut. For months, Winthrop and the Bay Colony leaders conferred in secrecy trying to reach agreement. When they did, Winthrop's claim was admitted, but Massachusetts settlers were allowed to continue going to the settlements already existing. Winthrop himself went with his party by sea to found Saybrook and build a fort there, completely ignoring Dutch claims to the spot. The site was chosen as much for trading potential as anything else. Thus the fourth town in the wilderness came into being.

Until Winthrop arrived, no settlement in Connecticut had any piece of paper from any English authority giving it a claim to its land. The leaders had bought it from the Indians, but the English Crown did not recognize the Indians' claim to it (a habit that European powers fell into all over the globe as they overrode primitive societies).

In 1637, the long-feared trouble with Indians did break out. A Pequot raiding party under their chief, or sachem, Sassacus, attacked Wethersfield and several settlers were killed. Two girls were taken captive. This overt hostility came from the Pequots' fear of greater encroachment by more English settlers on lands that they themselves had conquered. It was an ill-fated move on the part of the Pequots. The three towns, acting in concert, sent a force south and the result was their defeat in the largest battle fought in Connecticut's history (see Chapter 3).

During this trying time in Connecticut, English Puritans were having their difficulties at home. Opposition to their desired reforms of the Church of England had increased. Charles I was becoming more rigid in his outlook and the tide of emigrants from the home country increased. Most headed for Boston to get their bearings. As a consequence Boston and the surrounding towns were becoming crowded.

In 1638, a group of English immigrants arrived in Boston and left shortly to found New Haven under the leadership of Puritan John Davenport. They had found Massachusetts too "liberal" for their religious taste and wanted to create a pure theocracy. Henry Whitfield arrived in 1639, to found Guilford. The year before

Guilford was settled the leaders of the Hartford colony had begun to feel they were without a government. The Warwick patent described lands and claimed sovereignty but gave no ordered measures for governing the area. Reliance on Massachusetts Bay for day-to-day operation was obviously impractical. So Connecticut found itself (as did Rhode Island) in the peculiar position of being relatively independent. All other colonies that the English had established in America had charters laying down the laws of government specifically. And it was understood that they were under the sovereignty of the English government and the authority of the Board of Trade. This board, in England, began almost at once to complain about the loose nature of the bond between Connecticut and the Crown. In Connecticut, the result of these complaints was the realization that unless the three towns of Hartford, Windsor, and Wethersfield joined themselves under some formal governing body and set of laws, the English government would force a governor and his laws upon them. Leaders in the three towns met and drew up the original Constitution of Connecticut, calling it the Fundamental Orders. They were signed and became effective on January 14, 1639. The Orders established the supremacy of the General Court over town authority, provided for the election of officials and the raising of revenue through taxes. There was no mention of loyalty to the Crown.

Many claims have been made for the Fundamental Orders of Connecticut, the highest being that they formed the first governing document that admitted that the free consent of the citizens was the source of all governmental legitimacy. Such weighty historical evaluations came later, however. From 1639, when the Orders were adopted, until 1662, when Charles II issued the Connecticut Charter, the Fundamental Orders served as the sole basis of government. It is not known who wrote them, whether a committee, a small select group, or one man. Their precepts, however, are so lucidly stated that the accolade for composing them is traditionally given to Roger Ludlow of Windsor, who was a trained lawyer from Oxford.

By the time the Connecticut Charter was issued in 1662, there were seventeen settlements in Connecticut, and interestingly enough all but one, Farmington, were located either on the shores of Long Island Sound or the Connecticut River. For during this time, trade was what kept the settlements alive and growing. The principal items they had to send to England, Boston, or New York were tobacco, agricultural products, furs, and timber.

The Hartford colony of three towns had grown and absorbed others as they came into being. The New Haven colony had also expanded but was less successful economically. That colony had its own covenant, or fundamental orders, which established a theocracy and drew all its guiding laws from biblical sources. To the dismay of New Haven leaders, the 1662 charter included them in the Connecticut colony. Charles II had a rather vague idea of the geography and the charter describes the territory of the river colony (hereafter the Connecticut colony) as from Massachusetts south to the sea and from Narragansett Bay west to the "South Seas"—which meant the Pacific Ocean. And that certainly included New Haven. Unable to mount an effective protest, the New Haven colonists saw that they either had to join the Hartford group or risk being taken over by New York. The New Haven leaders reluctantly chose the former course and joined the Connecticut colony in 1665.

### King Philip's War

Following the destruction of the Pequot tribe in 1637 the Mohegan sachem, Uncas, remained on the side of the whites. His warlike tendencies found expression in attacks on other Connecticut Indian tribes and Rhode Island Narragansetts from his home base in Fort Shantok, near Norwich. He captured and killed the Narragansett sachem, Miantonomo, in one attack on his forces near Fort Shantok and the Narragansetts never forgave him. They also began to distrust all court decisions of the whites—which somehow came out favoring the white side of any dispute. In Massachusetts, the Indian-white relationship was little better. The wise sachem, Massasoit, of the Wampanoags in eastern Massachusetts, counseled peace for many years but he died in 1662. His second son, Philip, became sachem of that tribe.

Throughout New England, English settlements spread and as they spread the whites acted less and less like brothers and more like rulers. By the mid-1670s the uneasiness was general. The incident that ignited the war, according to some historians, was the trial and execution of three Wampanoag Indians for the alleged murder of a Christian Indian.

The war that followed was, in effect, the last attempt of the Indian tribes of New England to throw off the rule of the whites. It was doomed from the start, since by that time the white settlers could field some 16,000 men while the most the Indians could muster in Massachusetts, Rhode Island, and Connecticut was about 3,500. In Connecticut, there were many alarms, marches, and countermarches. Uncas and his Mohegans fought on the white man's side—for Uncas's dream of allying with whites and so building an Indian empire from defeated tribes was still strong. The white troops frequently were ambushed in Massachusetts and Rhode Island. Connecticut troops never were, primarily because Uncas and his men knew the Indian method of fighting and forewarned Connecticut's patrols when an ambush threatened. And the only major damage done in Connecticut was the burning of Simsbury (see Simsbury, in Part II). When the war effectively ended in 1676, King Philip was dead and many of the surviving warriors from the various tribes fled westward into New York. From that time forward, Indian threats never amounted to more than individual problems with recalcitrant survivors.

### Boundaries and Jurisdiction

Connecticut had never had close ties or frequent communication with England or any arm of English government save the Board of Trade. The charter of Charles II provided the basis for its independence and the colony guarded it jealously. In New York, the governor, Edmund Andros, acting under the grant from the Duke of York, claimed that the area included in New York took in all land west of the Connecticut River. Andros came once to claim this land, which would have shattered the Connecticut colony, taken the New Haven towns, and effectively ended the career of the colony before it had really begun.

He threatened to attack the fort at Saybrook and his ships lay offshore for several days while he made his demands. It is reported he ran up the English flag to give his argument force and the Saybrook defenders simply ran up their English flag to state their legitimacy. Andros retreated. He was, according to historians, an authoritarian eager to acquire as much power as possible.

In England, worry over the French in Canada and a possible invasion of the New England colonies from that quarter made the Crown look for some means of uniting the separate New England colonies and producing a joint front in case such a French attack came. Charles II died in 1685, and his son, James II, was turning out to be an authoritarian who wanted to control everyone absolutely. He decreed that Sir Edmund Andros was to be governor of all the New England colonies. It was not a wise move.

## The Charter Oak

Connecticut appeared to submit to this royal decree and Andros arrived in October of 1687 in Hartford. Governor Treat, of Connecticut, called together as many members of the Assembly as could be hastily summoned and Andros demanded the charter. Its physical transfer would mark the end of the independence Connecticut had long enjoyed. In midafternoon of that fateful day, Governor Treat began a long speech. Andros waited through it, not quite certain what it was all about. As the afternoon ended and the October darkness fell, candles were brought. Treat talked on. At length the Connecticut governor finished and Andros called for the charter. It was brought—but no sooner did it arrive than all the candles were extinguished. Someone passed the charter out the window of the meeting hall and there one Captain Wadsworth, according to the legend that grew around the incident, took the charter and hid it in a hollow of a great oak tree not far off. No one could explain the matter to Andros's satisfaction. Everyone apologized. All submitted to his authority. All were terribly sorry that the candles had gone out and that the charter had disappeared. Andros left in a huff. But the charter remained in Connecticut.

His rule as governor of the New England colonies was short-lived. During the time he did govern, however, he displayed his authoritative nature, and among other unpopular pronouncements decreed that all land titles purchased from the Indians were worthless.

In England in 1688, James II's tyranny became more than the English could bear and the "Bloodless Revolution" of 1688–89 occurred. It amounted to James II fleeing to the continent and William and Mary of the Netherlands coming to rule in England (Mary being the daughter of James II by his first wife). Andros shortly was displaced as governor and Connecticut reverted to its former charter, which had been preserved.

## The Eighteenth Century

Despite vigorous trading, at which they were adept, Connecticut merchants, save in a few instances, led a hand-to-mouth existence. The basic item of export, agricultural products, was not in demand in England or on the continent and so the West Indies became the principal focus of trading efforts. Shipbuilding flourished on the shores of the Sound and up the rivers leading to it. But farmers soon discovered that it was difficult to make a living from Connecticut's soil. This, and the fact that the farming practices were destructive to the environment, kept the colony on a hand-to-mouth existence.

Gradually the geographical and political outline of what was to be the state of Connecticut took shape. Hartford and New Haven shared the honor of being the state capital as the Assembly met alternately in each city. Yale College, originally the Collegiate School, began holding classes first in Killingworth and later in Saybrook. In 1716 the college formally moved to New Haven and soon became known as Yale College in honor of an absentee benefactor. In 1709 the first printing press in Connecticut was in operation in New London. The able merchants, like Jonathan Trumbull, made fortunes and here and there mansions were built to commemorate the wealth. A poor but usable network of roads made traveling between the cities and New York and Boston less hazardous. Inns, taverns, coaches, a growing number of homes, and a few industrial plants such as sawmills and gristmills gave the colonists the feeling that they were on their way toward founding a civilized state.

Unfortunately for Connecticut, England would not permit man-ufacturing to develop in the colony. The powerful guilds would not issue licenses to permit production of many essential items— so Connecticut had to buy finished goods from the mother country. Relations with England sometimes became strained—but in times of crisis, Connecticut leaders pledged the colony's allegiance while continuing on an increasingly independent course.

Currency was scarce and the former crude method of barter gave way to a system of credits: farmer to village store to city merchant to exporter or importer in Boston or New York. Not until 1737 did the first coined currency appear in Connecticut: the Higley penny made in Simsbury by Samuel Higley from copper in a deposit found in what is now East Granby.

During this period and until the Revolutionary War, Connecti-cut supplied men for various wars that England found herself engaged in on this continent. All of them were against the French and whatever Indian allies the French had at the time. The cause for concern was real enough. In Europe, the French and English were perennially fighting and the quarrels spilled over into the New World. An obvious route for French invasion of the New England colonies was down the long valleys leading from the Canadian border: the Champlain valley and that of the Connecti-cut River, which offered a highway for troop movement down through Massachusetts into Connecticut. King William's War occurred in the late seventeenth century, Queen Anne's War in the early years of the eighteenth century, and King George's War in the fourth decade of the century. In the latter conflict (known in Europe as the War of the Austrian Succession) Connecticut troops and other colonial contingents sailed north and attacked the mighty French fortress at Louisburg on Cape Breton Island. The fort fell, only to be restored to French possession when the treaty ending that war in Europe was signed. The return of Louisburg to the French did not sit well with the Connecticut men who had fought to take it. The question of why Connecticut men should fight English wars occurred then and may well have created first thoughts about independence from England.

The entire struggle of the French to dominate the American

continent came to a conclusion with the French and Indian War, which involved Connecticut troops from 1755 to 1760.

The backbone of Connecticut's economy through the first three-quarters of the century was agriculture. Tobacco in the Connecticut River valley was a valuable crop. Pork and cattle, hemp, maize, flax, and vegetables all were raised and sold. Some towns specialized in a single crop. Wethersfield, for example, took to raising onions—and became known as Onion Town. Mulberry trees were imported in 1760 and silk manufacture flourished for fifty years, ending when a blight hit the mulberry trees. Wheat fell victim to a blight also and it, too, passed from the list of Connecticut products.

Industry began with gristmills, first to supply local citizens and then to sell surplus meal abroad. Iron was discovered in the western Connecticut towns of Salisbury, Sharon, and Kent and blast furnaces glowed twenty-four hours a day turning out refined metal for the needed arms and farm tools. Copper was mined in East Granby. Local marble, limestone, and granite made their appearance and brick making provided a building material, other than wood, for houses.

Throughout the pre-Revolutionary War years of the eighteenth century, Connecticut was growing. In population it climbed from 30,000 in 1701 to 197,842 in 1774. Westward expansion into the Susquehanna Valley of Pennsylvania—western lands claimed by Connecticut under its charter—relieved some of the stresses of population.

England increased taxes and the hated Stamp Act went into effect in November 1765. It required purchase of stamps to be placed on all legal and business documents, newspapers, and pamphlets—and even playing cards. This unpopular act helped to create the radical organization Sons of Liberty, which fought for its nonobservance and repeal. It also brought trade to a halt and British merchants finally got it repealed in Parliament. Other onerous taxes followed, however, and the political divisiveness produced Tories or Loyalists as opposed to the independence-minded Sons of Liberty or Whigs. In other colonies, the same divisions were appearing. And in July of 1774, the Connecticut Assembly met and chose three delegates to the First Continental

Congress: Roger Sherman, Silas Deane, and Eliphalet Dyer. The aim of the Congress was to protest the loss of liberty as Englishmen at the hands of the English government and the onerous tax policy that was injuring the economy. Connecticut, with all the other colonies, stood on the brink of war.

**The Revolutionary War**

When the break with England came, touched off by the Battle of Lexington and the famed "shot heard around the world," Connecticut men who favored independence literally dropped what they were doing on hearing the news and marched away to Boston. Singly, in small groups, or as hastily mustered militia, they walked or rode to the support of the neighbor colony, whose citizens shared Connecticut's desire for independence. Israel Putnam, plowing his land in Pomfret, heard the news and left his horses in the field, setting out for Boston without a backward glance. Boys of ten or twelve became drummers or fifers. Men of military age took rifle, powder, and shot and left dinners on tables. All told, more than 3,500 Connecticut men rushed to Massachusetts' aid.

During the years of the war, Connecticut served primarily as a base and a supplier of war materials. The men of military age went off to fight. Those who remained behind worked the iron furnaces of Salisbury, Sharon, and Kent, producing muskets and cannon and shot. Windsor homes, according to legend, were bereft of timepieces because the metal weights used to run their clocks were all melted down and made into bullets. The town of Litchfield, safe from coastal raids in northwest Connecticut, became a warehouse point. Governor Trumbull, of Lebanon, set up a supply headquarters in his retail store next to his home in that town and the small red building (still standing) became known as the War Office.

Tory support for the Crown was widespread and inevitably there were clashes between neighbors, between groups of Whigs and groups of Tories. In particular, some of the western towns of the state had more Tories than patriots. On the shore in Fairfield County towns, active aid went to the British who took Long Island

and held it as well as controlling the Sound with their naval power. In time, some Tories went to Long Island and led raiding parties back among their former friends and neighbors. It is difficult today to state with assurance which group was acting traitorously. Of course, the patriots felt the Tories were traitors and as the war tides turned in favor of the patriot cause, men and families who had committed themselves to a loyalist position found they had to abandon home and all their goods and flee, either to Canada, the West Indies, or back to England.

The General Assembly itself was divided at first. But Governor Trumbull, a dedicated patriot, managed finally to get Whigs or patriots elected and major divisiveness within the Assembly ceased.

Early in 1775, a Connecticut-sponsored expedition was mounted against Fort Ticonderoga on the New York side of Lake Champlain. The immediate reason for the mission was to procure cannon for the defense of Boston—the patriots then being short of heavy armament. Money and supplies were raised in Hartford by an unofficial group (the Assembly had yet to meet, and time was short). On April 29, 1775, a Captain Edward Mott and less than twenty men set out. A message had been sent ahead to Ethan Allen to organize some of his marauding Green Mountain Boys. Allen, himself a Connecticut native, did just that and when the Connecticut troops arrived a predawn attack was planned on the large fort. Matters became complicated by the arrival of Benedict Arnold (not yet a turncoat as history knows him) who spoke with the authority of the Committee of Safety in Massachusetts. He, Arnold, had military rank and authority to lead the expedition. Allen and Arnold argued and reached a compromise just before the attack. Since Allen's men would not be led by or fight for anyone but him, the de facto leadership remained with Allen. But Arnold marched on a par with him at the head of the rag-tag force. The men embarked in dilapidated boats in the dark hours before dawn on May 10, 1775. Fortunately for the patriots, Ticonderoga was in a sad state of disrepair. The garrison of British troops expected no attack and when Allen, Mott, Arnold, and their men arrived in the darkness they entered the fort through a great gap in one wall. Taken totally by surprise, the garrison surrendered—its commander roused and hauled out into the chill air in his nightshirt. When the befuddled British commander asked by what authority the patriots had taken this action, the legendary Allen is reported to have roared, "In the name of the great Jehovah and the Continental Congress." Which answer seemed to satisfy the shivering British commander.

Farther up the lake, Crown Point was also fortified and occupied by a British garrison. Colonel Seth Warner, of Roxbury, Connecticut, led a force there and repeated Allen's success at Ticonderoga. The cannon were hauled to Boston—no mean feat in that time when roads were very nearly nonexistent.

While the cannon were of immediate importance, the fact is that by neutralizing Ticonderoga and Crown Point, the Connecticut-inspired expedition denied the British access to the lake and the approach by land down from Canada. Psychologically, the campaign gave all the colonies a lift, for it was one of the first major successes of the war.

At the Battle of Bunker Hill, in June of 1775, General Putnam and Captain Knowlton led Connecticut troops in that initial blooding. Actually fought on Breed's Hill, the battle was a critical event. It became a point of no return in the overall conflict. The British suffered heavy losses but won the field. It served notice that the colonial militia could and would fight. And it was in this battle that Connecticut's General Putnam contributed the phrase to American folklore about "not firing until you can see the whites of their eyes."

Connecticut's position between Boston and New York, and the absence of strategic targets within the colony, helped turn it into a supply depot for the Continental Army. The leaders of Connecticut met in Governor Trumbull's store in Lebanon nearly 1,200 times to plan shipping, raise troops, and discuss the supply of arms and food to the fighting troops. Couriers, awaiting orders and dispatches, often sat on the rude counter and swung their spurred heels against the planking beneath. Those scarred planks are now on view in the Connecticut Historical Society Museum.

Earlier than most colonies, Connecticut called for independence from England and the formation of a new nation. The Continental Congress, meeting in mid-1776 (fourteen months after the outbreak at Lexington), finally drew up a resolution calling for independence. It had been anticipated by many Connecticut preachers and political leaders. Governor Trumbull himself had written, "Affairs are hastening fast to a Crisis, and the approaching Campaign will, in all Probability, determine forever, the Fate of *America.*" When the Declaration of Independence was drawn up, Connecticut's four representatives to the convention signed it eagerly: Samuel Huntington, Roger Sherman, William Williams, and Oliver Wolcott.

### Battles in Connecticut

In actuality, Connecticut only experienced minor battles and skirmishes with the British. Towns along the shore feared landings from British ships, which controlled Long Island Sound. And after the British occupied Long Island itself, the fear intensified. The General Assembly directed that small garrisons of men be placed at the most likely points of attack. What came, at first, was a series of British raids with two goals in mind: provisions and nuisance value. The need for provisions was real enough, however, and several towns were raided, particularly along the shores of Fairfield County in the southwest corner of the state. In these, the British frequently were helped by Tories who led small raiding parties ashore and pointed out barns and fields where grain and cattle were to be found.

Eager but ill-equipped patriots set out in fleets of small boats to intercept British supply ships and smaller warships as they sailed in the Sound at night. On one occasion a fleet of whaleboats filled with zealous patriots rowed across the Sound, dragged the boats to the Atlantic side, launched them, and rowed down the coast to stage a counterraid on a British encampment.

In April of 1777, General Howe dispatched General Tryon with some 2,000 men and artillery to attack Danbury, a storage and warehouse point for patriot arms and supplies. The troops landed in Westport and marched inland, spending the night of the twenty-fifth–twenty-sixth in Weston. Alarmed citizens guessed the mission and word reached Danbury early on the twenty-sixth that Tryon was on his way. Defense was impossible as only about 250 militia could be rounded up in time. Tryon took the town. Tory houses were marked so they would not be destroyed but many patriot homes and barns went up in flames. General Tryon, ensconced comfortably in the Nehemiah Dibble house on South Street, waited for his troops to finish the job. In their search, however, the troops found stores of rum and they set about consuming it. Tryon began to worry. His soldiers were drunk and the American militia, he feared, was gathering unseen on the road to the south, which he had to travel to return to the ships. He ordered his troops out of Danbury and hurried southward.

His fears were realized as some 600 men under Benedict Arnold and General Wooster blocked his way. There were rear-guard actions and a stand made in Ridgefield. For a time it appeared the Americans had cut off and would capture the entire British force. But British marines, driving inland from the shore, turned the tide and the Redcoats reached their ships. Not, however, without suffering enough casualties to make them more cautious in the future.

General Tryon was not finished in Connecticut. He raided Greenwich and, since his men outnumbered the available militia under General Putnam, "won" the engagement and accomplished his objective, which was to destroy a salt works.

Next, with other commanders, Tryon attacked New Haven. The avowed purpose was to divert Washington in New York but an element of retaliation for privateering raids on British ships was always present. Men of the towns of East Haven, West Haven, and New Haven, combined with Yale students, formed the defense of the center of New Haven. Some American artillery was also available and that spirited group delayed the British advances, so that by the time the center of town was gained, Tryon again worried about his line of retreat. In return for not burning New Haven, the British were promised a safe exit, which they promptly made. Going to Fairfield, General Tryon landed his troops there and burned over 200 buildings. He repeated this performance at Norwalk, destroying more than 250 buildings and five ships.

The most brutal battle in Connecticut occurred in New London and Groton, across New London harbor. Thirty-two British ships appeared on September 6, 1781 and a force of about 1,700 men disembarked. Part of the force attacked Fort Trumbull in New London, which was undermanned. Benedict Arnold—now a turncoat—led the British troops in the New London attack. He knew Fort Trumbull was designed to repel attack only from the sea, so he ordered his men ashore up the harbor and they approached the rear of the badly defended fort. It fell almost immediately and the British began burning buildings. They destroyed shipping and supplies, and when the wind shifted, nearly all of central New London went up in flames.

Across the harbor, Fort Griswold came under attack by 800 veteran British troops who stormed the strong defense. Their leaders had demanded that the patriot forces surrender but Colonel Ledyard, commanding the fort, refused. The British took heavy losses in overcoming the fort but when they overran it Ledyard called for his men to surrender. He himself surrendered his sword to a British officer, who immediately ran him through with it. The British troops rioted and massacred over 80 Americans who had thrown down their arms. A wagon bearing American wounded from the fray got out of control and plummeted down the steep hillside facing the harbor, killing more Americans.

In the last months of the war, the British were vitally engaged elsewhere and the attacks on Connecticut ceased. In April 1783 all the colony celebrated an end to eight years of war. The leaders who had guided the colony through the war knew, however, that much work lay ahead. Connecticut had to become part of a new nation.

### Connecticut in an Emerging Nation

The end of the war brought many problems to Connecticut. Like the other former colonies, Connecticut was operating under a heavy debt. Paper money issued by the colony became worth not much more than the paper itself—and bore out the then popular phrase "not worth a Continental." The patrician and very conservative government realized that the war taxes and laws were honored now more in the breach than the observance, so they repealed them. And there was the entire question of a central government. Delegates were chosen to represent Connecticut in the Annapolis Convention of 1786 and the Constitutional Convention held in Philadelphia in 1787. Roger Sherman, Oliver Ellsworth, and William Samuel Johnson were selected. In Connecticut there was great debate about the desirability of a strong central government—as there was in many other regions. All of Connecticut's delegates returned from Philadelphia convinced that the newly drawn constitution of a federal government ought to be accepted. After much discussion among Connecticut leaders and assemblymen, it was. Roger Sherman, at the signing of the Constitution, had the unique distinction of being the only man who had signed all the important documents creating the United States: the Articles of Association of 1774, the Declaration of Independence, the Articles of Confederation, and the Constitution. Connecticut ratified the Constitution in 1788 and became the fifth state in the new Union to do so.

The ruling (and practically speaking, only) political party then was composed of the same men from leading families who had "run" the colony and the war effort. They were known as Federalists and for several decades ruled without opposition of any serious nature. Following the war, this ruling party (with counterparts in other colonies) gradually reinstated theocratic measures, to the annoyance of the backsliders who either had joined other sects like the Baptists, Anglicans, or Quakers or lapsed into secularity. And such was the rule of the Federalists that many Connecticut citizens migrated to Vermont and into the Western Reserve lands long ago claimed by the colony under the old charter which, with a dreamlike quality, fixed the western border of Connecticut on the shores of the Pacific Ocean.

This emigration from Connecticut cleared out many dissidents and malcontents, in the view of the theocratic Federalists. They had been upset since 1740, when a revival and reform movement called the "Great Awakening" had swept the colony and reduced the power of the theocratic leaders. The subsequent emigration partially restored that power and old Puritan conformism got a new lease on life. It set the pattern of acceptable behavior for 150 years.

**The War of 1812**

No New England state wanted the War of 1812. With trade picking up after the Revolutionary War and some measure of prosperity returning, the taking on of England again seemed to them the height of folly. So strongly did Connecticut feel about this that the Assembly declared a federal draft law unconstitutional and forbade federal officers to recruit around Hartford. Leaders referred to the war contemptuously as "Mr. Madison's War" and the governor refused to allow Connecticut militia to serve outside the state. In general, of course, the war was a naval one. Trading vessels from Connecticut became privateers and any British merchant ship was regarded as their fair prey—with the attendant loot, if all went well. There were only two British attacks on Connecticut towns. In April of 1814 the British sailed up the Connecticut River, landing marines at what presently is Essex. Some small ships, a sail loft, and a number of houses were burned. In that same year, on August 9, a British fleet appeared off the shores of Stonington and a more serious battle ensued. The British commander, Captain Thomas Hardy, warned the citizens of Stonington that he was going to attack and burn the town and advised them to get out. Thus irritated, the Stonington citizens decided to stay and fight. First they set tar barrels afire to alert militia who were stationed some distance away. Then they manned their artillery: two eighteen-pound guns and a four-pounder. A British force tried to land on the ninth and again on the tenth but a militia regiment under Colonel William Randolph turned them back. The British then contented themselves with bombarding the community. All told, according to an eyewitness, sixty tons of cannonballs fell on the town and the Stonington artillery returned the fire. The American casualties amounted to one wounded while the British suffered many casualties. One ship was severely damaged and the British finally withdrew. That engagement inspired the line, "It cost the King ten thousand pounds to have a dash at Stonington." The two eighteen-pounders are still in Stonington—and still pointing toward the sea.

## Into the Industrial Age

The War of 1812 brought almost a complete halt to the expanding trade that was helping Connecticut to its economic feet. The British blockade of Long Island Sound had been effective. When the Treaty of Ghent was signed on Christmas Eve of 1814, Connecticut citizens were immensely relieved. They had not liked the war in the first place, but at least it was over. The great age of trade for the Connecticut River towns, however, was ended and what survived was centered in the shore ports. Whaling blossomed as a business in New London and ships from Stonington, Stamford, and New Haven sought the fur of seals in far places and the oil of whales, which then was lighting the world's lamps.

Far more important to the future of Connecticut, however, was the rise of industry spurred by ingenious inventions and shrewd Yankee marketing. In the decades of the nineteenth century, Connecticut towns became famous for particular products: Danbury produced hats; Waterbury and Torrington manufactured brass products; Thomaston produced clocks; Meriden, silver, and so on and on.

Shortly after the War of 1812, New Haven, still feeling subordinate to Hartford, launched the famous Farmington Canal project, which was to be a substitute Connecticut River and tap the rich raw materials to the north. The Erie Canal had opened and been proven a huge success, so New Haven investors went heavily into the canal that was to reach into Massachusetts. Construction proceeded northward through Hamden, Cheshire, Southington, Bristol, Plainville, Farmington, Avon, Simsbury, East Granby, Granby, and Suffield. It opened in 1828 and within a few years, disasters in the form of leaks, sabotage, and dike failures put the whole expensive dream into history books. The investors went broke. The future of all canals, of course, was finally decided by the appearance of the railroads.

Hartford, in those years, began its insurance industry and worked so hard at it that today some forty insurance company headquarters are established there. New Haven found economic revival in mass-production techniques and the arrival of Eli

Whitney to exploit them. He set up an arms-manufacturing plant, and arms became one of several major industries in that city.

When the Civil War came, Connecticut sent its sons to the south with those of other northern states, and Connecticut industry became one of the leading factors in overwhelming the Confederacy. The repeating rifle, developed by Christopher Miner Spencer, of Windsor, was finally forced through, past the resistance of the ordnance experts in the Union Army, and came into the field in the late years of the war. It prompted the Confederates who encountered it to remark, "The Yanks load on Sunday for the rest of the week."

By the time the Civil War was over, the pattern of skilled industries had become a hallmark of Connecticut. And the state absorbed the flood of immigrants from Europe during the following decades, ending for all time the dominance of the "leading families" and the history of Connecticut as a stronghold of Anglo-Saxon citizenry. Today, all the towns and cities, save the most remote, are made up of a healthy mixture of ethnic origins. Aircraft, aerospace, electronics, watches, delicately wrought silver, and many other products help give the state its number one ranking in per capita income.

Over those nineteenth-century years and up to the present, Connecticut laws have tended to be conservative in the view of many citizens. If the history of the state is any guide, Connecticut will move with all due deliberation, but it *will* move and, as frequently has happened, surprise many people by approving liberating legislation while maintaining a very conservative countenance.

# 3
# INDIANS

In 1614, when Adriaen Block, the Dutch explorer, sailed up the Connecticut River he came upon a large encampment of Indians, well fortified and apparently on their home ground. These were later called Podunks, though Block for some unknown reason called them Nawaas. It was the first reported contact of whites with what were to be called the "savages" in all the early records.

The meeting was peaceful. Block then sailed back down the river and on eastward to Narragansett Bay, where he made contact with the Indians there, the large and influential tribe of Narragansetts. In sailing to Narragansett Bay, Block discovered that Long Island Sound was not a "deep bay" as was then believed, but that it opened to the sea at the eastward end.

The indefatigable Dutch immediately saw an opportunity for trade. A peaceful tribe of Indians was living up the Connecticut River and it was navigable; at the mouth of the river the way lay open across the sea to European markets.

They bought land from the then dominant and warlike Pequot-Mohegans who claimed to have conquered most of the Connecticut River valley lands. And in 1633 the Dutch built a trading post on a strip of land on the west shore of the river where Hartford now stands. Historians believe the exact location was at the mouth of the Little or Park River where it empties into the Connecticut. The Dutch forbade any fighting on the land (their aim was trade, not conquest) and they built a fort called the "House of Good

Hope" or "House of Hope." Just to make sure there was no fighting they mounted two cannon within the fort.

Tentative efforts had been made in 1631 by Connecticut Indians to get English settlers from Massachusetts to come to the Connecticut River valley. The offer came from Indians who had been conquered by the warlike Pequot-Mohegans. Their reasoning was that the English with their guns could help them regain their ancestral lands and keep the Pequot-Mohegans at bay. Not until late in 1633, however, was there any formal move on the part of the English. That fall an exploratory party sailed up the Connecticut River past the Dutch fort, despite protestations from the Dutch, and established a trading post at Windsor. During the same year a Captain John Oldham explored the Connecticut River below Hartford, made contact with the Indians there, and returned to report that he had found a good area for exploration, trade, and possible settlement. In 1634 a group from Massachusetts settled Wethersfield.

In 1635 first settlers arrived to found Hartford—and they were soon joined by the famous Reverend Thomas Hooker and his overland party in 1636. And in 1635, Saybrook was settled in disregard of a Dutch claim at that location at the mouth of the Connecticut River. In all these cases the English bought land from the river tribes that had suffered conquest by the Pequot-Mohegans—and in so doing the seeds of eventual trouble were sown.

The Dutch had bought from the supposed conquerors of the land; the English from the conquered. Who owned the land? Who had more legitimate claim? Whoever did, the Pequot-Mohegans believed they owned it and they were the dominant tribe in Connecticut.

Ethnologists classify Indian tribes, subtribes, and clans by linguistic affinity. This loose and sometimes broad classification is convenient for scholarly purposes but does little to help the amateur untangle the various tribes. One of the most widespread of these linguistically similar groups is the Algonquian or Algonkian. It is to this group that all Connecticut tribes belong.

All but one of the tribes in Connecticut were long established on their home grounds—and their total population has been estimated at about six thousand. In northeastern Connecticut (and

southern Massachusetts) lived the peaceful Nipmucks. The Podunks lived from South Windsor northward on the east side of the
Connecticut River; the Saukiogs and Poquonocks inhabited the
west side of the river from Wethersfield north; the Wangunks on
both sides of the river in the Middletown, Haddam, and East
Haddam region; at the mouth of the Connecticut on the west
were Hammonassets and on the east, Nehantics or Niantics;
Quinnipiacs lived along the shore in the New Haven region with
the Montowese inland just to the north. East of the Quinnipiacs
there lived the Menunketucks. Along the western shores of
Fairfield County there were the Paugussets and the Siwanogs. The
Tunxis occupied the New Britain, Farmington, Avon region west of
the Saukiogs, of which they were a subtribe. All these tribes had
occupied their territories long before the Dutch or English arrived.

The Pequot-Mohegan tribe occupied southeastern Connecticut.
Of Mohican origin and coming from the Taconic Mountain
section of New York State, they fought their way eastward and
down the east side of the Connecticut River, some time in the late
sixteenth century. Battles with the Podunks, the Nipmucks, and
the Nehantics or Niantics proved their dominance and they were
feared and hated by other Connecticut tribes. It was they who sold
land to the Dutch in the region around Hartford which they
claimed by right of conquest. The Pequot-Mohegans had, in fact,
conquered the Podunks, the Saukiogs, and the Nipmucks, and
they had split the Nehantic tribe in two as they settled in
southeastern Connecticut. The eastern group went to the Narragansett stronghold in Rhode Island while the western Nehantics
remained uneasily on the patch of ground to the east of the
Connecticut River at its mouth. Whatever the situation was in
Connecticut before the arrival of the Pequot-Mohegans, it was not
the same after their turbulent entry into the region's history.

Connecticut Indians were not nomads. Their villages were
permanent save in two instances. If the hunting in the surrounding
woods or the fishing in the streams, rivers, or the sea failed, they
would move the entire tribe to new grounds. And many tribes had
seasonal homes; in summer they would move, lock, stock, and
barrel, to the seashore for shellfish and more abundant fishing.
Clams, lobsters, and oysters were taken, fish caught in weirs, and

all that could not be eaten there was smoked or dried for winter use.

The work of the women was the planting of maize, the harvesting, the gathering of nuts, roots, and herbs from the meadows and forests. The men hunted and fished. Tools and utensils were crude. Wooden bowls and spoons were laboriously carved. Stone hatchets and hoes, pitch-lined elm-bark cooking pots, wooden mortars, and pestles for grinding corn—these and few other implements served their needs. The bow and arrow and tomahawk and wooden-headed or stone-headed club served them in war. In summer, dress for the men was a skin breechclout or trousers, for the women a skirt made of skin. Young children wore nothing. In winter, shirts, blouses, and furs protected them. Footwear was the ubiquitous moccasin, decorated frequently with shell beads.

Tribal leaders were called sachems and lesser leaders sagamores. And leadership was inherited, so succession of kings, princes, and princesses paralleled the more elaborate European structure of monarchy. Succession was not by primogeniture, however, although inherited leadership was kept within a "royal" family. Lesser leaders voted on which "prince" or "princess" they preferred. The sachem, moreover, was not an absolute ruler. He and his council of sagamores decided questions and rarely was action taken unless the council was unanimous. To the confusion of historians, the royalty of different tribes frequently intermarried, and so bonds were formed between unrelated tribes. And since the Indians had no written language (other than their enigmatic legend-bearing wampum), white inquirers had a difficult time getting tribal patterns straight. As a matter of fact, they are still finding it difficult.

In religious matters, the Indian was pantheistic and there were subtleties that escaped (and still escape) the prejudiced Christian observer. Certainly the first whites the Indians met, in the form of Christian zealots, were prejudiced to the point of blindness. Puritans pointed in horror, for example, at the custom of torturing prisoners, though in their own recent history, Englishmen had burned heretics at the stake, hanged, drawn, and quartered prisoners, applied the rack and the screw to force confessions or information from heretic or enemy prisoners. They never understood the Indian attitude toward bravery and death. A brave prisoner undergoing torture and laughing at his pain was a profoundly exalting experience for the onlooker. The Indian admired bravery, second only to the keeping of his word. He accepted death and admired a foe who would meet death bravely. The elements of vengefulness and punishment were not present in Indian torture unless the subject had committed a crime. And despite popular legend, scalping was unknown to Connecticut Indians—until whites put bounties on dead Indians and paid for the scalplock as proof of destruction—which, in fact, proved nothing, since scalping a live captive or wounded enemy did not necessarily cause his death.

Least understood by the whites was the Indians' concept of land and land ownership. To the Indian, land was held to belong to all. A territory might be staked out for hunting by a tribe, but no one believed the tribe "owned" the land as Europeans conceived of ownership. All land, in fact all life, was sacred and not susceptible of private ownership. Thus when the Dutch bought a strip of land from the Pequot-Mohegans in the Hartford region, they believed they owned it. And they set up rules concerning behavior on "their" land: no weapons, no fighting, no killing—just profitable trade. And from this nearly all the Indian trouble in Connecticut flowed.

Not long after the House of Good Hope was built, some Pequot-Mohegan braves killed enemy Indians on the land of the Dutch. In retaliation, the Dutch, as one historian delicately put it, "contrived to dispatch" the Pequot-Mohegan sachem, Wopigwooit, and several braves. In choosing a new sachem, the Indians voted on several princely candidates. In the case of the Pequot-Mohegans, after the murder of Wopigwooit, his son Sassacus was chosen. A losing candidate was a sagamore named Uncas, who did not like the selection. Proud, ambitious, crafty, intelligent, and brave, Uncas was to become the outstanding Indian of Connecticut during the course of his long life.

Naturally, the Dutch murder of his father forced Sassacus to avenge his death and for a year or two war was waged fitfully between the Dutch and the Pequot-Mohegans. Uncas, meanwhile, withdrew from the Pequots under Sassacus, moved to the northern edge of the territory with a few dissidents, and took the name "Mohegan" for his group. It was, after all, the original name of the Pequot tribe when they were in New York and is a variant spelling of "Mohican," the parent tribe. The name "Pequot," which means destroyer, was applied to the Mohegans by the other Connecticut tribes who had been defeated by them.

Connecticut settlements at Windsor, Wethersfield, Hartford, and Saybrook in these early years were under the control of Massachusetts Bay Colony, whose leaders believed they were empowered by their charter to govern the Connecticut River territory. And in all dealings with the Indians, all matters of importance had to be settled in Boston. This fact of government was in part responsible for considerable misunderstanding, which began to erupt in a very short time.

A trader-adventurer, Captain Stone, and his crew sailing from Massachusetts to trade along the shore with Pequots were killed. Then another trader, John Oldham, was found in his small ship, murdered off Block Island. It is clear that Pequots killed Captain Stone but whether justifiably so or not remains unclear. His ship blew up when powder casks took fire, so no evidence or English survivors could set the matter straight. Oldham's death probably came at the hands of Narragansetts, but the English accused the Pequots.

To punish the Indians, the Massachusetts government sent out a small force under John Endicott. A man of poor judgment, he burned vacated Indian villages, roused the Pequots' anger, and did nothing but stir up trouble. He went back to Boston. The Pequot sachem, Sassacus, decided he could drive the English from the land forever, so he began a hit and run war, attacking first the fort at Saybrook, driving everyone inside the fort while he burned crops and buildings. He next attacked Wethersfield in what has been called the Wethersfield Massacre. Eight people were killed and two white girls taken captive. Cattle were slaughtered and crops destroyed.

Thoroughly alarmed, the English upriver in the Hartford settlements and officials in Boston began to gather a force to destroy the Pequot forts at Groton and end the war. Windsor's Captain

John Mason was chosen to lead the force with men from his town, Hartford, and Wethersfield. Boston began raising men and dispatched a preliminary force under a Captain Daniel Patrick overland to join Mason.

Uncas, watching from the sidelines, saw his chance for power. He joined the English forces against his former tribe, the Pequots. His sixty warriors joined the approximately ninety English troops at Saybrook and on May 29, 1637, several ships carrying this force sailed eastward toward the Pequot strongholds.

Captain Mason planned not to confront the Pequots head on by sailing into New London Harbor, but to sail on by to Rhode Island and march back overland through Narragansett territory to take the forts by surprise. His march proved successful and he even picked up supporting troops from the Narragansetts and the defeated Niantics—none of whom liked the aggressive Pequots.

The English attacked the Pequots' eastern fort two hours before dawn one morning and caught the Indians completely by surprise. Mason and a detachment of his men entered one gate and shortly after the battle began another English detachment entered the opposite one.

Mason realized that his troops inside the fort might well be trapped there. And as the Indians began to awake and fight back, the likelihood grew. So Mason took a torch and set fire to the wigwams. A strong wind sent a sheet of flame across the entire enclosure and Mason and his men retreated outside the gates to kill or capture the Indians as they fled the flames.

The women and children within the fort could not flee. They died by fire inside. The men, some burning like torches, climbed the palisade walls and were shot as they topped the burning logs. Those who managed to get out were killed. Only seven captives were taken; four hundred died.

Captain Underhill later wrote, "Great and doleful was the bloody sight, to the view of young soldiers who had never been in war to see so many souls lie gasping on the ground so thick in some places that you could hardly pass along." When Governor Bradford of the Plymouth colony heard of the victory he wrote, "It was a fearful sight to see them frying in the fire and the streams of blood quenching the same and horrible was the stink and stench thereof. But the victory seemed a sweet sacrifice and they gave praise thereof to God."

The Pequot sachem, Sassacus, had been in the other fort and he and about three hundred Pequots were unaware of the destruction of most of the tribe. When the facts were learned, the Pequots turned on Sassacus, accusing him of a failure of leadership. The English victory filled them with fear and they decided to leave their country forever. Accordingly, the entire tribe set out along the shore, traveling to the west.

The progress of the Pequots was not swift, since they marched with their children. They crossed the Connecticut River after killing three white men and continued on through the country of the Hammonassets. Mason, meanwhile, had been reinforced by a total of 140 Massachusetts men, 20 under Captain Patrick and 120 under Captain Stoughton. The General Court at Hartford, hearing of the success, sent Roger Ludlow with 40 more men to find and support Mason.

The growing English force had struck fear in all tribes in Connecticut. The war power of the whites (which could outwit and exterminate so many Pequots) appeared overwhelming. Mason and about 20 men went ashore from their ships and, with Uncas and his Mohegans, tracked the fleeing Pequots while the ships sailed slowly along the coast with the other troops.

The outcome of this expedition was never in doubt. At Southport in the town of Fairfield, Mason's men sighted the fleeing Pequots. They were on the edge of a large swamp just north of Southport harbor. As the English drew near, all the Pequots disappeared in the swamp. The English forces surrounded the area, sealing off escape routes. One Thomas Stanton, who could speak the Pequot language, entered the swamp against orders and returned shortly leading 200 old men, women, and children. Then the trapped warriors tried to break through the English lines. Sharp fights followed. Some 70 braves managed to escape, including Sassacus. One hundred and eighty captives were taken. Some were turned over to the Indian allies—the Mohegans and Narragansetts; others were sent into slavery in Massachusetts or shipped to the West Indies, where their fate was the same. Today a marker beside U.S. 1 in Southport is the sole commemoration of the battle that saw the total destruction of the Pequots: The Great Swamp Fight here ended the Pequot War on July 13, 1637.

Uncas, the Mohegan, now rose to the pinnacle of his power. He successfully fought other tribes and always managed to stay in the good graces of the English. He conquered and killed the famous sachem of the Narragansetts, Miantonomo; he battled the Podunks again and continued to work at building an empire that he would rule. When the last great Indian attempt to repulse the white invasion (King Philip's War), broke out in 1675, Uncas again stayed on the side of the English. On one occasion when the Narragansetts had besieged Uncas and his men in their fort, Uncas was rescued by a white force sent out by John Mason, then in command at Saybrook. A Lieutenant Leffingwell arrived and the English presence persuaded the Narragansetts to withdraw. Uncas died in 1683. He has been regarded as a traitor to his people, a renegade, a wily enemy, a good strategist, an opportunist, and a brave man. Whatever the view, he was the last outstanding Connecticut Indian.

As the seventeenth century drew to a close, the coming of more and more white settlers had the expected result on Indian populations. They died from smallpox, from venereal disease, and from just being pushed from their own territory. Little regard was paid to their welfare until the numbers had dwindled below the survival level. And as the years passed, more of them intermarried with the whites.

From a population estimated at six thousand in the seventeenth century, Connecticut Indians have reached the following level on Connecticut's remaining four Indian reservations:

Trumbull, Golden Hill Reservation (1 building lot)    2
North Stonington, Eastern Pequot Reservation (224 acres)    12
Ledyard, Western Pequot Reservation (184 acres)    4
Kent, Schaghticoke Reservation (400 acres)    3

And although some 2,200 men and women today claim Indian lineage, the number of pure blood Indians is pitiably small.

# 4

# TOPOGRAPHY AND GEOLOGY

Small though it is, Connecticut has a diverse topography, with several strikingly dramatic features. There are hills and small mountains in the west and northwest section of the state, a broad low river plain through which the Connecticut River meanders in the central portion before it surprisingly turns east into a rising, undulating eastern plateau. The main divisions of the state, in fact, are known as the Western Highland, Central Lowland, and Eastern Highland.

## The Western Highland

A visitor driving from Danbury, north along U.S. Rte. 7, soon begins to feel that he is in the mountains. The road that runs along a valley floor is flanked in Kent and farther north by steeply rising mountainous slopes. These are the southern ends of the larger and higher ranges of mountains in Massachusetts and Vermont. Those on the western side of the Housatonic can be thought of as the foothills of the Taconic Mountains, which rise farther west in New York State. They are not high, as mountains go, but in the towns of northwestern Connecticut there are peaks that give the industrious hiker a spectacular view of the surrounding countryside. Bear Mountain, in Salisbury, is the highest in the state at 2,322 feet. Others in the northwest are: Gridley, Bald (Ball) Mountain, Mt. Riga, Mt. Tom, Canaan Mountain, and Ivy Mountain.

The eastern part of this highland section is not so mountainous as it is around Goshen and Cornwall. There are, however, many high rugged hills and ridges (running north-south) that interrupt the undulating fields and meadows of the countryside. Talcott Mountain, for example, running through Simsbury, Avon, and Farmington, marks the eastern edge of the highland in that portion of the state.

Two major rivers, the Housatonic and the Naugatuck, drain the region whose highest point is in the northwest corner of the state. The land slopes gradually, about twenty feet per mile, to the shores of Long Island Sound.

Except for nineteenth-century industrial development in the Naugatuck River valley, the Western Highland has largely resisted man's excessive exploitation. One result is the preservation of some of the best scenery in the state and many square miles of virtual wilderness among the hills and mountains.

### The Central Lowland

Stretching from the Massachusetts border to Long Island Sound at New Haven is the central lowland of the state. North-south vehicular traffic through Connecticut from New York to Massachusetts, Vermont, and New Hampshire follows Interstate 91 up through the lowland from New Haven to Springfield, Massachusetts. The prospect gives the unwary passing visitor the impression that all of Connecticut is a lowland.

It is in this central valley that the best farmland in the state exists and here were its first settlements: Windsor, Wethersfield, and Hartford. To the Indians who formerly lived here, it was a beneficent river plain, and white settlers found it equally so. Tobacco is a major crop in this valley and like river-valley and flood plains the world over it is where human settlements first sprang up.

A peculiar intrusion in the Central Lowland gives the otherwise ordinary river plain a dramatic quality from near the shores of Long Island extending north to the Massachusetts border. These are trap ridges projecting above the almost flat plain and they are hard basaltic rock, resistant to erosion, that project above the flood plain of the Central Lowland area. This clifflike, upthrusting, reddish or green rock forms the East Rock and West Rock protrusions near New Haven, the Hanging Hills of Meriden, with a series of others extending north into Massachusetts.

The long broad valley of Connecticut's Central Lowland actually begins far to the north in the narrow valley separating Vermont and New Hampshire through which runs the Connecticut River on its course to Long Island Sound. The valley broadens in Massachusetts and when it reaches Connecticut, it is twenty miles wide; it narrows on the shore to a width of about five miles. The Connecticut River does not follow the lowland to the Sound. Surprisingly it veers east into a valley of the Eastern Highland just south of Middletown.

## The Eastern Highland

This region, in the northern part of the state, lies to the east of the Connecticut River. In the southern part, it crosses the river and accounts for the hilly, ledgy character of such towns as Killingworth and Durham. With few exceptions, the Eastern Highland does not resemble the Western Highland. Traveling east from Portland, for example, on state Rte. 66, one is in the Eastern Highland immediately and, as you drive through East Hampton, Marlborough, Hebron, and Columbia, you get the impression that you are in a small boat crossing a sea of long undulating waves. The wide almost symmetrical ridges run north and south and you drive from one crest to a trough and on to the next crest. In many parts of this section north-south roads are laid out along the crests and from these roads you get the feeling of being on top of the entire region.

It is an area of big sky, for nothing obstructs the view. A westering sun hangs for seemingly endless time on the western edge of this world, sending long, slanting rays to illuminate everything. Exceptions to this rhythmic pattern of ridges are found along the easternmost section of the state in the Quinebaug River valley and in the southern part including the towns of Stonington and North Stonington. Here isolated hills intermingle with the rolling meadows and valleys, breaking the obvious pattern of ridges. From some of these, Lantern Hill, for example, in North Stonington, a climb to the top results in a well-earned view to the east and south that includes Long Island Sound, the offshore islands, and the Atlantic Ocean. The northern part of this highland region also has many scattered hills.

**The Rivers**

The present topography of Connecticut is carved from what was relatively close to a peneplain several million years ago. It was a sloping plain with its highest point in the northwest corner of the state. The slope is to the southeast. Such are the rocky ridges, however, that the river beds run north to south and the major rivers flow, however they meander, to Long Island Sound. One major exception is the Farmington River, although this water course, too, originally flowed north to south without deviation. Glacial deposits, however, obstructed its original path and forced it to turn northward through Farmington, Avon, and Simsbury, then eastward through Windsor until it found a new outlet into the broad-flowing Connecticut River.

The major river, of course, is the Connecticut. Its Indian name was *quinnehtukqut,* which means "beside the long tidal river"— and this name was accurate. The tidal effect of the ocean reaches up this river as far as Hartford, more than halfway to the Massachusetts border. The river is navigable up to the Enfield Rapids and these topographic facts controlled the activities of settlers in the earliest days. Another topographic feature of this major river accounts for a curious fact of the present: a sandbar near the mouth of the river on the Sound made navigation in the early days difficult but by no means impossible, although it has prevented deep draft vessels of the present day from entering. This situation made the mouth of the Connecticut one of the few major rivers where a large port could not be established. Thus Old Lyme, on the east side of the river, is a modest and quiet community; Old Saybrook, on the west side, is larger but is in no sense a port except for yachts and summer cruisers.

To the east of the Connecticut is the Thames River, which really is an estuarial river and is navigable up to Norwich. The Thames is formed by the confluence of the Quinebaug, Shetucket, and Yantic rivers. These rivers stretch inland—themselves being formed of smaller rivers to the north. They were used as a source of power for early mills and helped establish industry in that area.

The principal rivers in the western part of the state are the Housatonic and the Naugatuck. The Housatonic flows in some places like a mountain river through gorges and narrow valleys among the hills and mountains of Litchfield County, becoming a sedate, broad river only toward its mouth, which empties into Long Island Sound between Stratford and Milford. It is not navigable today very far upstream, but in olden days the river carried shipping from a lively inland port, Derby. The Naugatuck, unlike the upper reaches of the Housatonic, has been a major source of water power for industry for years and has turned the Naugatuck Valley into one of the state's most active industrial regions—with all the attendant problems of pollution that the nineteenth-century businessmen shortsightedly created. And there still remains much to be done about the Naugatuck from this point of view. It is not an attractive river until it joins the Housatonic in its final flow to the Sound.

The Quinnipiac River, with its headwaters near Plainville, flows south through Southington, Meriden, Wallingford, and North Haven to empty into the Sound at New Haven. Though smaller than the others, it was of great importance to the New Haven colony as a source of power in the early days.

With few exceptions, the tributaries of all these rivers flow in a southerly direction. The Mad River, however, flows west into the Still River at Winsted, and the Still River actually flows north to empty into the Farmington. In the northwest part of the state, the mountainous terrain dictates that some of the tributaries of the upper Housatonic flow either east or west to empty into that lively stream.

## Lakes and Ponds

Connecticut has well over a thousand lakes and ponds, created by two agencies: glacial and human. By far the greatest number of the lakes were produced by glaciation in different ways. The formation of kettles or potholes in the glacial debris that was filled with the melted glacier ground water is one way. Another was the deposition of glacial drift to choke small valleys, creating a dam that impounded melting glacier ice; these ponds are kept filled to this day by the natural drainage of the regions.

Over the years of Connecticut's history of white settlement, many manmade ponds and lakes have been created for two principal reasons: water supply for cattle or people and the development of a waterfall for water power, and latterly, hydroelectric power. Lake Candlewood, for example, in Fairfield and Litchfield counties is the largest manmade lake in the state, covering more than 5,000 acres. It was created in 1927 and is used both as a resort area and a source of hydroelectric generating power. Barkhamsted Reservoir, on the other hand, also manmade, is primarily a water supply source for the Hartford area. Both of these manmade lakes are huge and have had an effect on the topography of the state. Another large manmade water feature of the state is Lake Lillinonah, created by the damming of the Housatonic River for the generation of electric power. It is 1,900 acres in extent and the impounded water lies in the old river beds, rising to the slopes of hills surrounding the former course of the Housatonic and Shepaug rivers. It spreads now over parts of Newtown, Brookfield, New Milford, Bridgewater, and Southbury.

From these and other large bodies of water, the state's lakes and ponds range in size down to the ponds created by farmers as a source of water for livestock; a simple earth dam at some advantageous point along a stream bed suffices to create the pond.

Lakes formed naturally (i.e., by glacial action) are plentiful, too, throughout the state. Two of the largest are Bantam Lake in the towns of Litchfield and Morris, and Lake Waramaug in Warren, Washington, and Kent. Each of these lakes has been raised by manmade dams. With its 916 acres, Bantam Lake is the largest natural lake in Connecticut. For many years it has been a favorite resort spot and its shores are lined with cottages and houses.

**The Shore**

The southern edge of the state is a shoreline of about one hundred miles in length, discounting irregularities. With minor exceptions it is a rocky shore with few beaches of a size that characterize neighboring Rhode Island, for example. The sand beaches are for the most part confined to coves and inlets where the deposition of particles on a once-rocky shore has produced the beach. One of the few long beaches in Connecticut is Hammonasset State Park in Madison, where a two-mile stretch, under state control, forms the largest uninterrupted beach in the state.

The rocky character of the Connecticut shore plus the presence of Long Island itself a few miles to the south have kept the shore from changing radically in recent geologic time. Waves, however driven by storm winds, have too small a fetch to alter the shoreline much and the nature of that shore resists erosion much better than, say, the glacial moraine that constitutes the shores of Long Island itself and of neighboring Rhode Island.

The shore was originally formed by submergence—either by the sinking of the land surface or the rising ocean level, or both. Thus the ocean flooded stream mouths and valleys near the shore, producing the irregularity that exists today. The submergence is accountable for the appearance of rocky islets sprinkled here and there along the coast of the state. The Thimble Islands off Branford, for example, are composed of the tops of hard rock formations peeping above the present sea surface and many of the inlets along this section are reminiscent of the Maine coast, though in miniature, as sea waves advance and recede from well-defined rock headlands and small cliffs. The nature of the shore has allowed permanent homes to be built very close to the water's edge as on the western part of the shore in Guilford and in Southport. Stonington too has its share of old homes close to the water, and in fact the older part of that village is on a single headland jutting out from the adjacent shoreline and giving that town its Maine character. This rocky nature has restricted the summer-cottage-type development encountered in Rhode Island and Massachusetts to protected inlets where wooden pilings can be driven and built upon.

Technically, the mouths of all the major and minor rivers of Connecticut emptying into the sound and forming some of the indentations of the shore are estuaries. Viewed from the sea, for example, the Thames River can be seen as a deep estuary and not a true river at all. The tidal effects of the sea reach to the northernmost part of that river at Norwich; only dams prevent the tidal effect from being noticeable far up the Housatonic, as it is up the Thames and the Connecticut.

The marshlands where these great rivers meet the sea, and where the tides restrict the outward flow of water, were considered fit only to fill and build on in line with the blindly expansionist nineteenth-century philosophy. But having been seen recently as critical life sources for much of the sea itself, marshlands are now coming under permanent protection. These marshes are found in nearly all estuaries from Greenwich to Stonington along the shore. Two of the most extensive lie in the Quinnipiac Valley (New Haven) and the Connecticut Valley (Old Saybrook and Old Lyme). To reach them all, in general, follow the shoreline roads (south of U.S. 1) until you cross a bridge, large or small. By following the stream to the Sound you will find yourself in a tidal marsh zone with all its fascinating wildlife around you.

There still are many problems relating to the shore and man's use or abuse of it. Many of those problems originate, not on the shore, but farther inland where the polluting of streams through industrial and human waste begin to funnel the filth down the streams to the Sound. The Sound itself is under serious attack by garbage, oil, and solid waste. All one has to do is read early accounts of the teeming and apparently limitless sea life found along the shore and in its waters many years ago—and compare those accounts with today's store of sea life. Shellfish, lobsters, fish of all sorts filled the waters of the shore and the Sound then. Today the disappearance of some marine species and the diminution of others are the rule.

**Early Geology**

The principal topographic features of the land mass of Connecticut came into being very early in geologic time. The glacial period affected the topography, of course, but it did not give Connecticut its underlying character, that of the Eastern and Western highlands and the Central Lowland. All of that formation occurred or began to occur in Pre-Cambrian times some 620,000,000 years ago. Most of present-day Connecticut has always been above the sea surface but limestone deposits in the northwestern part of the state indicate that part of it was at one time beneath a shallow sea or bay. A similar situation apparently existed also in the eastern part of the state.

A major shifting of the earth's crust in the eastern part of North America occurred during Pre-Cambrian times and two more were to follow, both of them in the Paleozoic Era 230,000,000 to 500,000,000 years ago. These periods of crustal shifting affected a wide area in the eastern part of the North American continent. Mountain ranges were created and in the ensuing eons these mountains were worn down by rain, wind, snows, and heat. The resulting debris formed, first loosely and then tightly, compacted areas of sedimentary rock like sandstone. Then in the following upheaval, these relatively soft beds of rock were folded, raised, crumpled, and often buried and subjected to great heat and pressure. Thus new rock forms were created; the sandstone became much harder. Such new rocks are called metamorphic. It is this metamorphic rock (chiefly gneiss and schist) that forms most of that found in both the Eastern and Western Highland areas of the state.

During that earliest period of formation, when the earth's crust shifted, the new mountains thus created are thought to have towered thousands of feet over what is now the essentially modest hilly terrain of the present state. Some geologists have called the peaks Alpine and they may have resembled the jagged, uneroded look of young mountain ranges today—like the Alps and our western Rocky Mountains.

The ranges that formed ran essentially north and south and were located on or above what are now the Eastern and Western Highland sections. This, then, was the character of Connecticut at the close of the Paleozoic Era. Erosion of the mountains began to fill the valleys with mud and sand and when sunlight evaporated the shallow waters some of the sediment was exposed and mud cracks left their telltale pattern in the later sedimentary rock. It was during this early Mesozoic Era, in the Triassic Period, some 200,000,000 years ago, that dinosaurs paddled about in the mud-flats and left their footprints, which we have uncovered today (see Rocky Hill). And it was also at this time that volcanic lava flowed upward through fissures in the earth's crust. This lava flow, in the Central Lowland area, spread like a sheet across the sand and mud plain. In the intervals between this activity, sedimentation continued so that the layers of lava, which are igneous rocks, were eventually covered by more sediment.

Toward the end of the Triassic Period, the entire land mass of Connecticut experienced a general uplift of the earth's crust. In the process a tilt occurred that produced great cracks or faults in the surface. The tilt gave a slope to the land from northwest to southeast. The faults were most noticeable in the Central Lowland. In both the Eastern and Western highlands, the rock structure withstood faulting better and, when it occurred, served only to give the mountains a more tumbled precipitous appearance. The lowland sandstone, however, faulted and exposed the layers of igneous rock and revealed the stratified sandstone sloping down to the east. Uplifted sections on one side of the fault rose higher than those on the other. The result was that mountain ranges again were created, characterized by clifflike edges on one face of a mountain and a long, regular slope on the other, where the valley surface was tilted.

By the end of the Mesozoic Era the entire face of Connecticut had been eroded to nearly a plane surface. The high Alps were gone and only their core remnants remained. The Central Lowland had filled up again with debris from the mountains, and the rivers flowed in sluggish meandering fashion over the nearly flat surface of the state, which was not very far above sea level. Then another uplift occurred in the Tertiary Period of the present Cenozoic Era, some 60,000,000 to 70,000,000 years ago.

This time, the uplift was gentle and produced few faults. The slope of the plane that was Connecticut pitched down from a high point in the northwestern part of the state toward the southeast. An important effect of this was to give all the streams and rivers added velocity, to turn them into new, boisterous streams with a great deal of energy. The result of the rejuvenation of the streams and rivers, plus the constant eroding effects of the rainfall, began to wear the tilted plane still further down. Naturally, the soft sandstone of the Central Lowland responded to the forces of erosion faster than the hard rocks of the east and west highlands. The result was the formation of the state much as it can be seen today. The tilted volcanic layers of igneous rock in the Central Lowland withstood erosion as the sedimentary rock of the lowland washed into the sea. These igneous protrusions are the East Rock and West Rock in New Haven, the Hanging Hills of Meriden, with Mt. Lamentation and various others to the north.

### The Effect of Glaciers

Connecticut is in the part of the continent that was covered by glaciers in the not-too-distant geologic past. The advance of the sheet of ice and its subsequent melting affected the topography of the state and gave us many characteristics still visible today. This is not to say that glaciers changed the face of Connecticut fundamentally. Both the highland sections and the Central Lowland were, and still are, in existence. But glaciers did put the finishing touches to the already formed landscape. The last of these embellishments occurred a little over ten thousand years ago. For several hundreds of thousands of years the ice that formed in Canada was pushed southward by the increasing weight of snow. Like highly viscous molasses, the ice flowed south under this pressure. It covered New England completely with a sheet of ice thick enough to bury Mt. Washington in New Hampshire, which is 6,288 feet above sea level. In its slow progress south, the glacier bulldozed all the soil from the mountains, hills, and valleys in Connecticut. Pushing it far south of the present shore of the state, the glacier scoured the rocks beneath it and in its depths carried rock and soil from points farther north. The soil of Vermont, New Hampshire, and Massachusetts was roiled into the ice. Huge boulders were encased in it. The footprint of this vast ice movement, so to speak, lies in the worn, polished bedrock it uncovered and the scratches made by debris within the ice scouring the rocks. These striations can be seen today in many exposed rock locations in the state.

After thousands more years the climate began to warm and the glacial ice sheet started to melt. The top and southern faces of the glacier were exposed to the heat and they melted slowly over the centuries. Almost all of Long Island represents the visible southern extension of the glacier—and probably lots of the original soil covering Connecticut. That elongated heap of sand and gravel is called a glacial moraine and represents the last push of the bulldozer blade made by the ice.

Had the ice been free of debris itself, it would have melted and left Connecticut a scoured rock surface devoid of any soil at all. But as the ice turned to water, the load of debris was dropped in valleys and gorges. All the soil in Connecticut today is of glacial origin, the result of ice-carried sand, gravel, "rock flour" (finely pulverized rock), and pebbles being left behind when the ice sheet melted. There were numerous additions to, and changes in, the landscape when the glacier retreated; its course of retreat was not regular. There were periods when little or no melting occurred; others when relatively rapid retreat produced other characteristics. Some are obvious and noticeable while others, to the layman, are not.

Waterfalls, for example, come from streams having either been dammed by glacial debris, say in a narrow valley, and having water impounded until it broke over the dam. Other falls come from damming that diverts the stream and forces the water to find a new path of release, perhaps over the edge of a granite cliff or ledge, thus forming a waterfall.

Boulders strewn across countless pastures and fields in Connecticut came, for the most part, from the melting ice sheet. Stuck like raisins in a cake during the glacial advance, the rocks dropped where the melting ice left them. And there must have been a lot of them, varying in size from less than a foot in diameter to large ones weighing hundreds of tons. These rocks came to rest on mountains, ledges, sand plains, upland fields—everywhere. They are rarely of the same rock as the ledge or outcrop they lie on, which indicates they were moved there by the ice. Connecticut farmers have made stone walls of the ones they could move, have made pastures for cows in fields so strewn with large rocks they could not be moved. And the largest of all, the erratics, can be found randomly over the landscape, defying movement completely. They are lying where they were put by the glacier. A number of erratics can be seen in Meriden's Hubbard Park on the trail to the northwest corner of Minor Lake.

Kettles are conical depressions in a surrounding gravel and till region. Some are filled with water and are recognized lakes and ponds; others are dry and noticeable only if the eye searches for them. The sand plain north of New Haven has many of these holes. They were made when chunks of the retreating glacier broke off and lay buried in the surrounding deposit from the glacier itself. When the chunk of ice melted it left a depression, and if the resulting water could not escape, a lake or pond was formed.

Drumlins are elliptically shaped low hills made of till (a mixture of sand, gravel, clay, and rock flour). They are low hills with their long dimensions lying in a north-south direction and are caused by the bottom of a glacier pushing a heap of debris together as it moves. Many can be seen around Pomfret and in New Britain. The character of the drumlins is smooth and almost perfectly convex when viewed from the long side.

A kame is a complex formation from the glacier; it is a series of interlocking mounds and ridges composed of sand and gravel with hollows in which melting ice left ponds and lakes in some instances. These usually formed in valleys where the retreat of the glacier's front and the attendant deposition of material was erratic. Examples of kames may be found in the Nepaug Valley west of Collinsville, in Glastonbury, Avon, and west of Chester.

Eskers are long, winding ridges of glacial drift formed in the following manner. A stream of melted glacier water running beneath the glacier itself would deposit material just as a stream on the surface would. But in the case of a subglacial stream, ice on either side of it would support the deposit, building up a kind of reverse stream bed. Instead of being below the ground surface surrounding it, it would be above that final surface. Examples of eskers can be found in Hartland, Burlington, and elsewhere in the state.

Sand plains, not very noticeable, are formed when the glacier front melts in an already wide and fairly level valley. Then the particles in the melted ice are spread over a wide area and evenly distributed. Both Cromwell and Wallingford are on such plains, which grow pine, cedar, and scrub oak today.

These, then, are the finishing touches the Ice Age gave to the state's appearance. The most obvious of these changes were laid down in the glacier's retreat or melting phase. They are with us today, and some of the debris carried to the state has been found to be useful for purposes other than agriculture.

## Commercial Use of Rocks and Minerals

Connecticut is not rich in valuable metallic ores. The two that have been mined successfully in the past, copper and iron, no longer are economical to take from the ground. Yet the history of two regions was formed by the presence of the two metal ores. Iron was first mined in 1740 in Salisbury, in the northwest corner of the state. Nearby towns also found iron-ore deposits and much of that refined iron went into weapons for the Revolutionary War. Fortunately, there also were deposits of lime in the area, for it had once been a sea floor. Lime is necessary to reduce iron ore to usably pure iron. Copper was discovered in the part of Simsbury that now is East Granby. The copper mine at Newgate became a prison and held all manner of colonial criminals. During the Revolutionary War, Tories and British prisoners of war were held in the dank, underground tunnels. While they were there, many of the prisoners were put to work digging out copper ore, but its quality was so poor that even with free labor the mining of ore was not a commercial success.

Here and there throughout the state more esoteric metals were mined on a small scale. Bismuth was found in Monroe, for example, and cobalt gave the name to a small community in the town of East Hampton.

In the matter of utilizing rock commercially, Connecticut has been more fortunate. Granite from quarries in the towns along Long Island Sound has been used in buildings throughout the state and in others as well. And the brown-colored sandstone, known as brownstone, from Portland quarries gave a building stone to New York City that inspired the name Brownstone Era in that city's history. The color of sandstone found in Portland and the more reddish color of stone in the Central Lowland area is caused by the presence of iron oxide and other metallic oxides in the formation of the relatively soft stone. Much of the mid-nineteenth-century architecture of Middletown, across the river from Portland, is fashioned of brownstone, as are many other buildings still standing throughout the state. The clays of glacial till in the Central Lowland around Windsor and New Haven, for example, gave brick-making materials that were exploited early in the state's history. And brick making continues today. Cement blocks made from reddish soil and building tile of the same materials produces colored blocks and tiles that have long been used for architectural embellishment on modern buildings.

By far the most important rock quarried in the state, however, is the igneous trap rock that was uplifted lava. This hard stone, crushed to various sizes, has provided an excellent road-building material for many years. The quarrying and selling of trap rock is carried on in many places. Trap-rock quarries may be found in New Haven, North Branford, Cheshire, East Granby, Plainville, and other locations in the Central Lowland.

**Mineral Collecting**

Connecticut offers many sites where rock hounds can chip for specimens. Some places are commercially operating quarries, some are abandoned quarries hidden away on hillsides. All, however, are on land owned by others and permission should be gained before invading the landscape with pick, chisel, and hammer. The following list of sites is representative of the many that exist throughout Connecticut.

Bethel: Pegmatite Quarry. Go to Codfish Hill Rd., which runs off U.S. 202. Turn left off this road on to Codfish Hill Rd. Extension, then right on a deadend road. Inquiry leads you to the quarry back in the woods where you can find many minerals including beryl, tourmaline, quartz, and uranophane.

Bristol: The Bristol Copper Mine. North on Jerome Ave. and right on Mine Hill Rd. A construction company occupies the mine site. Copper, malachite, and quartz among others can be found.

Brookfield: On U.S. 7 south of state Rte. 133 on the east side of the highway. You can see the quarry from the road. It is an operating quarry, where, with permission, you can find barite, garnet, hornblende, and talc.

Canaan: Two quarries in Falls Village on Sand Rd. are owned by the U.S. Gypsum Co. With permission you can look for talc, calcite, and other minerals associated with lime deposits.

Durham: On the south side of Rte. 68, west of Pent Rd., lies the Reed's Gap Quarry operated by New Haven Trap Rock Co., from which permission should be gained to scout about and locate amethyst, fluorite, calcite, and quartz.

East Hampton: This is a town rich in quarries. Selden Quarry yields quartz, manganapatite, and scheelite. It is located south of Cobalt on Rte. 151 two and a half miles, then east one-third of a mile to a dirt road leading off to the right. Two other quarries are located in Meshomasic State Forest (inquire in Cobalt for directions). They offer albite, quartz, and scheelite.

Glastonbury: Hollister, Howe, and Husband quarries in this town are located east of Rte. 17 on a dirt road near the Glastonbury-Portland town line. They offer albite, autunite, manganapatite, and quartz.

Haddam: In Hurd State Park, behind the picnic areas, the quarry dump (known as Hurd Park Quarry) is visible. Among the minerals: albite, chrysoberyl, columbite, and manganapatite.

Middletown: A lead-silver mine was once here and the dumps reward the searcher with calcite, fluorite, and galena. It is on a dirt road running westerly off Silver St.

Monroe: The Booth Bismuth Mine is on Barn Hill Rd. about five hundred feet off Rte. 110. A path leading north takes you to the mine entrance and the dumps where tailings can be examined for bismuth, manganapatite, and scheelite. The mine is no longer operated. Lane's Mine is on Elm St., about one and a half miles off Rte. 111. It lies behind a stucco house on the left side of the road.

Inquire at the house. Among minerals reported here are pyrite, bismuth, tungstite, and sphalerite.

North Canaan: The Canaan Limestone Quarry is just south of the junction of U.S. 7 and 44. Go east on Lower Rd. for about a mile and the quarry can be seen from there. Permission is required from the New England Lime Company to search for actinolite, calcite, pyrite, talc, serpentine, and other minerals.

North Stonington: Lantern Hill Quarry lies on Lantern Hill Rd. and is operated by the Ottowa Silica Co., from which permission is required. Quartz crystals of many kinds are the treasure to be looked for here.

Plainville: The Plainville Traprock Quarry is on Rte. 72, east of the junction of Rtes. 10 and 72. Datolite, prehnite, and calcite are among the minerals here.

Portland: Four quarries in the town make the region a happy hunting ground for rock hounds. Andrews and Hale quarries are on Quarry Rd., which runs off Rte. 17 north of its junction with Rte. 17A. Quartz, hyalite, spodumene, and some kunzite are among the minerals that have been found in the two quarries. Case Quarry yields blue beryl. It is east of Rte. 17. Take Isinglass Rd., opposite Quarry Rd., turn right on Thompson Hill Rd. to a crossroads, where you turn left, and go until you see power lines. Follow them up to the hilltop, where you will see the dumps. Strickland Quarry has many specimens from albite to zircon. From Rte. 66, go north on Rte. 17, then right on Bartlett Hill Extension. At the Collins Hill Rd. junction an unimproved road leads to the dumps.

Woodbury: The Woodbury Pegmatite Quarry has beryl, garnet, quartz, tourmaline, and others. Take Flanders Rd. off U.S. 6 and 202, which coincide here. Just over one and a half miles is a farmhouse, from which you can get both directions and permission.

# 5

# TREES, FLOWERS, AND SHRUBS

Although Connecticut is the third smallest state it possesses a surprising diversity of vegetation zones, ranging from a small mountainous section of country on the Massachusetts border in the towns of Canaan, Norfolk, and North Canaan to the shore towns along Long Island Sound, where tidal marsh plants flourish. The state has over 1,000 ponds and lakes, and more than 7,500 miles of streams and rivers. Among the lakes are many that have passed through their life cycle and become swamps, and here and there in the southern part of the state where the water table is high, seasonal swamps exist.

The vegetation in Connecticut today is entirely different from that of the state when the last glacier receded about twelve thousand years ago. Then northern or arctic vegetation probably covered most of the state. But as the warming of the earth continued and the seas rose, the shores were flooded and tidal marshes began to develop; the character of the trees and shrubs covering the state changed and developed more nearly to present-day appearance. Indians, who moved into the region soon after the ice retreated, left the woods alone for the most part. They were accustomed, however, to building fires to clear fields, and this practice plus naturally occurring fires due to lightning periodically burned over many hundreds of square miles. And so a kind of rhythm or balance of growth and destruction by fire developed. Indians made use of a few trees—their bark and some of the herbaceous plants for medicine, and tree bark and pitch to seal canoes. Many Connecticut Indians used dugout canoes laboriously burned and carved from tree trunks.

As white colonists settled the state, one of the first community concerns to develop was the sawmill. Coming as they did from England, most of the people were unaccustomed to building all wooden houses, for wood in the home country was scarce. But with the forests so plentiful and a cheap building material so easily procured, the practice of using wood for construction very early became the rule. Oak formed the frame of the houses and, at first, the clapboards. Oak also supplied flooring, particularly for the first floor, which got a lot of wear. Tulip wood and hard pine were often used on the upper floors while chestnut was used for the early plank-walled houses. Cabinetmakers made use of maple, oak, and white pine, which, in comparison to oak, worked easily and made fine paneling for rooms.

From the Indians the settlers picked up the habit of burning forests to clear land for cultivation, and as more and more land was required to feed the colonists, the forests were drastically reduced. Oddly, when public concern was aroused to protect forests from thoughtless and unnecessary burning, it had a deleterious effect on the forests themselves. Accustomed to occasional burning over, the ground beneath trees had remained relatively free of shrubs, vines, and other plants. But as setting fire to the woods was stopped, this forest floor vegetation became a tangled mass that grew to maturity. *Then* when lightning caused a fire, conflagrations were started that wiped out many acres of woodland.

Along the drowned shores of Long Island Sound, from Greenwich to Stonington, rivers and streams deposited the silt the waters had carried, and gradually the tidal marshes were created. With their building came the plants of the tidal marshes. These marshes exist, technically, from the low-tide mark to the point on shore where the highest of the high tides has ever lapped. And, technically, these marsh zones may be rather steep. For the most part, however, we see them as periodically drowned horizontal stretches of land near river mouths. The shore area that boasts the most extensive tidal marshes lies on both sides of the mouth of the

Connecticut River and westward. The towns of Lyme, Old Lyme, Old Saybrook, and Westbrook offer many acres of tidal marshes where saltwater grass, salt meadow grass, glasswort, sea lavender, and pink and purple gerardia prevail. On short, steepening slopes fringing the marshes, black grass, switch grass, and marsh elder flourish. Cattails, bulrushes, and sword grass grow there also.

At the topmost level of the tidal-marsh zone the marsh elder and sea myrtle grow as shrubs to heights of from two to five feet and herald the end of the marsh delineation.

The tidal-marsh areas in Connecticut are not extensive in relation to the total land area. For years they have been filled or ignored and polluted. Only recently have people living in the shore towns become aware of their importance to the health of the land and of much of the animal life of the shore. Wetlands presently are protected by state law but the enforcement of that law is causing many businessmen anguish as they see potentially buildable land denied them.

When a lake has run its life cycle, silting up until the depth of the water is reduced to a shallow pond or less, plant life of the swamps begins to grow. In some cases this occurs on the banks of once-active streams. Scattered throughout the state these swamps support royal fern, New York fern, sensitive fern, cattails, cranberry, tussock sedge, skunk cabbage, and white hellebore. Buttonbush, sweet pepper bush, and spicebush are found here in swamp forests. Trees found in these swamps and bogs include the red maple, white ash, tulip tree, and occasionally yellow birch, hackberry, and sycamore.

Moving away from swampy, moist areas of former lake beds and streams onto drier, higher ground brings one to the more common plants in the state—widespread and found in all but the highest ground in Connecticut.

On hillsides throughout Connecticut the mountain laurel (the state flower) blooms in June and along with it bloom the pink and white dogwoods. Many communities, notably Greenfield Hill in the town of Fairfield, have elaborate displays of dogwood trees that have been nurtured over the years. Beneath and around them frequently can be found huckleberry, blueberry, blackberry, and thimbleberry—which is black raspberry. Also here can be found pink azalea, viburnum, and poison ivy. In open land, three of the most common shrubs are sheep laurel, sweetfern, and bayberry. Occasionally pokeberry is found too. Witch hazel is common and it provides a commercial harvest for still-functioning witch hazel manufacture.

Wildflowers will be met in nearly every sort of habitat imaginable in Connecticut. A walk in the woodland areas in the early spring will reveal trailing arbutus, bloodroot, violets, liverleaf, wood and rue anemone, and white trillium. As spring advances you can find wild lily of the valley, wild geranium, white baneberry, Solomon's seal, maystar, sarsaparilla, and mayapple. In moist places along streams, in bogs or swampy woodlands, the lady slipper and skunk cabbage are readily found as are jack-in-the-pulpits, red trillium, wild columbine, trout lily, and marsh marigolds. Open land, either a patch of space in woodlands or the fields and meadows, will produce the buttercup, star thistle, Dutchman's breeches, wild strawberry, daisies, coltsfoot, yarrow, clover, star thistle, Virginia spiderwort, bittersweet nightshade, spring beauty, cow vetch, and the ubiquitous dandelion.

When summer comes, woodlands yield other blossoms: the short-lived dayflower, which blooms and fades in one day, blue vervain, spotted wintergreen, partridge berry, Indian pipe, rattlesnake plantain, turtlehead, and the wood lily and touch-me-nots. Moist ground in bogs or along streams will grow the odd square-stem monkey flower, arrowhead, marsh mallow, smartweeds, and wild lettuce. Fields and meadows then are blossoming with horsenettle, Saint Johnswort, bull thistle, blue-eyed grass, Queen Anne's lace (or wild carrot), steeplebush, milkweed, meadow beauty, heal all, meadowsweet, pokeweed, and pearly everlasting. Black-eyed susans are all over the place.

As the summer wanes, what are thought of as fall flowers come into their own. The cardinal flower is out in bogs and moist ground then. Boneset, the white woodland aster, and the heath aster, along with joe-pye weed, goldenrod, sunflowers, and the late fringed gentian give color to the early autumn days.

Many of the wild growing flowers and weeds served early settlers either as herbs for flavoring and sources of teas or provided the only medicines to treat sickness or injury. Many have very early histories as useful plants. Heal all, for example, is a giveaway with its name and is a member of the mint family. Actually imported from Europe, in early days it was used to dress cuts and wounds of many kinds. Joy-pye weed has been known for its medicinal value for thousands of years under names less folksy than its present one. According to one report, the name it is known by here came from an Indian herb doctor named Joe Pye, who used the plant to treat fever victims in the Massachusetts colony. The bull thistle has been used for centuries to treat varicose veins. Saint Johnswort, of European reputation, was originally gathered there on Saint John's Eve and hung in doorways to ward off any evil that seemed threatening. It was used internally to treat "depression," since it was believed to be a stimulant and it was also used externally to heal wounds. Boneset was used to make a poultice that was applied to broken bones.

Pennyroyal and peppermint made teas—as did the young needles of white pine trees. Wine was made from the elderberry, black cherry, grape, gooseberry, and dandelion. Wild geraniums and primroses were employed as aromatics; lavender, tansy, and wormwood served as moth preventives. Even poison ivy saw service in producing ink.

Despite its highly urbanized regions and the relatively high density of population, 63 percent of the state is wooded. Indeed, driving in eastern Connecticut and in the hilly-to-mountainous western part, the sweep of forest, both deciduous and evergreen, fills the landscape. Litchfield County has more forest than any other, 401,000 acres. On a percentage basis, New London, Tolland, and Middlesex counties have 71 percent of their land surface covered by forests. And the least forested county, Hartford, is 49 percent forested. A hundred years ago, the state had only half as much land in forest.

Oak is the most widespread hardwood tree in Connecticut. It covers over 65 percent of the forested land. King of these deciduous trees is red oak; and the other varieties include white, scarlet, swamp white, post, black, and chestnut oak. Sugar maple, black birch, and white birch, poplar, beech, ash, and hickory are scattered throughout the state. The elm, formerly a symbol of New England, has virtually disappeared in Connecticut owing to the elm blight. Willow, cherry, American linden, gray birch, and ironwood are also to be seen. Among the evergreens, the hemlock is widespread as are white pine, red pine, and cedar on the higher elevations.

# 6
# WILDLIFE

When the first English settlers arrived in Connecticut, they found the forests, rivers, lakes, and ocean teeming with wildlife. Salmon and shad swarmed upriver seasonally and along the shores of Long Island Sound oysters, clams, mussels, lobster, crab, and a wide variety of saltwater fish were theirs for the taking. In woodlands, bear and deer, squirrel and rabbit, raccoon and possum all were there. It seemed that a limitless supply of food was at hand. As fields were cultivated and flocks of sheep and herds of cows became common in the village areas, some of the predatory animals caused damage to the livestock. The cougar or panther was still roaming Connecticut then; the wolf, the Canada lynx, and the bobcat were here. Bears, foxes, martens, weasels, and raccoons raided henhouses. Worst of all perhaps were the rattlesnakes. These were present in such quantity as to prove a hazard to sheep, horses, cows, and people. Norwich and Glastonbury were notorious for the density of the rattlesnake population. In one community bounties were offered; in another, citizens were required to bring in dead rattlesnakes or pay a small "fine" to hire someone else to do it.

Man began, slowly at first, to kill off the "pests" or the "vermin," as some people called them. As settlements grew, the bear, who never cared much for the smell of men anyway, became less and less visible. Its former presence was widespread, however, and lives on in the legend of an aging bear hunter who set out one morning to walk a short distance through the forest to a friend's house. At a turn in the trail, he found his way blocked by a rambunctious she bear and her cubs. Try as he might, the old man could not force the bear to leave the path and let him by. He showed up at home, tearful over his defeat by the animal he had hunted all his life.

The attitude of men in the seventeenth and eighteenth centuries toward the destructive animals might be understandable, since some species posed a threat to man's crops and livestock and therefore to his survival. So destructive animals were shot and when the nineteenth century brought trade, furbearing animals were killed for their pelts in large numbers. The beaver-fur hat industry that helped support the economy of Norwalk and Danbury wiped out the beaver for many years. They have been reintroduced and are now not uncommon in the northern parts of the state. And deer, once plentiful, have been thinned so much that today hunting them is heavily restricted. They can only be shot with bow and arrow or a shotgun on specified lands. So depleted have some species become that the state does not allow an open-hunting season on beaver, mink, muskrat, moose, otter, harbor seal, or Canada lynx. The trapping of some of these species is allowed, however, and until the very survival of these species is threatened, the trapper can make his rounds, for trapping still is a small industry in the state.

The most common wild mammals a visitor is likely to see include the woodchuck, gray squirrel (red squirrels are scarce), cottontail rabbit, chipmunk, porcupine, and skunk. Occasionally, on a back road, a flash of gray or red across your headlight beam may give you a glimpse of a fox and you may surprise a deer in an upland meadow. Your chances in Connecticut today, however, of coming within eyesight of a moose are nonexistent.

Snakes are as plentiful in Connecticut as elsewhere, yet all but two are perfectly harmless. Those two are the copperhead and the rattlesnake. The timber rattlesnake is found in upland, hilly country, while the northern copperhead lurks in lower damp places during the summer and among high, dry rocky outcroppings the rest of the time. Among the many harmless snakes you may come across in the state are the common water snake, brown snake, red-bellied, ribbon, common garter, eastern hognose, eastern ringneck, racer, smooth green, and rat snake.

Along the shore, the life of the sea and tidal marshes is abundant. In the marshlands and the river mouths you can find shellfish such as scallops, mussels, clams of many kinds, as well as snails, starfish, brittlestars, sea worms, sea cucumbers, sea mice, toads, tree frogs, and grass shrimp. A wide variety of crabs can be identified too: horseshoe crab, hermit crab, spider crab, blue, rock, green, mud fiddler, and others. Occasionally you may glimpse a muskrat in the brackish water.

On open beaches you will find deer mice, sand shrimp, ground fleas, seaweed hoppers, and sea worms, as well as horseshoe crabs, hermit crabs, and others. Starfish frequently are washed up and any receding wave may reveal a bump that turns out to be a horseshoe crab. In the water, on sandy bottoms, the sand eel may sometimes be seen.

Fish found in the salt waters of Long Island Sound and up the tidal rivers of the shore vary from the sand eels mentioned above to the often sought striped bass offshore. For swimmers, the danger of sharks is minimal. Although there have been six kinds of sharks reported in shallow coastal New England waters (sand, basking, ground, brown, and dusky shark plus the smooth dogfish), you are in about as much danger from a shark here as you are from being struck by a falling meteorite. In any event, the report of a shark's presence spreads quickly—and inaccurately—among bathers along any shore so you will have an abundance of advance misinformation on the presence of one should it stray into the area.

The game fish of the anglers includes the above-mentioned striped bass, and bluefish, chub, butterfish, mackerel, skate, and eels. Hake, mummichog, silversides, and Atlantic tomcod are sometimes taken. Not wanted on anglers' hooks are sea robins, sculpins, and toadfish—but they are caught just the same. A favorite fish for the nonmuscular fisherman is flounder, both summer and winter. Alewives and shad—in season—are traditionally caught and eaten in towns along the tidal rivers.

The small, abundant life to be found in Connecticut's lakes and streams is interesting and far easier to observe and identify than larger, rarer creatures. Five kinds of turtles are common: snapping turtle, stinkpot, spotted turtle, and the wood and painted turtles. There are mudpuppies, newts, the dusky and two-lined salamander, as well as frogs: pickerel frogs, green frogs, and the deep-throated bullfrog (see Windham).

Within these lakes, ponds, and streams there are many fish (some surviving naturally and others raised and stocked by the state). Brook trout, rainbow, brown, and lake trout are to be found. Largemouth and smallmouth bass abound, as do walleye, yellow perch, chain pickerel, and pike. White catfish have been introduced and are doing well, and in addition there are bluegills, sunfish, white perch, and brown bullheads.

In the bogs and marshes, snapping turtles also lurk (stay away from the head and don't misjudge how far that head can strike out from the shell) as does the painted turtle. Here too can be found the five-lined salamander and the four-toed variety; newts love bogs and marshes, as do green frogs. In the spring a shrill, plaintive pleasant chorus rises from stream sides, bogs, and swamps as the small spring peepers give forth their signal of the end of winter.

The small life of woods and open ground is all around you during any walk in the uplands or valleys. You may run across the box turtle and the common American toad. There is also the gray tree frog and the wood frog. The white-footed mouse is there—somewhere, being a timid animal. His timidity is shared by the five-lined skink. The Jefferson salamander along with the marbled and red-backed salamander can be located, and in the open spaces, the meadow vole.

Of all the forms of wildlife birds must surely lead the list in popularity. They appeal to the visual sense, both by their markings and color as well as by their graceful flight.

Along Connecticut's shore the ubiquitous herring gull screams, wheels, and drops over the shining water and the fringe of land. An occasional ring-billed gull can be spotted. The more dramatically marked common tern dips and skims and on very rare occasions a black-legged kittiwake or a black skimmer can be seen. Spotted sandpipers and an occasional sanderling hover over and scamper across the beaches. Lord of them all is the osprey. In the tidal rivers and marshes as well as in freshwater streams and ponds are rails, killdeer, woodcock, and snipe. Graceful, shy members of the heron family include the great blue, little blue, little green, and the black-crowned night heron. Both of the bitterns on the North American continent can be glimpsed although they are rare: the American bittern and the least bittern. These are even shyer than herons.

In both salt and fresh water seasonally come the grebes, mallards, teals (both blue- and green-winged) black- and pintail ducks, wood ducks, ring-necked ducks, the canvasback, and both the greater and lesser scaup.

Land birds of Connecticut are numerous and varied. Among the game birds are the ruffed grouse, quail or bob white, and the imported ring-necked pheasant. Predatory birds are owls (great horned, screech, barn, and barred, to name only a few) and hawks—the most common: the red-tailed and broad-winged. Of the carrion birds, the crow and the turkey buzzard are most frequently seen. Starlings are so numerous as to pose a threat to less hardy, primitive types. They have been known to drive out barn swallows from their annual nesting sites—which is sad, because there is nothing more touching than the sight of young swallows awkwardly trying their wings during the sunlit hours of an early summer evening. The raucous blue jay is here too, as are sparrows, juncos, warblers, thrushes, and a wide range of blackbirds. In early spring the coming of red-winged blackbirds with their comforting churring in thickets along brooks is a most rewarding experience. Grackles arrive noisily shortly after the red-winged blackbirds, and these glistening flocks are another herald of spring, as, of course, are the robins.

The colorful birds are plentiful too: the cardinal, scarlet tanager, oriole, grosbeak, redstart, and purple finch. Goldfinches and yellow warblers add their color to the scene. Less colorful and shyer are the brown thrasher and the wood thrush. Not at all shy are the many varieties of sparrows that appear. Woodpeckers, black and white warblers, and nuthatches walk calmly upside down on tree trunks searching for food. Catbirds and cowbirds, as well as the black-billed cuckoo, are aggressive birds, and when the hummingbirds arrive the summer has begun.

# 2

# The Towns and Cities of Connecticut

The first settlements in Connecticut were, or soon became, towns. As the population spread beyond town limits, the new centers of homes and farms became first parishes, and later evolved into new towns. Thus all the land area within the state finally was filled, border to border, with towns.

Several towns increased in population until the most populated part of it became a borough and then a city within the town borders. Continued growth produced finally the consolidated city and town whose borders matched and it thereafter was a single tax and political unit, a city.

Much of this great growth occurred in the nineteenth and early twentieth centuries when the flood of immigrants from Europe was at its height. In addition, the strong urban shift of the country's black and Puerto Rican populations has added to the ethnic and racial diversity of the state's cities. As a result, many of the industrial centers have a distinct ethnic character that lends variety to the state's otherwise dour Yankee foundations. The New Haven area, for example, has a large Italian population. New Britain and Bridgeport have Polish communities, and Waterbury has a large Lithuanian colony. Irish and Canadian immigrants are spread throughout the state, while Jewish settlement centers in Hartford and New Haven. In Colchester and Lebanon, Jewish farmers settled early and today form a prominent segment of the population. All these mixtures produce a variety of stores, churches, restaurants, and community festivities that retain the flavor of the ethnic origin but are full-bloodedly American in philosophy.

There are 169 towns and consolidated cities in Connecticut. A number of towns have boroughs within their borders and there still are some with cities within larger town borders. The city of Willimantic, for example, lies within the town of Windham, and the city of Winsted (a taxing unit only) is in the town of Winchester. Such cities as Hartford, Bridgeport, and Stamford have long since consolidated all functions of the town within the city structure.

The 169 towns and consolidated cities in the following section are listed and described in alphabetical order. If the name of a community for which you are searching is not the town name itself, you will find it in the appendix, where such communities (and the towns in which they are located) are listed.

In describing the cities and towns, effort was made to give the flavor of the community, its history, industrial accomplishments, and present appearance.

ANDOVER *(Tolland County. Rtes. into: U.S. 6; state 87, 316; 15.6 sq. mi.; 2,099 pop.)*
In the Eastern Highland section of the state, this small agricultural community was settled in 1718 and named for Andover, Massachusetts, in 1747 as a parish. Township came to Andover in 1848. Little has happened since its beginning to disturb the town. Only two incidents appear to have been recorded when "something happened." In 1760 a Captain Simon Smith passed through the town en route from Thompsonville and his home in New London. The captain had been serving in the French and Indian War and became ill on his journey. He fell from his horse and died of what Andover citizens believed was smallpox. To protect themselves from that dread disease they buried the captain, his horse, and all his gear, on the spot by the road where he fell. Today on Gilead Road in Andover a worn marker to his memory can be seen: "Loved yet unattended. All Alone. Sweetly repose beneath this humble stone ye last remains."

The other incident, cheerier, involved General Lafayette, who camped for three nights with a detachment of his men in the town on the land of Nathan Kingsbury, who entertained the French general in his home.

The town today partakes of the great sense of open sky characteristic of eastern Connecticut towns and little of modern life has come to spoil the community.

*To See and Do: (1)* Nathan Hale State Forest, northeast of the village center, offers hunting and hiking.

*(2)* The Townsend and Center cemeteries are ancient and have headstones dating from the seventeenth century.

ANSONIA *(New Haven County. Rtes. into: 8, 115, 243, 334; 6.2 sq. mi.; 21,160 pop.)*

A manufacturing city in the Naugatuck Valley, Ansonia was originally a part of Derby. In the seventeenth century the area was a wilderness inhabited by only a few hardy "pioneers" from the center of Derby. Its history during and prior to the Revolutionary War is a part of the parent town. The real beginnings of Ansonia, in fact, came from a controversy between one Anson G. Phelps and landowners in Derby. They would not sell him sites for proposed copper and brass mills—so he bought land in what is now his namesake city, Ansonia, and industrial development followed rapidly. That was in 1843, and from its founding Ansonia grew rapidly to city status. Today it still is a leading manufacturer of brass and copper products.

The industrial growth of the nineteenth century has given Ansonia its present appearance and there are few buildings still standing that predate the advent of Mr. Phelps. To help Phelps start his giant mills, Almon and Franklin Farrell, an enterprising father-and-son team, created a foundry in 1848 to produce his machinery (haulage from Pittsburgh being too costly) and that foundry became a worldwide enterprise that flourishes today. Like many Naugatuck Valley towns, Ansonia needed workers and the mid-nineteenth century immigration from all parts of Europe brought them, so that today their descendants are numerous in the factories, stores, and plants that make up the city. The city's most notable son (other than Anson Phelps) was David Humphreys, who was born there. He became a general in the Revolutionary War and, at Yorktown, accepted General Cornwallis' sword when the British surrendered.

*To See and Do: (1)* The Rev. Richard Mansfield House, 35 Jewett St. (Ansonia-Derby Historical Society). Moved from its original location across the street, this seventeenth-century house was the home of that clergyman who had the longest service of any Episcopal minister in the state: seventy-two years. It is furnished in the period and some of Rev. Mansfield's original papers are on display.

*(2)* David Humphreys House, Elm St. (Ansonia-Derby Historical

Society). This essentially eighteenth-century house is undergoing restoration and in all probability will be furnished in the period. It is the birthplace of David Humphreys (see above) who, in addition to generaling, was minister to both Spain and Portugal after the war and later became a successful businessman in the woolen industry.

(3) Olde Towne Burying Ground, Elm St.—across from the Humphreys House. Some of the oldest headstones in the community exist here as does a monument to the settlers who died in the Deerfield (Massachusetts) Massacre.

(4) Pork Hollow Monument, Wakelee Ave. A memorial to the region surrounding, which got its name after patriots buried food there to protect it from British raids during the Revolutionary War.

ASHFORD (Windham County. Rtes. into: I–86, Exit 104; U.S. 44, 44A; state 89; 40.3 sq. mi.; 2,156 pop. Other communities: Warrenville, West Ashford, Westford.)
Knowlton's Rangers of Revolutionary War fame were led by Colonel Knowlton of Ashford. With about seventy-five men he marched to Boston in time to support troops at the Battle of Bunker Hill. He was later killed covering a retreat of Washington's troops on Long Island. His grandnephew, Nathaniel Lyon, made a name for himself in later years (see Eastford).

Both Ashford and Warrenville have fine old houses near their small centers, and in the mid-nineteenth-century Westford became the location of a prosperous glass factory built and owned by a native, Michael Richmond. Today the quiet villages exist on agricultural activity, and both natives and visitors can enjoy the views from Rte. 89 in this sparsely settled town in the eastern highlands of Connecticut.

To See and Do: Fishing in Knowlton Pond, south of U.S. 44A, below West Ashford. Hiking in Natchaug State Forest (inquire locally), with the Nipmuck Trail crossing U.S. 44, 1.4 miles west of West Ashford. Hunting off Rte. 89 in the southern part of town in the 1,300-acre preserve of the Eastern Connecticut Sportsmen's

Association (see appendix), also in sections of the Natchaug State Forest, north of U.S. 44 and east of Rte. 89, below Westford.

*AVON (Hartford County. Rtes. into : U.S. 44, 202; state 10, 167, 177; 23.5 sq. mi.; 8,352 pop.)*
This open, residential community serves as a pleasant "bedroom" town for Hartford. The woodlands, fields, and rolling hills make excellent homesites.

In 1829, the ill-fated Farmington Canal was opened. It was to link all of northern New England to Long Island Sound via New Haven (see Cheshire). Manufacturers scurried to build plants along the proposed waterway, which passed through Avon. The burgeoning community grew so fast that it was incorporated in 1830 from its southerly parent town of Farmington. Alas, the canal failed and with it went Avon's chances of being labeled as an "industrial" town. Some remains of the canal are visible east of Old Farms Rd. less than a mile south of the junction of Old Farms and Country Club Rd. Today, Avon is experiencing growth of commercial and industrial properties, although development is strictly controlled by rigid zoning regulations.

Early settlers first came into the region in 1645 when Avon was a part of Farmington. The town is the location of a preparatory school, Avon Old Farms, whose architecture is of onsite quarried brownstone and hewn beams, giving the impression of a rural English village.

The Talcott Mountain Science Center is an educational facility supported by area towns and organizations. Located on a prominent peak of Avon Mountain, the center utilizes modern scientific equipment for the study of astronomy, meteorology, and geology. The Farmington River, flowing south and forming the western border of the town, makes a surprising bend below the town and flows northward through the eastern section.

*To See and Do: (1)* The Town Hall Complex, 60 West Main St., is a unique municipal facility. Formerly used for the manufacture of explosive cord, the buildings have two-foot-thick brownstone walls and are amidst a parklike setting.

*(2)* The Farmington River has good fishing and is well known for its excellent canoeing. Talcott Mountain State Park offers excellent hiking and picnicking.

*(3)* Horse Guard State Park, Rte. 167, is the home of the Governor's Horse Guard. The scenic rolling fields at the park provide grazing land for the horses that are used for official ceremonial events.

BARKHAMSTED *(Litchfield County. Rtes. into: U.S. 44; state 20, 179, 181, 219, 318; 39.0 sq. mi.; 2,066 pop. Other communities: Pleasant Valley, Riverton.)*
Incorporated in 1779 and named for an English town, Barkhamsted today is all country, with the huge Barkhamsted Reservoir splitting the township in two. A great proportion of the town is state forest (see below) and looks much as it did in the earliest days when one Molly Barber of Wethersfield eloped from her home with an Indian lover named Chaugham. They fled to Barkhamsted and built a home in the wilderness where, according to reports, permanent happiness set in. The home was known locally as the Barkhamsted Lighthouse, for Chaugham kept lamps burning brightly and weary stage drivers could spot it after dark and so get their bearings.

The small crossroads community of Pleasant Valley is one of the most aptly named in the state. It *is* pleasant. The few buildings comprising its center are grouped by a brook in a dell, where all the cares of the world appear to have been forgotten. And Riverton is the home of the famous Hitchcock chair. Here in 1818 Lambert (not Alfred) Hitchcock set up his chair factory, and his decorated chairs became popular. Today they are highly prized by lovers of nineteenth-century antiques. And today they are being reproduced to meet a demand that outruns the supply of original ones.

*To See and Do: (1)* Hitchcock Museum, Riverton. A fine collection of American antiques in various room arrangements makes an interesting visit. The pieces range from early-eighteenth to late-nineteenth century and of course include original Hitchcock chairs. The museum is in the old Union Church (Episcopal), built in 1829 of local granite and hewn oak and chestnut timbers.

*(2)* Hitchcock chair reproductions can be viewed in the making and then purchased at the factory in Riverton (see above).

*(3)* American Legion State Forest and People's State Forest (between Riverton and Pleasant Valley) total some 3,700 acres, where picnicking, hiking, fishing, and hunting can be enjoyed. There is also a snowmobile area in People's State Forest. On the eastern side of the reservoir, Tunxis Trail crosses Rte. 219 at 1.3 miles north of the Barkhamsted dam. Below the dam, just west of Rte. 219, boating with a launch site is available, and fishing can be enjoyed. West Hill Pond also offers fishing and a boat-launch site 3½ miles west of junction of U.S. 44 and Rte. 181.

BEACON FALLS *(New Haven County. Rtes. into: 8, 42; 9.8 sq. mi.; 3,546 pop.)*
This small town astride the Naugatuck River was once a thriving industrial community. It was settled in the seventeenth century and as industry in the state grew, it grew also, using the waterpower of the river to drive machinery in the early woolen mills. Following the Civil War, rubber footwear was manufactured here and it caught on. The period was the town's heyday. The footwear factory was so prosperous it took the fancy of the U.S. Rubber Company, which bought it—and promptly moved the plant to Naugatuck, to the north, which has reduced the town to being a warehouse depot and producer of metal hinges.

*To See and Do:* Naugatuck State Forest extends into the northern part of town, west of Rte. 8, and offers hiking, hunting, and picnicking on both sides of the Naugatuck River. The river, running through the forest here just west of Rte. 8, retains much of its charm, and industrial buildings do not intrude.

BERLIN *(Hartford County. Rtes. into: U.S. 5; state 9, 15, 71, 71A, 160, 364; 27.0 sq. mi.; 14,149 pop. Other communities: East Berlin, Kensington.)*

The ubiquitous "Yankee Pedlar" of bygone days got some of his impetus here when two Irish brothers, Edward and William Pattison, brought bright, shiny tinware to the attention of the colonial housewife in 1740. Using imported sheet tin they fashioned cheap household ware that beat pewter in price and appearance. They sold so much that they soon had saturated the market in Berlin, so they produced more and strapped it on their backs and headed for other communities in true peddler fashion.

Berlin kept in the forefront of Connecticut manufacturing through the eighteenth and nineteenth centuries. In fact, New Britain, a larger present-day manufacturing center, is really a spin-off of Berlin, for it was once part of the town. And while Eli Whitney is often credited with "inventing" interchangeable parts, one Simeon North started making horse pistols and secured a government contract for 20,000, which were to "correspond so exactly that . . . any part . . . may be fitted to any other pistol of the twenty thousand." So sure was North of his methods of manufacture that he agreed to supply the pistols for seven dollars apiece.

The tradition of manufacturing has been kept up and the town is devoted to the production of everything from aircraft parts to clay pots.

The Congregational Church in Kensington had the first organ installed in a New England church and the first of what were to be hundreds of Civil War monuments went up in the same church-yard in 1863, dedicated to Kensington men who had died at Antietam, Cold Harbor, and Andersonville.

The name of the town, by the way, is pronounced "Burr'-lin," *not* like its namesake in Germany.

*To See and Do:* Lamentation Mountain State Park, east of U.S. 5 and state 15 on the southern edge of town (47 acres). Hiking here, and on the Metacomet Trail, which passes through the east edge of the park. Boating and fishing on Silver Lake west of the park and U.S. 5 (launch site). Access area located at northwest end of lake about 1 mile west of Berlin Turnpike (Rtes. 5 and 15).) State fish hatchery on Rte. 71 in the southern part of town. Golf at the Timberlin Golf Club on Southington Rd., in nearby Kensington.

BETHANY *(New Haven County. Rtes. into: 42, 63, 69; 21.0 sq. mi.; 3,857 pop.)*

Law and order prevails now in this suburban and partially rural town near New Haven, but in 1780 things were different. Patriots led by a Captain Dayton came from Long Island to live in Bethany. Long Island Tories had made it too hot for them. The Tories, in fact, would not leave Dayton and his men alone. Seven of them under the command of a Loyalist officer invaded Dayton's home while he was away on a journey. They bound and gagged Dayton's wife and ransacked his home, taking or destroying 5,000 pounds' worth of goods. Eventually the Tories were caught and sent to Newgate Prison (see East Granby).

The town has a rugged topography with Beacon Hill (south of Rte. 63 in the northwest corner of town) being its highest point. From atop a large boulder on its summit, views of surrounding towns and the Naugatuck River Valley can be had.

*To See and Do:* Part of Naugatuck State Forest extends into the town near Beacon Hill, north of Rte. 42, offering hiking and picnicking.

BETHEL *(Fairfield County. Rtes. into: I–84, Exit 8; U.S. 6, 202, 202A; state 53, 58; 17.0 sq. mi.; 10,945 pop.)*

Named from the Hebrew, meaning "House of God," Bethel was incorporated from Danbury in 1855 and Danbury is still the "parent" town. The hills and valleys of Bethel's rugged terrain are dotted with houses of people who work in Danbury. The main street of the town has a relaxed village aspect and a walk along it is pleasant.

Bethel's first citizen was Phineas T. Barnum of circus fame (see Bridgeport). Late in his career, Barnum lived up to his reputation and gave a monument to himself—an eighteen-foot bronze fountain—to the town. It was erected in Barnum Square on Greenwood Ave. but required so much water it finally was dismantled.

Original industries included hat making—which made Danbury famous—and hat making persisted well into the twentieth century. Today, the industry fluctuates as hats are either in or out. Electronics, chemicals and wire production help diversify the town's industrial activity.

*To See and Do: (1)* The Israel Putnam Memorial State Park extends into the southern section of Bethel (Rte. 58) and the war museum and historic site, though in Redding, can be partially claimed by the town. Hiking, fishing, and picnicking may be enjoyed in the park's 183 acres. Golf at the Terre Haute Golf Course off Rte. 53.

*(2)* East Swamp, north of U.S. 202 (for exact directions, inquire locally), allows hunting in season on eighty-two acres.

*(3)* The Bethel Public Library is housed in an interesting Greek Revival house on Greenwood Ave.

BETHLEHEM *(Litchfield County. Rtes. into: 61, 132; 19.7 sq. mi.; 1,923 pop.)*
Incorporated in 1787 as Bethlehem (which in Hebrew means "House of Bread"), the town post office here inevitably handles a great volume of Christmas mail for those who wish the postmark on their cards. The town was originally part of Woodbury's North Purchase, which was settled in 1734. It is a quiet, hilly town, where today, as earlier, the principal business is agriculture and dairying.

A Reverend Joseph Bellamy arrived in the area in 1738 and in 1740 began a fifty-year pastorate there. He was widely known and is reported to have preached in over two hundred places throughout New England. A monument to his service stands on the site of the first Bethlehem church, at the north end of the small, triangular green. The good reverend captivated many people with his eloquence and ran what amounted to a theological seminary in his home for many years.

Around the green today are eighteenth- and nineteenth-century buildings, and an air of tranquillity still encompasses the center.

*To See and Do:* Regina Laudis Priory Creche, Flanders Rd., south of the center about 1 mile. Housed in an eighteenth-century barn is a many-figured creche, which is the work of eighteenth-century

Neapolitan artists. Figures depict worshipers at the crib of the infant Jesus and include workmen, lords, beggars, ladies, servants, and peasants. It is unique in America. The priory was established following World War II by refugees from Europe. They are Sisters of the Benedictine Order, and form a contemplative, semi-enclosed community.

BLOOMFIELD *(Hartford County. Rtes. into: 178, 185, 187, 189, 218, 305; 26.4 sq. mi.; 18,301 pop. Other communities: Blue Hills, North Bloomfield.)*

In recent years, Bloomfield has become the home of several major businesses that formerly were located in Hartford. The new commercial architecture set off on the rolling hills of the town is pleasing. Aside from being a headquarters town for businesses, Bloomfield is a residential suburb of Hartford itself. Its small green and old roads have few old houses that have not undergone unfortunate "modernization" if not total obliteration. The region was settled originally in the seventeenth century but remained a parish until Farmington, Windsor, and Simsbury contributed bits of themselves to form what was first called Wintonbury. Its present name came from a Hartford family of local fame.

Bloomfield's or Wintonbury's most illustrious son probably was James G. Batterson. He was the architect of the soldier's monument at Gettysburg and he built the present state capitol building in Hartford. In addition, he founded the Traveler's Insurance Company.

*To See and Do:* Penwood State Park (north off Rte. 185) of 787 acres offers hiking and picnicking. The Metacomet Trail passes through the park and parallels the western border of the town on a high trap-rock escarpment. Hiking and picnicking also in 557-acre Talcott Mountain State Park in the northwestern corner of town near junction of Rtes. 187 and 189. Fishing in Barber Pond (inquire locally for directions).

BOLTON *(Tolland County. Rtes. into: I–84; U.S. 6, 44A; state 85; 15.5 sq. mi.; 3,691 pop.)*
Settled in 1716 and incorporated four years later, Bolton was named either for Bolton, Lancashire, or the Duke of Bolton. Its high, open hilly aspect becomes downright mountainous in the northern part, where Bolton Mountain and Bolton Notch are sites of former quarries. Garnets and other worthwhile stones were quarried here.

Bolton center is a pleasant country residential grouping with a plain white Congregational church displaying modest dignity. Several late-eighteenth- and early-nineteenth-century homes along Bolton Center Rd. make a pleasant scene with distant views of the rolling land of eastern Connecticut visible behind them.

*To See and Do:* Bolton Notch State Park (U.S. 6 and 44A) is undeveloped, but hiking in the rugged area gives a feeling of mountain walking. Gay City State Park, west of Rte. 85, extends into the southern edge of town and there are swimming, fishing, hiking, and picnicking available. Bolton Lakes offer fishing (boat-launch site) north side of U.S. 44A, about 1 mile east of Bolton Notch. Hunting can be enjoyed in the Manchester Sportsmen's Association preserve (1,321 acres—see appendix) and in the 654-acre Bolton Area one-half mile north of the Bolton-Hebron town line and west of Rte. 85. There is also fishing in Bolton Notch Pond, west of Bolton Notch, on the north side of U.S. 44A.

BOZRAH *(New London County. Rtes. into: 2, 32, 87, 163; 20.0 sq. mi.; 2,036 pop. Other communities: Fitchville, Gilman.)*
The post office is in Fitchville, as is the Town Hall, a handsome granite building with white trimmed windows. Fitchville itself is a textile mill town and the workers' houses, large frame duplexes, line old Rte. 2 through the community. Gilman is a small cluster of well-kept houses on a quiet side road that has an air of tranquillity about it.

The town name from the Hebrew, meaning "Enclosure" came from a Bible-quoting native who was locally known as "The Prophet." When the town was incorporated from Norwich in 1786 the good burghers remembered his quotation from Isaiah, which included the word *bozrah.*

*To See and Do:* Gardner Lake, west of Rte. 163, in the southwest corner of town, offers boating with a launch site and fishing (see Salem). Hunting in the Norwich Fish and Game Association and Wewecus Hill Farmers Areas (see appendix) north of Rte. 82 and along Rte. 2.


BRANFORD *(New Haven County. Rtes. into: I–95, Exits 53 through 56—also called the Connecticut Turnpike; U.S. 1; state 80, 100, 139, 142, 146; 27.9 sq. mi.; 20,444 pop. Other communities: Stony Creek, Pine Orchard, Indian Neck, Short Beach.)*
The area known to the Indians on the Long Island shore as Totoket was purchased by the New Haven colony in 1638. Named Brentford for the English town, it has come down as Branford and so it remains today.

In 1665 when the New Haven colony was absorbed by the Connecticut colony (Hartford region) some of Branford's residents were so incensed that they packed up and moved to New Jersey, where they founded a town called Newark.

Reaching from an unsurpassed shore on Long Island Sound up into gently rolling northern hills, Branford today is largely residential although the American Wire Company has a large factory near the railroad and several light industries function in the town.

The green in the center of town has, at its eastern end, Trinity Episcopal Church, a Gothic adaptation made of wood. The large columned Town Hall separates Trinity from the white-spired red brick Congregational Church, while on the west end of the green the Baptist Church, organized in the town in 1837, is a traditional Greek Revival white-clapboarded, black-shuttered meeting house with a short, square belfry. Also on the green is a small, white school building with a short tower topped by a quaint cupola. The worn white clapboards and small-paned twelve-over-twelve windows speak more eloquently of the town's past history than any other building on the green.

*To See and Do: (1)* Boat trips among the Thimble Islands. This cluster of nearly thirty islets off Stony Creek gives a down-east, coast-of-Maine feeling. But they are not gray New England granite. They're pink, and a few have private summer homes perched among the cedars surrounded by rocky shores. During good weather in the late spring, summer, and early fall, excursions can be taken among them by boat from the Town Dock at the foot of Thimble Island Rd. in Stony Creek. Legend attaches itself to the islands. Captain Kidd in 1699 was making a fast getaway from authorities in his sloop, *San Antonio.* Fearing capture, he went ashore on one of the Thimble Islands and buried some of his stolen treasure. But which island? And where? To this day no one knows, although searchers have been scouring the region for years.

*(2)* Branford Trolley Museum (see East Haven, oddly enough).

*(3)* Blackstone Memorial Library Museum, West Main St. This large, almost overpowering library was built in 1896. A museum on an upper floor displays Indian artifacts and articles pertinent to the early history of the town.

*(4)* Drives around Branford. The most scenic area is along the shore where Rtes. 142 and 146 wind through wetlands, the shore communities, and wooded rocky hills, with occasional views out over Long Island Sound. East from the green in the center of town a number of eighteenth-century houses line the Boston Post Road (U.S. 1).

*(5)* Regulated hunting is available in the northern part of Branford and fishing (with permission of the New Haven Water Company) in Lake Saltonstall on the west border of the town, over which Rte. I–95 passes.

*(6)* Town beaches. Policy varies regarding nonresident use. Check with the town hall.


BRIDGEPORT *(Fairfield County. Rtes. into: I–95, which is also the Connecticut Turnpike here, Exits 25 through 30; U.S. 1; state 8, 25, 127; 17.5 sq. mi.; 156,542 pop.)*
Exceeded in population only by Hartford and in manufacturing by none, Bridgeport is a leading city in the state. Its haphazard growth as it plunged into industrial activity in 1840 remains

evident today by the insoluble problem of its main street. But off that occluded traffic artery, new buildings of striking design are making the downtown section less unsightly.

Settlers from Fairfield and Stratford moved into what is now Bridgeport in the middle of the seventeenth century, having purchased land from the Pequonnock Indians for a few bushels of corn and several blankets. The settlers made a treaty with the Indians, with a reservation for them—and as might be expected, went back on their word, crowding them out.

The town was for a time called Stratfield and Newfield but when a drawbridge was built over the Pequonnock River, its name became Bridgeport. In the eighteenth and early-nineteenth centuries the town "went to sea" in trade and whaling vessels like nearly all other seaports in New England. But with the coming of the railroads an industrial boom began that has pushed the city to the top as an industrial and manufacturing center. Like other Connecticut towns, Bridgeport also has its share of firsts. Elias Howe, inventor of the sewing machine, set up his plant here only to be scoffed out of business. England took him in, and took him in other ways, too, and he returned, broke, to Bridgeport to find other manufacturers infringing on his patent. He fought in the courts for many years before receiving his rights under the original patent, and died in his early middle years, probably as a result of the strains of his long fight. A horseless carriage was built in Bridgeport in 1895 and in 1902 the Locomobile Company began producing automobiles and continued until 1929. The American Gramophone Company in Bridgeport manufactured the first records in the United States. The name later became the Columbia Phonograph Company.

One of the leading early citizens of Bridgeport was Phineas T. Barnum, of circus fame and fortune. To Bridgeport he is more than the showman, however. He was the town's leading citizen in the nineteenth century, providing parks, serving as mayor, straightening out railroad service (Oh Phineas, thou shouldst be living at this hour!), bringing industry to the city and persuading the federal government to dredge the harbor for use by deep-water vessels. Though born in Bethel, he made Bridgeport his home and today a statue of him in Seaside Park (a 200-acre tract he gave to the city) at the seaward end of Main St. serves as a memorial to him. Barnum is buried in Bridgeport's Mt. Grove Cemetery.

One of Barnum's prize circus attractions, General Tom Thumb, a midget, was a native of Bridgeport and his wedding to Lavinia Warren, a midget lady, in 1863 took Bridgeport citizens' minds off the Civil War.

Now, every summer in late June, Bridgeport decks itself out in an annual Barnum Festival with more than two dozen events, including parade, fireworks, art and music shows, and a Midway. The festival has been described as the largest civic celebration in the northeast.

During the Revolutionary War, Bridgeport was still part of Stratford and like that and other towns along the shores of Long Island Sound, the inhabitants were often harassed by minor raids and by Tory trading with the British. The return of smallpox-infected prisoners by the British under a truce flag at Stratford Point brought the scourge to that community in 1777.

*To See and Do:* (1) The Barnum Museum, Gilbert and Union Sts. Aptly located in an ornate "Romanesque" building planned by Barnum himself, the museum houses a history of circus life complete with posters and a mounted baby elephant. The William R. Brinley Model Circus is here also. Half a million hand-carved animals, performers, and circus equipment offer a startling display that can be put into motion. It required forty-two years to complete. Another exhibit is a model Alpine village made by a Swiss watchmaker, Joseph Begmann, over a hundred years ago— and it still "runs like a clock."

(2) Museum of Art, Science, and Industry, 4450 Park Ave. The unique aim of this museum is to relate apparently dissimilar human activities by showing the art in such early and late industries as period furniture and contemporary design. Participatory exhibits (push the button, watch what happens), modern paintings and sculpture by such masters as Calder, Picasso, Weber, and Lipschitz. A planetarium plus science-history and science-explaining displays help attract 150,000 visitors a year. The John Brooks House (a 1788 dwelling) will be moved to the museum site

and furnished with items already within the museum's collection.

*(3)* Beardsley Park and Zoo, Noble St. A bird and mammal house is open to visitors in this park, one of thirty-three municipal parks in the city.

*(4)* Sacred Heart University, 5229 Park Ave. A liberal arts institution of just over 2,000 students offers among other attractions the usual college programs of drama and music periodically. The campus of tasteful modern buildings is worth a pleasant stroll.

*(5)* University of Bridgeport, 380 University Ave. A new nine-story Arts-Humanities Center has a 900-seat Little Theatre and a 200-seat Experimental Theatre where dramatic productions are given. An art gallery and outdoor sculpture garden and music-recital halls give space to these arts for presentations on a usual college schedule.

*(6)* Klein Memorial Auditorium, 910 Fairfield Ave. The Bridgeport Symphony presents concerts on a regularly scheduled program.

*(7)* Wonderland of Ice, Beardsley Park, where hockey games, ice shows, and public skating are available.

*(8)* Seaside Park, end of Main St. Originally donated to the city by P. T. Barnum, this 200-acre strip of shore has long been a recreational spot for Bridgeport citizens and visitors. There are concessions and public bathhouses. Picnicking and sunbathing are summer-long activities. Swimming has been hampered recently as pollution levels of the water in Long Island Sound rise above the danger point. Saltwater fishing is available in the Pequonnock River estuary and in the Sound itself.

*(9)* Housatonic Museum of Contemporary Art, 510 Barnum Ave. Changing exhibits of modern art.

*10)* Polka Dot Playhouse, Pleasure Beach. In a new 250-seat building, Playhouse people stage productions on a regular basis.


BRIDGEWATER *(Litchfield County. Rtes. into: 67, 133; 16.3 sq. mi.; 1,277 pop.)*
A pleasant agricultural and summer community whose southern

tip is defined by the junction of the Housatonic and Shepaug rivers, Bridgewater was named descriptively: a bridge over a river. Named in 1803, the town originally was part of New Milford to the north, and its history before and during the Revolutionary War was New Milford's.

A forerunner of premium selling flourished in Bridgewater and put the town on the map. Charles B. Thompson offered premiums for soap selling about 1870 and since he had dolls to offer for premiums, little girls all over the country sold soap and more soap to get a doll. So large was the demand for soap that Thompson had to set up a factory in Bridgewater, instead of buying from manufacturers, and shipping both soap and dolls. This was the only large industry the town ever saw. On Thompson's passing, Bridgewater returned to agricultural pursuits and catering to summer visitors, many of whom made the town their permanent home. From its roads there are many excellent views to be savored in leisurely fashion and along these roads are farmhouses of the early nineteenth century.

*To See and Do: (1)* The Captain's House, Main St. (Bridgewater Historical Society). The small, quaint nineteenth-century house with eyebrow windows to let light enter the attic was, for a while, the home of one William Dickson Burnham. As a boy of fourteen, Burnham went to sea as a cabin boy aboard a packet. By the time he was thirty-seven, he had risen to become a master mariner licensed to skipper any size ship, sail or steam, on all the seas of the world. He later became founder and president of the Hawaiian Steamship Line and probably is Bridgewater's most successful former citizen. The house is furnished as a small country store.

*(2)* The Elijah Peck House (1820), Main St.—next to the Captain's House. Former home of a Bridgewater storekeeper, the house has furnishings appropriate to the early years of the nineteenth century.

*(3)* Fishing in Lake Lillinonah—a man-made lake on the Housatonic River, northeast of Rte. 133. There is a boat-launch site available on the Bridgewater side of the bridge, over which Rte. 133 passes.

BRISTOL *(Hartford County. Rtes. into: U.S. 6, 202; state 69, 72, 229; 26.6 sq. mi.; 55,487 pop.)*
This busy industrial city has followed the industrial revolution from its beginnings. The area was part of Farmington, and although land was divided up in the seventeenth century, settlers did not build there until the first decades of the eighteenth century. The name comes from Bristol, England, and was taken in 1785. Prior to that time it was known as New Cambridge.

In the early years of the nineteenth century as many as fifty clock manufacturers were working on clocks or clock parts and the first known clockmaker, Gideon Roberts, was making clocks as early as 1790. Works then were of wood but as industrial know-how increased and metal became available, clocks and other precision machinery were produced here. Bristol had its share of inventors and innovators as the machine age dawned and the first watches with jewel bearings were made here. Perhaps the oddest invention to come out of Bristol was the collapsible steel fishing rod. It was invented by Everett Horton, a Bristol mechanic who wanted to sneak away from his wife and go fishing on Sunday. With the rod telescoped shut he could hide it under his coat. With the rod hidden, Horton also escaped the attention of constables who were looking for Sabbath-breaking citizens, like the errant angler.

Clocks, like most fine machinery of the time, were purchased only by the rich. But when mass production techniques became available they were quickly adopted by Bristol manufacturers and the cheap kitchen clock was produced by the thousands for mass purchase.

The skills of those early times remain in Bristol and today ball bearings, timing devices, electric motors, and many other precision items are produced.

In its rush into the technological twentieth century, Bristol has obliterated most of the old landmarks and buildings that enhance less bustling towns. This, plus the influx of European immigrants during the middle decades of the nineteenth century, has produced a growing, changing Yankee town more attuned to the business future than the aesthetic of the past.

*To See and Do: (1)* American Clock and Watch Museum, 100 Maple St. Located in the Miles Lewis House, which was built in 1801 when clockmaking really flourished in Bristol, the museum has over 450 clocks of American manufacture and a watch collection of 200 timepieces that shows the craftsmanship of the early workers. In addition there is a horological library and material relating to the early clockmakers in the town.

*(2)* Bristol Nurseries, Pinehurst Rd. Acres of chrysanthemums blossom here in the autumn, and this growing industry has sparked an annual festival in October of each year.

*(3)* Cedar Lake, west of Wolcott Rd. (Rte. 69), in the southwestern part of the city, offers boating and swimming. Also considered by Bristol citizens as part of their scene is Lake Compounce (Lake Rd. heading toward Southington), where boating and swimming and an amusement park offer recreation. The 2,500-acre Bristol Fish and Game Club land (see appendix) gives nimrods a chance, while golfers can play at the Red Stone Hill Golf Club on Red Stone Hill Rd.

**BROOKFIELD** *(Fairfield County. Rtes. into: U.S. 7; state 25, 133; 19.8 sq. mi.; 9,688 pop. Other communities: Brookfield Center.)*
Settled about 1700, Brookfield was originally a part of Danbury, New Milford, and Newtown. Much traveled U.S. 7 and Rte. 25 meet at Brookfield, while Brookfield Center is east of U.S. 7 at the junction of Rtes. 25 and 133. Both communities have their share of eighteenth- and nineteenth-century houses. Brick and frame, the early houses can be admired on Pocono Rd., Long Meadow Rd., and on U.S. 7 itself, as well as in the centers.

The town today is largely residential and there are apartment complexes and housing developments. The Congregational Church at Brookfield Center (west side of Rte. 25) was built in 1854. It represents a trim example of Greek Revival country church architecture. The library facing it (formerly the town hall) is a small, quaint building built in 1876 that gives this road junction much of its charm.

North of Brookfield Center, on Rte. 25 and south of it, are good views to the west, and many back roads of the town (like Obtuse

Rd. and Dingle-Brook Rd.) offer views of distant hills as well as old farm houses.

The Revolutionary War history of Brookfield is that of its parent towns and the parish, as it then was, sent men to the defense of Danbury when the British attacked that larger community (see Danbury). Early gristmills and sawmills and ironworks became the industries of Brookfield, and today light manufacturing, printing, and electronic assembly plants make up the industrial life of the town.

*To See and Do:* Candlewood Lake, which lies on the west edge of Brookfield, west of U.S. 7, offers a full range of summer lake activities. Lake Lillinonah (Rte. 133) is a manmade lake on the Housatonic River (see Bridgewater). Fishing and boating can be enjoyed there. Hunting in 1,475-acre Brookfield Sportsmen's Club (see appendix). Golfers can play at the Brookfield Golf Club, in Brookfield Center.

BROOKLYN *(Windham County. Rtes. into: U.S. 6; state 169, 205; 28.7 sq. mi.; 4,965 pop. Other communities: East Brooklyn.)*
Most eastern Connecticut towns along the Quinebaug River have had early evidence of their settlement wiped out by the rush of nineteenth-century mercantilism. Not so Brooklyn. The green and the surrounding massive houses, some of twin-chimney design that are characteristic of this region, still give a real sense of history.

The land that is now Brooklyn was bought first in the seventeenth century by a Cromwellian officer, Sir John Blackwell. Sale and resale followed without owner occupancy and the town was finally named Brooklyn or Brook Line from the Quinebaug River, which formed its eastern boundary.

The ubiquitous General Israel Putnam figures prominently in the early history of the town. He lived in Brooklyn when that part of it where his farm was located was officially in the town of Pomfret, to the north. Putnam, a staunch patriot, was the political enemy though a good neighbor of another Brooklynite of equal strength, Godfrey Malbone. Southern born, aristocratic, Tory, and slaveholder, Malbone opposed the Revolutionary War and as a staunch Anglican finally, in 1771, caused to be built the outstanding architectural gem of the town today, the Episcopal Church (east side of Church St. opposite junction of Brown Rd.). Practically unchanged, this building's value can hardly be overestimated. The box pews inside have walnut paneled doors and backs, just as they existed before the Revolutionary War. Its exterior is unaltered though obviously some boards and shutters have been replaced over the more than two hundred years it has been standing. It is the oldest Episcopal church in the oldest diocese in the United States.

Another building of interest is the Unitarian Church, on the green itself. Built also in 1771 as a Congregational church, it "changed hands" in 1819. The exterior remains much as it has always been, but alterations of the interior lessen its architectural value somewhat. General Putnam was bell-ringer in this church until he left for the war.

Story and legend surround Israel Putnam. It was when plowing one fine day that he heard of the call for help from Lexington, where the Minutemen were hard pressed. He left his plow in the field and without changing clothes set out to the scene of the action. He returned and raised a regiment and was in the Battle of Bunker Hill and many later Revolutionary War engagements. In his last years he lived with his son, Israel Putnam, Jr., whose house still stands on Spaulding Rd. At his funeral, the eulogist summed up Putnam's life: "He loved war for the sake of peace and freedom; he loved the battlefield because he loved his farm." The statue of Putnam and the good general's grave are located on Rte. 169, a short distance south of the village center.

Industry came to Brooklyn as to nearly all other Connecticut towns, but fortunately for Brooklyn itself, the mills were built on the Quinebaug River, where East Brooklyn grew as the manufacturing center. Proof that millhands did not always live in squalor is evident in East Brooklyn in Quebec Village (south of U.S. 6). A cluster of connected "apartments" built for workers in the latter half of the nineteenth century stand in an area off Elm St. They are sturdy brick 1½-story "apartments" that housed the families, and granite door and windowsills with some brick arches above doors and windows tell of money well spent to give workers accommodations. Some of the units are lived in today and a casual glance could mistake the long row of apartments for a more modern structure.

*To See and Do:* (1) Hunting is offered in the Brooklyn Shooting Grounds (see appendix). Also in the northern part of town is the Brooklyn Ski Area, Church St., 2 miles east of town. Blackwell's Brook, which crosses U.S. 6 about 1 mile northwest of the center is state-stocked for fishing.

(2) Drives along Tatnic Rd., Wolf Den Rd., and Church St. will be rewarding for architecture buffs. And the top of Tatnic Hill affords all-around views of the countryside.

BURLINGTON *(Hartford County. Rtes. into: 4, 69, 179; 30.6 sq. mi.; 4,070 pop. Other communities: Whigville.)*
Rugged hills that characterize the terrain of Burlington inhibited its early settlement when that area was a part of Farmington. But about 1740, land was cleared and several families moved in. Copper was discovered in the southern part of the town and although rich pockets were inducement enough to start mining, they soon played out and the workings failed several times. But those efforts created the small community of Whigville, whose name came from the Whig political party of the time.

Burlington was the home (and is the burying place) of Katherine Cole Gaylord, who went with her husband to Westmoreland, Pennsylvania, only to see him slain in the Wyoming Valley massacre of 1776. With her three children she walked back to her home in Connecticut. A memorial gravestone exists today in the cemetery in Burlington

*To See and Do:* State Fish Hatchery off Rte. 4, east of the center, is open to visitors. Nassahegon State Forest (1,226 acres) south of Rte. 4, in the geographical center of town, offers hunting, hiking, and picnicking; while the Farmington River, on the town's eastern border, offers fishing. The Tunxis Trail passes through, crossing Rte. 4, just over a mile east of the center.

CANAAN *(Litchfield County. Rtes. into: U.S. 7; state 63, 112, 126; 33.4 sq. mi.; 971 pop. Other communities: Falls Village, Huntsville, Lime Rock Station, Lower City, South Canaan.)*

Falls Village, which is the chief community of the town, lies along the Housatonic River and, as might be expected, adjacent to a source of falling water as an early source of power. The first industry in this rugged hilly town was lumbering but that quickly gave way to iron processing when the rich ore of the Litchfield hills was discovered. Iron, in fact, was hauled to blast furnaces and forges in carts, saddlebags, and baskets, to make everyone rich, and for years debts were paid and produce purchased in terms of iron as local currency.

There are ruins today of eighteenth-century iron furnaces on Lower Rd. and the existing eighteenth-century homes in the town are reminders of successful iron-producing families. South Canaan has outstanding views of nearby mountains—including Canaan Mountain, Mt. Riga, Monument Mountain, and Bear Mountain. The village also has an outstanding Congregational church, built in 1804, with a largely unaltered interior.

Over forty years ago Canaan attracted the attention of Jacques Gordon, who had been concert master of the Chicago Symphony Orchestra. He set up a foundation, concert hall, and school on what has become Music Mountain, south and east of Falls Village. Here music students come each summer and study undistracted by urban temptations. Concerts are given for the public during the summer session.

*To See and Do: (1)* Falls Village–Canaan Historical Society Museum, Main St., Falls Village. Costumes and local artifacts are displayed in the small museum.

*(2)* Beebe Hill School, Rte. 7 and Beebe Hill Rd. (Canaan Historical Society). A restored one-room district school.

*(3)* Music Mountain, Falls Village. Summer concerts of chamber music.

*(4)* Housatonic State Forest. Hunting and hiking are enjoyed here and the nationally known Appalachian Trail passes through, crossing Rte. 112 just east of the Housatonic River. There is fishing

available in the Housatonic River and golf may be played at the nine-hole course at Canaan Country Club on South Canaan Rd.


CANTERBURY *(Windham County. Rtes. into: 14, 14A, 169; 40.0 sq. mi.; 2,673 pop. Other communities: Westminster.)*
In 1697 a Major James Fitch moved deep into the wilderness of what is now Canterbury and set up a trading post. His influence for many years dominated the region and he got on with Indians, traders, and travelers alike. He had, in effect, set up a fiefdom in the wilderness and he resented what he must have felt were "usurping settlers" who came after him. But in 1703 Canterbury was set off from its parent town, Plainfield, to the east of the Quinebaug River and incorporated. Its name comes from Chaucer's Canterbury, but there is little resemblance, as the wide fields of this community and its quiet village green give no hint of grandeur.

It is the birthplace of Moses Cleveland, who surveyed and laid out a town in the Western Reserve lands and named it Cleveland (Ohio).

Industry came to Canterbury and then faded, since no railroads found their way to the town and Finnish workers who had been brought over to enlarge the rope and textile businesses turned to agriculture to make a living.

Canterbury's most famous building is the Prudence Crandall House (southwest corner of the green). It is a monument to the endless bigotry of mankind. Miss Crandall, a Quaker from Rhode Island, bought the house and opened a young ladies' school in 1832. When a black girl applied for admission Quaker Crandall admitted her and the trouble began. The townspeople tried to force the black girl out. Angered, Prudence Crandall discharged all the white girls and announced her school was for blacks only. Town meetings, demonstrations, rock throwing, window breaking, and court suits followed. Miss Crandall was, in effect, driven out of her home. She was tried twice for breaking a hastily passed Black Law prohibiting black children from out of state being educated without town permission. Both times she was convicted but finally the Supreme Court of Errors reversed the convictions. Whatever legal victory Miss Crandall finally had, she no longer had her school and her liberalism was stifled. The house today is owned by the Connecticut Historical Commission but is not yet open to the public.

*To See and Do:* Hunting and fishing are offered along the Quinebaug River, which forms the eastern border of the town.

CANTON *(Hartford County. Rtes. into: U.S. 44; state 25, 179, 309; 25.0 sq. mi.; 6,868 pop. Other communities: Canton Center, Collinsville, North Canton.)*

The west part of Simsbury, which became Canton, was called Suffrage by Simsbury citizens. The name sprang from the reported sufferings of settlers in that wilderness to the west in 1740. When it became a town in 1806 its present name sprang, according to records, from one of two sources. Either it was Canton, China, or, more likely, a Swiss canton, an independent, self-governing community though a part of a larger federation.

Early industry tapped the apparently limitless forests; and resin and pitch were sent to shipbuilding centers. The farming was difficult, so Canton citizens turned an apple crop to cider and then turned the cider to brandy. At one time eight commercial cider-brandy distilleries were operating in the town. If nothing else, this gave ministers endless subject matter for sermons on the evils of drink. Yet a cider depot in the town was kept for the sole purpose of refreshing churchgoers.

One of the original industries to flourish in Canton was the world's first ax factory, in Collinsville, owned by William Wells and his cousins, Samuel and David Collins—hence the community's name. Together the three men brought prosperity to that thriving community with a very simple idea. Why not make axes *before* people needed them and have them instantly available? Early farmers either made their own ax blades and handles or stood around the smith's forge while he beat an ax head into shape. From the time the Collins' factory opened, getting an ax became a simple trip to the general store, which carried a varied supply.

Industry today in the area includes chemicals, wrought iron, and brass products. The town is a mixture of rural and residential neighborhoods.

*To See and Do: (1)* Canton Historical Museum, 11 Front St., Collinsville (Canton Historical Society). Housed in the former nineteenth-century plow-manufacturing building belonging then to the Collins Company, the wide-ranging museum displays Victorian furnished rooms, industry of the period, a country store, barber shop, and blacksmith shop, with farm tools and machinery on the lower level. There are rotating exhibits including displays of dolls, costumes, toys and games, and jewelry—all of the period.

*(2)* Golf may be enjoyed at the Canton Public Golf Course, at the junction of U.S. 44 and state 177, and fishing in the Farmington River.

*(3)* Roaring Brook Nature Center, Gracey Rd. (west of Rte. 177). One hundred acres of woodland, fields, meadows; two ponds and a stream; with trails and signs identifying the types of plants, trees, and animals to be seen.

CHAPLIN *(Windham County. Rtes. into: U.S. 6; state 198; 19.8 sq. mi.; 1,631 pop. Other communities: South Chaplin.)*
Settled by Deacon Benjamin Chaplin as a parish of Mansfield, the community was named in 1809. It is a small rural town and Chaplin St., its main thoroughfare, is lined with good examples of early nineteenth-century houses, the Congregational Church, and an old burial ground where Deacon Chaplin was buried.

Its principal economic mainstay today is agriculture though in former days, sawmills, gristmills, hat and boot manufacture, and silkworm culture made it a thriving industrial center. The silkworm boom died here as in other towns when a blight wiped out the necessary mulberry trees.

*To See and Do:* Goodwin, Natchaug, and Mansfield Hollow State Forests spread into large portions of the town, where hiking, boating, picnicking, and fishing can be enjoyed. Hunting is available in Mansfield Shooting Grounds (see appendix). The

Natchaug River, which flows through town, crossing Rte. 198 just north of South Chaplin, offers fishing.

**CHESHIRE** *(New Haven County. Rtes. into: I–84; state 10, 42, 68, 70; 33.0 sq. mi.; 19,051 pop.)*
Among many other towns in the state, Cheshire hoped to benefit by the opening of the Farmington Canal, a scheme to connect northern New England to Long Island Sound at New Haven by a waterway that would ignore the Connecticut River and make the New Haven planners and financiers rich. Sections of the canal, when completed, were opened, and Cheshire was on the first leg of it to enjoy the benefits of a short run down the canal with the agricultural products that were Cheshire's chief contribution to the economy. Soon washouts and squabbles, dike failures, and lawsuits combined to sink the Farmington Canal forever, but for a brief time one could see large ships apparently floating over the highlands of northern Cheshire in a most unusual procession.

Now principally a residential town, Cheshire serves as a suburb for New Haven, Meriden, and Waterbury. Agriculture is still its principal native industry, though brass goods and heavy machinery make up some of its income. Copper mining and barite production in the early days was enough to draw one hundred miners from Cornwall in England to work the diggings, on Jinny's Hill Rd., but in 1878 with western copper and railroads combining, the mining in Cheshire was finished.

Cheshire Academy, formerly the Episcopal Academy, was started in 1796, and when the churchmen moved on to found Trinity College, Hartford, a preparatory school occupied the surviving buildings and is in operation on Main St. to this day. The center of Cheshire is stretched along Main St. and opposite its triangular green is an outstanding Congregational church built in 1826 and designed after the Milford church, a Hoadley structure. Its Ionic columns and tall spire were reproduced in other towns in the state.

*To See and Do:* Hunting in the Meriden Rod and Gun Club and Meriden Farmer's Area; 3,551 acres (see appendix).

CHESTER *(Middlesex County. Rtes. into: 9, 9A, 148; 15.9 sq. mi.; 2,982 pop.)*
Today this quiet town on the west bank of the broad Connecticut River, a few miles north of the river mouth, gives no hint of a somewhat raucous past. Sheep raising started some of the uproar. Sheep would congregate beneath the Second Congregational Church during services and set up such a bleating the men had to come out and shoo them away. Next, the young people inside the church began experimenting with harmony singing, to the dismay of their parents, who shied from such modern ideas. Somehow Chester survived.

Water-powered gristmills and sawmills operated in town in the seventeenth century, and the late eighteenth century saw the rise of shipbuilding. The nineteenth century brought manufacturing of many sorts, particularly the making of thousands of inkstands, which provided a livelihood for Chester citizens. Samuel Silliman, a native, developed three types of inkwells (which earned him the title "Father of the Modern Inkwell")—a school inkstand, a desk type, and a pocket inkwell for soldiers. Today electronic teaching equipment and wire and metal manufacturing provide the incomes. Also knitting needles.

Some eighteenth-century homes and many handsome nineteenth-century ones make the quiet streets of the town attractive. In the center, on Rte. 148, stores and shops are somewhat overpowered by a large, handsome granite building with white columns. It was once a bank. Today, unquestionably, it is the area's most elaborate liquor store. The Old Town Hall—in public use since 1793—is now restored and serves as a community center.

*To See and Do:* (1) Ride the Chester-Hadlyme ferry, which began operation in 1769. Follow Rte. 148 to the west bank of the Connecticut River and the ferry landing. The small vessel holds only a few cars, but in crossing the river striking views up and down stream can be appreciated.

(2) Cedar Lake, west of the center on Rte. 148, offers boating, fishing, and swimming. Cockaponset State Forest, some 15,000 acres, reaches into the central and western portion of the town and is available for hiking, picnicking, hunting, and fishing.

Fishing is also available in Pataconk Lake in the state forest area, 3 miles north of Rte. 148 on Cedar Lake Rd., and hunting in the Pataconk Fish and Game Association area (see appendix).

**CLINTON** *(Middlesex County. Rtes. into: I–95, which is the Connecticut Turnpike here, Exits 63 and 64; U.S. 1; state 81; 17.2 sq. mi.; 10,269 pop.)*
Settled in 1667, the town was originally part of Killingworth but became a separate town in 1838 and drew its name from De Witt Clinton.

In 1701 Abraham Pierson, the Congregational minister, began classes in his parsonage. These educational efforts were called the Collegiate School. The school was formally based in Old Saybrook, moving from there to New Haven, where its name changed to Yale.

A 1706 graduate of the Collegiate School (while it was in Old Saybrook) was Jared Eliot, who became Clinton's first citizen and most outstanding resident. He was Congregational minister there for the rest of his life and preached some 4,000 sermons, not missing at least one sermon a Sunday for forty years. Not content with saving souls, Eliot studied medicine and became, according to one report, the leading physician in New England. He branched out even further and went into animal and agricultural matters, writing many treatises on farming. Still of a probing nature, Eliot found a way to convert the black sand then abundant on the coast into usable iron. For this he was made a member of the Royal Society of London.

The shore of Clinton harbor now is crowded with summer boats and a few fishing vessels. In the nineteenth century large ships lying offshore loaded cargo for the West Indies, as in many other coastal and river towns in the state. The present dock area at the foot of Commerce St. is more reminiscent of a placid fishing village than of a bustling port.

*To See and Do: (1)* Stanton House, 63 E. Main St. (U.S. 1). This large two-chimney house built in 1789 is now a museum containing antique furniture, china, and glass. The added ell on the east end gives it more formality than one would expect in a small village.

*(2)* Drives into parts of Clinton reveal its olden times better than its traffic-crowded Main St. East of the Stanton House on Main St., Waterside Lane goes its narrow way between older homes shaded by maples. It gives a real sense of the early days. A small bridge over a stream leads to the Clinton Town Beach. Farther east along Main St., Liberty St. turns left beyond a small green whereon is a cannon manned in 1812 by Gideon Kelsey in a one-man defense of the town against the raiding British. Up Liberty St. are several old Cape Cod houses, and that area before crossing the railroad gives a feel for early times. North of the Connecticut Turnpike, on Rte. 81, and up Walnut Hill Rd., opposite the high school, leads you to Cow Hill Rd. and in a small triangular space at the junction of Airline Rd. stands a small one-room school house built around 1800.

*(3)* William Stanton Andrews Town Hall, U.S. 1, in the center. This multipurpose building contains, in addition to a public auditorium, a museum room maintained by the Clinton Historical Society. The room is built to colonial specifications, with hand-hewn beams and large fireplace, and displays accoutrements of the early settlers.

*(4)* Town beaches. Policy varies regarding nonresident use. Check with the town hall.


COLCHESTER *(New London County. Rtes. into: 2, 16, 85, 149; 48.7 sq. mi.; 6,603 pop. Other communities: Westchester.)*
Settled in 1699, the town was named for Colchester, in Essex, England. The large green today has a number of eighteenth-century houses on two treelined sides and stores on the others. In the nineteenth century a large rubber factory brought industrial prosperity to the heretofore agricultural town and, now, though the rubber plant is gone, plastics and clothes manufacture give an industrial look to several sections of the village.

In the center, Bacon Academy, founded in 1803, once rivaled Phillips Exeter as a preparatory school and students from all over the country came to rural Colchester. Its founding was a bequest of an ill-regarded farmer, Pierpont Bacon, who worked hard, saved his money, and was called "Stingy Old Bacon" by his neighbors—until his will was read and Bacon Academy got its start. Now he's a hero.

*To See and Do: (1)* Just about opposite the southeast corner of the green is a small one-room gambrel-roofed cottage, its red-painted clapboards and wavy roof line marking it now as one of the oldest structures left in town. Its date: 1702.

*(2)* Comstock Covered Bridge, over Salmon River, community of Westchester (junction Rtes. 16 and 149). One of three remaining covered bridges in the state. Covered bridges were not covered for the benefit of Grandma Moses pictures or for any other charm. They were covered to keep from scaring horses, which, on uncovered bridges, could see darn well they were about to fall off.

*(3)* Day Pond State Park, off Rte. 149, north of Westchester Center, offers fishing, hiking, and swimming, while Salmon River State Forest, which reaches into that part of town, offers hiking and hunting. A public boat-launch site at Pickerel Lake, reached by going west off Rte. 16, south of junction with Rte. 149, serves the floating angler.

COLEBROOK *(Litchfield County. Rtes. into: 8, 182, 182A, 183; 33.0 sq. mi.; 1,020 pop. Other communities: North Colebrook, Roberts-ville.)*
The region of the town was named for a town in Devonshire in 1726 but was not settled until 1765. Local legends in Colebrook run thin. But how's this? Some farmers, it is said, in 1796 plowed up three large tusks and two four-foot thigh bones that were over twelve inches in circumference. But since they reportedly disintegrated on exposure to the air, proof of that legend has long since vanished.

Today Colebrook is quiet. Agriculture and outdoor sports are the chief activities with fishing well in the lead (see below). Perhaps the fishing is what inspired Colebrook native Eb Jenks many years ago to produce the first American-made steel fish-hooks in his workshop.

*To See and Do: (1)* Underwood House or Seymour Inn (1816) in the small village center (Colebrook Historical Society). Museum and home of the historical society; local artifacts and memorabilia.

*(2)* Hunting in Tunxis State Forest and Algonquin State Forest off Rte. 8. Fishing in the Colebrook Flood Control Pool (east side of Rte. 8, near Massachusetts border), in Sandy Brook, and Colebrook River Reservoir where, on the east bank, there is a boat-launching site.

COLUMBIA *(Tolland County. Rtes. into: U.S. 6; state 66, 87; 21.8 sq. mi.; 3,129 pop.)*
Long before it was given the patriotic name (1804), the town, formerly a part of Lebanon, missed a chance to be as well known as, say, Hanover, New Hampshire. Here in 1755 Rev. Eleazer Wheelock started a school for Indians and named it Moor's Indian Charity School in honor of a donor from Mansfield. The school grew but Columbia townspeople did not take kindly to the idea of increasing numbers of students in the town. So Wheelock looked for a new campus. Money was not a problem. One of his "savage" graduates, Samson Occum, had preached in England and raised quite a lot of money. Much of it came from the Earl of Dartmouth. So Wheelock removed to Hanover and Dartmouth was born. Little wonder the college symbol is an Indian.

Today the quiet green among eighteenth- and nineteenth-century houses basks in country calm. Behind the Congregational Church is Wheelock's old school building.

*To See and Do:* Drives north and west on Rte. 87 bring you to Columbia Lake, one of the largest manmade lakes in the state (375 acres). The water was impounded by a dam in 1865 and is now town-owned.

CORNWALL *(Litchfield County. Rtes. into: U.S. 7; state 4, 43, 45, 63, 125, 128; 46.8 sq. mi.; 1,177 pop. Other communities: Cornwall Bridge, Cornwall Center, Cornwall Hollow, West Cornwall.)*
Steep hills, deep valleys, and it is cold in the winter in Cornwall. In

early days, first settlers (in 1740 when the town was incorporated) had difficulty surviving the winters. Stories have come down of cattle requiring hot broth to survive the low temperatures and of children freezing to death in their beds at night. Today, fortunately, such dangers are slight. The hills of Cornwall and the roads running through the beautiful town afford views from many locations. And in summer the dark, tree-shaded dells are cool and quiet.

Cornwall is the site of the first foreign mission school in the United States, begun in 1817 by Edwin Dwight. Sandwich Islanders (or Hawaiians, as we would call them today) were educated here, and later, Indians. The present quaint American Gothic Lutheran Church is on the site of the long-ago school on Bolton Hill Road. The Congregational Church, a stone's throw away, is a good example of Greek Revival church architecture in a rural setting. Scattered throughout the communities are a number of early nineteenth-century homes and the pace of that period seems to permeate the town. Summer draws many seasonal residents to homes away from home.

*To See and Do: (1)* Cornwall Museum, Cornwall Village (Cornwall Historical Society). Permanent exhibits of local items and a collection of history books on town affairs are available.

*(2)* Mohawk Mountain State Park south of Rte. 4 in the eastern part of town offers 260 acres for picnicking and hiking, plus skiing and snowmobiling in winter. Housatonic State Forest has parts scattered about the town, principally in the southeastern and northern sections, and offers hiking and hunting, and the famous Appalachian Trail winds through the town crossing Rte. 7 five miles south of Cornwall Bridge. Wyantenock State Forest also offers hunting, while fishing is available in the Housatonic River, which forms the western border of town, Cream Hill Pond (south of Cornwall Hollow, Rte. 43), and Mohawk Pond in the state forest south of Rte. 4.

*(3)* Covered Bridge, West Cornwall, Rtes. 7 and 128. This is one of three remaining in the state.

COVENTRY *(Tolland County. Rtes. into: U.S. 44A; state 31; 37.3 sq. mi.; 8,140 pop. Other communities: North Coventry.)*
Named for Coventry, England, this "Lake District" town has woods, hills, lakes, and ponds that proved attractive to settlers in the last quarter of the seventeenth century. It was incorporated in 1712 and four years later it began to augment agricultural income with industries. A gristmill was an obvious necessity and it came into being. Later an iron forge was built. At the beginning of the nineteenth century water power was used to power textile mills; in addition factories made metal products and glass—some of which is now prized by collectors. As the railroad bypassed Coventry, the industries in town dwindled, but there are now silk and machine parts manufactured in the town.

There are quite a few eighteenth- and early nineteenth-century homes both in the village and out along the scenic, winding roads; and Coventry, like many small Connecticut towns, would be comparatively undistinguished save for the life of one young man who was born and raised in the town. His body today lies in an unmarked grave beneath the asphalt jungle of New York City. His name was Nathan Hale, and he was twenty-one when the British hanged him as a spy. A graduate of Yale, soft-spoken, and handsome, he had many friends in college and in the places he taught briefly after his graduation from college. But then came the Revolutionary War and he was a patriot. He joined the famed elite group of Knowlton's Rangers and when Washington needed information on Long Island behind the British lines, Hale was the only volunteer. A spy at that time was regarded with contempt but Hale put usefulness to his country above personal feeling and went. He was nearly away from British territory when he was captured, and his statement before being hanged has come down to us as an integral part of American lore. It is reported that on the scaffold he said, "I regret that I have but one life to lose for my country."

*To See and Do: (1)* Nathan Hale Homestead, South St. (Antiquarian and Landmarks Society). The Hale Homestead was built in 1776 by Deacon Hale, father of Nathan. The earlier home where Nathan was born no longer stands but it was near the present house, which is said to have some timbers from that earlier home used in its construction. The ten rooms are completely furnished as they might have been when lived in by the Hales, who were there until 1832. Many of the items are original to the house. Some of Nathan Hale's boyhood belongings are there on display.

(2) Nathan Hale State Forest (south of Rte. 31, west of village of South Coventry) offers hiking, and there is hunting in the Nathan Hale State Forest Management Area (700 acres). Two-mile-long Lake Wamgumbaug has fishing and a boat-launching site, as does Bolton Lakes (west of Rte. 31, in the northwest corner of the town). There is also fishing in Eagleville Lake, on Rte. 275 just on the Coventry-Mansfield town line.

CROMWELL *(Middlesex County. Rtes. into: I–91, Exit 21; state 3, 9, 99; 13.5 sq. mi.; 7,400 pop. Other communities: North Cromwell.)* Named for Oliver Cromwell belatedly, in 1851 when it was incorporated from Middletown, this small riverside community first was a shipbuilding center. Today flower nurseries are the leading industry. The town is a residential community oriented toward Middletown to the south and Hartford to the north. A number of old houses in disrepair still exist on River Rd., running beside the Connecticut River, which is the town's eastern boundary.

*To See and Do:* Hunting in 500-acre Cromwell Meadows (see appendix) and golfing at the Edgewood Golf Club, on Golf Rd.

DANBURY *(Fairfield County. Rtes. into: I–84, Exits 1 through 8; U.S. 6, 7, 202; state 35, 37, 39; 44.0 sq. mi.; 50,781 pop. Other communities: Germantown, Mill Plain.)* Named from Danbury, in Chelmsford, England, the city was settled in 1685 and incorporated in 1702. Its first nickname was Beantown —from beans grown there along with other vegetables that were taken, first by horseback and later by wagon, over a primitive road to be traded in Norwalk—from which most of Danbury's first settlers came. The second and more lasting nickname came after hat making became a leading Danbury industry before the Revolutionary War. English hatters wanted the monopoly and the controversy over the right of colonists to make hats was one more log on the fire of rebellion. In 1880, 20,000 hats came from Danbury and Hat City became its name. It has kept it ever since, growing from small village status to town, to borough, to city in 1889. And its growth shows in the clutter of streets and highways, which has been partially relieved by redevelopment and Rte. I–84. Today other industries have replaced hat making but chances are good Danbury will remain Hat City forever.

During the Revolutionary War Danbury was a military-supply base for the American forces, and the British, in 1777 under General Tryon, marched up from the shores of Long Island Sound and burned and looted the place—sparing Tory homes that were well marked as well as the Episcopal Church. As those trying days approached one local minister, Ebeneezer Baldwin, preached an astonishing sermon in which he flayed the British parliament and government, and smote them hip and thigh, verbally. Carried away by his own vehemence, he went on to prophesy that the new country would be founded on principals of freedom and liberty and when 200 years had passed would have a population of 192,000,000.

Many Connecticut citizens do not think of hats when Danbury is mentioned. They think, instead, of the Danbury Fair, one of the oldest fairs in Connecticut—and one of the larger ones in New England. Precisely when it began is in question, but it was an annual event shortly after the end of the War of 1812. Except for the interruption of World War II, it has been going strong ever since. In its early days, country folk and city slickers rubbed elbows at the fair, where farm families came bringing food for a week in their wagons, with cattle, sheep, and pigs in tow for display and hoped-for blue ribbons. More streamlined today and with less distinction between city and country people, the fair is an annual event that draws farmers (now in vans, buses and trailers rather than buckboards) and city visitors to the fair grounds on I–84 instead of on unpaved roads.

*To See and Do: (1)* Danbury Scott–Fanton Museum and Historical Society, 43 Main St. There are three buildings on this site open to visitors: The David Taylor House (1750); The Dodd or Barnum House (1770); Huntington Hall, a modern display building. The Taylor House, a twin-chimney colonial, contains period furniture, costumes, Indian artifacts, maps, and utensils. Exhibits are changed periodically. The house is one of the few pre-Revolutionary buildings in town; it was spared the British torch because it was owned by a Tory. The Dodd or Barnum House is actually one of the town's earliest hat shops, where busy Danburians helped create the image of Hat City. Huntington Hall displays art, science, and industrial material pertinent to Danbury.

*(2)* Wooster Mountain State Park on either side of U.S. 7 offers part of its 327-acre site to skeet shooters, and the rest of the undeveloped area is open to nonshooters for a wilderness walk. Candlewood Lake reaches into the northern part of Danbury, east of Rte. 37, where boating (with a launch site), fishing, and swimming can be enjoyed. A public access area is located west of U.S. 7, about a mile north of its junction with I–84; follow signs or ask locally.

*(3)* Lake Kenosia (70 acres) offers good fishing and can be reached easily, for it is located just off U.S. 202, about 2 miles west of the junction of Rtes. 202 and 7.

DARIEN *(Fairfield County. Rtes. into: I–95, which is the Connecticut Turnpike here, Exits 10 through 13; U.S. 1; state 106, 124, 136; 14.9 sq. mi.; 20,411 pop. Other communities: Noroton, Noroton Heights.)*
Originally part of Stamford to the west, Darien was settled with its parent town in 1641. The section that was to become Darien was called Middlesex Parish and was incorporated under its present name in 1820. The name may refer to the Isthmus separating the Atlantic and Pacific oceans. At the time of its settlement, Darien and Stamford were on the real frontier and the fear of Indian attack persuaded inhabitants to fortify the settlement. Like many other settlements on the sound, a river mouth offered good land and food from the sea. The Noroton River, now forming the

western boundary of the town, drew the first settlers. Goodwives River and Five Mile River were next settled and an old Indian trail became the King's Highway when the first mail was sent from New York to Boston in 1672.

So Darien is an ancient town, although today it is largely a "bedroom" suburb for New York commuters who, while no longer fearing Indian attack, worry not a little about the arrival and departure of the Penn Central Railroad's morning and evening trains.

During the Revolutionary War many members of Middlesex Parish remained loyal to the King and so, as Tories, left their homes and joined British forces on Long Island. From time to time they led raids on their former friends and the conflict was bitter. Seven boatloads of Tories and British landed in Scotch (now Scott's) Cove on July 21, 1781. They surrounded a church, where morning service was being held, and the call for the worshipers to surrender came in recognizable tones from one of the parishioner's former neighbors, a Captain Frost. Men and boys were tied two by two and marched to the boats. Some were taken away and languished in prison for five months under such conditions that six of them died. When peace came, the Tories dared not return to their homes but fled to Canada. Understandably.

In the eighteenth and early-nineteenth centuries, Darien was an agricultural and then an industrial (principally shopping) community. But as the twentieth century approached, its advantages as a seashore resort became evident and shorefront cottages on a rather large scale were built. Long Neck, Great Neck, Contentment Island (formerly called Contention Island) were settled. Gradually the town took on its present coloration as a residential community, although more than fifty eighteenth- and early-nineteenth-century homes remain. They are scattered throughout the town among the newer modern homes.

*To See and Do: (1)* Bates-Scofield Homestead, 45 Old King's Highway North (Darien Historical Society). One of the unspoiled eighteenth-century homes remaining in town, it was moved to its present site in 1964. Costumes, manuscripts, and folklore of the region are offered here.

*(2)* Milestone Village Museum, 1844 Boston Post Rd. This unique museum has eleven restored historic houses, some thirty stores and craft shops just as they were. There are costumes, textiles, and marine items.

*(3)* Town beaches. Policy varies regarding nonresident use. Check with the town hall.

DEEP RIVER *(Middlesex County. Rtes. into: 9, 9A, 80, 145, 154; 14.2 sq. mi.; 3,690 pop. Other communities: Winthrop.)*
This small community has a national following. It is the scene of the Annual Ancient Muster of Fife and Drum Corps each July. Units arrive from as far away as Virginia and Ohio to compete and the roll of drums and shrill, plaintive, stirring music of fifes fill the streets as the parade moves to the grounds where each unit competes in style and complexity of musical presentation. Costumed in Revolutionary War, War of 1812, or Civil War regalia, the corps create a thumbnail review of U.S. military and naval history unmatched anywhere in the country.

When the muster is over, Deep River returns to its status of a small, Connecticut town. Its busy Main St. (9A) is lined with stores, nineteenth-century brick factories, and some now spruced-up older homes. Several marinas and shipyards on the Connecticut River and meandering inlets recall its busier days as a ship center, as were nearly all the lower river towns.

*To See and Do: (1)* The Stone House, South Main St. (Deep River Historical Society). Built in 1840 for Deacon Ezra Southworth and his new wife, the dwelling remained in Southworth hands until 1947, when it was given to the Historical Society. Made of quarried granite and set well back from the thoroughfare, it exemplifies the rural luxury of the latter half of the nineteenth century. On display in its spacious interior are marine items relating to the history of the Connecticut River and the shipping that gave it prosperity.

*(2)* Cockaponset State Forest (Rte. 145, north of Rte. 80) lies partially in the western part of town, and hiking and picnicking are available. Fishing and boating can be enjoyed on the Connecticut River.

DERBY *(New Haven County. Rtes. into: 8, 34, 115, 188, 243, 334; 5.3 sq. mi.; 12,599 pop.)*

A manufacturing town in the Naugatuck Valley, Derby was settled early as a trading post in 1642. The reason was that the town lies at the junction of the Housatonic and Naugatuck rivers and the waterways then were unimpeded by dams. As a settlement it really got underway in 1675 and among its first activities was a brisk trade with the West Indies and the use of water power from its two rivers to serve industries. Derby got an industrial boost in 1870 when the Housatonic Dam was completed just upstream from the bridge connecting Derby to Shelton. This ended the town's history as a port but ensured power for new manufacturing. As industry grew during the last century, Derby took a leading role in developments. Today, heavy metal goods (forgings, castings, etc.) are produced along with magazines, rubber goods, textiles, and a variety of other products.

Immigrants settled in Derby as they did in other valley towns during this period and they have helped make Derby a productive town. The architecture along the main thoroughfare (Rte. 34) reflects the heyday of the town's growth. The brick façades of stores and office buildings are of the latter part of the nineteenth century. Turning up Elizabeth St. off Rte. 34 brings one to an unexpectedly pleasant green amidst the brickwork of the town. On the west side is the Second Congregational Church, a good example of mid-nineteenth-century church design. On the same side of the green is the Sterling Opera House, built in 1889. For many years it served as a cultural center for the region. Today it is awaiting restoration and stands as an imposing Victorian structure, a monument to that era. Derby's most notable son unquestionably was Commodore Isaac Hull, who commanded the U.S.S. *Constitution*, or "Old Ironsides," during the War of 1812.

*To See and Do: (1)* Colonial Cemetery, Derby Ave. An ancient burying ground where the remains of Derby founders, pioneers, and sea captains are buried. It is maintained as a historic site by the Uptown Burying Association.

*(2)* Osbornedale State Park, on the north side of Rte. 34, upriver

of the center. This 350-acre park offers picnicking, swimming, and winter sports.

DURHAM *(Middlesex County. Rtes. into: 17, 68, 77, 79; 23.3 sq. mi.; 4,489 pop.)*
Landseekers from Guilford settled this farming community in 1699, when it was called Coginchaug by the Indians. Named for the town and county of Durham in northern England, the town today is a spruced-up agricultural community with a little light industry. Its green, on the west side of Rte. 17, in the center of town, has nicely restored eighteenth- and nineteenth-century homes. The character of the town is clearly evident all summer long as fairs, auctions, antique shows, and horse and pony pulls crowd the calendar. There are nice views to the west through the center of town as the land falls steeply away into north-south valleys. It is the birthplace of Moses Austin, who helped colonize Texas. His son, Stephen, carried on after Moses's death. Result: the state capital of Texas, Austin, named after the Durham emigrant. And there is the legend of the two churches, each vying with the other to build the taller steeple. The South Church won. Not long after, a windstorm tore off the taller steeple, turned it over, and drove its needlelike spire straight down into the prideful edifice. It is said that the congregation got the point.

*To See and Do: (1)* Hiking in two undeveloped state parks: Millers Pond (northeast corner of the town) and Trimountain (southwest corner). The Mattabesett Trail winds through town, crossing Rte. 17 just east of Pistapaug Pond.
*(2)* Hunting in 556-acre Durham Meadows (see appendix).

EASTFORD *(Windham County. Rtes. into: U.S. 44; state 171, 198; 28.6 sq. mi.; 922 pop. Other communities: North Ashford, Phoenix-ville.)*
Originally a part of Ashford, the town contains the village of North Ashford—which may explain things. High, open country typical of northeastern Connecticut prevails in this rural community where views are good and no one gets in the way of them. As may be

expected, dairy farming, horticulture, and wood products are the chief industries, although some metal fabricating is done here.

First citizen of Eastford must be Nathaniel Lyon, whose birthplace is in the town. A graduate of West Point, he took part in the Seminole Indian War and the Mexican War of 1845. By the time the Civil War broke out he was a general, and died leading a charge of 5,000 Union troops against more than 20,000 Confederates. Thousands of people from all over Connecticut attended his funeral in the town and today a monument to his accomplishments can be seen in the southern part of town off Rte. 198.

*To See and Do:* Natchaug State Forest astride Rte. 44, east of Phoenixville, offers hiking, picnicking, and fishing on more than 10,000 acres. Hunting in Yale Forest (see appendix). Fishing in Hall's Pond, west of Rte. 198, in the southern section of town. Buell's Greenhouse, in the village, will prove of interest to those for whom the African violet has charm.

EAST GRANBY *(Hartford County. Rtes. into: 20, 187, 189; 17.4 sq. mi.; 3,532 pop.)*
Formerly part of Granby—which in turn was part of Simsbury—the town has a history dating from the seventeenth century, when it was known as Turkey Hill. And as early as 1705 the section proved to be valuable with the discovery of copper. Iron ore also was discovered but Britain's refusal to allow colonists to refine either the copper or iron resulted in bootleg products and a virtual stoppage of mining for a while. The copper mine eventually turned into a prison (see below) but even with convict labor the low-quality remaining ore could not be refined at a profit.

Agriculture, tobacco growing, and dairying have long sustained citizens above ground in this still essentially rural town. Dr. Samuel Higley, a resident of what is now East Granby, mined his own copper and produced the first copper money made in the colonies. His Higley Copper or Penny served for many years and today an original one is a rare treasure. John Higley, Samuel's son, discovered a steel-making process and tried to produce steel from local iron deposits, but costs were too high and he could not make a go of that business. Another "first" of which East Granbians are proud is the development of a successful silverplating process in 1843 by the Cowles Manufacturing Company.

Despite all the inventive activity, East Granby remained largely an agricultural community and today it mingles agriculture with a residential aspect for workers at nearby Bradley International Airport and not-too-distant Hartford.

*To See and Do: (1)* Old Newgate Prison, north of Rte. 20, west of the center on Newgate Rd. (Connecticut State Historical Commission). In 1773, when the copper mine that had been in production for over sixty-five years became unprofitable, the Connecticut colony authorities decided that the dank tunnels and underground rooms would make an excellent abode for burglars, horse thieves, counterfeiters, and other unsavory characters. So they turned the mine into a prison and erected walls and administrative buildings around the shaft. Named Newgate for its namesake in London, the prison soon had an assortment of inmates who were at first required to mine copper. But even with free labor, the operation proved to cost more than it made. Conditions in the mine as a prison were as horrifying as the most active imagination can conceive. Chained down, wet, miserable, fighting rats, having food dropped to them through trap doors, the prisoners survived as best they could—though many did not. During the Revolutionary War, Tories were imprisoned here, and toward the end of the war, captured British troops.

Despite its deep tunnels and dungeons, despite the strong thick rock walls surrounding it, the prison was not escapeproof. A number of men managed to escape, and there were uprisings against the foul treatment they were undergoing. In 1776, Newgate became officially a state prison and it held prisoners until 1827, when it was abandoned. Today a journey through the mine tunnels will give anyone a sense of what it must have been like to live underground in Old Newgate Prison.

*(2)* Golf at the Copper Hill Country Club, on Copper Hill Rd.

EAST HADDAM *(Middlesex County. Rtes. into: 82, 149, 151, 156; 57.6 sq. mi.; 4,676 pop. Other communities: Bashan, Little Haddam, Millington, Moodus, North Plain.)*

The Indians called it "Mackimoodus," which meant "place of noises," and only in the early part of the eighteenth century did East Haddam get its present name. The Haddam East Society, formed of Haddam citizens across the river, asked for a church as early as 1697 but none was forthcoming until after 1700. Struggling settlers did not have their own proper graveyard until the problem of crossing the ice-strewn Connecticut River in winter for funerals became overwhelming.

The present large town borders the Connecticut River and the land rises steeply to the west. Some roads run through noticeable ravines to the meadows and woods of the sprawling eastern section of the town. Today the town is largely residential, although a few plants turn out nylon and cotton twine, fishnets, and electrical components. There are several camps and resorts within the town, on Rtes. 149 and 151. In earlier days, East Haddam was a shipping point with wharves on the river, and a fishing industry boomed with salmon and shad providing a harvest.

The mysterious noises, first noticed by the Indians, were called, in the eighteenth and nineteenth centuries, "Moodus noises." They were thought to be audible waves set up by earth tremors. But they proved to be relatively harmless. The only damage reported in early times was ruined turkey egg settings and broken china.

*To See and Do: (1)* The Goodspeed Opera House, east end of bridge over the Connecticut River. Built by William Goodspeed in the heyday of river steamboats, the Goodspeed Opera House drew people from all over Connecticut. Resort hotels flourished along the river bank in East Haddam. Restored today by enthusiastic citizens, it presents a unique picture of entertainment life in the late nineteenth century. Plays, musicals, and films make up its program now in this small but delightful center of miniaturized elegance.

*(2)* Amasa Day House, Main St., Moodus, junction of Rtes. 149 and 151 (Antiquarian and Landmarks Society). This trim Federal house with twin chimneys was built in 1816. The house is furnished with Day-family heirlooms from the period 1800 to the 1840s. Each of the seven rooms has been restored with the correct period colors and fabrics. In addition to family artifacts, there are

collections of ceramics, early iron, children's toys, mirrors, and clocks.

*(3)* Nathan Hale Schoolhouse, off Rte. 149, on a hilltop just north of the Opera House (Sons of the Revolution). Nathan Hale taught school here in the winter of 1773–74. The schoolhouse is visible upriver from the bridge crossing the Connecticut River.

*(4)* Gillette Castle. (See Lyme.)

*(5)* Devil's Hopyard State Park, off Rte. 82, north of North Plains. On Eight Mile River and with lovely Chapman Falls, this 860-acre park offers fishing, hiking, picnicking, and camping. The curious park name has a legendary origin. Hops were believed to have been grown there and possibly soaked in potholes worn in the rocks below Chapman Falls. And the Devil was believed to have sat above Chapman Falls playing, of all things, his violin, while directing witches below as they mixed magic potions (beer?).

*(6)* Summer Sightseeing Cruises on the Connecticut River and Long Island Sound from Goodspeed Landing on a 400-passenger power boat.

*(7)* Fishing can be enjoyed on Bashan Lake (take Mt. Parnassus Rd. off Rte. 82, follow signs), Moodus Reservoir (south of Rte. 149, above village of Moodus), Pickerel Pond (north of Rte. 149, near Colchester), and Shaw Lake or Hayward Lake (in the northeast corner of town), all of which have boat-launch sites. Hunting in Wopowag Management Area (see appendix) on 473 acres and also at Haddam Neck on the Connecticut River (94 acres). Golfers can use the Banner Lodge Course, on Banner Rd., in Moodus.


EAST HAMPTON *(Middlesex County. Rtes. into: 16, 66, 151, 196; 36.8 sq. mi.; 7,078 pop. Other communities: Cobalt, Middle Haddam.)*

Called "Pocotopaug" by the Indians, the town was named Chatham in 1767 for William Pitt, Earl of Chatham. The name later was changed to East Hampton.

In 1808, William Barton set up what is believed to be the first bell-making factory in the United States. Sleigh bells, cowbells, church bells—you name it and he made it. Millions of bells have come from the town since that time, and apprentices of Barton learned their trade and then began their own businesses. Over the years as many as thirty bell-making firms were known in the town. Today one remains, Bevin Brothers Manufacturing Co., on Bevin Rd., founded in 1832 by apprentices of the bell-happy Mr. Barton. Little wonder East Hampton had the nickname "Belltown."

Cobalt, a small village in town on the eastern edge (Rte. 66) gained its livelihood briefly and its name permanently from cobalt mines in the region. Ore-separation problems brought this industry to a halt, but the surrounding country is good rock-hound land.

Middle Haddam (Rte. 151), on the Connecticut River, once was a thriving shipbuilding center. London packets and China tea clippers came down the ways into the river. One builder, Thomas Child, built 237 ships here. Today the Middle Haddam Library, with its curious corbeled overhang, is reminiscent of those shipbuilding days.

*To See and Do: (1)* Congregational Church, East Hampton Green. As handsome an example of elaborate nineteenth-century church architecture as can be found, with what must be one of the most imposing spires in the state, well-displayed on a slight rise above the street.

*(2)* Below the church on the street level is a huge boulder with four plaques on it. One for the dead in the Revolution and War of 1812; and one each for the Civil War, Spanish-American War, and World War I. The stone was moved there from neighboring Marlborough, requiring fifteen yoke of oxen to do it.

*(3)* Lake Pocotopaug. A large resort lake on Rte. 66, northeast of the village with islands, sailboats, public recreation, beaches, and fishing. In early days so many Indians drowned in the lake that "big medicine" to save tribe members required the chief's daughter to be sacrificed by drowning. While her father weighed the demand from the priest, his daughter, who had overheard the demand, did the job herself. Local legend has it that following her self-sacrifice no one drowned in the lake until the turn of the present century.

*(4)* Hurd State Park (810 acres), off Rte. 151, going south of Middle Haddam, offers boating, hiking, and picnicking, and has

camping shelters. There is hunting and hiking available in that part of Salmon River State Forest that enters the southeastern part of the town (Rte. 16). Hunting can also be enjoyed in the 5,000-acre Belltown Sportsmen's Club area (see appendix).

EAST HARTFORD *(Hartford County. Rtes. into: I–84, I–86; U.S. 5, 6, 44; state 2; 18.1 sq. mi.; 57,583 pop. Other communities: Burnside, Hockanum, Hillstown.)*

Now a residential and industrial community, East Hartford was taken from Hartford across the river and made a separate town in 1783. In the seventeenth century it was the location of the now vanished Podunk Indians, one of whose sachems asked the Massachusetts Englishmen in 1631 to come and settle in the valley of "the broad river" (Connecticut River). His reason was simple: to gain the protection of the English against the feared and hated Pequots, who raided up from Norwich on any slight pretext (see Chapter 3). The Podunks had a fort in the Hockanum River valley and early settler William Hill was killed by Indians in the Narragansett War. Several seventeenth-century homes then "across the river" from Hartford were fortified to protect the farming settlers from Indian raids.

At the outset of the Revolutionary War, in April 1775, the citizens of East Hartford raised a company of forty-nine men to help Massachusetts' troops, and a number of them remained in the patriot forces. French General Rochambeau and his troops were quartered in East Hartford for a time, and the troops' paymaster kept silver in the Forbes house. So rare was silver in the colonies at that time that when the French troops were paid the name Silver Lane was applied to the road near their encampment —and Silver Lane it remains today. At the corner of Silver Lane and Lawrence St. is a boulder with a bronze tablet commemorating the French encampment.

East Hartford early turned to industry. Farming vanished. Today United Aircraft's Pratt and Whitney Division is a major member of the more than one hundred industries in the town.

Very few unspoiled early houses linger in East Hartford. The

Forbes house, on Silver Lane, where the French silver was stored still remains, however, as do several others.

*To See and Do: (1)* Wickham Park, on the eastern edge of town, offers pleasant walks through Oriental gardens and affords a commanding view of the Connecticut River valley.

*(2)* Golf can be enjoyed at the East Hartford Golf Club, on Long Hill St.

EAST HAVEN *(New Haven County. Rtes. into: I–95, Exit 51; U.S. 1; state 80, 100, 142; 12.6 sq. mi.; 25,120 pop. Other communities: Foxon, Momauguin, Short Beach.)*
This small, crowded town (originally part of New Haven) reaches from the shore, where beach cottages abound, northward into hilly country where some agriculture is still carried on. Originally the settlement was named Iron Works Village, since it is the site of the first ironworks in Connecticut and the third to be built in the entire country. The date: November 29, 1655. Bog iron from North Haven was carted or shipped laboriously to the furnace and shaped into useful tools in a nearby forge.

*To See and Do: (1)* The Old Stone Church (Main and High Sts.) was built before the Revolution. The site was bought by the Congregationalists for twenty-six pounds, eight shillings, and a penny, and the congregation then set to work building their meeting house as the churches were first called. The stone is a sandstone conglomerate and the mortar was made from the usual sand and burned shell lime. The walls measure seventy by fifty feet not counting the belfry. The meeting house was dedicated late in 1774 on the eve of the Revolution. It has endured, with several changes of course, for two hundred years. The British searched it for silver, a tornado hit it, the people altered it, but it remains.

*(2)* Branford Trolley Museum, 17 River St. (Branford Electric Railway Association). A collection of trolleys for nostalgic oldsters and strange vehicles for the innocent young, the electric railway

cars preserved in the museum mark a milestone in transportation history. Rides for wonderstruck visitors are available on a stretch of track to Short Beach in Branford—tracks the cars used to travel not too many years ago.

*(3)* Town beaches. Policy varies regarding nonresident use. Check with the town hall.


EAST LYME *(New London County. Rtes. into: I–95, Exits 72 through 76, which is also U.S. 1 here; state 51, 156, 161; 34.8 sq. mi.; 11,399 pop. Other communities: Black Point, Crescent Beach, Flanders, Giant's Neck Beach, Niantic.)*
In 1647, a romantic adventure occurred in the present town that lingers on in the name of Bride's Brook. Young Jonathan Rudd and his fiancée were waiting for the magistrate to come to marry them. It was winter and a great blizzard kept the official away. Rudd appealed to Governor John Winthrop, then in nearby New London—then officially under the jurisdiction of Massachusetts. The Connecticut couple from Saybrook finally were married in the snow on the western edge of Bride's Brook. Across, on the eastern shore, stood Winthrop, powerless to cross and marry them in Connecticut. But his words carried well and the ceremony was performed. A historic marker now marks Bride's Brook where it flows under Rte. 156.

This ancient town (originally part of Saybrook Plantation) became its present self in 1816, and the crowded summer resort shore brings thousands of visitors in season. But back away from the beaches and highways all remains rural and quiet. And in these back areas can be found many examples of eighteenth-century architecture.

*To See and Do: (1)* Thomas Lee House, Rte. 156, Niantic (East Lyme Historical Society). This large lean-to house is one of the oldest frame houses in the state, and the best information is that part of it was built around 1660 by Thomas Lee, 2nd, or Ensign Lee, as he was called. Lee's father and mother died on the voyage to Boston in 1641. The children and grandparents made their way to the Saybrook Plantation, which brought Ensign Lee to this region.

The house has fascinated architectural historians for many years. Rooms were added and the front of the house reversed in the eighteenth century when the road was changed to run behind the original south-facing structure. In nearly its original primitive state with unpainted weathered clapboards, it is a strange, hypnotic ghost from long ago.

Next to the Lee House stands the Little Boston School, built later but earning a reputation for scholastic excellence that prompted people to call it the Boston school in deference to that city's eminence as a seat of learning.

*(2)* Rocky Neck State Park, Rte. 156. The 562-acre park has an outstanding crescent-shaped beach that borders the Sound. Camping facilities are available and fishing, hiking, and picnicking are proffered activities. Pataganset Lake (1 mile north of Flanders Village, north of Rte. 51) and Power Lake, west of Pataganset Lake ($2\frac{1}{2}$ miles north of Rte. 51), have fishing; boat launch sites available. Nehantic State Forest, west of Rte. 161 in the northern part of town, allows hiking, picnicking, fishing, and hunting. Fishing in Dodge Pond (in village of Niantic, north of Rte. 156 and west of Rte. 161) and Gorton's Ponds (off Rte. 161, south of I–95), both of which have boat launch sites.

*(3)* Town beaches. Policy varies regarding nonresident use. Check with the town hall.

EASTON *(Fairfield County. Rtes. into: 58, 59, 136; 28.8 sq. mi.; 4,885 pop.)*
A residential community of exurbanites, Easton has the Fairfield County atmosphere of being at once rural and sophisticated. Settled by Fairfield people in 1757, its name of North Fairfield was altered to Easton (as being the east part of Weston) in 1845. It was the home of Samuel Staples, who established in 1798 the Staples Free Academy. The school was widely known in New England and Samuel Staples is buried in the town. His academy building served for many years as a community building. The open meadowed river and stream valley today are sprinkled with new and older homes among the wooded hills.

EAST WINDSOR *(Hartford County. Rtes. into: I–91—the first two exits east of the Connecticut River above Hartford; U.S. 5; state 140, 191; 26.8 sq. mi.; 8,153 pop. Other communities: Broad Brook, Melrose, Scantic, Warehouse Point, Windsorville.)*

The town, oddly, has no center named East Windsor. Indian troubles marked the first phase of the town's history. Originally part of Windsor (as were Ellington and South Windsor), the river-valley fields were farmed early in the seventeenth century—but the farmers went to their homes across the river at night because of fear of Indian attack. The apocryphal story persists of one farmer who was stacking hay on a summer afternoon when an Indian, panic-stricken, ran from the woods toward him asking for help. The farmer tossed several forkfuls of hay over the Indian, who lay hidden while his enemy Indian pursuers were directed farther on by the quick-thinking farmer. All such troubles culminated in King Philip's War in 1675, and when that subsided, white settlers moved in.

Tobacco as a crop on the lowlands of the river valley brought East Windsor to comparative affluence many years ago and for many years more of its land, proportionately, was used for tobacco growing than that of any other town in the state. From early summer, fields blanketed with gauzelike netting nurture the tobacco, and unpainted tobacco barns dot the fields and roadsides of the town. Another early industry was the manufacture of whiskey and gin. In 1816 there were six large distilleries in the town, going full blast year-round.

Warehouse Point (I–91) flanks the river, and got its name as a storage place for cargoes portaged around Enfield Rapids and loaded on flatbottomed boats in Thompsonville to the north. From there, the shallow draft boats were poled to Springfield, Massachusetts.

*To See and Do:* (1) Connecticut Electric Railway Association, Warehouse Point, North Rd. A museum of electric streetcars and rail equipment dating from 1880 to 1950. The association has films, documents, and lectures on transportation history. Rides available.

(2) Scantic Academy Museum, Rte. 191, Warehouse Point (East Windsor Historical Society). One of the many private schools that

flourished in Connecticut when "public" schooling failed. The academy was built in 1817. It houses artifacts connected with agriculture, transportation, and industry.

(3) Fishing is available on the east and south shores of Broad Brook Mill Pond, just south of junction of Rtes. 191 and 140; golfing at the Tobacco Valley Country Club on U.S. 5 at Warehouse Pt. The Flaherty Field Trial Area (see appendix) permits hunting save when field trials are in progress. Hunting is also permitted in the East Windsor–Enfield Farmer's Area (see appendix) and the South Windsor Area.


ELLINGTON *(Tolland County. Rtes. into: 30, 32, 74, 83, 140, 286; 34.8 sq. mi.; 7,707 pop. Other communities: Crystal Lake, Sadds Mill, Windermere.)*
Settled in 1717, chartered as a town in 1786, Ellington was named for a town in Yorkshire, England. The town was and is largely agricultural and there are today large farms visible from all its main roads. Ellington center on Rte. 140 (and just west of north-south running Rte. 83) is a quiet, leisurely village. The early-nineteenth-century Federal Congregational Church facing the small green has a rather heavy portico with modillions on its pediment and that of the main building. Quoined corners of wood add to the rural elegance.

Crystal Lake in the northeastern corner of the town is a popular summer center and long ago when trolleys were operating, summer visitors came from as far away as Hartford aboard the "trolley" for an afternoon's picnicking, bathing, and boating.

Windermere is an early mill community that came into being with the rise of textile manufacturing in the area. Sadds Mill is the location of an early gristmill, named for the family that operated the mill.

*To See and Do: (1)* Boating and fishing in Crystal Lake (Rte. 30). Hunting and hiking in Shenipsit State Forest (6,181 acres), off Rtes. 140 and 83, in the northern section of town. The Tolland Shooting Preserve, some 15,000 acres all told, reaches deep into central and eastern Ellington, where hunting is permitted.

ENFIELD *(Hartford County. Rtes. into: I–91, last 4 exits before the Massachusetts border; state 190, 191, 192, 220; 33.8 sq. mi.; 46,189 pop. Other communities: Hazardville, North Thompsonville, Scitico, Thompsonville.)*

Originally a Massachusetts town and named for Enfield, in Middlesex, England, the community seceded from the Bay State and became part of Connecticut in 1749, in the settlement of one of the interminable border disputes. Enfield originally included Somers to the east.

Congregationalism and gin coexisted in Enfield in its earlier days. Here Jonathan Edwards preached his famous "Sinners in the hands of an angry God" sermon that literally scared the hell out of his congregation and sparked a revival called "The Great Awakening," which shook all the colonies. And there were numerous gin distilleries operating here, too—some twenty-one in the region.

Enfield was headquarters of the Bigelow-Sanford Carpet Co. and the town's rug and carpet making has been in operation since 1828. Enfield also is the headquarters of the Society for the Detection of Horse Thieves and Robbers—a 150-year-old organization that was ever on the alert and kept saddled horses ready and waiting to pursue felons.

*To See and Do: (1)* Old Town Hall, Enfield St. This presently vacant building, whose fate is not yet decided, dates from 1775. It was remodeled in the nineteenth century and the Greek Revival portico is the outstanding evidence of that change. The building served as the Enfield Town Hall until the new one was built. Before that it was the Congregational Church (and stood approximately on the site of the present church across the street). On April 20, 1775, a worship service was interrupted by a far-from-peaceful drumbeat. A Captain Thomas Abbey marched around the church and told the startled congregation that the British had fired on Minutemen at Lexington. The war was on. Today the memorial statue of Captain Abbey stands before the present Congregational Church.

*(2)* Fishing for shad is an Enfield tradition. The Enfield dam, on the upper reaches of the Connecticut River in the state, draws

shad and shad fishermen from all over. The season begins in late April and goes into June. Shore and boat fishing are both popular.

ESSEX *(Middlesex County. Rtes. into: 9, Exits 3, 4; 9A, 153, 154; 12.2 sq. mi.; 4,911 pop. Other communities: Centerbrook, Ivoryton.)*
No matter how far from the Connecticut River bank an Essex citizen may be, he is conscious of that great river leading to the Sound. Of all the Connecticut River towns that have a maritime past, Essex has retained the most of that heritage. A shipbuilding center from 1720 to the mid-nineteenth century, Essex today is a yacht haven known all along the Sound and to Martha's Vineyard and Nantucket. The summer season brings the sloops, ketches, and schooners to moorings and berths along its busy waterfront. And at the foot of Main St. on the river bank there is a small reminder of the British raid in 1814 when, as a shipbuilding center, the town drew the attention of a British naval squadron that was blockading the Sound. A small detachment of British marines in small craft came to burn the shipping being produced in North Cove and along the shore. Altogether they destroyed some twenty-two vessels. Among them was the *Osage,* a name taken by an inn on Main St., and that name is still one that greets a visitor driving down along the curving road to the center of town.

Settled as part of Saybrook originally in 1690, the region had drawn the attention of the proprietors of Saybrook as early as 1648, when parts of it were purchased for future use. What drew settlers in the first place was the agricultural possibilities of the river plain along those shores. But timber and ships became the main "trade" in the early years of the eighteenth century, and when the Revolutionary War broke out, the *Oliver Cromwell,* a 24-gun ship built in the town, was purchased and donated to patriot forces by the citizens of Essex.

Among the early industries, one has continued to flourish. The E. E. Dickinson Co. still produces witch hazel and ships it all over the world. The making of piano keys and parts in the community now called Ivoryton became world-known, and although plastic has replaced ivory, that industry draws piano manufacturing experts from Europe and all over the United States to the small town.

Essex today is a sophisticated town that has drawn middle- to upper-income retirees. Some have opened modern shops and native and immigrant alike wait with mixed emotions the arrival of the yachting crowd in the summer. In winter the shipyards and marine engine works form a substantial part of the town's business and they enter the summer frenzy with everyone else when that season arrives.

*To See and Do: (1)* Lieutenant William Pratt House, 20 West Ave. (Society for the Preservation of New England Antiquities). The main building fronting West Avenue is from the mid-eighteenth century but the original one-room building, which was enlarged to four rooms with a gambrel roof, dates from the seventeenth. The interior is restored and features furnishings of the period with excellent building details visible in the rooms.

*(2)* Probably the most rewarding experience in Essex is a slow walk along Main St. down to the river and back up again. The street is lined with houses, most of them from the Federal period in the early years of the nineteenth century. A few small eighteenth-century homes and shops remain, and the entire street gives an almost picturebook atmosphere to the center.

*(3)* The Ivoryton Playhouse. Summer theater brings star billings to the small theater in Ivoryton. For many years it has been on the summer circuit and continues to draw large crowds.

*(4)* Steam train rides are available from Essex Junction just west of the Rte. 9 junction with Rte. 153. Train buffs will delight in the leisurely trip to Deep River and return along abandoned tracks of the Connecticut Valley railroad. You can even make a boat connection in Deep River with the *Yankee Clipper* for a two-hour scenic cruise on the river. Return connections are made with the train and an entire afternoon of fun on old-fashioned transport returns you to the "good old days." Plans are to extend the line north to Chester and south to Old Saybrook.

FAIRFIELD *(Fairfield County. Rtes. into: I–95, which is the Connecticut Turnpike here, Exits 19 through 24; U.S. 1; state 15, which is the Merritt Pkwy., 58, 59, 136; 30.6 sq. mi.; 56,487 pop. Other communities: Southport.)*

An early town, it was settled in 1639, and is parent town to the nearby later towns of Weston, Easton, and Redding. The first settler saw Fairfield in 1637 as a member of the English force pursuing the last remnant of the Pequot tribe that was wiped out in Sasqua Swamp (south of U.S. 1, across from Hull's Highway) near Southport (see Chapter 3). He was Roger Ludlow and he returned two years after the battle to live there.

Part residential and part industrial (in the eastern edges near Bridgeport), Fairfield also has charming uphill sections such as Greenfield Hill, where an annual dogwood festival celebrates that flowering tree in the spring. U.S. 1, which is the Boston Post Road, has the traffic and shopping clutter now familiar in all American towns. Fortunately, the Boston Post Road bypassed the old green, which allows the green to survive as a pleasant reminder of colonial days. There are many pre-Revolutionary War homes scattered in the town and a sampling of later Federal and Greek Revival homes. An outstanding building is the Fairfield Academy on the Old Post Road. Built in 1804, its style reflects the concern for architectural elegance in the first years of the nation's life in contrast to earlier, mere "survival" structures.

The shore community of Southport is known as a social address and a yachting center. Long Island yachtsmen know it well.

During the Revolutionary War, British naval vessels harassed the rebel-held shores along Fairfield, and one Captain Caleb Brewster led a fleet of whaleboats that put out from Fairfield to annoy British ships in the Sound. He was effective at this, capturing or burning quite a number of larger vessels. The British kept Fairfield under their observation and doubtless in their minds. In July 1779, General Tryon, a ruthless British commander, landed Hessian troops and attacked New Haven (see New Haven). Following that attack he landed at Fairfield, catching the town by surprise, and occupied it. Under his direction systematic looting and burning began. When it was over, all public buildings and nearly two hundred homes had been destroyed. After the war, as was the custom, citizens who had lost property were offered a tract in Connecticut's "Western Lands" in Ohio. In the case of the Fairfield citizens, the tract amounted to half a million acres. Several such instances in other Connecticut towns (including burned New Haven) resulted in migrations westward to the compensatory gift of free land.

The vigor of Fairfield did not suffer too much in the attack. Houses were rebuilt and the green, after a short time, was restored to its former beauty.

*To See and Do:* (1) Historical Museum, 636 Old Post Rd. (Fairfield Historical Society). Paintings, glassware, lusterware, newspapers, and manuscripts of the colonial period and of local origin. Also, a 5,000-volume library available for research purposes on the premises.

(2) Birdcraft Museum, 314 Unquowa Rd. A collection of 2,000 mounted bird and mammal specimens plus some 50 decoys on display from a private collection.

(3) Natural History Museum, Larsen Sanctuary, 2325 Burr St. (Audubon Society). Permanent and temporary exhibits in the museum with wildlife visible on the nature trails of the sanctuary.

(4) University Playhouse, Fairfield University, North Benson Rd. Seasonal productions of the University Players as well as community drama groups. Also art exhibits, music, art, foreign and folk festivals and, in addition, the usual collegiate athletic events.

(5) Walking tour of the old center. Old taverns, the 1790 town hall, homes, and churches can best be viewed around the center by picking up a small mimeographed sheet from the Fairfield Historical Society (see above) that directs a leisurely and rewarding stroll.

(6) Fishing and boating may be enjoyed on Long Island Sound from two public boat basins. Fishing also in Mohegan Lake. Golfers can swing on the Fairfield Wheeler Golf Course.

(7) Town beaches. Policy varies regarding nonresident use. Check with the town hall.


FARMINGTON *(Hartford County. Rtes. into: I–84, Exits 37, 38, 39; U.S. 6, 202; state 4, 10, 167, 177; 28.7 sq. mi.; 14,390 pop. Other communities: Unionville.)*
An important early town (1645), Farmington was the first "inland" town west of Hartford—i.e., not bordering on the Connecticut

River in the central section of the state. It also was a "parent" town, contributing much of its then extensive lands to form all or part of nine later towns in the state. Until 1771, however, Farmington extended from Simsbury south to Wallingford, and it was the largest town in Hartford County.

Today Farmington occupies a top place among historic and well-to-do towns in Connecticut. It is the home of the widely known and highly fashionable girls' boarding school Miss Porter's; its many old houses and mansions span the seventeenth, eighteenth, and nineteenth centuries—with several Georgian Revivals built in the early years of the twentieth century.

In terms of industry, Farmington has gone through several distinct phases. Agriculture was practiced from the seventeenth century onward but as early as 1700 industries began to rise. Before the Revolutionary War, however, Farmington remained principally agricultural. And since it abutted the western boundary of Hartford (what is now West Hartford), little fear of being wiped out by Indians existed at first and settlers spread over the rolling hills of the town. One Indian incident occurred, however, which led Farmington to take elaborate precautions against attack. Indians apparently murdered a Farmington settler in 1657. As a result, no more than two Indians at a time were allowed in a settler's home—and they had to be unarmed. Later, after the Deerfield, Massachusetts, massacre, seven Farmington houses were fortified and an armed garrison was set up. Later still a new church was built, with barred doors and windows and "guard seats" inside, where armed men sat during meetings. Atop the church a cupola was built where a lookout kept watch. Yet no attack came—perhaps because the Indians were aware of the precautions.

After the Revolutionary War industrial activity spurted upward with the advent of the Farmington Canal in 1828, but troubles beset the venture from the outset and financial disaster was not far behind. During its operation, though, Farmington got temporary benefit from the ill-fated venture. Clocks, candles, carriages, linen, and hats came from the town. An East Indies trading company formed and trading and shipping took many Farmington men into the large world of international commerce. This soon gave

Farmington a cultural lead over neighboring towns that it has never relinquished. In the early years of the twentieth century Farmington became a social address to be reckoned with and industry was not encouraged to expand as ruinously as it did in other Connecticut towns.

Today there is industry in the town, but most of it is of the "light" type that does not engulf a community. Farmington is chiefly noted now as a "village of homes" and many of its citizens work in Hartford. It is by no means a satellite of that larger community, however. In fact, one report perhaps characterizes Farmington with flip, democratic accuracy. "When people in Hartford make it," so the report goes, "they move to West Hartford. And when they *really* make it, they move to Farmington."

*To See and Do:* (1) The Farmington Museum (formerly the Stanley-Whitman House), 37 High St. (Farmington Village Green and Library Association). This is an outstanding house, one of the rare seventeenth-century homes, fully restored, in the state. Its probable date of construction is 1660. This style of house is a survival of Elizabethan or Jacobean architecture transplanted from England by the earliest settlers. The overhanging second story with its drops or pendants have no purpose other than decoration—despite legends of a "garrison overhang" that survive the Indian days.

The interior of the house is a typical central chimney design with the huge stone chimney taking up all of the center of the house. Originally the house was of the "two room plan" with two rooms on the ground floor, a front stairway, and two rooms above. The lean-to that turned it into a "saltbox" was added later and the great chimney burrowed into to provide another flue for the fireplace in the new room. The fireplaces in the two "front" rooms are all original masonry. The leanto is thought to have been added about 1760. In keeping with the custom of the time, a buttery (unheated) occupied one end of the room and a "borning" or "birth and death" room occupied the other end of the lean-to. The generous room between became the kitchen and dining room.

The house is superbly furnished with seventeenth-century items. A fireproof wing has been added, and it is used to exhibit old manuscripts, glass, china, silver, and pewter, all from the Farmington area. An old wagon shed adjoins the house and antique farm and craft implements are displayed there. An herb garden at the back door is typical of those in colonial days, when cooking and medicinal herbs were all "home grown."

*(2)* A walk in Farmington along Main St. and along Farmington Ave. will give a good sampling of the early houses of the town and illustrate why it is called the village of homes.

*(3)* Hill-Stead Museum, 671 Farmington Ave. The museum displays paintings by Manet, Monet, Degas, Cassatt, Whistler, and many other famous artists. Also on display are decorative arts, graphics, and sculpture as well as glass, books, and china.

*(4)* The Triangle Playhouse, Farmington Ave. A summer stock company that performs seasonally.

*(5)* The Farmington River, which winds down and back through the town, offers fishing, as does Batterson Park Pond (with a boat-launch site). Hunting is allowed in what is designated as the Farmington Area (state-owned land), north of U.S. 6 and east of Rte. 177. Golf may be played at the Tunxis Plantation Country Club and the Westwoods Country Club.

FRANKLIN *(New London County. Rtes. into: 32, 87, 207; 20.0 sq. mi.; 1,356 pop. Other communities: North Franklin.)*
Both Franklin and North Franklin are quiet and small enough to be overlooked, but set among the ridges and hills of east-central Connecticut they offer a haven from city life. The homes in the town are widely scattered now and they were just as widely scattered in the eighteenth and nineteenth centuries, when Samuel Nott, a Congregational minister, responded to complaints about the poor state of the schooling afforded Franklin youngsters. He lived in Franklin for an astonishing seventy years (1782–1852) and tutored some three hundred Franklin children, forty of whom went on to college. His wife matched his instruction of the boys with suitable training for the girls of that period. Minister Nott was, and is, Franklin's first citizen.

And a legend persists here of the Bloody Apple Tree. A Yankee peddler was murdered, his pack looted, and his bloody body found the next day beneath an apple tree on Michah Rood's farm. Rood was suspected but no proof ever was unearthed. The peddler, it is believed, drew down a curse upon the farm. When the apple tree bore fruit, the pulp had bright red spots in it. And Rood's fortunes ebbed. He died a pauper. Natives claim there is a tree on the self-same farm now that has red stains in the apple blossoms and bears fruit with the telltale stain.

*To See and Do: (1)* Fishing in Beaver Brook (crosses Rte. 207 four times east of N. Franklin). Hunting in Lebanon-Franklin Preserve, Sprague Rod and Gun Club, and Franklin Swamp (see appendix).

GLASTONBURY *(Hartford County. Rtes. into: 2, 17, 83, 94, 160; 52.5 sq. mi.; 20,651 pop. Other communities: Addison, Buckingham, East Glastonbury, South Glastonbury.)*
For lovers of old houses, Glastonbury offers an abundance of savoring. Three centuries of architecture can be viewed in Glastonbury and in its outlying communities of South Glastonbury and Buckingham (Eastbury). Settled as part of Wethersfield before the middle of the seventeenth century, the town was named from Glastonbury in Somerset, England. Incorporated as a separate town in 1690, it took its present name two years later and was spelled at that time "Glassenbury."

A hint of modern rhetoric comes from a resolution passed by the town meeting in 1774, when they decried the passage of the Tea Tax as "subversive of the rights and liberties of the British Americans, unconstitutional, and oppressive." And when the townspeople heard that the Battle of Lexington had been fought, they immediately sent a company Boston-ward to the rescue.

Women's Lib could well note the activities of one Mrs. Hannah Smith, wife of a minister, who drew up and signed along with some forty Glastonbury women what is alleged to be the first petition against slavery. The document was presented to Congress by John Quincy Adams. Hannah Smith's daughters were five in number. And they took up the cause of women's rights vigorously, refusing to pay taxes on property they owned, since they were not allowed to vote. Angry town leaders seized cows in payment. And the angry daughters, it was said, bought them back again. Sympathizers sent money gifts to the "Smith sisters," who were being so sorely tried by the male chauvinists of the period.

Agriculture was an early industry in the large, rural town and eventually mills and factories began to dot the town. Among the agricultural successes was peach growing, which reached a peak around 1900 when a determined citizen proved peaches did not have to come from Georgia to be good. One crop sold from his orchards for $100,000. And it has been estimated that 40 percent of the poultry raised in the United States had its origin in one farm in the town: Arbor Acres raised White Rocks.

State Route 2 has marred the face of Glastonbury and although it provides easy access for Hartford commuters, it lessens the open charm of the town. Walking south on Main St., however, past the shopping areas, a visitor can view old houses to his heart's content. And almost any drive back off the main roads, or into Buckingham or South Glastonbury, will bring architectural rewards.

Despite legend to the contrary, South Glastonbury does not truly have a Rattlesnake Hunt Club. South Glastonbury, otherwise known as Nayaug, is becoming known for its put-ons. Among its instant legends: a rattlesnake crossing, and a green on which there is a sign stating, "357 Years Ago On This Very Spot, Nothing Happened." It is also said that Nayaug has petitioned the federal government to be recognized as the fifty-first state and has elected a governor and other officials; and that, periodically, they aim a Revolutionary War cannon at the Town Office Building in Glastonbury and shoot it off in protest against high taxes.

*To See and Do: (1)* Welles-Shipman-Ward House, 972 Main St., South Glastonbury (Glastonbury Historical Society). Built around the middle of the eighteenth century, the house is one of many fine examples in the town. Fortunately, you can go into this one. Both externally and internally the house has many rewards for the colonial house buff and the furnishings are in keeping with its period.

*(2)* Old Town Hall Museum, Main and Hubbard Sts. (Glastonbury Historical Society). Historical exhibits relative to the town are

on display. In addition, some homes may be visited by appointment.

*(3)* Meshomasic State Forest extends into the town in the southern area off Rte. 2, and fishing and hiking are available here. And if rattlesnakes are of interest to you, there are samples to be found in this region. Hunters can find game both in the Meshomasic State Forest and in the Glastonbury Sportsmen's Association of some 2,400 acres (see appendix). The Shenipsit Trail (crossing Rte. 94 east of Bailey St.), for experienced hikers, winds through the state forest and along through the eastern edge of town among the hills, the views from which are far-reaching. Fishing also can be enjoyed in Angus Park Pond (on Fisher Hill Rd.) and golfers are welcome on the Minnechaug Golf Course, on Manchester Rd. The Glastonbury–Rocky Hill Ferry offers an interesting way to cross the Connecticut River going to or from the town.

**GOSHEN** *(Litchfield County. Rtes. into: 4, 63, 272; 45.6 sq. mi.; 1,351 pop. Other communities: West Goshen.)*
Named for Goshen in Egypt, this sparsely settled hill town was sold at auction (lot by lot) in 1737 and was incorporated in 1739. Goshen sent its sons to the Revolutionary War and was haunted by the threat of smallpox from returnees, as were other Connecticut towns. Isolated "pesthouses" were set up for the last days or slow recovery of the stricken men. Goshen had three such houses.

Dairy farming and cheese production were the industries of Goshen and many of its expert cheesemakers migrated to Wisconsin and helped get that industry started there. And today agriculture and dairy farming keep the scenic town going economically. Summer homes now bring city people to the unspoiled countryside and help the economy too.

*To See and Do: (1)* Historical Museum, Eagle Academy, Old Middle Rd. (Goshen Historical Society). Displays of pewter, rocks, and shells plus Indian artifacts and local historical items.

*(2)* Hall Meadow State Park (Rte. 272) stretches into Goshen from neighboring Torrington and offers fishing, hiking, picnicking, and swimming as well as winter sports. Boating (with launch sites)

and fishing are available in Tyler Pond (northeast of Rte. 4), fishing in West Side Pond (off Rte. 63), Dog Pond, and Mohawk Pond (off Rte. 4; follow highway signs). Hunting in 1,172-acre Goshen Rod and Gun Club Preserve (see appendix).

GRANBY *(Hartford County. Rtes. into: 10, 20, 189, 219; 41.3 sq. mi.; 6,150 pop. Other communities: North Granby, West Granby.)*
Named for the Marquis of Granby, the town was settled first in 1660 and incorporated in 1786. Before its settlement the area occupied a border zone between two different and frequently warring Indian nations: the Algonquians to the east and south and the Mohawks (Iroquois) to the north and west. This made settling Granby hazardous. One result was a hardy type of citizen who rarely turned away from trouble.

As in the past, the principal industries today in Granby are tobacco growing, agricultural products, and dairying. Long ago the U.S. government praised the bucolic village and held it up as an example of rurality at its best and recommended it as a model for other rural villages to follow. The town's broad main street with the village green and older country homes gives the town a look of Tom Sawyer tranquillity and evokes thoughts of the good old days. Today Granby is home for a growing number of city workers who like the feel of olden times without suffering economic handicap to savor it.

*To See and Do:* (1) Abijah Rowe House, 208 Salmon Brook St. (Granby Historical Society). Exhibits pertinent to the history of Granby are on display, plus a 600-volume library of genealogical materials and local history. In addition to this house there are others privately owned on the same street and a leisurely walk or drive along it and other older streets in town would be worthwhile to view the exteriors.

*(2)* Scenic drives are pleasant along the east and west branches of Salmon Brook River, on Rtes. 189 and 20, respectively. The east branch is stocked for fishing, too.

*(3)* Enders State Forest, on Rte. 19, offers hiking and picnicking in its 1,400 acres.

GREENWICH *(Fairfield County. Rtes. into: I–95, Exits 2 through 5; U.S. 1; state 15, which is the Connecticut Turnpike; 50.6 sq. mi.; 59,755 pop. Other communities: Banksville, Byram, Cos Cob, Glenville, North Mianus, Old Greenwich, Quaker Ridge, Riverside, Round Hill, and Stanwich.)*

The origins of Greenwich were turbulent. The Dutch, under Adriaen Block, put up a temporary settlement on the shores of what now is Greenwich in 1614, but not until 1640 did permanent English settlers move in and buy land from the local Indians. These two men, David Patrick and Robert Feake, from Watertown, Massachusetts, acted under the authority of the New Haven colony. The Dutch, however, eyed that land and incited Indians with rum to attack the English. Receiving no aid from the New Haven fathers, the settlers sought protection from the Dutch. So Greenwich passed under Dutch control until 1656 when it reverted, once and for all, to a Connecticut town under English rule. Named for Greenwich, England, the town was incorporated in 1665 but despite its naming it was known for many years as Horseneck.

Greenwich leaders today describe their town as the "premier residential community in America" and certainly with its location near New York City (while lying outside New York State where personal income tax plagues the rich) and possessing both shoreline and hillside, it has advantages. For Greenwich, as a town, is not well-off. It is not "wealthy." It is rich. A drive along its estate-lined residential streets quickly convinces even the best-heeled citizen from Shaker Heights or the proper address in Dallas to this effect. And despite its early colonial New England beginnings, Greenwich has little of the frugal quality associated with New England towns.

The northern part of town is hilly and bridle paths crisscross over the hills, the highest of which is six hundred feet above sea level. There, and on other hilltops, residents have views of Long Island Sound. The small communities in the large town are very nearly self-contained; each has its shopping and service areas. Those near the shore exist cheek-by-jowl with neighboring communities while those to the north are separate and more distinct, being somewhat isolated by the hills and rolling meadows.

During the Revolutionary War, General Israel Putnam, an ubiquitous hero of Connecticut in that war (see Redding, Pomfret), was in Greenwich (or Horseneck, as he referred to it) when the British under General Tryon (fairly ubiquitous himself; see New Haven, Fairfield, Danbury) marched into view. Realizing his troops were outnumbered, Putnam ordered his men to scatter, jumped on his horse and, pursued hotly by mounted British troops, plunged himself and his horse over a nearby precipice to escape. The British dared not follow and so the legend of General Putnam's daring escape was born. For escape he did, to fight another day.

*To See and Do:* (1) The Bush-Holley House, 39 Strickland Rd., Cos Cob (Greenwich Historical Society). Believed to have been built in the latter part of the seventeenth century, the house has been added to and changed over the years, as might be expected. During its restoration, early wallpaper with the tax stamp of George II on it was discovered as well as a stone stairway and old bake ovens. It is furnished with articles of the period, and collections of glass, china, silver, maps, and documents are exhibited.

(2) The Putnam Cottage, 243 East Putnam Ave., Greenwich (Daughters of the American Revolution). Known also as the Knapp Tavern, this is the house in which General Putnam was staying on his visit to Greenwich when the British surprised him (see above). Although the chimney restoration above the roof is inadequate, the exterior does speak of early architecture. It is thought to have been built around 1730 and the plate overhang suggests this as do the rounded or "boat bottom" shingles, some of which are original. Furniture and paintings of the eighteenth century are on display and some General Putnam memorabilia is on exhibit.

(3) Bruce Museum, Steamboat Rd., Greenwich. A history and science museum with thousands of exhibits forming one of the best faunal collections in the East; live birds and mammals; ecological displays emphasizing the local area; art gallery containing nineteenth-century European and seventeenth-century Italian paintings, Near Eastern pottery, porcelains and ivory from India, China, and Japan; science museum containing graphic representa-

tion of the solar system, comets, meteorites, eclipses, formation and eruption of volcanoes, intercontinental missiles and satellite carriers; history museum containing Indian artifacts.

(4) Audubon Nature Center, Riversville Rd. at John St., Quaker Ridge. Nature trails. Special courses offered during the summer months.

(5) Drives along estate-lined streets reveal many examples of affluent architectural tastes. Going north off Putnam Ave. (U.S. 1) on Deerfield Dr. onto Lake Ave. or on Greenwich, Maple, or Park Aves. brings you to the well-kept lawns and homes. Greenwich Ave. or Indian Field Rd., south of Putnam Ave., will take you to the shore, where harbors and yachts abound.

6) Town beaches. Policy regarding use by nonresidents varies. Check with the town hall.


GRISWOLD *(New London County. Rtes. into: Connecticut Turn-pike, which is state 52; 12, 138, 164, 165, 201; 37.6 sq. mi.; 7,763 pop. Other communities: Doaneville, Glasgo, Hopeville, Jewett City, Pachaug.)*

In an area called Pachaug by the Indians, the town of Griswold (with no village center named Griswold) was taken from Preston to the south in 1815. Its history, however, reaches back to the seventeenth century, when the first white settlers moved in.

Jewett City, the main community of the town, was named after its leading citizen in 1771, who used the water power of the Quinebaug River to begin the town's industry. As early as 1682 settlers came in and by the early years of the eighteenth century had established gristmills, an iron foundry, and other businesses.

The Revolutionary War drew over two hundred men from the small community and eleven officers served with distinction from brigadier general down to captain. In 1824, on his great, sad farewell tour of the infant country, Lafayette returned to Griswold overnight and noticed an old man sitting silently watching the proceedings. With emotion, the aging Frenchman greeted Captain Fanning, an old comrade, as Lafayette put it.

Today light industry is concentrated in Jewett City and most of the population lives in or near that community. The eastern part of the town is rugged, and sparsely settled.

*To See and Do: (1)* Hopeville Pond State Park (Rte. 201, near village of Hopeville) offers hiking, fishing, boating, swimming, picnicking, and camping in its 554 acres. Pachaug State Forest, east of the park, offers wilderness hiking in its more than 20,000 acres. There is fishing in Pachaug Pond (south of Rte. 138, in the eastern part of town) and Glasgo Pond (one-half mile north of junction of Rtes. 201 and 165), where there is a boat-launch site.

GROTON *(New London County. Rtes. into: I–95; U.S. 1; state 12, 27, 117, 184, 215; 38.3 sq. mi.; 38,244 pop. Other communities: Burnetts Corner, Center Groton, Groton Long Point, Noank, Poquonock Bridge, West Mystic.)*
With three of its four boundaries at the edge of the water, Groton understandably has a seafaring heritage. Incorporated from New London (of which it was the eastern part) the town fronts on the Sound, has the Thames River for a western border and Mystic River for its eastern. Like neighboring towns, Groton has marginal agricultural possibilities and so its men turned early to the sea: to fish, to trade, or to build ships.

Today that heritage of the sea is continued in the presence of a large Navy submarine base along the Thames, the presence of Electric Boat (Division of General Dynamics), and the notification to incoming visitors that they are approaching the submarine capital of the world. Eastbound traffic going across the Gold Star Memorial Bridge is confronted today with a maze of lanes and turnoffs that can prove confusing. And a drive down the eastern bank of the Thames past Electric Boat does nothing to relieve the impression of clutter and more than enough traffic. By turning uphill off the river, however, you can drive a few blocks to the residential portion of Groton Heights (Monument Ave.) and reach Fort Griswold (see below), high above the river and free of exhaust suffocation.

Relief from the clutter of downtown Groton can also be found in the outlying hills and communities. Noank, for example (Rte. 215), is an almost undisturbed fishing village, protected by its location on a small peninsula from encroachments of superhighways. Fishing vessels, yachts, lobster pots, gear of the sea, all combine with the tidy white houses of the nineteenth century to produce a tranquillity impossible to find along the western shores of the town. Noank is what people mean when they sigh for the good old days.

The western half of the city of Mystic lies in Groton (see Stonington) and much the same charm as Noank exists there but on a somewhat larger scale. If you turn north off U.S. 1 just west of the bridge over the Mystic River onto Gravel St. you will go past as tidy a row of homes of the seafaring period as one could find. They range from cottages to elaborate captains' houses.

And this seafaring heritage is real. Joseph Holmes, for example, held what probably is a record in sailing safely around Cape Horn. He "doubled" the Horn (went east then returned west) a total of more than eighty times. And one Groton skipper sailed fifteen months for whale and came back with a cargo sold for more than $150,000 in a ship that cost, outfitted and ready to go, less than $36,000. And another sailed to Callao en route to Chile to find a revolution going on; he got out of that and ran into pirates, who boarded his ship and forced him to navigate theirs. He escaped from them and returned in his own ship back to Callao—where another uproar was in progress. He was taken off by a U.S. Navy warship and, disgusted with his luck, sold his ship and returned to Groton. The sea legends go on and on.

*To See and Do: (1)* Fort Griswold State Park and Groton Monument, Monument Ave. One of the most brutal and tragic engagements of the entire Revolutionary War occurred at the fort on September 6, 1781. The fort, manned by about 50 men, became the target of attack for about 800 British regulars landed by ship on the New London side of the Thames River. Earlier that morning, the fort fired two cannon shots upon sighting the British naval squadron lying at the mouth of the river. This was the signal for alarm that was to call citizen soldiers, the militia, from their homes and farms in the village of Groton. But the British knew the signal.

They also knew that three shots signaled good news—and no cause for alarm. Before the last echo of the second shot from the fort died away, the British fired a single shot—making the villagers believe that all was well and some good tidings might be learned that day. This act was the first in a long series throughout that bloody time—and it was all made possible by the inside knowledge of turncoat Benedict Arnold, who led the British forces. At the last moment before the British attacked some hundred more men were gathered, all untrained, making a total in the fort of about 150. Twice the British demanded surrender, and twice the garrison, under Colonel William Ledyard, consulted and refused the demand.

As the British troops, two regiments, stormed the fort, General Benedict Arnold watched the progress of the battle from New London. The fort was soon taken, as its defenses had not been completed. Seeing that he had lost, Colonel Ledyard ordered his men to throw down their arms and surrender. The British officer then in command shouted "Who commands this fort?" Colonel Ledyard replied, "I did, sir, but you do now," and handed over his sword.

By all the rules of warfare, the British had won, the battle was over. But the British continued to fire. The British commander used Colonel Ledyard's sword to run the American commander through. The British fired and bayoneted all Americans who were standing. They entered the barracks and continued to kill the troops who had already surrendered. They looted bodies and extended their killing and pillaging to several homes in the town outside the fort itself.

When it finally was over, the American bodies were so mutilated their families had difficulty identifying them; and of that battle, at the 250th anniversary of the slaughter (1931), the orator presiding said, "In the whole military history of the United States from Colonial Days down through World War [I], there is no example of greater courage and devotion than was shown by the heroes of Fort Griswold."

Today the wind blows softly through the grasses covering the redoubt, and outside the fort a granite monument, an obelisk, 22 feet square at its base and 134 feet high, commemorates the battle.

From its top a commanding view of Long Island Sound, offshore islands, and the Thames River estuary can be seen. Nearby is Monument House, a museum, where relics of the battles, Indian artifacts, costumes, and whaling gear are on display.

(2) Boat rides on the Thames River, 86 Fairview Ave., which is a dock just north of the Gold Star Memorial Bridge. Regular boat rides on the busy Thames River show off Groton and New London to advantage.

(3) U.S. Naval Submarine Base. Follow signs on the east side of the Gold Star Memorial Bridge. Guided tours of the base and entrance to the famed Submarine Library.

(4) Noank Museum, 19 Sylvan St., Noank (Noank Historical Society). A small, quiet museum reflecting the sea orientation of this small village. Also on display are Indian artifacts and items relevant to the history of the village.

(5) Mystic Art Gallery, Water St., Mystic. A riverside art gallery on the banks of the Mystic River.

(6) Indian Museum, Old Mystic, north of I-95 on Rte. 27. An Indian and colonial research center with a library of Indian history.

(7) Golfing can be enjoyed on the Shennecossett Golf Course, on Plant St.

(8) Town beaches. Policy varies regarding nonresident use. Check with the town hall.


GUILFORD *(New Haven County. Rtes. into: I-95, which is the Connecticut Turnpike here, Exits 57, 58, 59; U.S. 1; state 77, 146; 47.6 sq. mi.; 12,033 pop.)*
This early town named for Guildord, in Surrey, has one of the most beautiful of New England's many village greens. Great care is taken to preserve it and the surrounding buildings, which range from early eighteenth century to late nineteenth century. Guilford, in fact, probably has more eighteenth-century homes than any comparably sized Connecticut town.

Settled in 1639 by Reverend Henry Whitfield, vicar of Ockley parish St. Margaret's Church in Surrey until 1638, the town "fathers" consisted of twenty-five young families, mostly from Surrey and Kent farming regions. The colonists landed in New

Haven in July 1639 and bought the land that is now Guilford from the Squaw Sachem of the Menunketuck Indians.

Guilford joined the New Haven colony four years after its founding and one of its original settlers, William Leete, became governor of the New Haven colony and, later, governor of the Connecticut colony (Hartford region) when New Haven was absorbed by its northern neighbor. Most of the original twenty-five family heads were farmers and at first this was the principal industry of the town. Being on the Boston Post Road, the main stage route between Boston and New York, the town grew rather rapidly during the eighteenth century and attracted artisans who developed a variety of industries. By 1747 there were two corn mills, two fulling mills, a sawmill, a shipyard, and a shoe manufacturer. Being on the shores of Long Island Sound, Guilford early developed a fishing industry and some trade was established with Boston and New York ports. Later ships went to the West Indies. A carriage maker flourished in town until 1837 and a foundry was established in the 1800s that still operates. Local granite deposits were discovered and quarries opened that supplied stone for the base of the Statue of Liberty and for many abutments of New York bridges—including those of the Brooklyn Bridge.

The Revolutionary War scarcely touched Guilford directly—it was one of the few towns on the Sound that escaped any serious raiding by the British. But in May 1777, feeling in Guilford ran high about raids on neighboring towns and a group under Colonel Miegs set out in whaleboats to "have a go" at the redcoats. They rowed from Sachem's Head to Plum Gut, dragged the boats overland to the ocean side of Long Island, launched them, and rowed to within a short distance of a British base at Sag Harbor. They took the British by surprise and burned ten transports, a hundred tons of hay, wharves, and one eight-gun schooner. Within twenty-four hours all the Guilford men were home, unharmed. The British retaliated with a landing in June but were driven off quickly. The only damage inflicted was the burning of two houses on Leete's Island.

One Guilford farmer of the eighteenth century contributed his name to the American language. He believed devoutly in democracy and campaigned for so many offices in the town government that the phrase "running like Sam Hill" became a phrase still used today. His name: Sam Hill.

Today the town, stretching from the shore of the Sound north to wooded and granite-ledged uplands, has thirty-one industries ranging from castings and chemicals to candlemaking. It is the home of many people who work in New Haven, a short twenty-minute drive to the west. Yale professors and still-working farmers mingle at town meetings and the names that came over with Henry Whitfield still are found in today's phone book: names such as Leete, Chittenden, Bishop, and Parmelee.

A place name persists in Guilford that was established even before the town in 1639. It is Sachem's Head, a promontory jutting out into the Sound. The name does not spring from a contraction of headland, as might be expected, but from an Indian war that occurred in 1637 (see Chapter 3). The Pequots, under Sachem Sassacus, had terrorized whites and enemy Indians alike along the eastern Connecticut shore for some time. This culminated in the Pequot War two years before Whitfield landed here. A fleeing band of Pequots was attacked and defeated on the land now called Sachem's Head by dissident tribe members and some whites. A captured Pequot was executed by Uncas and his Mohegans. The head of the Pequot was cut off and wedged in the fork of an oak tree on that rocky promontory, where it remained for years, "a ghastly object of terror and superstition," according to one historian, and inspiring the present name of that part of Guilford.

*To See and Do: (1)* The Henry Whitfield Museum, Old Whitfield St. (Connecticut Historical Commission). This home of Henry Whitfield, begun in 1639, served as meeting house, fort, and residence during the first years of the colony's existence. It is locally known as The Old Stone House and until 1899 was a private residence. It is of late medieval English style, built of stone quarried from a ledge several hundred yards east of the site, along what is now called Lover's Lane. As a residence, with various owners over the centuries, it underwent many changes but was reconstructed in 1937. It is the oldest stone dwelling in New England and is furnished as a seventeenth-century home.

*(2)* The Griswold House, Boston St. (Guilford Keeping Society). An outstanding example of mid-eighteenth-century architecture, this white saltbox on a slight hill, fronted by a white fence, is frequently photographed and has become a New England signature. Built in 1735 by Thomas Griswold, it was occupied by Griswold descendants until 1958. Early wallpaper in the parlors and the furnishings give an authentic glimpse of eighteenth-century life. The house contains many artifacts from Guilford history.

*(3)* The Hyland House, Boston St. (Dorothy Whitfield Historical Society). This early leanto (1660) with first-floor overhang was built originally as a two-room (two up, two down) house. The leanto probably was added by one Ebeneezer Parmelee around 1720. In adding it, Parmelee enclosed a back casement window and some of the original clapboarding. The casement windows visible on the front of the house were modeled on the covered, and so preserved, original. Despite the fact that the summer beams have been removed from the original part, the rooms and furnishings give an authentic impression of seventeenth-century life.

*(4)* The Westwoods. Almost 3,000 acres of woods, marsh, and rocky ledges, with marked trails for hikers and a bridle trail for horseback riding. The land is partially state owned (Cockaponset State Forest) and partially held by private owners. There is a fine hemlock-tulip poplar forest with the usual growths of oak, hickory, and maple common to New England. Geologically, the entire area is underlaid with granite, which projects out over the entire area. There are low-lying escarpments in the southern part and tall cliffs in the northernmost end. A number of trails are marked through the preserve, ranging from easy walks to more difficult hikes. There is no camping in Westwoods. It is strictly for short hikes of a day's duration. Permission is required to light any fires, since the aim of the sponsoring Guilford Conservation Commission is the preservation of the trees and total ecosystem for enjoyment by everyone. Forest fires are the greatest threat to this end.

The main entrance now is on Peddlers Road, which is west of the town center on the Boston Post Road (U.S. 1). Other entry points are on Moose Hill Rd., Dunk Rock Rd., and right off Leete's

Island Rd. (Rte. 146) just before the road turns sharp left under the railroad bridge. Detailed maps and descriptions of the trails can be obtained in the town hall, on the east side of the green.

*(5)* Walks around Guilford. For a look at the many antique houses in the town, take very nearly any street leading off the green and turn as you choose. Especially noteworthy is Fair St. (west from the green on Broad St., take first right). On the west side of Fair St. to the Boston Post Rd. are seven eighteenth-century houses in a row, most of which were built at a slight angle to the street to take advantage of southern sun in the winter.

*(6)* There is fishing in Quonnipaug Lake in North Guilford (Rte. 77) and hunting in the Guilford Sportsmen's Association (see appendix).

*(7)* Town beaches. Policy varies regarding nonresident use. Check with the town hall.


HADDAM *(Middlesex County. Rtes. into: 9, Exits 6 and 7; 9A, 81; 46.7 sq. mi.; 4,934 pop. Other communities: Higganum.)*
This is the only town bordering the Connecticut River that ignores the river as a boundary. The town straddles it. The main part is to the west; the part across the river is called Haddam Neck. The name itself comes from Much Haddam, in Hertfordshire, England.

With the completion of new Rte. 9, the old road (now 9A) along the river sees little traffic. But a leisurely drive along it through the centers of Haddam and Higganum will be pleasant. Along some sections there are beautiful views of the river and the former shipbuilding, seafaring, and fishing life of the community can be sensed. Shad and salmon were the fish and, though salmon are gone, shad make their annual appearance and are eagerly sought. During the shad season local restaurants serve the fish and roe as a special delicacy and shad bakes are common among community organizations.

In Haddam, the old state jail and the town hall are of gray granite, which indicates another native industry: quarrying. Boatloads or bargeloads of the stone were sent down river. Lead was also mined in Haddam and provided Revolutionary War bullets.

*Right*. Completed in 1963, the Beinecke Rare Book and Manuscript Library at Yale University is a modern windowless building with panels of translucent marble.

*Below*. The Farmington Museum, a National Historic Landmark in Farmington, was built in 1666 and is furnished with rare pieces of early American furniture.

*Above left.* Fishing facilities in Connecticut are good, particularly the shad fishing at the Enfield Dam, while along the coast there are plenty of docks *(far right)* to house small fishing craft.

*Upper center.* The Buttolph-Williams home in Wethersfield was built in the 17th century and is furnished with early American pieces. *Right.* The Hill-Stead Museum in Farmington has a fine collection of paintings by Manet, Monet, Degas and Cassatt as well as collections of glass, china, furniture and books.

*Left.* Glastonbury's typical New England Main Street is softened with a dusting

Connecticut offers good swimming both along the shore or in the many lakes found throughout the state. *Below.* A lighthouse marks the shoreline near Ocean Beach. *Above.* Swimmers enjoy the lake at Mt. Tom State Park located just southwest of Litchfield.

*Left.* The Captain James Boxton Fife and Drum Corps marches in the Deep River Annual Ancient Muster. *Below left.* Visitors and residents enjoy the Hamburg Fair held every August.

*Below.* The square-rigger *Joseph W. Conrad* is one of the many interesting ships on display at the Mystic Seaport in Mystic.

The Kingsnorth House, a fine example of colonial architecture, was built in 1643. Today it is a private home in Guilford.

*Above*. This quarried sandstone building is part of Avon Old Farms, a boys' preparatory school in Avon. *Below*. Built around 1772, this colonial store in Norwichtown is open to visitors.

*Above.* Constitutional Plaza, overlooking the Connecticut River in Hartford, is an outstanding example of modern city architecture.

*Opposite.* The Downes Memorial Clock Tower at Trinity College, Hartford, was completed in November, 1958.

Haddam Neck, across the river, is a placid bypassed district now except for the Yankee Atomic Power Plant (see below). Haddam Neck was also the home of an astonishing black, Venture Smith. Son of a king in Guinea, he was captured by enemy tribesmen, sold into slavery, and eventually given his freedom by his master, an American sea captain. Venture Smith was a huge man. He settled in Haddam Neck and tradition has it that he could cut four hundred cords of wood in a few weeks, had shoulders so broad he had to enter doorways on an angle. And he learned the Yankee meaning of thrift. In his later years he owned a hundred acres, three houses, and some twenty trading vessels. He died in 1805, and is buried in the Congregational Church Cemetery.

*To See and Do: (1)* The Thankful Arnold House, Hayden Hill Rd. (Haddam Historical Society). Built some time between 1795 and 1810, this excellently restored and furnished home gives a real feeling of the earlier days.

*(2)* Connecticut Yankee Atomic Power Plant, Haddam Neck. This first of Connecticut atomic plants is open to the public. Groups, with advance notice, can have a tour extolling the wonders of atomic energy and describing how everything works.

*(3)* Higganum Reservoir State Park (just west of Rte. 81 in Village of Higganum) has 147 acres with fishing and hiking. Haddam Island State Park, in midriver, offers mainly escape from the mainland. Haddam Meadows State Park, on the west shore of the river (165 acres), offers boating, hunting, fishing, picnicking, and winter sports. Hurd State Park and George P. Seymour State Park, on the east side of the Connecticut River, have hiking, picnicking, and camping (shelters). Hunting is allowed on Haddam Neck, Higganum Meadows, and in the Higganum-Haddam Rod and Gun Club. Cockaponset State Forest (a few campsites) spreads throughout much of Haddam, and hiking, hunting, and fishing are allowed there. There is hunting in the 473-acre Wopowog Management Area (see appendix).

HAMDEN *(New Haven County. Rtes. into: U.S. 5; state 10, 15, which is the Wilbur Cross Pkwy.; 33.0 sq. mi.; 49,357 pop. Other communities: Augerville, Centerville, Hamden Plains, Highwood, Mt. Carmel, Spring Glen, Whitneyville.)*
In its southern portion, the town is indistinguishable from New Haven as the residential areas and thoroughfares merge. In the northern parts, however, a more open aspect prevails and the rugged topography in the western portion rises as high as 880 feet. Most residents are employed in the New Haven urban region. First settled in 1638 (as part of the original New Haven colony), the town was separated from New Haven in 1786 and named for John Hampden, a Puritan English patriot of Cromwellian days.

In 1798 Eli Whitney, inventor of the cotton gin, began producing muskets under contract to the U.S. government in what is now Whitneyville. In doing this he shares honors with others in the development of mass-production techniques including line as- sembly, precision gauges, machine tools, and, according to some reports, interchangeable parts.

*To See and Do: (1)* The Jonathan Dickerman House, Mt. Carmel Ave. (Hamden Historical Society). This one-story house has two interesting architectural features: a leanto addition that gives it a miniaturized saltbox appearance and the curving front projection of the roof, which is a Dutch influence. It appears on Connecticut houses near ports where trade with the early New York Dutch brought this small evidence of appreciation among some Con- necticut home builders.

The Dickerman family, long residents of the New Haven colony, became leaders in Hamden when it was incorporated. Eighteen Dickermans have served as Selectmen of the town.

The interior of the house is furnished in the period with a homelike display of china and glass in a corner cupboard. Brick fireplaces attest to the early production of this building material in the area. Outside, the garden-herbarium is as it would have been during the earliest years of the house.

*(2)* Sleeping Giant State Park (Whitney Ave., Rte. 10) offers over 1,300 acres of trails, woods, and views from a high rock formation that looks from a distance like the form of a man sleeping on his

back. A trail system has been developed that offers long and short walks, and campsites are available. Part of Naugatuck State Forest (west of Rte. 10, in the northern part of town) offers more hiking. Brooksvale Recreation Park offers 170 acres for hiking, skating, and skiing. Both East Rock and West Rock parks lie partially in Hamden, though they belong to New Haven (see New Haven). Hunting is permitted in a 3,600-acre area of the Hamden Fish and Game Protective Association (see appendix). Golf can be enjoyed at the Laurel View Golf Course (West Shepard Ave.) and the Meadowbrook Golf Course (Dixwell Ave.).

**HAMPTON** *(Windham County. Rtes. into: U.S. 6; state 97; 25.3 sq. mi.; 1,129 pop. Other communities: Clark's Corner.)*
This small, pleasant rural community, settled in 1712, has the distinction of lying to the east of its namesake town, East Hampton. Most of the village is strung along Rte. 97 and fine eighteenth- and nineteenth-century homes set well back from the road give it great attractiveness. And from this state highway you can see a "far piece" easterly to ridges beyond a wide, gentle valley. The Congregational Church on the west side of Rte. 97 in the "center" was built on an eighteenth-century frame and the present square-towered structure with its heavy Greek portico dates from 1840. Just south of the church on the east side of the road stands the home of former Connecticut Governor Chauncey Cleveland. It is an imposing building, somewhat pretentious amid Hampton's rural charm. South and east of the church lies Howard Valley, where can be found an old Baptist church, a number of older homes, the remains of several gristmills—an altogether pleasant area to inspect at a very leisurely pace.

*To See and Do:* The James L. Goodwin and Natchaug State Forests cover most of the central and northwestern part of town. There is ample acreage for hiking, picnicking, and fishing (Hampton Reservoir and Pine Acres Lake).

**HARTFORD** *(Hartford County. Rtes. into: I-84, I-91; U.S. 5, 6, 44; state 4, 15, 185, 187, 189; 18.4 sq. mi.; 157,600 pop.)*

In the geographical and political center of Connecticut is Hartford, the state capital and, according to its boosters, the insurance capital of the world. Its location, on the Connecticut River, which is navigable to the sea, was a stroke of luck for its early settlers. This, and the fact that it lies near the center of what was eventually to become the state of Connecticut, assured its dominance both in the early days and the present. Today its refurbished skyline with the gold-plated capitol-building dome can be seen for miles across the central lowland and river plain on which it is built.

The first white settlers were actually the Dutch, though their "settlement" consisted primarily of a trading post, the House of Hope, or Fort Good Hope. It was active around 1633, under Commissary Van Curler. As the English began to move into the region, founding Windsor to the north and Wethersfield to the south, the Dutch found themselves outflanked. Within a few years they gave up and sailed downriver to the sea and New Amsterdam (New York).

As the third oldest permanent settlement in the state, Hartford had an auspicious beginning. In 1635 petitioners from the crowded Boston-Newtowne (Cambridge) area asked to leave and be allowed to find lands of their own. The most favorable reports they had of the western wilderness concerned Suckiag, as the Indians termed the area which is now Hartford. These reports had come in 1633 and 1634 from explorers who hoped to engage in trade with the Indians while keeping their eyes peeled for likely settling spots. The place called Suckiag became, briefly, New-towne in late 1635. The first English settlers, led by a John Steel and numbering about sixty, were concerned mainly with shelter and food for the winter and they lived in dugouts. Despite the fact that they had neighbors in Windsor and Wethersfield, the help they could get was doubtful, since those pioneers were also struggling through the cold months. In the spring of 1636 Thomas Hooker led a group of additional families, believed to number about one hundred people, on the two-week journey overland from Cambridge to join Steel and his people. Two years later Suckiag, or Newtowne, was renamed Hartford.

From the first, Hartford dominated the towns of Windsor and Wethersfield. And when the settlers learned they were no longer under the jurisdiction of the Massachusetts Bay colony, the question of governing themselves became paramount. In 1638 representatives of the "river towns," as they have been called, met in Hartford and drew up what is regarded as the first written constitution: the Fundamental Orders of Connecticut. Its new, revolutionary concept was that all governmental authority rested on the free consent of the people.

The banding together of the three neighboring towns created what was first known as the Hartford colony; it later became known as the Connecticut colony. From its founding, Hartford was in a favorable position for trade. The Connecticut River led to the sea and was navigable. Above Hartford were the Enfield Rapids, which meant Hartford was nearly at the upper limit of the river for seagoing ships. North of the rapids stretched the wilderness, where riches were to be gathered: furs from the Indians, wood products, timber for ships, and fish and game. In addition, the river plain surrounding Hartford was fertile. Tobacco was a valuable and marketable crop as were all agricultural products.

The settlers of Hartford were shrewd men, Puritans whose ethic included a good profit. And they began making it at the outset. By 1662 there were fourteen towns in the flourishing Connecticut colony. And in 1665, the New Haven colony with its six towns reluctantly became a part of the larger, more fortunate community. From that time forward the history of Hartford became the history of Connecticut in all larger aspects and as such is treated in Chapter 2.

Shipping and trade from Hartford reached its zenith in the eighteenth century; its demise can be marked by the War of 1812, when British ships blockaded river traffic and, in fact, nearly all of Long Island Sound. For the river towns this meant an end to the era of European and West Indian trade forever. What shipping survived the war gradually rose again in those ports directly on Long Island Sound.

One outgrowth of the shipping era, however, had far-reaching consequences for Hartford. As ships went out, they frequently were financed by men who stayed behind. As is natural, the men whose money was invested in the hazardous venture worried a great deal about fire, shipwrecks, and storms. So the investors (or speculators) created a crude form of marine insurance. They agreed to reimburse losses jointly in return for a greater profit in the event that the ship returned. With the end of shipping, the infant insurance industry turned to fire insurance for buildings and homes. The Hartford Fire Insurance Company was begun in 1810 and Aetna in 1819. Things proceeded nicely in the profit department until December 16, 1835. On that night, in New York City, with the temperature at seventeen below zero and a northwest wind howling through the streets, a fire broke out in a wooden building. Flames spread and a major catastrophe was on the way. When at last the fire was controlled and put out (by dynamiting a path wide enough to keep the flames from igniting more buildings) six hundred buildings had been destroyed in a seventeen-block area of New York. News of the disaster reached Hartford and insurance executives turned pale at the information. New York insurance companies had immediately gone into bankruptcy, since they could not pay the claims. The then president of the Hartford Fire Insurance Company was Eliphalet Terry. He went by sleigh to New York City and in the scene of desolation announced dramatically that Hartford Fire Insurance Company would pay all losses of its customers. Seen by some as a tremendous example of business integrity and by others as a shrewd Yankee move for business, the action nonetheless resulted in a boom in Hartford insurance. New policies flowed in. The total loss in the New York fire was around $17,000,000. Hartford's claims amounted to less than $65,000. Whatever the motivation or combination of motivations of the businessmen, the reputation of Hartford insurance companies grew throughout the nineteenth century. They weathered similar disasters in Boston, Jacksonville, Chicago, and San Francisco in the earthquake of 1906. In that great disaster, insurance claims amounting to $15,000,000 were promptly paid and it brought Hartford the reputation of being the insurance capital of the world. Today the home offices of forty insurance companies are located in Hartford. Among them are the familiar names of Hartford Fire, Aetna, Travelers, and many others.

The industrial history of Hartford, like that of New Haven, shows a rise after the War of 1812. The city is the home of the famed Colt revolver. The factory, established in 1852, still operates in the city.

Organs and aircraft engines (Pratt & Whitney, now in East Hartford) are world-known products of the Connecticut city.

No city in Connecticut is more representative of latter-day Puritanism than Hartford. It has lived and evolved for more than three hundred years, escaping the ameliorating effects of easy summer existence on the shore, the influence of larger, more distant urban centers like New York City and Boston, and it has guarded and enlarged its capital with unshakable Yankee prudence. It is a shrewd city, in business terms. Despite its small size, nationally, as a city, Hartford has more experience with money than any comparable community in the nation, thanks largely to the insurance business. Large sums are discussed as casually in this Yankee city as in Wall Street, Washington, or oil-rich Dallas. The difference is that in Hartford there is little ostentation and no conspicuous waste—which could prove deceptive to the outsider.

Like Dallas, Hartford is a city run by business. Here, however, it is banking and insurance, not oil. Tightly knit and structured, the leaders decide many things on their own and usually get what they want. Public outcries are rare, since the leadership carefully avoids false steps or too much publicity. Born as a theocracy in stern authoritarian Puritanism, Hartford has kept the same self-righteous attitude it had then as it changed to a plutocracy.

*To See and Do: (1)* Old State House, 800 Main St. (city of Hartford). One of the few eighteenth-century buildings remaining in the city, the old state house was designed by Charles Bulfinch in the last decade of the eighteenth century. Charles Bulfinch was from Boston and designed the famous state house there. Its Federal style was at that time a fresh new evolution of the fully developed Georgian architecture of the period. Now under the care of the Connecticut Historical Society, the building has been restored and furnished as nearly as possible to appear just as it did in 1796, when it was first occupied. The first floor served as a courtroom for both the local and superior courts and provided office space for the governor, comptroller, and treasurer. The House and Senate chambers were on the second floor. The building was used by both the city and the state for many years. When a city hall was built in 1827, the state alone used the building. In 1879 the present Capitol building was occupied and city government moved back into the old state house until 1915. Many important events in Connecticut history occurred within the building. The Hartford Convention of 1814 met in the Senate chamber and the Constitutional Conventions of 1818 and 1965 held sessions in the building. In 1824 the aging Lafayette was honored in the building while he was on his farewell tour of the United States.

(2) The State Capitol, Capitol Ave. and Trinity St. This imposing building of marble and granite stands on what now is appropriately known as Capitol Hill, overlooking Bushnell Park. In 1872 the city of Hartford, vying with New Haven, purchased the site from Trinity College in an effort to induce the state to make its permanent home in Hartford. A design competition was held, attracting the notable architects of the day. *The Hartford Courant* stated that what was being sought was a "showy and sensational" building. Richard M. Upjohn, willing architect, laid out a spectacular yet dignified edifice, a kaleidoscope of eclecticism in its architectural styles. Construction was completed in 1879 at the cost of more than two and a half million dollars. The twelve-sided dome can be seen from afar, being finished with gold leaf. Once topping the dome was a bronze sculpture, the "Genius of Connecticut," by Randolph Rogers. The statue was removed in 1938 because of the approaching hurricane of that year. In a patriotic gesture, the bronze sculpture was melted down during World War II for war use. A small replica is exhibited inside the Capitol. The interior of the Capitol is rich in variety of spaces and textures, bright and gloomy, colorful, gold, and silver. Stair rails and door knobs are of brass, and the extensive use of marble is particularly effective. The main mass of the building is flanked by two multistory wings on the east and west ends. The first floor contains offices and displays of Connecticut flags and other memorabilia from the history of the state. The governor's office is on the second floor, near the House of Representatives' chamber. The third floor houses Senate chambers and the senators' offices and hearing rooms, while committee rooms occupy the fourth floor. The small fifth floor contains a cafeteria, legislators' dining room, and storage area.

*(3)* Connecticut State Library, 231 Capitol Ave. (opposite the Capitol building). Built in 1910 in Italian Renaissance style, the imposing building is entered via a long flight of broad steps flanked by two large sculptural groups. A half-million volumes comprise the library proper but archival material contains two million manuscripts dealing with law, the social sciences, and genealogy, and including official state papers and those relating to the history of the state dating from 1636. The building contains a history museum where displays of governors' portraits, Indian artifacts, and military relics can be seen. In the museum also is the Newcomb clock collection commemorating one of Connecticut's early industries and the Colt firearm collection—more than one thousand guns depicting the development of Colt weapons from the first revolvers through automatic rifles to aircraft machineguns.

*(4)* Nook Farm (Mark Twain House–Harriet Beecher Stowe House), 77 Forest Rd. Three houses and two carriage houses, all of approximately the same period, comprise this interesting group. In the latter half of the nineteenth century, Mark Twain and Harriet Beecher Stowe brought international fame to the cluster and neighborhood. There is a parking area on the south side of Farmington Ave., just west of the Mark Twain House. One of the carriage houses has been converted to a visitors' center where tickets may be bought and souvenirs purchased.

*(A)* The Mark Twain House. The flamboyant Mark Twain lived in a flamboyant house. The red and yellow brick house is in the Victorian-Gothic style and represents all the elaboration of that period. The twenty-room structure was Twain's home from 1874 to 1879. Reminiscent of Twain's Mississippi Riverboat days is an addition in the rear modeled after the pilot house of a long-ago steamboat. With characteristic perversity, Twain laid out the servants' quarters in the front of the house overlooking Farmington Ave. so the servants could keep up with gossip and who went where without traipsing through the house to check on passersby. Twain claimed it saved the rugs. The house contains a 500-volume library of first editions and foreign translations of Twain's work as well as a photographic file on Mark Twain, his family, and friends in the Hartford region.

*(B)* Harriet Beecher Stowe House. A modest house, by contrast

to Mark Twain's, this Victorian brick home was Harriet Beecher Stowe's from 1873 to 1896 and was built in 1871. Memorabilia of the author of *Uncle Tom's Cabin* is on display.

*(C)* The Day House. This Victorian mansion has been converted to a library covering the period 1840–1900 and runs to nearly 10,000 volumes. In addition there are 50,000 manuscripts available for study by qualified scholars.

*(5)* Wadsworth Atheneum, 600 Main St. This is one of the finest medium-sized museums in the country. It was the first free public art museum in the United States. The museum contains the J. P. Morgan collection of antique bronzes, European porcelain, and silver; also on display are pieces of the famed Wallace Nutting collection of early American furniture, with rooms furnished in the period of the eighteenth and nineteenth centuries. There are European paintings from A.D. 1400 to the present in the art galleries, with special galleries devoted to Middle Ages and Renaissance art, a court of European tapestries, arms, and armor. Early Central and South American art occupies other rooms. Ship models, ballet design, and costume displays, Oriental art, Pilgrim furniture, costumes, and furniture can also be seen. There is also a reading room where the 11,000-volume library of art reference books may be utilized.

*(6)* The Connecticut Historical Society, 1 Elizabeth St. Founded in 1825, the private society is handsomely housed on an 8-acre estate in the former Curtis Veeder mansion. There is now a parking lot, a 250-seat auditorium, and 30,000 square feet of new display space in a new building attached to the original structure. Numerous bequests of furniture collections make its rooms of seventeenth- and eighteenth-century work outstanding displays. Some of the finest cabinetmakers in Connecticut are represented. There are also some six hundred portraits ranging from the seventeenth to the twentieth century as well as early engravings by such masters as Abel Buell and Amos Doolittle. More than six hundred lithographs from the Kellogg Brothers firm cover the period from 1830–70. Clocks by Daniel Burnap, Eli Terry, Joseph Carpenter, and Simeon Jocylen are also owned and displayed by the society. Exhibitions are always being changed and only about

10 percent of the society's material is visible in the display rooms at any one time. Silver, pewter, toys, glass, pottery, and stoneware add to the interest of the exhibitions. For those interested in particular items of furniture, glass, etc., it is nice to know they can be admitted to storage rooms for examination of the entire "line" of their interest. Some 70,000 volumes comprise the society's library with one and a half million manuscripts, 3,500 bound volumes of newspapers, plus almost literally uncounted thousands of broadsides, maps, prints, and photographs. There is also a large genealogical collection on New England families and their descendants in regions of Connecticut migration (e.g., Ohio).

*(7)* Trinity College, Summit Ave. This presently nonsectarian college grew from the first Episcopal college in New England—first known as Washington College when it was established in 1823. It took its present name in 1845 and in the 1870s moved to its present location, selling its original site to the city, which offered the land as an inducement to the state for the new State Capitol Building. Trinity's Long Walk is an excellent example of college architecture of the period, which tended to mimic the style of Oxford and Cambridge in England. Trinity College Chapel is the purest form of Gothic architecture in the state, with painstaking care given to all details to reproduce the perpendicular style common to English church architecture. The interior is especially noteworthy with carvings both in stone and wood. The buttressed tower, visible from many places in and around Hartford, is an outstanding accomplishment and develops in visitors familiar with English churches a genuine twitch of nostalgia.

The Austen Arts Center, on the Trinity College campus, has changing exhibits of paintings and prints. It frequently is well worth a visit.

*(8)* Center Congregational Church and Ancient Burial Ground, Main and Gold Sts. The church, built in 1807, is probably from a design by Daniel Wadsworth, who had apparently seen St.-Martin's-in-the-Fields, in London. The exterior is elaborately embellished with classical motifs and urns at balcony levels. The interior, redone in 1852, has more delicate work, including an interesting barrel-vaulted ceiling. The church society that built Center Church

is the oldest in the state, having been formed in 1632. On Gold St., behind the church, is the ancient burial ground which was in use between 1640 and the early 1800s.

*(9)* Bushnell Memorial Hall, 166 Capitol Ave. Built in 1930 of brick and limestone, the large, massive building is a typical example of institutional Georgian Revival. Once inside, visitors may enjoy a running series of events in the large auditorium along with loyal Hartford citizens. Acoustics have been hailed as excellent, particularly for symphonic programs. Also, the Hartford Stage Company, 65 Kinsky St. at Constitution Plaza, offers excellent theatrical productions.

*(10)* Charter Oak Memorial, corner of Charter Oak Ave. and Charter Oak Pl. The granite column erected in 1906 is "near" the site of the famed Charter Oak (see Chapter 2), which is revered by all pious Nutmeggers. The tree itself, apparently a giant with a trunk circumference of thirty-three feet, blew down in 1856. Pieces of the tree became great prizes and various articles (such as the speaker's chair in the state Senate chamber) were carved from it. But if all the items reportedly made from the one tree really *were,* the tree—however large—would have had to be considerably larger.

*(11)* Constitution Plaza. New bank and insurance buildings clustered in a modern arrangement in the plaza give the twelve-acre site Hartford's distinctively new downtown look. The most striking building is the Phoenix Mutual Building, which has a double-bowed outline sheathed in green glass. Christmas finds elaborate lighting in the plaza, but it offers a pleasant stroll any time of the year.

*(12)* Parks. Hartford has six major parks and more than forty smaller parks and public squares. *Elizabeth Park,* just west of the city line at Prospect St. and Asylum Ave., contains the famous rose gardens, as well as a natural pond where one can feed ducks and goldfish in spring and summer, and ice skate in winter. *Keeney Park* is a heavily wooded area just north of the center city. Tower Ave. runs through its center; North Main St. leads to the zoo entrance. It offers an eighteen-hole golf course and a delightful children's zoo, Sherwood Forest, patterned after Robin Hood's

domain. *Goodwin Park*, at the city's southern border, is reached by traveling south on Maple Ave. It has both eighteen- and nine-hole golf courses, an ice-skating pond, and recreation spots. *Pope Park*, off Park St., offers the expected recreation areas and is a good place to picnic, for fireplaces are available. *Colt Park* is most notable for its history. It was originally the 114-acre estate of Samuel and Elizabeth Colt; Samuel was the inventor of the Colt revolver, and his factory and housing for workers still stands. Just west of the park area, on Wethersfield Ave., is their home, Armsmear, specified to be used by widows of Episcopal clergymen. The land area is being eaten away by Interstate 91 and by the city for the building of a new school, but much of it yet remains. The park offers an artificial ice rink and contains Dillon Stadium, place of football games, rock concerts, and other events. The park is reached by following Wethersfield Ave. to Wawarme Ave. *Bushnell Park*, where the State Capitol is located, was laid out in 1853 by Dr. Horace Bushnell and Frederick Law Olmsted, designer of Central Park in New York and the first landscape architect in the United States. One of the earliest public parks in the nation, it has many monuments and memorials, in sculpture and tablets, the most interesting of which is the arch at Trinity and Ford Sts. Designed by George Keller and dedicated to the soldiers and sailors of the Civil War, it was given to the city by the citizens of Hartford. The bas relief around the turrets offers an interesting assemblage of the various professions involved in the war. Bushnell Park is bounded by Asylum St., Trinity St., Jewell St., Elm St., and Capitol Ave.

HARTLAND *(Hartford County. Rtes. into: 20, 179, 181; 34.5 sq. mi.; 1,303 pop. Other communities: East Hartland, West Hartland.)*
A situation exists in the town that represents one of the more endearing traits of Yankee character. The village of West Hartland is east of Hartland, and logic be damned. One local historian remarked proudly that Hartland was the only town in the state that showed a consistent population decline from the first U.S. census onward. We can only hope he finished his remark before everyone

had left. Until 1940 the gentleman's boast was correct but things are picking up in Hartland today, as it offers wonderful scenic landscape for summer homes and true rural existence. Hills, hollows, and forest are the marks of Hartland. The town is almost bisected by the huge manmade Barkhamsted Reservoir. To get to East Hartland from Hartland requires driving north almost to the Massachusetts line on Rte. 20, around the top of the reservoir and so on through forests to East Hartland. Though a long drive, it is a pretty one, and well worth the time.

*To See and Do:* Tunxis State Forest and People's State Forest cover a major portion of the town and offer fishing, hunting, hiking, and picnicking. There is a boat-launch site on Howells Pond (1½ miles off Rte. 20, northwest of West Hartland) in Tunxis Forest. Hunting also is permitted in the 4,500-acre Metropolitan District Area (see appendix).

HARWINTON *(Litchfield County. Rtes. into: 4, 8, 72, 118, 222; 31.4 sq. mi.; 4,318 pop.)*
In the Revolutionary War, Harwinton had a large number of patriots who either went to war or, barring that, harassed Tories whenever possible. Reports come down that there was only one Tory in the entire town, so you can imagine what a life *he* led. Near Chippen's Hill a large cave retains to this day the name Tory Den. Allegedly traitorous loyalists met and plotted evil doings there.

The first settler in what is now Harwinton was a Captain Daniel Messenger, who moved into the region in 1730. Part of the town had been deeded to men of Hartford and part to proprietors in Windsor and Farmington. So when the naming of the town took place it came out "Har" for Hartford, "win" for Windsor, and "ton" for Farmington. Hence Harwinton.

Agriculture, some foundry work, and light manufacture now comprise the industry of the essentially rural town. With its location in relatively high terrain, Harwinton has become an attractive home for commuting residents who work in Bristol and Hartford.

*To See and Do:* Mattatuck State Forest on the western edge of town offers hiking, picnicking, and regulated hunting. Hunting is also available on the 1,308 acres of the Harwinton Rod and Gun Club (see appendix).

HEBRON *(Tolland County. Rtes. into: 66, 85, 94, 207, 316; 37.5 sq. mi.; 3,815 pop. Other communities: Amston, Gilead.)*
Settled in 1704, Hebron's name comes from some form of Hebrew meaning "league" or "association," depending on which authority is consulted. Its quiet country existence on the undulations of this part of Connecticut was disrupted during the Revolution when excited patriots tarred, feathered, and rode out of town on a rail one Samuel Peters, Tory and cleric, who called their actions treasonable. Rev. Peters fled to England and wrote a preposterous book entitled *History of Connecticut* in which he "got back" at the colonists by wildly distorting life in Connecticut. Disbelieved here, it was widely held to be accurate in England and contributed further to English smugness.

Hebron today is a crossroads center at the junction of 66 and 85, where churches and a few older houses nicely spaced almost define visually the term "country quiet." Just south of the center is St. Peter's Church, a red brick structure dating from 1825 with the tower at the west end, the entry at the east end. The small graveyard behind the church and the weathered brick are reminiscent of country churches in the Tideland area of Virginia.

Gilead, a small cluster of well-kept houses and a simple west-facing Congregational church, lies north of the center, on Rte. 85, where everyone always has a view of rolling hills to the west. Amston was named after Charles Ams, who owned a silk mill there and gave the community its reason to be.

*To See and Do:* Gay City State Park (1514 acres), bordering Rte. 85 in the northern part of town, offers fishing, hiking, swimming, and picnicking. Holbrook Pond (east of Rte. 85, 1.4 miles north of Hebron village) has hunting and fishing, and there is a boat-launching site. Golf can be enjoyed at Blackledge Country Club, on West St., and the Tallwood Country Club, on Rte. 85.

KENT *(Litchfield County. Rtes. into: U.S. 7; state 341; 49.5 sq. mi.; 1,900 pop. Other communities: Bull's Bridge, Flanders, Kent Furnace, Macedonia, North Kent, South Kent.)*

The Housatonic River runs smack through the town, from northeast to southwest, and the main road (U.S. 7) runs along the river-valley floor, which is broad and contains the agricultural land of the town. Steep hills rise precipitately on either side of the valley. Several decades ago Kent was "discovered" by country-hungry city people and vacationers, so that today many of its citizens are transplanted urbanites. Hikers and naturalists and a great many painters know Kent well. George Inness and William S. Jewett, for example, both painted the Kent hills and valley long ago.

Like its neighboring towns, Kent enjoyed the iron-production boom that began early in the eighteenth century and continued, in some cases, through the Civil War. Three blast furnaces were operating at one time in the town and metal for rifles made at Harpers Ferry and Springfield came from the iron mine in the town. During the Revolutionary War, Kent men formed two companies to fight the British and reportedly these troops went to the aid of neighboring Danbury, when it was attacked (see Danbury). Surprisingly, a local tribe of Indians, the Schaghticokes, contributed a hundred braves to help the patriot cause. Reportedly they served as a signal troop, sending drum and fire and smoke signals along the shores of the state to the back hills—in code the British probably never broke.

Kent is also the home of Kent School, a preparatory school that has gained national attention both through the rigorous discipline of its founder, the late Father Sill, and through the efforts of its crews, many of whom have competed in the Henley Regatta in England. Today, any visitor in the spring or early summer may catch a glimpse of crews practicing on the waters of the Housatonic River there.

*To See and Do: (1)* The Sloane-Stanley Museum, Kent Furnace, U.S. 7. (State of Connecticut). The ruins of one of Kent's blast furnaces suggested the location and purpose of this museum. On display in the recently constructed building are antique tools of all descriptions, made of wood and iron, hand carved and hand forged. Down the slope toward the river rises the ruin of the great blast furnace itself, made of granite, its outline unimpaired by time. When in operation, fires were kept going day and night. If the fire went out and the half-smelted ore cooled, the furnace had to be abandoned and another one built.

*(2)* Covered Bridge, west of Bull's Bridge, a crossroad hamlet on U.S. 7. One of the last remaining covered bridges in Connecticut.

*(3)* Kent Falls State Park, east side of U.S. 7, in the north part of town. The most beautiful waterfalls in the state, according to some reports, makes this park especially inviting. A 200-foot drop in less than a quarter-mile of the stream bed produces cascades of water that can be enjoyed while picnicking there. Hiking, camping, and fishing are also available on the 275-acre site. Macedonia Brook State Park (2,300 acres) offers the same amenities. It is located on the west side of the Housatonic River, north of Rte. 341. Wyantenock State Forest, in the north-central part of town (east of U.S. 7, northwest of Rte. 341), offers hunting and hiking. The Appalachian Trail enters Connecticut here from New York State and passes through Macedonia State Park. Fishing in the Housatonic River, Waramaug Lake, and Hatch Pond (South Kent); also North Spectacle Lake and South Spectacle Lake lying north and south respectively of Rte. 341 in the eastern part of town.

KILLINGLY *(Windham County. Connecticut Turnpike, north on Danielson Connector, which is Rte. 52; U.S. 6; state 12, 21, 101; 50.0 sq. mi.; 13,573 pop. Other communities: Attawaugan, Borough of Danielson, Dayville, East Killingly, Elmville, Ballouville, Rogers.)*
The town was purchased early from the Indians, settled in 1700, and named from Killingly Manor in Yorkshire. The Indians, of the harmless Nipmuck tribe, later regretted the low price they had accepted, succumbed to fecklessness, and took to sitting on settlers' doorways, smiling wanly and hoping to be fed.

An overlooked candidate for Women's Lib attention was a native of Killingly. Mrs. Mary Kies invented an improvement for weaving straw with silk or thread. She was the first woman applicant for a patent that was granted. The then First Lady, Dolley Madison, sent her a congratulatory note.

The Quinebaug River forms the western boundary of the town, and mills were primary industries for many years. In 1836 its nickname was Curtain Town, and it led all other Connecticut towns in producing cotton cloth. Early mills employed entire families on a dawn-to-dusk workday schedule. A sample wage went like this: father, a dollar a day for twelve hours' work; mother, thirty-five cents; children, twenty-one cents. Annual income: four to six hundred dollars per year. Today industries centered largely in Danielson produce yarns, canvas, wood and leather products, helicopter air frames, and molded rubber products. And wages are better.

The rocky, wooded hills of the town contain an interesting old quarry. It lies on Whetstone Brook, not far from Killingly Center. Indians from as far west as Michigan used to come to quarry the whetstone that helped shape arrowheads and other stone utensils.

*To See and Do:* Old Furnace State Park, with 101 acres, offers fishing, shelters, and picnicking facilities. Fishing on Quinebaug Lake (Wauregan Reservoir), Alexander Lake, and Killingly Pond (inquire locally). Regulated hunting and fishing around Tetrault Pond. Hunting in the 269-acre Ross Marsh Management Area (see appendix), and golfers can play at Woodlawn Country Club in Danielson.

KILLINGWORTH *(Middlesex County. Rtes. 80, 81, 148; 36.0 sq. mi.; 2,435 pop.)*
Founded in 1667, Killingworth originally reached to the shore, including the present town of Clinton. The name is a corruption supposedly of Kenilworth (Castle), in Warwickshire, England. Today you can drive through and never know you have passed the center. This might be considered the junction of Rtes. 80 and 81 but the true "center" is spread along Rte. 81, north of 80. A small store, garage, town hall, church, and school *are* the center. There is some farming in the town but it is mainly residential and wooded.

Two legendary figures still find currency in Killingworth. One, in legend and fact, tinkered with currency and became a convicted counterfeiter in colonial days. But Abel Buell, as his name was, had at first a local and then a wider reputation as a genius. He engraved the first map of America and among other accomplishments altered five-pound notes. Curious Peeping Tom neighbors caught him at it (by mounting a ladder and watching him through an upstairs window of his home). Yet the King's Attorney, after Buell's conviction, carried out only the most adumbrated letter of the law, which required ear cropping, branding, and life-imprisonment. The tip of Abel's ear was snipped off, held on his tongue to keep it warm, and then replaced, where it grew back, good as new. The "C" for counterfeiter, to be branded on his forehead, was lightly done above the hairline, and his imprisonment was shortly terminated when Buell invented the first lapidary machine in America, made a gold ring with it, and sent it as a gift to King's Attorney Griswold, who shortly secured Buell's release.

The other figure, more shadowy, was Goodie Wee, a witch who caused, as all good witches do, milk to sour and lumber to slide from wagons.

*To See and Do: (1)* Chatfield Hollow State Park, Rte. 80, west of Rte. 81. This 356-acre park has swimming, hiking, fishing (Schreeder Pond), winter sports, and picnic facilities. Several gravel roads are good for extended walks leading into the surrounding ledgy countryside beyond the park boundaries.

*(2)* Congregational Church, Rte. 81, north of 80. Widely known as an example of late Federal architecture, the building was erected in 1820. The center door is Greek in influence while the doors on either side are Adamesque. Both interior and exterior are worth attention. An Episcopal church in the woods stands alone west of Durham Rd. (Rte. 148, west of Rte. 81). Watch for sign.

*(3)* Drives through Killingworth reveal here and there eighteenth-century cottages and fine examples of early nineteenth-century dwellings. Several are located just north and south of Rte. 80 on Rte. 81. And both centuries of building are represented on quaintly named Roast Meat Hill Road (first right going east on Rte. 80, beyond Rte. 81).

LEBANON *(New London County. Rtes. into: 16, 87, 207, 289; 56.1 sq. mi.; 3,804 pop. Other communities: Chestnut Hill, Exeter, Goshen Hill, Liberty Hill.)*

No other country town has produced or entertained as many notable people as Lebanon, which began its history in 1697 and drew its name from biblical association. Its high, hilly landscape offers a bleak view in midwinter and drew from the chilled lips of Duc de Lauzun, assigned winter quarters there during the Revolution, the remark that "Siberia alone can be compared to Lebanon."

The good duke followed orders however, and his troop of cavalry whiled away the idle months parading on the town green to the delight of the villagers. During the Revolution, Lebanon citizens were much more than spectators, however. One farmer, Miller Gay, who was an ardent drummer, left his hoe standing in a corn row and with a hasty good-bye to his wife followed Captain Clark, another Lebanon citizen, to Lexington and eventually to Bunker Hill. First citizen of the town was Jonathan Trumbull, whose family had gained wealth in trade with the West Indies. Lebanon was the family headquarters and there were branch offices in East Haddam, Norwich, and Wethersfield (all shipping ports then).

Six years before the Declaration of Independence, in 1770, citizens of Lebanon wrote up a "declaration of rights and principles" in response to news about the Boston Massacre, and when the war came, Jonathan Trumbull, who was governor of the Connecticut colony, was the only colonial governor to throw in his lot with the patriots. He also threw the wealth of his estates into the cause. He became a counselor to General Washington and something like the chief supply officer of the war. His home and a small office (see below) became the meeting place for Revolutionary leaders, men whose names are known to all of us now: George Washington, John Jay, John Adams, Benjamin Franklin, Generals Putnam and Knox, the Marquis de Lafayette, and Count Rochambeau as well as the aforementioned goose-pimpled Duc de Lauzun.

Some hint of Jonathan Trumbull's importance comes from the story that when Washington was wintering in at Valley Forge and his men were starving, Trumbull arranged for three hundred cattle on the hoof to be taken to the troops—an incredible feat in midwinter during that fateful period. Of Trumbull, Washington later wrote, "But for Jonathan Trumbull, the war could not have been carried to a successful conclusion." Ammunition, cannon muskets, uniforms, wagons, food, horses—all the necessities to wage war were Jonathan Trumbull's concern. He was Lebanon's and Connecticut's outstanding Revolutionary War figure—and became first governor of the state after the war.

One William Williams was also a citizen of Lebanon, and it was he who drafted the declaration of rights and principles in 1770. He went on to be a signer of the Declaration of Independence when that document was written.

*To See and Do: (1)* Jonathan Trumbull House, second house north of junction of Main St. and Colchester Rd., Rte. 207, west side (Connecticut Daughters of the Revolution). Built by Jonathan's father, Captain Joseph Trumbull, in 1735, the building was moved in 1830 a short distance to its present site. It was dragged there on skids, using several yoke of oxen. Pedimented windows on the first floor, matching the door pediment, are unusual and the house gives the appearance of being a typical central-chimney dwelling—which is deceptive. There is a center hall in it, and the fireplaces in three chimneys heat the rooms. The chimneys merge in the attic and one stack only is visible above the roof. Interior shutters and paneling are of interest, as is Governor Trumbull's private office on the five-bedroom second floor. It is a small room with one small window set high in the wall. Legend has it that this was done so no British sniper could shoot the governor while he was at his desk. Since there was a price on Trumbull's head during the war, the legend has credibility.

*(2)* War Office, second building north of Trumbull House. This small, red two-room building was Trumbull's business office. During the Revolution Governor Trumbull turned it into his supply office and it was then connected with his house by a tunnel. In addition to meeting national and military leaders here, Trumbull met with the Connecticut Council of Safety some 1,200 times, when discussions of troop drafting, outfitting warships, and security matters took place; supplies were packed here, and

records kept. Booted and spurred couriers waited orders, swinging their heels against the counter panel—a part of which is preserved and on display in the Connecticut Historical Society Museum (see Hartford).

*(3)* Old Burial Ground, northeast of the center on Rte. 207, just across Susquetonscut Brook. Here are the graves of Jonathan Trumbull and William Williams as well as many other Revolutionary War citizens of Lebanon. Here also are the graves of Governor Jonathan Trumbull, Jr., and Governor Joseph Trumbull. (Lebanon is also the birthplace of two other Connecticut governors: Clark Bissel and William Buckingham.)

*(4)* Congregational Church, junction of 87 and 207. Built in 1807 by John Trumbull, son of Jonathan Trumbull, Sr., the church is notable for being the first with a recessed entry, having brick columns in front, and being one of the earliest brick churches. John Trumbull was an artist known today as a portraitist and painter of Revolutionary War scenes and personalities.

*(5)* Hunting in Lebanon-Franklin Shooting Grounds, some 12,000 acres, Bartlett Brook Management Area, Pease Brook Area (see appendix). There is fishing in Williams Pond, off Rte. 207, in the northwestern corner of town.

LEDYARD *(New London County. Rtes. into: 2, 12, 117, 214; 40.5 sq. mi.; 14,387 pop. Other communities: Gales Ferry.)*
Originally North Groton Society, the town is oriented toward the sea, as the navigable Thames River (see New London for local pronunciation) forms the western border of the town and its most developed community, Gales Ferry, is on the river bank. Shipyards operated here in the nineteenth century, and during the War of 1812 Stephen Decatur was blockaded this far upriver by a squadron of British warships. The site of the fort built by Decatur to protect his ships still exists on a hilltop near the river.

Gales Ferry, a quiet village of considerable charm, today serves as the training headquarters of the Yale crew each early summer as they prepare to row against arch rivals from Harvard (see New London).

Eastward, Ledyard develops quickly into a rural town, where

farming is the principal activity. Such industry as there is is situated along the river. The town's most notable son, Bishop Samuel Seabury, was born here in 1729 (see Woodbury). The town's name comes from Col. William Ledyard, who was killed in the Battle of Groton Heights (see Groton).

*To See and Do: (1)* Nathan Lester House, off Rte. 12 (town of Ledyard). A good example of eighteenth-century house architecture of the region.

*(2)* Stoddard Hill State Park, on the west side of Rte. 12, north of Rte. 214, with 55 acres, offers boating and fishing on the Thames. There are picnicking facilities available. Lantern Hill Pond, Long Pond, and Whitford Pond, off Lantern Hill Road, 1 mile south of Rte. 2, in the northeastern edge of town, offer fishing with boat-launch sites available at the first two ponds. The Pequot Hiking Trail passes through the northern part of town, crossing Rte. 214 just south of its junction with Rte. 2. Hunting in Rose Hill Management Area's 413 acres (east of Rte. 117, south of Rte. 2 to Thomas Rd.).

LISBON *(New London County. Rtes. into: Connecticut Turnpike, Exit 84; state 12, 138, 169; 16.5 sq. mi.; 2,808 pop. Other communities: Newent.)*
Jabez and Joseph Perkins bought land in that section of Norwich then named Newent. They were merchants whose ships sailed to European ports, and the town drew its name later from Lisbon, Portugal, in indirect recognition of the Perkins brothers' far-flung interests. Agriculture is the chief in-town occupation now, and workers from Norwich people the hilly farm community, giving parts of it a suburban aspect.

Long ago a coincidence of living had a Revolutionary War hero, Captain Oliver Arnold, living side by side with a Reverend David Hale. The captain was brother of traitor Benedict Arnold and the Reverend was the brother of patriot martyr, Nathan Hale.

*To See and Do:* Golf can be enjoyed at the Lisbon Country Club, on Kendall Rd.

LITCHFIELD *(Litchfield County. Rtes. into: 25, 63, 118, 209, 254; 57.3 sq. mi.; 7,399 pop. Other communities: Bantam, East Litchfield, Milton, Northfield.)*

Circumstance, design, and accident have made Litchfield the almost ideal New England village. The circumstance is its geographical location; the design is that of its founders; and the accident was the trend of industry location during the days of railroad influence.

Named from Litchfield, in Staffordshire, England, and incorporated in 1719, the town's founders, who came from the already settled communities of Hartford and Windsor, conceived and eventually laid out the broad green and the avenues that persist to this day. The spaciousness of their concept is the more startling when you realize they were looking at wilderness that is now the center of the village.

For they were on the frontier of wilderness to the west when they began the village. Hostile Indians captured one of the original settlers but he managed to escape and return to his family. Another, not so fortunate, was scalped at the edge of town. Five houses were fortified, stockades built, and sentries posted. Bit by bit, the wilderness was pushed back and gradually the threat of Indian attack faded. Farms sprouted out in the land that was bought for fifteen pounds by the original Hartford and Windsor purchasers. Gristmills, blacksmiths, and other small industries sprang up to supply the necessities of village life in those days.

Geographically, Litchfield is on broad upland meadows and not far from metallic deposits that contributed to its importance in the Revolutionary War. When that war came, the town was feverishly patriotic. So intense was the feeling that one minister allowed women to spin yarn on the Sabbath. By virtue of its location, Litchfield became a storehouse for military supplies and a source of armaments.

When the British took New York, the route for troops and supplies near the coast between New England and Pennsylvania was cut off. Litchfield lay on the alternate route and it became an important point on that line of supply and communication. General Washington visited the town five times during those war years to confer with leaders and check on supplies.

Ethan Allen was born in Litchfield and although he was regarded by more conservative citizens as a rapscallion, he is now claimed proudly as a native. His victory in taking Fort Ticonderoga and securing the important waterway of Lake Champlain for patriot use was an important contribution to the final victory.

On several occasions detachments of men were mustered from among Litchfield citizens to go to some threatened town. Perhaps the most revealing was the group of the fourteen last able-bodied men in town to rush to the defense of Danbury on April 27, 1777. Altogether, 504 men of Litchfield served in the Revolutionary War, and their spirit was best expressed by the engraved statement on the sword of one of them, Colonel Fisher Gay. It read, "Freedom or Death."

For a "frontier" town, Litchfield attracted a great number of the best families from other Connecticut towns. And they, or their Litchfield-born children, accomplished astonishing things.

Judge Tapping Reeve, for example, established the first law school in the United States (see below). An unusual man for his time, Judge Reeve worried about the plight of women in those unliberated times and he wrote the first serious, questioning, and defining volume on domestic relations published in the United States.

Sarah Pierce, a native of Litchfield, became a pioneer in the education of women. Her school was the first to offer higher education for girls. Over forty years some three thousand women attended her school.

Oliver Wolcott and Oliver Wolcott, Jr., lived in the town. Harriet Beecher Stowe attended Miss Pierce's school. Henry Ward Beecher was born there.

Industrially, Litchfield began as many Connecticut towns did: by using water power and brain power. Inventions and factories began to sprout in the town, and Julius Deming, a merchant, moved to Litchfield and began a thriving business that depended on his ships' cargoes from China. Goods were hauled from the coast and a number of stores sold his wares in Litchfield and neighboring towns.

With the coming of the railroad in the nineteenth century, accident played its part in preserving the "old" Litchfield. The river valley towns got the major rail lines and industry folded up in Litchfield and followed the iron horse to the Naugatuck and Housatonic valleys, where Connecticut's industrial towns still function. This left Litchfield high and dry. So it dozed through the years, content with a memorable past. Its eighteenth-century character and charm were ensured.

*To See and Do:* *(1)* The entire center of Litchfield (technically the Borough of Litchfield) is now a Historic District. This means that the eighteenth-century charm of the buildings and homes will be preserved for all time. A walk around this center will do more to inform visitors of the way colonial times were than any artificial exhibition. The homes are still lived in by Litchfield citizens—who are accustomed to wandering visitors gazing into the past.

*(2)* Tapping Reeve House (1773) and First Law School, South St. (Litchfield Historical Society). Judge Tapping Reeve's house is furnished in the period and gives a true reflection of the time during which he ran the law school, a small, one-room clapboard structure nearby, set among flower beds and shade trees. Undoubtedly many of his students sat with him in his home. The law school has been described as the "fountainhead of law in America." Among its graduates there were to be eventually three Supreme Court justices, twenty-eight senators, over a hundred representatives, three vice-presidents, plus fourteen governors and sixteen state chief justices. The small building truly is the cradle of law in America.

*(3)* The Congregational Church, East St. Built in 1829, the church is an almost identical replica of those designed in Milford (by David Hoadley), Cheshire, and Southington. It is representative of the finest period of New England church architecture and probably is the most photographed church in Connecticut.

*(4)* Litchfield Historical Society Museum, East St. This attractively laid-out building displays outstanding examples of earliest American pewter, furniture, pottery, silverware, paintings, and costumes.

*(5)* Litchfield Nature Center and Museum, south of Rte. 25. Habitat groups of native flora and fauna plus exhibits of the botanical and geological history of the area make this museum a worthwhile interlude in the historical town.

*(6)* Heritance House, Sawmill Rd., south of Milton. This early eighteenth-century home is unique among houses open to the public. Reservations are required and small parties are urged to spend an afternoon "living" in the eighteenth century. Candles and fires supply light. The owners live in the manner of Litchfield's early years, eschewing twentieth-century trappings. Naturally, all interior and exterior parts of the house environment are in keeping with the time when Peter Buell brought his bride to the then newly constructed house.

*(7)* Mattatuck State Forest (east of Rte. 254, in the southern part of town) offers hiking, hunting, and fishing. There is also hunting in the Torrington Fish and Game Area's 4,635 acres (see appendix). Humaston Brook State Park has picnic facilities. Bantam Lake, southeast of Bantam, offers boating and fishing, while the Northfield Cutlery Company Pond, Northfield Brook Impoundment, and Mt. Tom Pond (off Rte. 25), with its boat launch area, also offer fishing. Golfing is available at the Stonybrook Golf Course, on Milton Rd., and for snowmobile enthusiasts there are two privately operated grounds: Cozy Hills and White Memorial, both off Rte. 25.

LYME *(New London County. Rtes. into: 82, 148, 156; 33.0 sq. mi.; 1,484 pop. Other communities: Hadlyme, Hamburg, North Lyme.)* The town is, for the most part, open country with excellent views of the Connecticut River along Rte. 156. The low-lying river plain indented with sunlit inlets is a haven for yachts during the summer season. East of Rte. 156, farms and rising hills make a beautiful rural scene. Eight Mile River flows into Hamburg Cove and you pass through the small center of Hamburg just about where it does. Vacation homes and farms dot the hills and line the river shore. There is little industry in the town and, having once driven through it, one can only say, "Thank heavens there isn't."

*To See and Do: (1)* Gillette Castle State Park, on the northern edge of town, off Rtes. 82 and 148. Part of this 171-acre park lies in East Haddam, but in fact state publications list it as in Lyme. No matter. The castle, which is visible from across the river, was built on a hilltop by actor William Gillette. Begun in 1914, it took five years to complete. Made of granite, fieldstone, and timber, its forty-two rooms are all designed differently and the details of its construction speak of bizarre taste with money to indulge it. Actor Gillette lived in his castle, fashioned after a remembered castle in Germany's Rhine Valley, and it was turned over to the state as a park in 1943. The hilltop park acreage also affords hiking, picnicking, and the enjoyment of views of the Connecticut River.

*(2)* Hadlyme-Chester Ferry. At river's edge, on Rte. 148, you can cross the Connecticut in season via a small car ferry, and from it, glimpse some of the views and sense some of the power of this large flowing body of water.

*(3)* Selden Neck State Park. Hunting for duck, in season, is permitted in this undeveloped state park on the Connecticut River, south of the village of Hadlyme. Nehantic State Forest in the central, uninhabited part of Lyme, offers hiking and picnicking. And there is boating, with a launch site, on Rogers Lake on the southern edge of town, reached by turning off Rte. 151 onto Grassy Hill Rd. Fishing may be enjoyed in Norwich Pond and Uncas Lake (both east of Rte. 156), both of which have boat-launch sites.


MADISON *(New Haven County. Rtes. into: I–95, which is the Connecticut Turnpike, Exits 60, 61, 62; U.S. 1; state 79, 80, 36.3 sq. mi.; 9,768 pop. Other communities: North Madison, Rockland.)*
Originally a part of Guilford to the west, Madison was first known as East Guilford. In 1826 the area was incorporated as a separate town and took the name from President James Madison. As a shore town, fishing and shipbuilding are a part of its past. In the early years of this century, the sandy shore was "discovered" by inland-dwelling Nutmeggers from such towns as Hartford and Waterbury. Summer homes soon lined the shore and the principal business of the community became servicing the summer people. Today, as a year-round town, Madison is largely residential.

North Madison is at the junction of Rtes. 79 and 80, and the small cluster of buildings is distinguished only by the Congregational Church, a spare, white meeting house with simple dignified lines.

*To See and Do: (1)* The Congregational Church (1838), on the green, is visible from U.S. 1 (Boston Post Rd.) at the end of two rows of tall trees. It is a perfect setting for this fine example of Greek Revival church architecture.

*(2)* Nathaniel Allis House, U.S. 1, east of business center (Madison Historical Society). This 1739 dwelling was originally a one-story building of four rooms. The second story was added, as were extra rooms in the back. In the 1860s more space was added by extending the house eastward, so you might say the building grew. The house has many fine pieces of furniture in rooms decorated in the period. A carriage house at the rear displays early farm tools, looms, Indian artifacts, and other items.

*(3)* Hammonasset State Beach Park, east of the center of town on U.S. 1 or Exit 62, off I–95. This two-mile long sandy beach is unique along Connecticut's varied coastline. Bathing and camping may be enjoyed and there are food concessions and bathhouses.

*(4)* Drives around Madison will reveal many eighteenth- and nineteenth-century houses of distinction. The south side of U.S. 1 at the green has a number of examples of good house architecture spanning two centuries, and a seventeenth-century home on U.S. 1 can be glimpsed behind evergreens east of the green. For a "feel" of the present town and its past, take a drive along Green Hill Rd. (take Wildwood Ave. north, off U.S. 1 in the western edge of town, which intersects Green Hill Rd., and drive east).

*(5)* Golf may be enjoyed at the Madison Country Club (Rte. 1).

*(6)* Town beaches. Policy varies regarding nonresident use. Check with the town hall.

MANCHESTER *(Hartford County. Rtes. into: I–86; U.S. 6, 44, 44A; state 30, 83; 27.2 sq. mi.; 47,994 pop. Other communities: Buckland, Highland Park, Manchester Green.)*
Manchester sprang from the parent town of Hartford by way of East Hartford, and it early developed into an industrial town. At

the Five Mile District of Hartford, to the east of the Connecticut River, the seventeenth-century settlers had to cope with Indians while they were developing the area. A sawmill was built in 1671 and a second one two years later. By 1741 Col. Joseph Pitkin, descendant of William Pitkin, one of the first settlers in the area, was running an ironworks. During those early years, water power from Hop Brook and the Hockanum River ran the mills and by 1775 paper was being produced in what had become known as Orford. By 1794 the town was on its way with a cotton mill. The Pitkin Glass Works (ruins of which are still visible at the corner of Parker and Putnam Sts.) was one of the many factories that were built and operated by the Pitkin family, who were dominant in Manchester business during the eighteenth century.

The nineteenth century saw the rise of the Cheney family, and they operated silk mills in the town, constructed many nineteenth-century mill houses for the workers (which still exist as private homes on Pleasant, Fairfield, West, and Ridge Sts.) and then built mansions for themselves along Hartford Rd. from Elm to Main St. Some are in Victorian or Georgian style, and they reflect the way rich people lived in the late-nineteenth and early-twentieth centuries.

As in many other industrial towns, Manchester has suffered either the loss of early buildings or their debasing "modernization." This leaves little in the way of eighteenth-century architecture to remind visitors of the lengthy past history of the city.

Manchester was the birthplace of Christopher Spencer (1833–1922), who as a young man worked in the Cheney mills. But he also developed into an inventor. He invented the Spencer repeating rifle and tried to sell it to the army during the Civil War. The army would not listen to him—even though his rifle could fire twenty-one shots a minute compared to the three a minute then fired by Union rifles. Spencer finally got an audience with Abraham Lincoln and, sharpshooter that Abe was, Spencer convinced him. When the rifles appeared in combat, the Rebels complained that the "Yankees load on Sunday for the rest of the week." By war's end, 200,000 Spencer rifles were in service.

*To See and Do: (1)* The Cheney Homestead, 106 Hartford Rd. (Manchester Historical Society). Permanent exhibits of local history are on display in the 1790 Cheney Homestead, headquarters of the society.

*(2)* Lutz Junior Museum, 126 Cedar St. Material of interest to young people (and older ones too) includes the natural and physical sciences, industry, history, and art.

*(3)* Golfing at the Manchester Country Club or the Red Rock Golf Course.

*(4)* Antique Auto Museum, Slater St. (off I–86). More than two dozen antique cars, restored and in running order, are displayed here.


MANSFIELD *(Tolland County. Rtes. into: U.S. 44A; state 31, 32, 89, 195, 320; 45.2 sq. mi.; 19,994 pop. Other communities: Eagleville, Gurleyville, Mansfield Center, Mansfield Depot, Mansfield Hollow, Merrow, Perkins Corner, Spring Hill, Storrs.)*
Despite the number of different communities, the large population of this rural eastern Connecticut town is largely due to the presence of the University of Connecticut at Storrs (see below).

One of the strangest industries in Connecticut had its beginnings here: silk production. In 1775 one Nathaniel Aspinwall brought mulberry trees to Mansfield, and began raising silk worms. And less than twenty years later, Connecticut became a silk-producing state in an attempt to supplant a sagging agricultural economy. (The sag was brought on by poor land in much of the state and unintelligent land use throughout the state.) The legislature offered bounties on mulberry trees and raw silk. Half an ounce of mulberry seed was sent to every town in Connecticut. Silk production soared until 1845, when a blight wiped out the mulberry trees. Yet some survived and silk still is produced in the state.

Mansfield Depot had its beginnings in its name, springing up around the train station. Today, with rail service abandoned, the station houses a gift shop. Mansfield itself is called Mansfield Four Corners, and that is about all it is (Rte. 44A). Spring Hill, a small hilltop village (Rte. 195), has the town hall and is the center of town government. These smaller communities have many older homes of the eighteenth and nineteenth centuries lining the main roads.

Origins of the University of Connecticut stem from 1881 when a gift from Augustus and Charles Storrs created Storrs Agricultural College. Today the university is a center of agricultural research and both arts and science colleges with an excellent reputation in many scholarly disciplines. The buildings reflect the tastes of a variety of modern, low-bid designs and if a single thread can be said to join the campus dormitories and classrooms it would be that of variety itself. There is no architectural cohesion evident and the only charm of the campus comes from its landscaped greensward and the changing, hilly terrain.

*To See and Do:* (1) Old Eagleville School, Rte. 32 and South Eagleville Rd. (Mansfield Historical Society Museum). Exhibits of rural living in the region covering a 200-year span, and textiles and costumes.

(2) University Campus. The Museum of Art has a fine collection of paintings, graphics, sculpture, and examples of decorative arts. Nutmeg Theater, a part of the Drama Department, presents excellent productions throughout the summer season. During regular sessions there are concerts, sporting events, and all other activities associated with a large university.

(3) Mansfield Hollow State Park (astride Rte. 89 north of Mansfield Center). Some 2,300 acres offer boating, hiking, hunting, picnicking, and fishing, with a boat-launch site on Naubesatuck Lake near Bassett's Bridge, $2\frac{1}{2}$ miles east of Mansfield Center. The Nipmuck Trail passes through town, crossing Rte. 195 just south of Spring Hill. There is also fishing in Eagleville Pond, west of Eagleville on Rte. 275.

MARLBOROUGH *(Hartford County. Rtes. into: 2, 66: 23.5 sq. mi.; 2,991 pop.)*
Settled in 1715, the town was named for the Duke of Marlborough in 1747. At the junction of old Rte. 2 and 66 there is the handsome, gambrel-roofed Marlborough Tavern, dating, according to some sources, from 1740. Among those who have stopped and been

entertained there are Presidents Jackson and Monroe. It still functions as a tavern today.

A rural town, Marlborough was the scene of frantic inventiveness in the nineteenth century. During that period of Connecticut's plunge into the industrial age apparently nearly every man, woman, and child was busy tinkering with something to make a fortune. Marlborough tinkerers produced, among other things: a bread knife, a washing machine, machine-made boxes, and wagon seats. Some of the patent-happy Marlboroughans got rich; most returned to farming. But at least they didn't tinker with the town's open rurality, which is a primary asset today.

*To See and Do:* Salmon River State Forest (6,102 acres) in the southern part of town offers hiking, hunting, fishing in Dickinson Brook, and picnicking. Fishing also is available in Terramuggus Lake on old Rte. 2 and Lake Rd., less than a mile from the center.

MERIDEN *(New Haven County. Rtes. into: I–91, Exits 18, 19; U.S. 5; state 15, which is the Wilbur Cross Pkwy., Exits 67, 66, 70, 71; 24.0 sq. mi.; 55,959 pop.)*
In 1661, Jonathan Gilbert of Hartford was granted a farm of 350 acres in what has since become the city of Meriden. To run his farm, Gilbert persuaded one Edward Higbee to plunge into that wilderness and get things going. Higbee generally is believed to be the first white settler to live in the area.

Like many Connecticut towns and cities, Meriden is known for a particular product. Meriden's is silverware. It is the headquarters of the International Silver Co., which got its small start in 1794 when Samuel Yale decided to go for broke and produce pewter buttons in a small shop. Fourteen years later Ashbell Griswold began making Britannia ware, an alloy that looks more like silver, although it is scorned by pewter fanciers today. Soon imitators cashed in on Griswold's success, and finally a number of small businesses combined to form the Meriden Brittania Co. The successor to this combine is the International Silver Co. and Meriden became known as The Silver City. Today, in addition to silverware, industry in Meriden includes electronics, machine tools and parts, plastics, clothing, nonferrous metal sheets, and printing equipment.

The population of Meriden is a peaceful, cooperative mixture of Yankee stock and later-arriving citizens from Britain and Europe. Like all New England towns, Meriden's beginnings were dominated by Yankees. Winston Churchill's great-great grandfather was the American Timothy Jerome, who lived in Meriden. His son, Samuel Jerome, fought in the Revolutionary War in the first great effort to dissolve the British Empire—a dissolution that great-grandson Winston vigorously opposed in post-World War II years. One commercial-minded Yankee, Amini Clark, joined the ranks of inventive Connecticut Yankees, and patented the first coffee mill. Prior to this event, coffee beans were pulverized with mortar and pestle. Following Clark's invention, soldiers' rifle stocks contained a small model of his invention to grind beans at nightfall after the day's march.

The long green in the center of the city was a training ground for patriot troops during the Revolution. Two old, now peaceful churches on the corner of Broad St. and E. Main St., once had a small disturbance. The Congregational Church (1831) had a rather soft-spoken minister when the adjacent Baptist Church (1847) was built. The Baptist minister of the moment was a loud-voiced exhorter. Fearing he would drown the quiet tones of their minister, the Congregationalists sought an injunction to prevent the next-door church from going up. Apparently they lost. The churches still stand, the severely plain Baptist one, and the more elaborate Congregational edifice, and harmony has reigned ever since.

*To See and Do: (1)* Hubbard Park and Castle Craig. West of the city center on a peculiar geological formation formed by two successive and tilted lava flows is Hubbard Park, built on those flows that are called the Hanging Hills. Walter Hubbard, a Meriden industrialist, bought the land, erected the landmark called Castle Craig, and in 1900 gave the park and tower to the city. From Castle Craig you can see, on a clear, unsmoggy day, the spires of New Haven, the waters of Long Island Sound, and the dark shores of Long Island to the south. Looking north, you can see into the rising hills of Massachusetts. The elevation is over one thousand feet, and there are nature trails, ponds, picnicking facilities, hiking paths, tennis, a small zoo, and swimming. For the myth-minded, there is the legend of the Black Dog that still haunts the craggy summits here. Should a person see this black dog on a visit, two more sightings of the dog are fated. On the first sight, the viewer will experience financial gain. On the second viewing, illness will strike. On the third viewing, death. To add to the hackle-raising legend, several people who have claimed to see the Black Dog have died mysteriously. The Black Dog, by the way, leaves no tracks either in snow or dirt, and he has been seen howling with no sound issuing from his gaping mouth.

*(2)* Andrews Homestead, 424 West Main St. (Meriden Historical Society). Built in 1760, this integral saltbox or leanto house has girt and plate overhangs and, with its massive central chimney, is typical of Connecticut house architecture of the period. Originally a farmhouse in the wilderness, the structure is now surrounded by the city. Inside, the five rooms are decorated and furnished in the period, and the walls are lined with antique glass and china plus samples of Meriden products over the years.

*(3)* West Peak State Park, adjacent to Hubbard Park in the Hanging Hills, offers hiking and picnicking. There is swimming in Hubbard Park, Ceppa Park, Beaver Lake, Cedar Park, and at the two high school pools. In the central part of town there are concerts in the music shell in season, and swimming and tennis in city parks. Fishing may be enjoyed in Beaver Pond and Silver Lake (which has a boat-launch site west of U.S. 5 on the north edge of the city). Black Pond, south of Rte. 66, in East Meriden, also has a boat-launch site. And there is golfing at Pleasant View Golf Course (Paddock Ave.) and Hunter Memorial Golf Course (Westfield Rd.).

MIDDLEBURY *(New Haven County. Rtes. into: I–84; state 63, 64, 188; 18.0 sq. mi.; 5,542 pop.)*
Ponds and hills characterize this still largely rural town midway between Waterbury and Woodbury—from which fact came its name. It is the home of Westover School for Girls. Founded in 1909 by a Miss Mary Hillard, it partakes of the gentility of Miss Porter's

School in Farmington and St. Margaret's School in Waterbury. The town green is small and pleasant, with a Congregational church built in 1839 with Greek motifs. Church, town hall, and the girls' school all give the center of the small town an air of tranquillity.

*To See and Do:* Lake Quassapaug, Rte. 64, west of center. Swimming and boating are available on this large lake. There is also a small, pleasant amusement park.

MIDDLEFIELD *(Middlesex County. Rtes. into: 66, 147, 157; 13.3 sq. mi.; 4,132 pop. Other communities: Baileyville, Rockfall.)*
Middlefield, whose name is descriptive, was originally part of Middletown and its early history follows that of the larger community. In the latter part of the eighteenth century, however, when the community had a meeting house of its own, the minister, Yale graduate Abner Benedict, struck a blow for the abolition of slavery. He persuaded all slaveholders in the town to free their slaves.

Various early manufacturing plants took advantage of the generous water power of the streams in the town. A gristmill, button factory, and nail plant (where the first cut nails in the United States were reportedly made) kept the community going. Two powder mills and a pistol-manufacturing plant added to the town's income. Today gun sights are still made in Middlefield as are ivory novelties, thermometers, and tools. The town has never "made it" in national terms. Perhaps the nearest it has ever come was the abortive Rock Festival of a few years ago at commercially operated Powder Ridge, a ski area.

There are, in the quiet residential areas of town, excellent views to the east toward the lower hills of the Connecticut River valley.

*To See and Do:* Wadsworth Falls State Park (southwest of city, on Rte. 157). The 285-acre park offers hiking, picnicking, swimming, and winter sports as well as fishing. Boating, with launch sites, is available in Black Pond, south of U.S. 66, about 2 miles east of I-91, and Beseck Lake, west side of Rte. 147, about 1¾ miles south of junction of Rtes. 66 and 147. Skiing at Powder Ridge (west of Rte. 157, in southwest corner of town) during the winter, with a varied program during the rest of the year. Hunting in Middlefield Fish and Game Club's 1,356 acres (see appendix). Golf can be enjoyed at the Indian Spring Golf Course, on Mack Rd., and the Lyman Meadow Golf Club, on Rte. 157.

MIDDLETOWN *(Middlesex County. Rtes. into: 9, 17, 66, 72, 157, 217; 42.9 sq. mi.; 36,924 pop.)*
Halfway between Hartford and Old Saybrook got Middletown its name in 1653. Its extraordinarily wide Main St. and the shaded campus of Wesleyan University give the town a peaceful air with little to indicate that it was the wealthiest town in all New England during the latter half of the eighteenth century. Middletown's wealth during that period sprang from shipping. It was a thriving port doing trade with the West Indies and, alas, in the slave trade also. Like Portland across the river, Middletown built ships. Lumber and farm produce were its outbound cargoes.

Colonists from Wethersfield and Hartford first settled the town and after a moribund hundred years of farming, the shipbuilding boom struck. In 1831 Wesleyan University was founded and brownstone from nearby Portland gave some still-existing build- ings their character. The affluence of the town, its trade with foreign ports, and the growth of the small but first-rate university combined to give Middletown a cultural leg up on its neighbors, and helped create a firm world view of matters that persists today.

*To See and Do: (1)* General Mansfield House, 151 Main St. (Middlesex County Historical Society). Examples of decorative arts are found in this 1810 house, which is furnished in the period of its building.

*(2)* Davison Art Center, 301 High St. (Wesleyan University). This is the Alsop House, dating from 1838–40, and is Italianate in treatment. It was during the mid-nineteenth century that diversi- fied architecture was carried to such lengths as this. The museum houses a fine, small collection containing works by Dürer, Rem- brandt, and Whistler.

*(3)* Submarine Library and Museum, 440 Washington St. On

display are memorabilia of the World War II submarine service and a collection of submarine models. There also is a research library on undersea matters.

(4) A walk or drive around the Wesleyan University campus will, at many points, give rewarding views of many samples of Victorian architecture and some eighteenth-century homes. High St. and Washington St. are best. Brownstone was widely used and the extent and direction of ornamental embellishment depended solely on the owner's or architect's whim.

(5) Fishing can be enjoyed on Crystal Lake (take Millbrook Rd. off Rte. 155, follow signs) and Dooley Pond (on Brush Hill Rd., east of Rte. 17), both of which have boat-launch sites. Crystal Lake also has swimming and picnicking facilities. Hunters can use the nearly 1,800 acres of the Middletown Sportsmen's Club Area (see appendix), the 1,300 acres of the Westfield Sportsmen's Club (see appendix), or the Cromwell Meadows Management Area of 486 acres (see appendix).


MILFORD *(New Haven County. Rtes. into: I–95, which also is the Connecticut Turnpike, Exits 34 through 40; U.S. 1; state 15, which also is the Wilbur Cross Pkwy., Exit 54; 121, 162; 23.5 sq. mi.; 50,858 pop. Other communities: Devon, Rivercliff, Woodmont.)*
The town had trouble with the Indians in the early days. So much so that a stockade a mile square, manned by guards, protected the village of the seventeenth century. One authority maintains that the Indians taunted the white men and bragged about keeping them penned up like pigs. Whatever the source of the trouble, there is no record of any white being killed by an Indian.

The founders of Milford came to Connecticut with the party that settled New Haven in 1638—with the exception of Peter Prudden, the settlement leader. He arrived from his Herefordshire parish after Davenport and Eaton's group got to New Haven. By 1639 they had bought land from the Indians and organized themselves in the rigid theocratic system of the time. Some idea of the degree of self-sanctification reached by the early theocrats comes in an often-reported vote of the Milford town meeting. The meeting first voted that the earth was the Lord's and the fullness thereof. The citizens then voted that the Lord had given the earth to the saints. To clinch matters, they voted, finally, that they were the saints. Little wonder they had trouble with the Indians.

The area they had purchased was astride the Wepawaug River and the fishing and agricultural possibilities were the principal attraction. Milford today still straddles the Wepawaug, but its growth has produced the usual traffic problems in the crowded center. Factories, business establishments, and homes cover the area where once Indians came to the shores of Long Island Sound to gorge themselves on oysters—leaving as their legacy to the white man a 24-acre area forming the largest oyster shell deposit in Connecticut. And oystering was an early industry of the white men. Until the streams and the shoal waters of the Sound were polluted by a heedless population, acres of underwater oyster farms brought wealth to the owners. Shipbuilding began early in Milford, in the seventeenth century, and it continued to flourish until the second decade of the nineteenth century. Today an assortment of metal-producing and electronic industries provide employment for Milford citizens.

A tragic passage of Revolutionary War history was written in Milford when two hundred American troops who had been prisoners of war were set loose on ice-covered Milford beaches. Some were in the last stages of sickness and could neither walk nor crawl further. The town mobilized to shelter and care for them only to discover that many of them had the dreaded smallpox. A Captain Stephen Stow, who had experience in many seagoing years in treating pox victims, volunteered to stay with the men and try to save them. Forty-six of the two hundred released prisoners died. And Captain Stow himself contracted the then untreatable disease and died also.

*To See and Do: (1)* The Eells-Stow House, 34 High St. (Milford Historical Society). Built in 1680 by Samuel Eells, the house has, contrary to symmetry-loving architects, an off-center door, and also an off-center chimney behind the roof ridge. Another unique external feature is the plate or second-story overhang minus a first-floor overhang. Letting the architects quarrel or puzzle, the house is of immense interest both architecturally and historically.

Inside is a flight of "dogleg stairs" that is quite unusual. And Captain Stow, of Revolutionary War fame (see above), bought and occupied the house in the eighteenth century. It was from this house that he went to the assistance of the sick patriots. Furnishings are of the period and permanent displays include one of Indian artifacts.

(2) Walk along West Main St. and see the two excellent churches near the eastern end of the street. The westernmost is the Congregational Church and is an excellent example of late Federal styling, having been built in 1823. It is believed to have been designed by David Hoadley, noted Connecticut architect, and has been widely copied. The easternmost, across the Wepawaug River, was the Plymouth Church and it was built in 1834. Its heavy, monumental character indicates the Greek Revival style. On the northeast corner of West Main and High Sts. is the Colonel Stephen Ford House. Ford settled in Milford in 1646 and for many years this building was a tavern. Its style does not indicate seventeenth-century architecture—rather it is mid-eighteenth in its present condition.

Off Prospect St. is the Old Burying Ground, one of the oldest in Connecticut. Here Captain Stow and the other smallpox victims share a common grave. Here, too, are the graves of Robert Treat, famed as a leader in King Philip's War (1675) and founder of Newark, N. J., as well as being Governor of Connecticut for thirty-two years; Jonathan Law, Governor of Connecticut for nine years from 1742; and Samuel Andrew, fifty years a minister, and a rector of Yale from its earliest time. Memorial Bridge, which crosses the Wepawaug River just east of the green, was built in 1895 to commemorate the town's original settlers. Their names and a brief personal history of each one are inscribed on the granite blocks of the structure.

(3) Duck hunting may be enjoyed at Milford Point on the Housatonic River shore (Charles E. Wheeler Wildlife Area, see appendix).

(4) Town beaches. Policy varies regarding nonresident use. Check with the city hall.

MONROE *(Fairfield County. Rtes. into: 25, 34, 59, 110, 111; 26.4 sq. mi.; 12,047 pop. Other communities: Stepney, Upper Stepney.)*
This residential community has many citizens who work in Bridgeport and many others who raise poultry or practice agriculture. There is little industry in the town, which was settled by people from Stratford and first had the name New Stratford. Named today for President James Monroe, the town has an attractive small triangular green at its center, where Rtes. 110 and 111 join.

Monroe was the site of a French encampment during the Revolution as the troops were going to join General Washington in June of 1781. The eastern part of the town is hilly, while the western part is open and virtually horizontal.

*To See and Do: (1)* Barn-Hill-East Village Schoolhouse, Monroe Center (Monroe Historical Society). The schoolhouse, dating from 1800, has on display costumes, mineral exhibits (a variety have been mined in the town, including bismuth), and archival material.

*(2)* Lake Zoar, Rte. 34, in the north part of town. Swimming, fishing, picnicking, and boating in this large manmade lake forming the northeastern corner of town (see Southbury for boat-launch site).

*(3)* Hunters can use the Bridgeport Hydraulic Area's state-leased 794 acres (see appendix).

MONTVILLE *(New London County. Rtes. into: Connecticut Turnpike, which is state 52, Exits 78, 79, 79A; state 32, 82, 85, 163; 43.9 sq. mi.; 15,662 pop. Other communities: Chesterfield, Massapeag, Mohegan, Oakdale, Uncasville.)*
Indian history lingers here with unusual persistence. Uncas, the Mohegan sachem, made common cause with white settlers in the seventeenth century, and sites of Indian forts, burial grounds, and other vestiges of their culture can be found. The communities of Uncasville and Mohegan carry on the Indian tradition in their names. In 1645 the Mohegans and Narragansetts were having at

one another, and the Rhode Island Reds, so to speak, had cornered Uncas and his men in their fort at Shantok Point and were starving them out. Canny Uncas sent a secret messenger by night to Saybrook and asked for the white man's help. While waiting for help to arrive, Uncas kept watch from a rocky ledge with a good view—and it has ever since been called Uncas Chair. Help did arrive and the wily Uncas was saved.

Eventually the area now Montville was claimed by the whites as part of New London but not until 1786 was the town a separate entity. Its hilly, high terrain induced the settlers to name the town after the French Mount-ville. Today it is still linked to New London as many of the townspeople work in that larger city.

Montville is the birthplace of a noted Indian, Samson Occum, who was the first ordained Indian minister. He preached among his fellow Indians and in 1766 made a trip to England where he raised $30,000 to aid his people. That fund helped found Dartmouth College (see Columbia).

*To See and Do: (1)* Tantaquidgeon Indian Museum (Rte. 32). This small granite museum displays Indian craftwork and stone tools and is a further reminder of the Indians in this region. It was built by John Tantaquidgeon and his son, both descendants of Tantaquidgeon, a lesser chief under Uncas.

*(2)* Fort Shantok State Park, east of Rte. 32, in the northern part of town. Remnants of the fort where Uncas and his men sweated out a siege (see above). Here is an old Indian burial ground with several ancient headstones and the Leffingwell monument in honor of the succoring officer from Saybrook who saved Uncas and his men. Picnicking. Views.

*(3)* Fishing in Gardner Lake, on Rte. 82, east of its junction with Rte. 354.


MORRIS *(Litchfield County. Rtes. into: 61, 63, 109, 209; 18.8 sq. mi.; 1,609 pop. Other communities: East Morris, Lakeside.)*
Summer folk account for a majority of taxes and income in Morris. This high, hilly town has a trimmed look that straight agricultural income cannot produce. Bantam Lake, the largest natural lake in

the state, dominates the town and its shores are lined with second homes from nearly all income brackets.

Originally part of Litchfield, the town was called South Farms and was so named a parish in the eighteenth century. James Morris, born in the parish, established the Morris Academy in 1790 and the well-known preparatory school, now coeducational, has many distinguished graduates. When township status came in 1859 the problem of name-choosing was not difficult.

*To See and Do:* (1) The James Morris Reading Room and Museum, Morris Academy. Dedicated to the town's benefactor, this building is open to the public.

(2) A pleasant scenic drive through Morris might begin on Rte. 109 at the eastern border, where you pass below the dam impounding water for the Morris Reservoir, through East Morris and Morris, to a right turn northward along the western shores of Bantam Lake.

(3) Fishing in Bantam Lake (Rte. 209) and Mt. Tom Pond, which has a boat-launch site (see Litchfield).

NAUGATUCK *(New Haven County. Rtes. into: 8, 63, 68; 16.2 sq. mi.; 23,034 pop. Other communities: Straitsville, Union City.)*
This heavily industrial nineteenth-century community astride the Naugatuck River got its start in 1843, when the brothers Charles and Henry Goodyear established a rubber mill in the town. The Goodyear process of vulcanizing rubber made the first widely marketed articles like rain shoes practical. The town has been a center of rubber manufacture ever since. In addition, Naugatuck today has manufacturers producing chemicals, plastics, aluminum, and iron products.

The area that now comprises the town was bought from the Indians in 1685 by Thomas Judd and John Stanley and it was known locally as Judd's Meadows when the first settlers moved in during the first decade of the eighteenth century. Its present name, one of the few towns in the state to have an Indian name, means "a tree" or "one tree" and was applied to the area as early as 1800, although town status did not come until 1844. Going east or west from the river, a visitor moves rapidly upward to steep hills where many homes are perched, away from factories and the highway that flank the riverbanks. The narrowness of the valley produced a catastrophe in 1955, when Hurricane Diane poured sixteen to twenty inches of rain on most of Connecticut. The tributaries of the Naugatuck and the Naugatuck itself erupted and thousands of people were made homeless as flood waters rose. The concentrated industry along the river was almost completely wrecked and the town lay prostrate. Even today driving on Rte. 8 by the river, unrepaired buildings and embankments are evident. The concrete flood-control works along the river near the town center, built after the flood, attest to the seriousness of the problem.

The rise of industrialism in the mid-nineteenth century brought German, Irish, Italian, and Polish immigrants to work in the factories. And today, Union City, off Rte. 8, north of the town center, has a large colony of Polish citizens. The industrial boom that continued into this century had another effect: the almost complete obliteration of early buildings. One of few remaining examples of early architecture is St. Michael's Episcopal Church (1875) and its parish house on Church St. at the intersection with Maple St. It is built of brick in the Gothic style and has a slate roof. Both church and parish house, which has a unique façade with an ogival double window in the center of the second story and four pilasters with carved brownstone pediments, are worth viewing.

*To See and Do:* The Naugatuck State Forest has hiking trails and picnic areas. It is best reached off Water St. via Rubber Ave. to Andrew Ave. This becomes Andrew Mountain Rd. Whittemore Glen State Park is undeveloped but offers hiking. Golf may be played at the Hop Brook Golf Course on North Church St.


NEW BRITAIN *(Hartford County. Rtes. into: I–84, Exits 35, 36; state 71, 71A, 72, 175; 13.3 sq. mi.; 83,441 pop.)*
The "Hardware City of the World," as it is called, was named as a parish in 1754 but did not receive formal town status until 1850. At

about that time, New Britain settled on a specialty of manufacture: hardware, and has held to it ever since. Tools, nuts, bolts, screws, and you-name-it in the hardware line are manufactured there today.

As its hardware manufacturing increased, New Britain needed more workers and they came as immigrants. Italian, Polish, Irish, Ukranian, and Swedish families moved in and the men went to work.

Unlike all other Connecticut mill towns, New Britain did not rely on water power to run its mills. Steam was early introduced, and the self-sufficient town grew to achieve its eminence in its field. Men and owners walked to work together; town problems were everyone's problems. When railroads came, New Britain's self-contained independence was expanded; other industries could then benefit from the tool-making capacity of the city.

With the twentieth century, and particularly the post-World War II period, more growth and modernization began to erode the nineteenth-century atmosphere of the city. Many of the old mills were torn down to make way for newer plants, and the dream of superhighways infected many New Britain citizens. Those interested in the historic buildings have mounted opposition to the obliteration of old-time New Britain, and the result likely will be some compromise between the forces for growth and those for historic preservation.

One of the best nineteenth-century downtown buildings is the City Hall at 13-35 West Main St., across from a small park. It was built in 1885 by Joseph Morrill Wells, who was Stanford White's principal assistant. It is a five-story brownstone building. Flanking it are two buildings which are smaller and now part of the office complex of the main building. Other areas where the nineteenth-century remains are on Vine, West Main, South High, Court, and Walnut Sts. A smaller area, south of Walnut St., includes Camp and School Sts.

One of New Britain's most beautiful sites is Walnut Hill Park, designed by Frederick Law Olmsted in the mid-nineteenth century. This first landscape architect, who also designed Central Park and the Boston Park System, worked his magic here also. From the hilltop site you can view nearly all of New Britain.

Fortunately, Olmsted's early influence in the planning of the city resulted in many open parks outside the central downtown region, and there is assurance that, whatever happens, a balance has been struck between pavement and park.

The city's most illustrious son was Elihu Burritt. Born in 1810, he apprenticed himself to a blacksmith at the age of fifteen and studied so hard, on and off work, that when he was thirty he had command of some fifty languages. He became interested in world peace and, going to Europe, sponsored conferences in Belgium, Germany, France, and England on the theme of universal brotherhood. For four years (1865–69) he was consular agent at Birmingham, England. He returned to New Britain, where he died. Today an imposing monument on Franklin Square commemorates his life struggle to achieve peace.

*To See and Do:* (1) Museum of American Art, 56 Lexington St. Nearly 1,500 pieces in the collection from oils through sculpture span the period from precolonial times (earliest painting: 1734) through present-day painters—and includes five Wyeths.

(2) Children's Museum, basement level of the Hawley (Children's) Memorial Library, 28 High St. The range here is wide, from natural science to dollhouses showing colonial, Victorian, and contemporary styles of architecture and furnishings. There are live animals and plants and exhibits of arts and crafts from different countries and times.

(3) Central Connecticut State College Museum, 1615 Stanley St. Displays range from archeology and anthropology through painting and sculpture to industry and models. Modern brick, concrete, and glass buildings make up this campus and there are the usual range of activities, many of which are open to public attendance.

(4) New Britain Symphony. Seasonal performances are given in Herbert Welte Hall, on the Central Connecticut College campus. The symphony grew from a college-community orchestra that proved successful. Other events such as art shows, lectures, and films are available in the usual campus schedule of college life.

(5) Park recreation. A full and vigorous recreation program in the city's thirty-eight parks includes swimming pools, tennis

courts, gardens, and nature trails, plus summer band concerts and music festivals in the modern Darius Miller Music Shell, in 98-acre Walnut Hill Park (West Main St.).

*(6)* Golf can be played at the Stanley Golf Course.


NEW CANAAN *(Fairfield County. Rtes. into: 15, which is the Merritt Pkwy., 106, 123, 124; 23.3 sq. mi.; 17,455 pop.)*

This New York-oriented, residential community is situated back from the shores of Long Island Sound on high hills from which a Sound view (highly prized) can be gained from some homes in the area. Originally part of both Stamford and Norwalk, New Canaan was settled in the first decade of the eighteenth century and incorporated in 1801.

An intense, closely knit community, New Canaan vies with neighboring towns for the mythical title of "most desirable" as a residential address. Denied extensive frontage on the Sound by its inland location, the town is determinedly "country" and great emphasis is placed on horticultural pursuits and horseback riding. There are extensive bridle paths, a Bridle Path Association, and a mounted troop for youngsters.

*To See and Do: (1)* Hanford-Silliman House and others, 13 Oenoke Rd. (New Canaan Historical Society). There are several buildings on this site. The Hanford-Silliman House, built in 1764 and altered later, is furnished as a home; the keeping room is primitive but the parlors reflect later elegance. The Town House, 1825, is the archive of the society where the library and genealogical records are kept, and there is a costume museum on the second floor. The John Rogers Studio memorializes that New Canaan sculptor and displays some of his works and family memorabilia. The Cody Drugstore, from the mid-nineteenth century, is furnished as an apothecary shop of that period. In addition there is an antique-tool museum on the premises. This complex is part of the Church Hill Historic District of the town, which includes a small park at Park and Main Sts. It was an eighteenth-century burial ground and is now called God's Acre. At the eastern tip of the triangular park is a World War I memorial. Facing the park is the Congregational Church, on Church Hill, the third meeting house built on the hill, erected in 1843. Another church, St. Michael's Lutheran Church, lies within the district on Oenoke Ridge, facing Park St.

*(2)* A drive through some streets of the town is rewarding for architectural buffs. A late-eighteenth-century house lies at the junction of Valley Rd. and Silvermine Rd. and, going west on Silvermine Rd. to Carter St., there is a mid-eighteenth-century leanto house on the southeast corner. Where Carter St. joins Clapboard Hill Rd. sits a Little Red Schoolhouse dating from 1865. South on Carter St., between Dabney Rd. and Buttery Rd., on the west side, are an eighteenth-century leanto and a nineteenth-century Italianate villa. All are privately owned.

*(3)* An Indian monument, junction of Ponus Ridge and Davenport Ridge Rds., on a small green. A rough stone monument that marks the home site and traditional tomb of Ponus, sachem of the Ripponam Indians.

*(4)* Silvermine Guild of Artists Museum, Silvermine Rd. More than 450 professional artists from the Guild display their work here. Changing shows continue year round and contain painting, sculpture, and graphics.

*(5)* New Canaan Nature Center, 144 Oenoke Ridge. A marsh diorama and live cold-blooded vertebrates of Connecticut are displayed in permanent exhibitions; Bird Sanctuary and Wildlife Preserve (Old Stamford Rd.) has nature trails and is maintained by the Audubon Society, which owns three others in the town: Henry Kelley Sanctuary Lowlands on Wahackme Rd.; the Henry Kelley Sanctuary Uplands, accessible from Hickory and Cedar Lanes; and the Rosebrook Sanctuary on Rosebrook Rd.


NEW FAIRFIELD *(Fairfield County. Rtes. into: 37, 39; 25.8 sq. mi.; 6,991 pop.)*
The town was settled by families from Fairfield via a grant made in 1707 and was incorporated in 1740. The area was the site of what was called the Big Basin, a valley area rich in timber. In 1927 the Big Basin was flooded by water impounded by dams and Candlewood Lake was created. It is the largest manmade lake in

Connecticut. Many legends are told of the Basin and the lumber-jacks who worked in it. Paul Bunyan and his blue ox play a part, and Perry Boney and his Littlest Store in the World, where only one customer at a time could get into the place. Perry Boney spoke of elves and fairies, and trudged to a distant store for supplies for his store. He trudged back with a full market basket to sell his wares—at exactly the same price he had paid for them. The store failed to open one day and, search high and low as they could, neighbors never found a trace of the storekeeper. Elves? And Charlie Munson's corn beer made from a secret recipe that died with him—but left a legend of extraordinary examples of courage by those who drank his beer.

All those stories lie today beneath the bright waters of Candle-wood Lake, where summer homes, water skiers, and swimmers give the Basin a different history to contend with.

Rurality is still the character of the community to the west of popular Candlewood Lake, and the hills, valleys, and ponds of the region make back-road driving a pleasure.

*To See and Do: (1)* The Candlewood Theatre offers a program of summer-stock productions seasonally.

*(2)* Hidden Valley Nature Center, Gillotti Rd. A natural history museum and wildlife sanctuary, where geology, Indian artifacts (there were many found in this region), minerals, and ornithology are uppermost. There is a nature trail for hiking and occasional programs for groups.

*(3)* Squantz Pond State Park, west of Rte. 39, in the northern part of town, offers 172 acres for fishing, hiking, swimming, and picnicking. Ball Pond, east of Rte. 39, in the southern part of town, offers boating, with a launch site (at the south end, with an access road south from Rtes. 39 and 37A), and fishing. Candlewood Lake itself turns almost the entire eastern section of the town into a water-sports area with a boat-launch site on Rte. 39 along the lake's western shore. Hunting is permitted in the Pootatuck State Forest.

NEW HARTFORD *(Litchfield County. Rtes. into: U.S. 44; state 25, 219; 38.3 sq. mi.; 3,970 pop. Other communities: Bakersville, Nepaug, Pine Meadow.)*

Settled and named in 1733, this quiet, rural town, as might be suspected, had as its original settlers families from Hartford itself. Satan's Kingdom, east of U.S. 44, north of the village center, was the lair of renegade Indians, blacks, and whites, who raided the settlements from time to time. There still is wild country in New Hartford, although manufacturers there now produce such domestic items as soda-dispensing machines, blenders, and guitars.

New Hartford's most famous son was Governor Marcus Holcomb, who served three successive two-year terms from 1915 to 1921. Like Governor Jonathan Trumbull during the Revolutionary War, he presided over the state with extraordinary powers during World War I.

*To See and Do: (1)* Nepaug State Forest, north of Rte. 25, in the southeastern part of town. Hiking, picnicking, and hunting are available. There is also hunting on the 1,308 acres of the Harwinton Rod and Gun Club, 2½ miles south of Bakersville, and in the Metropolitan District Area in the Greenwood Dam Section, north of New Hartford center. Boat-launch sites and fishing are available in Compensating Reservoir (Rte. 219) and West Hill Pond, in the northwest corner of the town. The Farmington River also is state stocked for fishing. Ski Sundown (Rte. 219), 2 miles north of New Hartford, is nearby for skiers. The Tunxis Trail runs through the eastern section of town, crossing Rte. 25 1½ miles east of Nepaug.

NEW HAVEN *(New Haven County. Rtes. into: I–91, Exits 6, 7, 8; I–95, Exits 45 through 50; U.S. 1, 5; state 10, 15 (which is the Wilbur Cross Pkwy.), 17, 34, 63, 67, 69, 80, 122, 142; 22.5 sq. mi.; 137,707 pop.)*
A cultural, educational, and industrial center serving nearly half a million people, New Haven is and has been for many years a leading urban center in the state. As the home of Yale University, its educational influence is dominant in Connecticut and its long-standing rivalry with Hartford, the state capital, goes back to the very beginnings of the New Haven colony in 1638 (see Chapter 2).

The Reverend John Davenport, Puritan and dissident English-man, came with Theophilus Eaton from England and landed in Boston. Reports that came to that city from the military force raised to vanquish once and for all the Pequot Indians (see Fairfield) gave Eaton, an astute and wealthy merchant, the infor-mation that a harbor existed at the mouth of the Quinnipiac River in the wilderness of that time. Exploration parties sent out from Boston confirmed that fact and the band of Puritans under Davenport and Eaton went to the spot and established what was first called Quinnipiac but soon was changed to New Haven Colony.

It was a theocracy from the start. The Bible was the law and English common law and all adulterating customs were banished. Harsh laws forced compliance with the church, which was the government. The laws were not written and hence cannot be referred to in detail. There was, as Davenport saw, no reason to write them: they were already in the Bible. So stringent was the enforcement that a husband who was seen to be kissing his wife "with appetite" on Sunday was hauled into court.

Within a short time after the founding of the colony its boundaries were increased by the absorption of Milford, Stamford, Guilford, and Southold, on Long Island across the Sound. The green was the center of this sprawling colony, which seemed to be on the verge of growth and prosperity through trade.

Trade was what had tempted Eaton to choose the harbor on the Sound as a place to form the colony. It lay between Boston and New Amsterdam (now New York City) and it was thought this would bring a profitable trade in furs and produce with those larger communities. Two initial ventures undertaken by the colony failed abysmally and brought it to near economic destruction. The first involved buying land from Indians on the coast of what is now Delaware and establishing a trading post. Much of the gold in New Haven Colony was put into this enterprise. The Dutch and Swedes in that area, however, forced the fifty families that had migrated to flee. The post was burned and all the gold was lost. Next, the New Haven leaders loaded a ship with goods and watched it sail out of the harbor bound for England and a profitable voyage. It was never heard from again. With their resources gone, the colony became what today we would call an economically depressed area. And this state of affairs persisted for many years.

In 1661 the colony of New Haven was visited by two men whose lives were to become woven into the history of the city. Edward Whalley and his son-in-law, William Goffe, both had signed the warrant for the arrest and execution of King Charles I in 1647. And in 1660, after the Cromwellian Protectorate was over and the monarchy restored under Charles II, son of the beheaded king, the lives of Whalley and Goffe (plus the lives of the others involved in the execution) were in danger. Both men fled from England to Boston, and when Charles II offered a hundred pounds' reward for each man, dead or alive, they took sanctuary in the New Haven area, for both were friends of John Davenport. The king sent two pursuivants to track Whalley and Goffe to death, but the men hid variously in the homes of friends in New Haven and Milford and, reportedly, Guilford as well. For a time they were hidden in what today is still called Judges' Cave in West Rock Park. Neither of the men was ever caught and they lived out their lives in hiding and under assumed names in Hadley, Massachusetts.

By 1673 a third regicide, John Dixwell, was in hiding in New Haven, spending the rest of his long life there under the name of James Davids. He married twice, the last time at sixty-nine, fathering three children before his death at eighty-two. His gravestone, simply marked "J.D.esqʳ," is at the rear of the Center Church building on the green.

At the beginning of the eighteenth century one event occurred that was to have long-range effects on New Haven. A small "school" called the Collegiate School was founded in 1701 in Old Saybrook. Its "tutors" taught in houses in Killingworth and later in Guilford and Old Saybrook; in 1716 the Collegiate School moved to New Haven and occupied a building on the west side of the green. Within a few years its name was changed. Today, Yale University is an integral part of the past and present of the city.

Long after Eaton and Davenport had died the dream that brought them to the mouth of the Quinnipiac River began to come true. The harbor saw more and more ships arriving and departing for Boston, New York, and the West Indies. The town population increased from 1,400 in 1748 to 8,000 by 1774. And New Haven reached city status in 1784.

The heyday of New Haven's shipping and trade came after the turn of the nineteenth century, when skippers eyed not only the Orient but the sealing business. Islands of the south Atlantic and southern Pacific were swarming with seals and their furs were valuable. Thousands of seal pelts returned in the holds of New Haven ships and were laid out to dry in the sun along the shore. The stench of those drying skins became almost a hallmark of the city in those days. Trade with South America and the Orient occupied the minds of skippers and shipowners in that period too. One ship, *The Neptune*, put out from New Haven under the command of a Captain Townsend; he had a cargo to trade and $500 for quick cash deals. Townsend sailed from New Haven to the West Indies, to the sealing grounds off the Falkland Islands, to the South Seas, to Shanghai, and back to New Haven. He was gone for two and a half years, but he returned with $250,000 worth of cargo. And he still had his $500 in cash in his pocket.

The War of 1812 put an end to trade from most American ports as the British blockaded them. Unemployed seamen were a common sight along the shores of the continent. New Haven was no exception.

Denied their share of trade, and envious of the goods flowing down the waterway of the Connecticut River making Hartford rich, New Haven leaders watched after the war as the Erie Canal in New York opened the interior of the continent there to safe trade. They schemed to build the Farmington Canal to get their share of profit from the hinterland areas. They also wanted to bypass Hartford and, in effect, build their own Connecticut River. The canal opened in 1828 but after only a few years operation it became a disaster as problems beyond the engineering capabilities of the day beset the enterprise. The Farmington Canal was a total failure. Its channel was used as a railroad right of way in places, passing beneath present-day Temple St. and Whitney Ave. just north of the green. Then the coming of the railroad changed New Haven's focus and complexion totally. Manufacture and industry began to rise in the city as it was doing all over the state. Eli Whitney came to New Haven and set up his arms factory, and by ingenious mass production methods produced interchangeable parts. He frequently is credited with being the father of mass-production techniques. Whether he, or someone else, first hit on the scheme, is immaterial. Whitney used the idea and his factory flourished. Other ingenious men, inventors and adaptors, abounded in the New Haven area and New Haven firsts include the truss bridge (1821); machine tools (1832); sulfur matches (1835); automatic revolver (1836); vulcanized rubber (1844); artificial ice (1849); machine stone crusher (1851); commercial telephone exchange (1878).

By the time the Civil War came, New Haven along with other major New England cities was able to provide arms and supplies to aid the Union cause, and the boom of those days continued into the twentieth century. In its industrial development, New Haven was not unique in Connecticut but was nearly always the leader in innovative techniques.

The mid-nineteenth century was the time of the second great wave of immigration to the United States (see Chapter 2) and New Haven received its share of the newcomers: Irish, Italian, German, Jews from Bavaria and Eastern Europe, with a sprinkling of other ethnic groups. The city grew under their impact and the homes stretched farther and farther from the center of town into Westville, east into Fair Haven, and north into what is today Hamden and North Haven. For although the town of New Haven was some 130 square miles in extent, bits of it were chipped off to form the present towns of Woodbridge, Orange, West Haven, Hamden, East Haven, and North Haven. Gradually the boundary of New Haven shrank to its present size. Large houses of the successful merchants and manufacturers grew up along Whitney Ave., St. Ronan St., Hillhouse Ave., and adjoining streets, and large homes still speak of affluence in the neighborhood. In its growth, the city flowed around the campus of Yale University, and as the years passed, the city and the university became inextricably intertwined.

As a modern urban region New Haven has had its share of urban problems. In fact, it still does. Much of the downtown section has been rebuilt over the past two decades, however, and new apartment buildings, new business centers, and new university buildings provide the present skyline. And there is enough architectural variety to blur the aesthetic eye. New Haven suffers from the apparently inescapable flaw in modern architectural thought: the personal expression, by many architects, of their personal philosophies in stone, steel, and concrete. The general styles of the past that gave harmonious groups of buildings to us are gone; individual styles prevail. Faced with such wide diversity in building styles, the visitor to New Haven should content himself with finding one or two that are pleasing to him.

The architecture of Yale University is also a mixture of styles old and new. They range from the handsome eighteenth-century Connecticut Hall, through neo-Gothic, Victorian, Georgian Revival, to contemporary expressions by world-known architects.

*To See and Do: (1)* The New Haven Green. The center of New Haven's nine original squares, the green retains its old proportion and a hint of its early flavor as the heart of a bustling community. Bounded by a potpourri of buildings ranging in styles attributable to most of the building periods of New Haven's more than three hundred years, its center is graced by three churches, all of them very early nineteenth century, while the lower section still functions as parade ground and civic gathering place.

*(2)* Trinity Church (Episcopal) at Temple and Chapel. Designed by Ithiel Town and built in 1815, the seam-faced traprock and brownstone trimmed Trinity is one of the first, if not the first, of the Gothic Revival churches built in the United States.

*(3)* Center Church (United Church of Christ), as its name implies, is centered on the green between Trinity and its own daughter church, United. This Georgian brick building was designed by Benjamin Asher and Ithiel Town. While built in 1812, it is the third building of the society on the green, covering part of the original burying ground, and its crypt contains 139 stones dating from 1687. The interior of this fine brick and wood building is beautifully proportioned and galleried on three sides. There is a Tiffany window memorializing Davenport's first sermon in the New Haven colony, and the church walls display commemorative

tablets for its distinguished ministers. At the back of Center Church are memorials for the colony's first governor, Theophilus Eaton, and the three "regicides," Dixwell, Whalley, and Goffe.

*(4)* United (North) Church (United Church of Christ), on the green, at the corner of Elm and Temple Sts. This delicate masterpiece of David Hoadley, built in 1814, is highly representative of the finest expression of Georgian colonial church architecture, with noteworthy interior paneling and furnishings.

*(5)* Three of the early residences that ringed the green still survive in the Elm St. block between Temple and College Sts. These eighteenth-century buildings, now affiliated with Yale, are the Elihu Club, the Graduates Club, and the Yale Faculty Club. The Ingersoll House, at the corner of Elm and Temple, also a Yale building, was built in 1830, while further east along Elm St. are the Bishop Mansion (1816) and the Jonathan Cook House (1804).

*(6)* Yale Colleges and Buildings. As many of the preceding items indicate, it is sometimes difficult to differentiate between strictly New Haven places of interest and Yale. Generally speaking, the areas immediately north and west of the green hold the bulk of the Yale buildings. Free, guided tours of the colleges are furnished during term-time weekends, leaving from Phelps Gateway, on College St., on the west side of the green. Yale's Information Office is located here, too, and tour schedules, maps, and information are available.

The oldest of the Yale buildings, Connecticut Hall, is in the Old Campus, entered through the Phelps Gateway. Carefully renovated, this former dormitory has been, since its completion in 1752, the college home of many distinguished graduates, including Eli Whitney, Nathan Hale, and Noah Webster. As the term "university" implies, Yale is made up of several colleges, most within walking distance of the green, although the Pierson-Sage Square, the School of Forestry, and the Yale Divinity School, along Prospect St., would be recommended only to the hardy hiker.

Many of Yale's buildings and dormitories are of either Gothic or Georgian design; some of those viewable from the Gothic Harkness Tower are Gothic in exterior appearance and Georgian within the quadrangle. Most of the colleges were built between

1918 and 1940. Since World War II the Yale buildings planned and erected have been "modern" in design, but carefully adapted to harmonize with the university atmosphere. The more successful are spectacular. Particularly noteworthy are the School of Art and Architecture, at Chapel and York Sts., designed by Paul Rudolph; Eero Saarinen's Morse and Ezra Stiles' colleges, bounded by York, Broadway, and Tower Parkway; his Co-op Building on Broadway; Gordon Bunshaft's controversial Beinecke Rare Book and Manuscript Library on Wall and High Sts. whose striking exterior is surpassed only by its interior; and out on the corner of Prospect and Sachem Sts., Saarinen's first Yale building, the 1957 David S. Ingalls Hockey Rink—the "Yale Whale." For a purist, with the exception of Connecticut Hall and its older residence buildings, these and buildings currently under construction are Yale's least derivative and most exciting buildings, however one might quibble with their "modern" intrusion.

*(7)* Hillhouse Ave. Once a road on the Hillhouse farm, this short, fine avenue still exhibits homes of the elegance that made it one of the loveliest streets in America in the middle 1800's. Most of the buildings now belong to Yale and are used as classrooms or official residences, one red brick house in the center of the block between Trumbull and Sachem Sts. serving as the residence of its president.

Here also, at 15 Hillhouse Ave., is the Yale Collection of Musical Instruments, over three hundred, dating from the sixteenth to nineteenth century and including several harpsichords.

*(8)* Grove Street Cemetery, Grove St., opposite High St. One of the first cemeteries to be laid out in family plots, established in 1797, it is the burial place of Noah Webster, Eli Whitney, Samuel Morse, and other distinguished New Haven citizens, including most of the past presidents of Yale.

*(9)* Wooster Square, four blocks east of the green, on Chapel St. Once known as the lower green, this square still has several houses facing it dating from when it was one of "the" residential areas around 1840, and the area is now a historic district. Particularly noticeable is the iron grillwork decorating several of these pre-Civil War houses, which were built for summer use by

Southern planters. Later to become and remain the heart of New Haven's large Italian community, the square has a commemorative statue of Christopher Columbus.

*(10)* Defenders Monument, at the juncture of Columbus and Congress Aves. Here a commemorative statue grouping immortalizes those town and gown defenders of New Haven who held the West River Bridge against the advancing British in 1779. Fortunately for the town, the British looked the situation over and rerouted themselves over another less vigorously defended bridge, giving the militia more time to regroup and fight.

*(11)* The Pardee-Morris House (New Haven Colony Historical Society), a good drive away from the green, at 325 Lighthouse Rd., well to the east along New Haven Harbor. One of the oldest surviving houses in New Haven, the Morris House was rebuilt in 1780, incorporating the ruins of a 1671 building burned by the British in 1779. The kitchen ell, built in 1767, survived the fire, and displays hewn oak beams and a sink cut from solid rock. A long, narrow, vaulted-ceiling ballroom was added over the west wing about 1800.

*(12)* New Haven Colony Historical Society, 114 Whitney Ave. A museum commemorating New Haven history from its days as a colony. The collection includes early silver, glass, toys, ship models, and Eli Whitney's cotton gin as well as a genealogical and historical library.

*(13)* Yale University Art Gallery, 1111 Chapel St. Presently housed in a modern building, this was the first American university art gallery to be established, and houses a fine collection, ranging through African and pre-Columbian sculpture; archeological materials, including frescoes and a third-century baptistry from the excavations at Dura Europos in Syria; Oriental art; European art from the medieval period through the eighteenth century; nineteenth-century American and British paintings; the early "modern" painting and sculpture collection of the Société Anonyme; and the outstanding Garvan collection of early American furniture and silver.

*(14)* Peabody Museum of Natural History (Yale University), 170 Whitney Ave. A wide-ranging collection, with a spectacular dinosaur hall, extremely well-done dioramas of North American

birds and small animals in their natural environment, and Indian artifacts and exhibits.

*(15)* Sterling Memorial Library (Yale University), High St., between Elm and Wall. Rotating exhibits in the main hall of materials such as cuneiform tablets and rare manuscripts.

*(16)* Beinecke Rare Book and Manuscript Library (Yale University), Wall and High Sts. On exhibit are rare books, including an Audubon drawing folio and a Gutenberg Bible.

*(17)* Winchester Gun Museum, 275 Winchester Ave. at the corner of Munson St. Guns and more guns from the fourteenth century to the present, well and carefully displayed.

*(18)* The Southern New England Telephone Company Exhibit, 227 Church St. A replica of the world's first commercial telephone exchange as it appeared when it was opened in New Haven in 1878, in addition to other exhibits of telephones and their complex operation.

*(19)* East and West Rock Parks (city of New Haven). Red trap-rock memorials to the age of glaciers, both East and West Rock offer fine views of New Haven and its surrounding countryside. East Rock, dominated by the rocketlike Soldiers and Sailors Monument, offers hiking and picnicking within the city limits. West Rock, further away, also offers hiking and a drive to Judges' Cave, a hiding place for the regicides (see above) Edward Whalley and William Goffe.

*(20)* West Rock Nature Center (city of New Haven), forty acres. Trails, picnic area, and a living collection of caged small animals and birds indigenous to the area, built and run with the help of young volunteers.

*(21)* Lighthouse Point Park, Lighthouse Rd. (city of New Haven). The municipal beach, with bathhouses, picnic areas, and sports facilities. Also on the grounds is the octagonal lighthouse, which served the harbor from 1840 to 1877, a ninety-foot-high white-painted East Haven sandstone and North Haven brick structure.

*(22)* Varied smaller parks are available for walks and drives through the New Haven area, including Edgewood, Edgerton, Fort Wooster, and Nathan Hale Park, which also offers picnic facilities.

Sports are available through all seasons in various parks and city facilities, with tennis at College Woods, Bowen Field, and Edgewood Park and also some Yale facilities. Edgewood Park has the Coogan Pavilion for ice skating, which may also be enjoyed at the Trowbridge Rink, Blake Field Rink, and the Municipal Golf Course. Swimming is available at the high school pools in addition to Lighthouse Park, while there are boat launches at Lighthouse and Fort Hale parks. For golfers the Alling Memorial Golf Course is at 35 Eastern St. in the Fair Haven section.

*(23)* The Shubert Theater, 247 College St. With a long history of being one of "the" theaters for pre-Broadway openings, the Shubert is still an important house of the legitimate-theater circuit.

*(24)* The Long Wharf Theatre, Frontage Rd. (Exit 46 off the Connecticut Turnpike). The home of a good professional repertory group, this theater with its four hundred seats and open-stage design brings the immediacy of "live" action directly to its audience.

*(25)* The Yale School of Drama, 222 York St. Varied and vigorous student presentations, both premieres and revivals; with offerings on the main stage and workshops in the Experimental Theater. The Yale Repertory Theater is located at 1120 Chapel St. in a converted church building.

*(26)* Woolsey Hall, College and Grove Sts. (Yale University). Tickets for the Woolsey Hall Concert Series or the New Haven Symphony are difficult to come by, but worth trying for. Some are turned in by those unable to make a specific concert and are made available at the box office one half hour before concert time.

*(27)* Sprague Hall. College and Wall Sts. (Yale University). The Chamber Music Series of the Yale School of Music offers five evening concerts during the season by visiting, and outstanding, chamber groups.

*(28)* The Payne Whitney Gymnasium, Tower Parkway and Dixwell Ave. (Yale University). The university sports events may be found in its Sports Schedules, available at the athletic ticket office here.

The Yale Bowl, Derby Ave. (Yale University). College and professional football as scheduled.

*(29)* Chapel Square, south side of green. A two-story covered shopping mall, office tower, and a high rise hotel make up downtown New Haven's most modern commercial center. The

mall is linked to two department stores and a parking garage to complete the complex.

*(30)* Veterans' Memorial Coliseum and Knights of Columbus Building, George and Orange Sts. Designed by Roche, Dinkeloo and Associates, the two buildings—one office and one recreational—are linked by the use of identical structural materials. The coliseum seats 10,900 spectators and houses 2,400 cars. The recreation schedule includes ice hockey, ice shows, basketball, circuses, stage shows, expositions, and symphonic programs. The office building, which is the national headquarters of the Knights of Columbus, is too large to be ignored. It is admired by those who have never distinguished between quantity and quality.

NEWINGTON *(Hartford County. Rtes. into: U.S. 5; state 15, 173, 175, 176; 13.2 sq. mi.; 26,037 pop.)*
Sandwiched between Hartford and New Britain, this town of respectably early origins is today primarily a suburb of both cities. Residential developments cover the hills where once many farms gave the town a truly rural air. Only one or two large farms now manage to exist in the suburban community.

Known in the seventeenth century as Wethersfield West Society, the town grew from just the few scattered homesteads that were there early in the eighteenth century. During the Revolutionary War, over one hundred men from Newington served. One of the earliest public libraries was begun here in 1752 and throughout the eighteenth century Newington flourished as a literate, agricultural Yankee town. The early material is still in the present library. One by one the large, gracious homes disappeared and all that remains that can be viewed by the public is, oddly, not in Newington, but in the Metropolitan Museum in New York, where a room of Charles Churchill's home is on display in the American Wing. His Newington home had seven fireplaces, one of which was, according to report, large enough to take a whole ox for roasting.

*To See and Do:* American Radio Relay League Museum of Amateur Radio, 225 North Main St. Radio buffs and historians can see early radio transmitters and receivers, and there is a 5,000-volume library for research into the history of ham radio and related subjects.

NEW LONDON *(New London County. Rtes. into: I–95; U.S. 1, which coincides with the interstate highway here, 1–A; state 32, 85, 213; 6.3 sq. mi.; 31,630 pop.)*
The city was once much bigger. Both neighboring Groton and Waterford were originally part of New London, which was first settled in 1646. John Winthrop, Jr., of Massachusetts received a grant of Fisher's Island and later of land "at or near Pequot," which is what the English settlers called New London and its environs at that time.

The name New London was bestowed after some dispute with the General Court. The settlers saw their city as a great industrial port. They had good reason for that view. New London, stretching along the western side of the Thames River (pronounced here Thaymes, not Tems), was one of the best deep-water ports in New England—and some say along the entire Atlantic coast, with the exception of New York City. The Thames actually is a drowned valley, deep and wide near the coast, and navigable up to Norwich. New London's history centers for the most part around this principal feature.

As early as the seventeenth century inland farmers saw the advantages of the port and hauled their produce overland to the dockside for shipment. Fishing became a local industry and in the eighteenth century the city began its love affair with whaling. Except for the interruption of the Revolutionary War and the War of 1812, New London whalers roamed the seven seas for more than one hundred years. Actually, whaling rights were granted in the seventeenth century, although only for "Connecticut waters," but by the 1860s nearly eighty vessels fitted for whaling sailed from the home port of New London. This was just one ship less than the number registered in the most famous whaling port of New England history: New Bedford, Massachusetts. Whale oil to light the world's lamps and whalebone were the prizes, and fortunes were made on voyages of one to five years. On the discovery of crude oil in Pennsylvania in 1859 the need for whale oil declined and whaling began to die as a major industry.

The Revolutionary War saw New London ships turn to privateering, and more privateers slipped out of New London to attack British merchant ships than from any other New England port. In fact, the trouble they caused the British prompted the attack on New London in September of 1781. Twenty-four British ships with eight hundred troops aboard paid New London a nearly fatal visit (see Chapter 2).

During the War of 1812 New London was blockaded by British ships for almost two years, and Commodore Decatur was bottled up with his ships above New London on the Thames (see Ledyard). New London citizens grew accustomed to the sight of lurking British ships, and when the war ended and the news reached New London on February 21, 1815, the British came ashore and a Peace Ball was given in the Court House, an outstanding building that is in use today, on Huntington St. at the top of State St.

Since its great whaling days New London has had shore industries but shipbuilding remains a major contributor to the economy of the city. Textiles and wood products are other important industries, but the basic reason for the city's prominence still lies in sea matters. The U.S. Navy has long made New London one of its principal bases on the northeast coast, with the submarine base across the river in Groton and an underwater systems center at old Fort Trumbull. The U.S. Coast Guard Academy trains officers on the west bank of the Thames and each June the river is the scene of the Yale-Harvard regatta.

The downtown section of New London (State St.) is in need of a thorough face lifting, but other pleasant avenues, leading along the Thames on the high ground of the city, open to residential areas south toward the sound, where large houses line the streets and overlook the water. Nearly all residential streets have some buildings of eighteenth- or nineteenth-century vintage that are worth a leisurely drive of inspection. And in the house at 325 Pequot Ave., Eugene O'Neill lived and wrote his first plays.

*To See and Do:* (1) The Hempstead House, 11 Hempstead St., north of Jay St. (U.S. 1A) (Antiquarian and Landmarks Society). Built in 1678 by Joshua Hempstead, only son of Robert Hempstead, a founder of New London, this house was expanded in 1728 and was lived in by Hempstead heirs until 1937. It is one of the few houses to have escaped the British attack in 1781 and today is the oldest house in the city. It is furnished in the period of the late-seventeenth and early-eighteenth centuries. Few museums give a more definite feel of authenticity than this one.

Also on the property is the Nathaniel Hempstead House, or what was formerly called the Huguenot House, because it was built by Huguenots under the direction of Nathaniel Hempstead in 1751. It too is the property of the Antiquarian and Landmarks Society and plans are going forward to restore and open it to the public.

(2) The Shaw Mansion, 11 Blinman St. (New London County Historical Society). This home of Captain Nathaniel Shaw was built in 1756 and the stone for it was quarried on Captain Shaw's property by displaced Acadians who had descended on New London at that time. The house served as a naval headquarters for all of Connecticut during the Revolutionary War. The British partially destroyed the house in their raid but most of the present main structure is original. Furnishings are fitting for such a home and the china, silver, and books are augmented by an excellent collection of letters and manuscripts.

(3) Lyman Allyn Museum, 100 Mohegan Ave., at the corner of Williams St. A handsome building on landscaped grounds houses American and English antiques, both furniture and silver, plus costumes, dolls, toys, Mediterranean antiques, and paintings by both American and European masters. There is also a 7,000-volume library of art history books with emphasis on drawings and decorative arts.

(4) The Old Town Mill, Mill St. just off Main St. Originally built by John Winthrop, Jr., in 1650, the first—and, for a long time, only—mill in New London today is a faithful reconstruction of the original. Some of the timbers in it are believed to be from the original structure.

(5) Nathan Hale Schoolhouse, Mill St. In 1774, when it was built,

the school was located on the southeastern corner of State and Union Sts. In this building Nathan Hale taught from March 1744 to July 1755, and it was from this employment in this building that he went to join the patriot forces that led to his death by hanging as a spy against the British.

*(6)* Ye Ancientist Burial Ground, 190 Huntington St. The oldest cemetery in New London has markers dating back to the seventeenth century and contains the remains of a number of New London's prominent early citizens. It is said to be the place where Benedict Arnold watched his British troops burning New London.

*(7)* Whale Oil Row, east side of Huntington St., north of State St. Four astonishing Greek Revival houses (1830), which resulted from wealth gained in the whaling days of New London. It is believed to be the only such group of houses standing in the United States.

*(8)* New London County Court House, Huntington St. at the top of State St. This handsome Georgian building has served as a courthouse for nearly two hundred years. Built in 1784, it was where the Peace Ball was held when the War of 1812 ended. Relieved New Londoners entertained officers of the formerly blockading British fleet.

*(9)* Thames Science Center, Inc., Gallows Lane. A natural history museum that appeals to children and contains shells, minerals, stuffed birds, native live wild animals, saltwater aquariums, and fossils. There also is a library of natural history books and magazines for use in the building.

*(10)* Connecticut Arboretum, west of the Connecticut College campus on Williams St. A collection of some three hundred varieties of plants on seventy acres for botany buffs. The college campus itself, overlooking the Thames, is pleasant and trim, with gray stone buildings rising from manicured lawns on the hilltop. Each summer the college offers a series of dance concerts.

*(11)* Herbert F. Moran Nature Center and Zoo, Chester St. A zoo for adults and a zoo for children. Also on the property, a nature center and camp.

*(12)* U.S. Coast Guard Academy, Mohegan Ave. The grounds are open to visitors, and occasional parades and musical concerts enliven the campus. Seasonal collegiate athletics.

*(13)* Block Island Ferry, at the foot of State St. The car ferry to Block Island makes a good summer-day excursion.

*(14)* Ocean Beach Park, at the foot of Ocean Ave. Called by its boosters "New England's most beautiful beach," the curving sand shore and mile-long boardwalk make it a major summer attraction. In addition to ocean bathing there is a large swimming pool and the expected concessions.

NEW MILFORD *(Litchfield County. Rtes. into: U.S. 7; state 25, 39, 55, 109; 64.8 sq. mi.; 14,601 pop. Other communities: Boardman's Bridge, Gaylordsville, Lower Merryall, Marble Dale, Northville, Park Lane, Upper Merryall.)*
A "parent" town, which was first settled in 1707, New Milford supplied all the land for neighboring Bridgewater and half the land for Brookfield, which were incorporated from it. New Milford also is the shopping and industrial center for much of the surrounding region.

Tobacco was one of the early sources of wealth in the town and many fine brick homes from the first years of the nineteenth century are still standing in outlying agricultural communities and districts. Today, U.S. 7 is the main artery through the town and, fortunately, the town center is across the Housatonic River from the highway and safe from traffic snarls. The center is built on hills, and the long narrow green is pleasantly shaded, with a World War I tank ensconced on the southern end. Several churches flank the eastern edge and they are separated by a number of gracious older homes of the nineteenth century. The west side of this pleasant spot has stores and shops along the street.

The leading historical figure claiming New Milford as home was Roger Sherman. This extraordinary man moved to New Milford in 1743 at the age of twenty-two and, unable to attend Yale, studied by himself, devouring books and earning a living as a cobbler. It is said that he read with the book propped against his cobbler's bench until finally he was admitted to the bar. After serving in a number of town offices, he rose in the state government, went to New Haven, and later had an important say in the framing of the U.S. Constitution. He is the only Connecticut man whose signature is found on all the key documents of this nation's founding: the Declaration of Independence, the Articles of Confederation, the Articles of Association, and the Constitution.

As in many western Connecticut towns, Indian legends abound, and Lovers Leap (where Farm Brook joins the Housatonic River) is where Lillinonah, daughter of Chief Waramaug, and her white sweetheart perished. She, despairing of his return from his home, canoed down the Housatonic River to a dangerous gorge replete with rapids in the southern part of town. As she approached the white water, she threw away her paddle. At that instant, her white lover appeared on a rocky path above the falls. She called to him and he leaped in to save her. Both died on the rocks of the rapids.

*To See and Do: (1)* New Milford Historical Museum, 6 Aspetuck Ave. (New Milford Historical Society). Exhibits include glass, china, portraits, costumes, dolls, furniture, and historical records.

*(2)* Candlewood Lake reaches into the southwestern part of town, west of U.S. 7, and a full range of summer water sports is available. There is hunting in the New Milford Sportsmen's Association tracts scattered along the Housatonic in the Merryall and Second Hill sections, above Boardman Bridge. The Housatonic and the Aspetuck Rivers offer fishing, as does Lake Lillinonah, with its boat-launch site on the north shore of the impoundment, east of Rte. 133. The Candlewood Valley Country Club is available for golfers.

NEWTOWN *(Fairfield County. Rtes. into: I–84; U.S. 6, 202; state 25, 34; 60.4 sq. mi.; 16,942 pop. Other communities: Botsford, Dodgingtown, Hattertown, Hawleyville, Huntingtown, Sandy Hook.)*
The broad Main St. of this handsome rural town is lined with large well-kept houses of the late-eighteenth and the nineteenth centuries. They are set back from the road and shaded by large maples just as the original proprietors planned in 1705. Coming from Stratford, those pioneers envisioned a spacious and peaceful community set on the rolling ridges of this section of Connecticut. Appropriately, the name chosen was Newtown. Their planning paid dividends and the sense of spaciousness is jealously guarded

by its present inhabitants, many of whom came from urban areas in search of just such quietude.

At the outbreak of the Revolutionary War, the town surprised many people by voting against the "rebellion." There were many loyalists in the community and for a time they prevailed. At a town meeting in February 1775, the Tory leaders went on record that they did "publickly disapprove of and protest against said Congress." Further, they believed that what the Congress was doing was unconstitutional, subversive of their real liberties, and, worse yet, tended toward "licentiousness." In November of that year, some two hundred patriots invaded Newtown, stayed two days, and spent the time "reducing and disarming said tories." By 1777 the Tory sentiments had decreased and from then until the end of the war Newtown fulfilled its quotas in both men and supplies. Rochambeau's troops encamped in the town going and returning from battles. While in Newtown they may have used the weathercock on the Congregational Church as a target for rifle practice. The bullet-ridden weathercock can be seen today on the later building (1818) on the west side of Rte. 25 at the junction of Church Hill Rd.

There is an air of affluent country living in the center of Newtown and the community has benefited by endowments and buildings given and constructed by former citizens. The Georgian Revival brick town hall, for example, with auditorium theater, kitchen, and gymnasium was given by Mary Elizabeth Hawley in 1930. The library (south of the center on Rte. 25) is in a handsome twin-chimney brick Georgian-style building. The smaller communities of Hawleyville and Sandy Hook offer a less tailored appearance than the Main St. of Newtown's center. In Sandy Hook (Rte. 34, east of the center) the buildings are less pretentious and late-eighteenth-century homes cluster close to the roads. It is in these communities that Newtown's few industries function (as well as south of the center on Rte. 25). They include the manufacture of fire hose, copper tubing, pressure gauges, and cardboard cartons. Hattertown, a small, quiet crossroad community, got its name, as might be expected, from the manufacture of hats in earlier times. Dodgingtown's name came from a more colorful past: a haven for peddlers, traders, and others "on the dodge" from the law.

*To See and Do:* Paugussett State Forest, east of Rte. 34, on the Housatonic River, offers fishing, hunting, and hiking. Lake Zoar—an impoundment of the Housatonic River—just south of the state forest offers boating (launch site: see Southbury), swimming, and fishing. Fishing also in Lake Lillinonah, north of I-84 (see New Milford).

NORFOLK *(Litchfield County. Rtes. into: U.S. 44; state 182, 272; 46.7 sq. mi.; 2,073 pop. Other communities: North, South, and West Norfolks.)*
It took a while to get settlers into Norfolk. The General Court tried to sell pieces of the town for many years before it all was taken. One reason was that Norfolk's land was less suitable for agriculture than some communities nearer established centers like Hartford, Windsor, and Simsbury, where the settlers came from. Though named (for Norfolk County, England) in 1738, the town was not incorporated for twenty years. And the agricultural going was so bad that the community turned to producing maple sugar, 21,000 pounds in a single season. The rise of Norfolk to its present estate as a rich summer colony was due largely to a remarkable family whose patriarch, Joseph Battell, moved to Norfolk and built a mansion from trading profits in 1800. The fortune built by the father was used by two sons, Joseph Battell, Jr., and Robbins Battell to become scholars. Robbins took an interest in music and brought concerts to the small town in the Berkshire foothills. This attracted wealthy summer folk who, liking the mountains, built large estates and helped the community become known as the Lenox (Mass.) of Connecticut. It remains today much unchanged. Until 1925 summer concerts in the Music Shed behind the Battell mansion were the event of the summer. The tradition is carried on today by the Yale Summer Music School.

*To See and Do: (1)* Norfolk Historical Society Museum, Village Green, Norfolk. Exhibits include the decorative arts, costumes, folklore, maps, and manuscripts.

*(2)* Concerts seasonally in the Music Shed (see above) and the Yale Summer Music School.

*(3)* Campbell Falls State Park with 102 acres, on Rte. 272, in North Norfolk offers hiking, picnicking, and fishing. Dennis Hill State Park, south of the center, on Rte. 272, offers picnicking and hiking on 240 acres. Haystack Mountain State Park, with 225 acres northwest of the center between U.S. 44 and Rte. 272, offers fishing, picnicking, and hiking. Wood Creek Pond has boating (with a launch site) and fishing. Access: 1 mile east of Rte. 72, off Doolittle Pond Rd. With the rise of cross-country skiing, the town attracts its share of winter-sports enthusiasts.

*(4)* A walk about the center of Norfolk would be pleasant. At the north end of the small, triangular green is the Richardsonian-style library, designed by George Keller in 1888. Going up North St. from the green (Rte. 272) to Old Colony Rd.—a distance of about $\frac{1}{2}$ mile—brings you to a Greek Revival house, a Gothic-style house, and on the north side of Old Colony Rd., the 1764 Stevens House. Drives on Shepard Rd., Maple Ave., or Laurel Way will give a good indication of the town's beauty. The hilly terrain tempts further back-road excursions.

NORTH BRANFORD *(New Haven County. Rtes. into: 17, 22, 80, 139, 150; 26.8 sq. mi.; 10,778 pop. Other communities: Northford.)* A district of Branford originally, the community reached town status in 1831. Both North Branford Center and Northford are essentially residential, and the green in Northford has a number of pleasant eighteenth-century houses near it. Much of the rest of the town has a surprisingly rural quality for a community so near the city of New Haven. A major industry in town is the processing of traprock for roadways. This lava that flowed upward near the surface in ancient times is broken to proper size and hauled away, endlessly, in huge trucks along Rte. 80, just west of the center.

*To See and Do: (1)* Red School House (1805), Old Post Rd. (Northford Historical Society). Exhibits of eighteenth- and nineteenth-century books and town memorabilia.

*(2)* Golfers can play at the Rolling Acres Golf Club, on Rte. 80, and Twin Lakes Golf Course, on Twin Lakes Rd. Hunting in the Suburban Sportsmen's Association (see appendix).

*(3)* Visitors are allowed to inspect the large dam at Lake Gaillard—a reservoir—and enjoy the views.

NORTH CANAAN *(Litchfield County. Rtes. into: U.S. 7, 44; 19.6 sq. mi.; 3,045 pop. Other communities: Canaan, Canaan Valley, East Canaan, Sodom.)*
Originally part of Canaan to the south, this small town on the Massachusetts border contains the village of Canaan (which can prove confusing) and is actually the earliest settled part of the area embodied in the two towns. At the junction of U.S. 44 and 7, the village is a shopping point for the rural region. The first settler, Captain Isaac Lawrence of Plainfield, came here in 1738 and wintered over in a dugout with his wife and children until spring. The town was incorporated from Canaan in 1858.

Snug, tucked away, quiet, and peaceful, North Canaan has survived amid the hills; and its citizens have made their living from quarrying stone, agriculture, and earlier, making two-ton anchors from ore in surrounding areas. Today magnesium and calcium-bearing ores mined here are refined to produce those metals while other light manufacture takes up the slack in the economy.

In East Canaan an industrial monument marks the site of an old iron forge, which was worked by one Samuel Forbes and Ethan Allen before Ethan moved north to Vermont.

*To See and Do: (1)* Housatonic State Forest reaches into the southern part of the town, east of U.S. 7, where hunting and hiking may be enjoyed. You may, in fact, do a lot of hiking nearly anywhere in North Canaan—including climbing Canaan Mountain (near Canaan Village) where all-around views are the reward.

*(2)* C. H. Pease Nature Museum, Douglas Library. Displays of specimens of native animals.

NORTH HAVEN *(New Haven County. Rtes. into: I–91, Exits 9, 12; U.S. 5; state 17, 22; 21.0 sq. mi.; 22,194 pop. Other communities: Montowese.)*

A residential and manufacturing town formerly part of the New Haven colony, North Haven was an early shipbuilding and brick-making center. Bricks from its kilns remain today in pre-Revolutionary homes in contrast to other communities, where stone is the fireplace material.

North Haven's outstanding citizen in Revolutionary War times was Benjamin Trumbull. A Calvinist minister of firm conviction, he was an ardent patriot and after one fire-eating sermon signed up members of his congregation at the communion table for the rebel forces. He himself served as chaplain and headed a volunteer company in several campaigns. Following the war he wrote *A History of the United States* and *A History of Connecticut*, which were widely read. Since the New Haven colony was a theocracy, it is not surprising that church records in Montowese reveal that a small girl was excommunicated because she was discovered skipping rope in front of the church one Sunday morning.

Today, the town green is surrounded by some suburban homes, but there are a number of eighteenth- and early nineteenth-century houses there also and a faint echo of the past remains.

*To See and Do:* Wharton Brook State Park, between I–91 and U.S. 5, on the northern edge of town. Fishing, hiking, picnicking, swimming, and winter sports are available.

NORTH STONINGTON *(New London County. Rtes. into: I–95; state 2, 49, 184, 201, 216: 56.3 sq. mi.; 3,748 pop. Other communities: Clarks Falls, Laurel Glen.)*

There is the look of all New England in the town's stone-fenced, stony fields and, as might be suspected, its name came from that characteristic of the land. Incorporated in 1807, North Stonington is mostly farm and hill country. The center is quaint and quiet with a mixture of eighteenth- and nineteenth-century buildings. The post office is a small country Federal-style building; a red-painted village store and adjacent white town hall—all in the small village scale—make this an attractive spot. West of these buildings is the expected Congregational Church (1846) with rather ornate columns in the full-blown Greek Revival style. The second stage of the three-stage church tower is columned also.

Clarks Falls, on the eastern edge of town just off Rte. 216, is an even smaller collection of homes. Here a gristmill still operates and is open on Sundays to sell stone-ground flour to baking purists.

There are more graveyards in the flinty earth of North Stonington than in any other town in the state; more than ninety (mostly family plots) hold the remains of past citizens. Some can be seen near the old farmhouses on the country roads north and east of the village center (see also Stonington).

*To See and Do: (1)* Lantern Hill, used first as an Indian lookout and later a signal point where patriots burned barrels of tar to forewarn Stonington men of the approach of British ships during the War of 1812. From this 580-foot mass of quartz and granite you can see Long Island, Block Island, and miles of surrounding countryside on a clear day. The quartz outcroppings, glittering in daylight, produced its name and were said to be used as a navigational aid by sailors on the Sound. East of the junction of Rtes. 2 and 216, about 0.2 miles, is a road running south. About two hundred yards on this road brings you to an unsigned but very visible trail leading to the summit. The climb is somewhat arduous but not hazardous.

*(2)* Pachaug State Forest on either side of Rte. 49, in the northern part of town, offers boating, fishing, hiking, and picnicking, and the Narragansett Trail passes through here, crossing Rte. 2 just south of the junction with Rte. 201. Fishing (with boat-launch sites) is available on many of the town's lakes: Lake of Isles, Anderson's Pond, Billings Lake, Lantern Hill Pond, Long Pond, and Wyassup Lake (inquire locally). Hunting is permitted in Assekonk Swamp (see appendix).

NORWALK *(Fairfield County. Rtes. into: I–95, which also is the Connecticut Turnpike, Exits 14, 15, 16; state 15, which also is the*

*Merritt Pkwy., Exits 38, 39, 40; U.S. 1, 7; state 53, 123, 136; 27.7 sq.*
*mi.; 40,113 pop. Other communities: Rowayton.)*
Little of the early "town" settled in 1649 remains—thanks in part at least to the British. Named (as only one of two towns are) from an unspellable word of Indian origin, "Noyank" phonetically, the town of Norwalk was purchased for a rather small sum from the Indians and, as was the custom in those times, with measured distance along the shore and "one Indian day walk" into the interior. How fast the Indian walked is not recorded.

The settlement grew and shipping and oyster fishing were among its earliest industries. By the time the Revolutionary War broke out, artisans were making watches and clocks, paper and nails, and the oystering was still prospering. The war overtook Norwalk in 1779, when 2,500 British troops landed on Calf Pasture Beach with the help of incorrigible Tories and proceeded to burn the town. They burned churches, houses, barns, ships' factories—everything they could lay the torch to. Some 400 patriots hastily organized and tried to withstand the assault but were driven back. When the fire was over most of the town and all of the stores of food were gone. After the war, citizens who had lost everything were offered land in the Western Reserve and they set forth by wagon train to that wilderness where they founded the present town of Norwalk, Ohio.

The town's position along the coast made it a favorite target of such raids during the war, but afterward it helped develop a shipping industry and trade with distant ports. As a stop on the old coach road between New York and Boston, Norwalk had its share of early inns, taverns, and travelers. During the nineteenth century the town—which rapidly was becoming a city—developed characteristic industries and gained a reputation second only to Danbury in the production of hats, at that time the beaver hats of the fashionable men. One hat, for seven dollars, was supposed to last a lifetime, but the beaver fur wore off the edges and one James Knapp changed the course of hat history by experimenting with a block that was rounded—and the derby hat was born.

One notable military leader, Colonel Thomas Fitch, a son of native son, Governor Thomas Fitch, inadvertently helped create a popular tune as old as this country: "Yankee Doodle." Leading some irregularly uniformed colonial troops to support the British in the French and Indian War started the whole thing. To give the ragged volunteers some semblance of uniformity, each man stuck a chicken feather in his hatband and when a British surgeon saw them he extemporized and the lines were born—including "stuck a feather in his hat and called it macaroni." Macaroni was the slang of the day for a dude, dandy, or fop. Colonel Fitch's home in Norwalk—no longer standing—was called the Yankee Doodle House for many years thereafter.

Today Norwalk is victim of the crowded nineteenth-century reliance on the railroad, which runs yet through the older downtown district. Industry is Norwalk's reason for existence, and while old red brick factories still exist, new and modern plants are rising in less-crowded areas. The city now prides itself on being an important center for research, development, and the manufacture of advanced products for aircraft, submarines, and space vehicles. Also present in today's Norwalk is a large electrical industry and industrial and consumer-product manufacturers.

*To See and Do: (1)* Lockwood-Mathews Mansion Museum, 295 West Ave. The ultimate in Victorian architecture, this four-story mansion has more than sixty rooms and fourteen baths. Double-walled construction gives it the feeling of a fortress, as it did when it was finished in 1868 at a cost of $2,000,000. A private reservoir supplied the house with water, and the entire structure was the idea of financier LeGrand Lockwood, a Norwalk native who made his money in New York. The Paris-trained architect Detlef Lienau designed the huge building and the interiors were done by a bevy of designers, among them Leon Marcotte and Christian Herter. Imported finishes, woods, and marbles were worked and carved and put in place in a display of affluence belonging to an age that has passed.

Demolition threatened the gaudy building in 1958 but it was such a conspicuous bangle that citizens marshaled state and federal help to save and restore the mansion. It still is in the process of being restored and those who are committed to it swear it is all worthwhile. If dreams of opulence in the Victorian tradition haunt you, you should see this museum.

*(2)* Karamuseum, 133 Lexington Ave. An art center, zoo, and nature center, plus an aquarium.

*(3)* Old MacDonald Farm, 768 Connecticut Ave. This is a children's farmland, nature center, and zoo. Antiques and imports are sold in an old-fashioned general store.

*(4)* There are facilities along the Sound for boating and saltwater fishing offshore among the spate of islands lying outside the harbors and coves forming the southern boundary of the city. Golf can be played at the Oak Hills Park Golf Course, on Fillow St.

*(5)* Town beaches. Policy varies regarding nonresident use. Check with the city hall.

NORWICH *(New London County. Rtes. into: Connecticut Turnpike, which is also Rte. 52; state 2, 12, 32, 82, 87, 97, 165, 169; 27.1 sq. mi.; 41,739 pop. Other communities: Greenville, Norwichtown, Occum, Taftville, Yantic.)*

This is a major Connecticut city, rich in history and with a great deal to see. It lies at the junction of the Quinebaug, Yantic, and Shetucket rivers to form what is called the Thames River. Do not let the complex of highways and roads leading to the downtown section put you off. It is confusing but fortunately this is not the historic Norwich. It is the commercial center and shipping area of the nineteenth century, when the navigable Thames was alive with ships. The oldest architecture here in the center is mid- to late-nineteenth century, when Norwich was a full-blown city.

The original grant of land was a purchase from Uncas, Mohegan war chief or sachem, and in 1659 the General Court of the Connecticut colony approved the settlement of the region by families from Saybrook. In 1660 the court added the proviso that "Uncas . . . and Indians and successors shall be supplied with sufficient planting ground at all times." As a result, Indian history mingles with white history in this region (see Montville).

A little more than a hundred years after its founding Norwich began to blossom industrially. At the head of the Thames River (pronounced with "Th," not "Tems") the city was an ideal shipping point and shipbuilding location. Ships that put to sea brought skilled craftsmen from London. Watch and clock making became early businesses. The usual way to approach Norwich in those days of no or horrendous roads was via the Thames, and not until many years later did roads, then railroads, displace the river as the principal path of approach. In Norwichtown, the oldest section of the original settlement (see below), one Dr. Daniel Lathrop opened what is believed to be the first apothecary shop in the state and drew customers from as far away as the Naugatuck Valley. The first paper mill (1766) in the state began here and in 1772 a stoneware company opened its doors. Textiles, coming near the close of the century, put Norwich in the front rank of industrial towns of the state.

The Revolutionary War saw hundreds of Norwich men leaving for the defense of hard-pressed Massachusetts. As a port and a major community in Connecticut, Norwich became a supply storage point and a source of arms and war material. Tory and British troop prisoners were kept in confinement in Norwich. As might be expected, the town's civil and military leaders were in close contact both with General Washington and his staff and Governor Trumbull as well (see Lebanon).

The true heyday of Norwich development came in the first half of the nineteenth century—as it did to most of the eastern seaboard of the young country. Demands of the Civil War increased manufacturing here and guns (Smith and Wesson in 1853) were produced by the thousands. The older ornate buildings visible today in the business center attest to that booming period.

Textiles and paper still are manufactured in Norwich, as well as shoes, candles, plastics, chemicals, wire products, and plumbing equipment. It is, as it has been for two centuries, an industrial city. Fortunately, the older parts of the city (Norwichtown, Bean Hill) were not seriously disturbed by the nineteenth-century boom period, nor have they been obliterated by the commercial activities of the twentieth. Away from the narrow downtown streets are broad avenues lined with excellent examples of three centuries of architecture and historic districts (see below) that guarantee permanent conservation of the oldest and best buildings in the city.

As in all old communities, curious fact and fanciful legend mingle. Norwich is known for barrel burning. Barrels, once an important product of the town, were strung like beads on a string hauled to the top of mast-high poles on Thanksgiving Day. And with more barrels stacked about the base, the entire monument was set afire after darkness fell. Competition was strong and various "teams" of local boys would fight to get the prime position on a hill from which onlookers from miles around would gather annually to view the celebrative conflagrations.

A more recent legend concerns the washing away of the Methodist Chapel in 1823 in one of the periodic floodings that took place on the Yantic and Shetucket rivers. According to the story, the church, candles still alight in the windows, went bobbing down the Thames, to the astonishment of incoming sea captains.

*To See and Do: (1)* The Leffingwell Inn, 345 Washington St. (Society of the Founders of Norwich). The earliest part of this unique structure dates, according to some experts, to 1675. And that part was built by one Stephen Backus, who sold it to Ensign Thomas Leffingwell in 1700. A year later, Thomas Leffingwell got permission to operate the house as a tavern or inn. Around 1715 another leanto house was moved to the site and joined to the original building in the form it presently appears. A grandson, Christopher Leffingwell, inherited the inn and it was this man who made the strongest impact on the community and the state. He established, among other things, the first paper mill in Connecticut, a stocking factory and a pottery mill on Bean Hill, a chocolate mill, clothiers shop, dye shop, and a fulling mill.

During the Revolutionary War, Colonel Christopher Leffingwell's Inn was a gathering place for leaders and citizens of the community, state, and nation. General Washington stayed at the inn and Colonel Christopher was consulted by the national leader and Governor Jonathan Trumbull of Connecticut on many occasions.

The inn today is one of the most meticulous restorations in New England, the work for which was completed in 1960 by John J. Stone. The building itself is really all that is needed to tempt a visitor. But on display is an outstanding collection of furnishings, pewter, silver, swords, and clocks made by Norwich craftsmen.

*(2)* Norwichtown Historic District. The Leffingwell Inn is at the southern apex of an almost triangular area which includes more than fifty houses, schools, and offices, plus the Leffingwell Inn. The historic houses are sprinkled among structures of later date and are roughly enclosed by the following streets: Town, West Town (a distance of about half a mile), East Town, Huntington Lane, Scotland Rd., and Washington St. A small group of five houses on Harland Rd., counting from Town St., is also in the Historic District. All of these buildings, except the Leffingwell Inn, are closed to the public. The best thing to do is park your car and walk along these streets. Particular attention should be called to the Norwichtown Green, where all but one or two of the buildings are of great interest. They date from the seventeenth century through the nineteenth. Signs on most of the important buildings help you fix their dates.

*(3)* Royal Mohegan Burial Ground, Sachem St. (off Washington to the right if you are southbound). This small plot with the granite monument and the few other headstones marks the burial ground of great sachems of the Mohegans—among them Uncas, considered to be the most influential of them all.

*(4)* Yantic Falls, Indian Leap, Yantic St. From the Royal Burial Ground, continue west on Sachem St. and turn left on Yantic St. The street slopes down and curves, following the river course. Don't pass along the street too hurriedly because the mill houses on either side are of great interest. The brick "apartments" for workers in old mills below the falls and some individual structures or duplexes are outstanding examples of late-eighteenth- and early-nineteenth-century craftsmanship. There is a footbridge over the falls to the unused railroad across the Yantic River. Water from the dam plunges into a narrow gorge, and it was from the high promontory on the west bank that beleaguered Narragansetts are supposed to have chosen to leap into the roaring water rather than submit to capture by their enemies, the Mohegans. Hence the name Indian Leap.

*(5)* Slater Museum, 108 Crescent St. This is just east of Broadway where Washington St. and Broadway diverge. Norwich Free Academy, one of three such schools still operating in the state, is endowed (see Colchester; Woodstock) and is the high school of

the town—which pays tuition to have Norwich students attend. On the grounds is the Slater Museum and Converse Art Gallery, where displays of Renaissance sculpture and furniture may be seen, and a fine collection of Oriental art.

*(6)* Mohegan Park and Memorial Rose Garden, east of Washington and Broadway (follow signs). The park consists of 350 acres in the middle of the city devoted to healthful recreation: swimming, hiking, and tennis. There also is a small zoo, where deer, foxes, a Russian black bear, and a white peacock (of all things) can be admired. Rose gardens are also here and there are flowers to beguile a visitor from May to November.

*(7)* Backus House and Rockwell House, 42 Rockwell St. (Faith Trumbull Chapter, DAR). Nathaniel Backus House (1750) and Rockwell House (1818) are both museums. The Backus House is much changed from its original architecture, although some interior aspects are of the dated period. It contains furniture, old glass, china, and early paintings and chairs that have historical importance. The Rockwell House, next door, has early-American furniture, costumes, rare crewel work, antique toys, children's clothing, and many other items.

*(8)* The Norwich Fish and Game Association offers hunting west of the Connecticut Turnpike on over 3,000 acres in the southwestern corner of the city. There is also fishing in Bog Meadow Reservoir and Mohegan Park Pond. Golfers can play at the Norwich Golf Club, on West Thames St.

OLD LYME *(New London County. Rtes. into: I–95, Exits 70, 71; U.S. 1; state 51, 156; 27.1 sq. mi.; 4,964 pop. Other communities: Black Hall, Laysville, Sound View, South Lyme.)*
Yesterday Old Lyme was a seafaring town where ships were built, captains' families lived, and the sea and the navigable river formed two of its boundaries. Today these boundaries remain and small boats ply the river and the Sound, but the great days of sail and the China trade are over. Old Lyme dozes peacefully among the relics of the past, the widow walks, the white clapboarded homes watched over by the tall spire of the Congregational Church. Its winding roads along the shore and among the hills are flanked by

sedate colonial homes and its chief industry is catering to summer colonists.

The beginnings of the Revolutionary War saw Old Lyme in an uproar. Rev. Stephen Johnson followed the news of the hated Stamp Act with a fiery sermon in which he asked rhetorically, "And why not Tax us for the Light of the Sun, the Air we breathe, and the Ground we are Buried in?" Rhetorical the question may have been, but it stands up today as well as yesterday. Angry patriots guarded the coastline of Old Lyme and after the Boston Tea Party managed to stage one of their own when a peddler bringing a load of English tea to sell was stopped and his stock of tea burned on the spot.

Originally part of Saybrook, and called East Saybrook, Old Lyme (including what is today Lyme and East Lyme) was set off in 1665. Old Lyme took its present name in 1857, two years after separation from Lyme to the north. In so doing Old Lyme retained the most settled part of the larger original town called Lyme. Roads leading to the coast are lined with modest homes, some built as beach cottages and later converted to year-round dwellings.

From early times, Old Lyme has had bad luck with its church. By 1738 three edifices had been put up in succession, and the third one was hit by lightning in 1815. The fourth one faced the green in town and was regarded as a beautiful building architecturally, but in 1907 that church burned to the ground. The present one is an exact copy and is highly regarded as one of the state's most beautiful churches.

*To See and Do: (1)* Florence Griswold House, Lyme St. (Lyme Historical Society–Florence Griswold Association, Inc.). The building is of as much interest as its contents of toys, dolls, doll houses, children's books, costumes, china, and glass. Built in 1817, the large, ornate house is a fine example of Georgian architecture. Designed by Samuel Belcher, it has a large portico supported by four columns, a fanlighted front door made visible from the street by a slight separation of the two middle columns. In 1900 Florence Griswold, daughter of the sea captain who bought it in 1841, turned it into an art center. Artists from far and wide came there to paint and some of their efforts are visible today on the paneling inside. For many years it was known simply as Miss Florence's and artists known and unknown were assured a welcome.

(2) Lyme Art Gallery, Lyme St., next door to the Florence Griswold House. Results of the work of many of Miss Florence's protégés are hung here and seasonal showing of work makes it an active place in the summer.

(3) Rogers Lake offers boating with a launch site (Grassy Hill Rd. off Rte. 51) and fishing. Waterfowl hunting on Great Island and Lord's Cove (see appendix) on the Connecticut River and on Seldon's Island.

(4) Town beaches. Policy varies regarding nonresident use. Check with the town hall.

OLD SAYBROOK *(Middlesex County. Rtes. into: I–95, Exits 66, 67, 68; state 9, 154; 18.3 sq. mi.; 8,468 pop. Other communities or districts: Fenwick, Saybrook Point.)*
The town was named for Viscount Saye and Lord Brooke, two of three "Friends of Warwick" who formed a company to settle and exploit lands here under a patent of James I to the Earl of Warwick. The dream was a rich man's feudal kingdom in the New World, which came to naught. But a fort was built and the original lands of the Saybrook Plantation, which were much more extensive than the present town area, were made safe from Dutch possession. It was a case of the English pushing the Dutch out, really. Adriaen Block, the Dutch explorer, found the land first, and the Dutch traded with Indians as far up the Connecticut River as the Enfield Rapids. The only members of the wealth-seeking English syndicate who came to Old Saybrook were Colonel Fenwick and his wife, Lady Alice. The fort is gone; the oldest houses gone. All that remains of that early time is the grave of Lady Fenwick. She died in childbirth after seven years in the wilderness waiting for the "feudal kingdom" to be realized. Her grave can be seen today in Cypress Cemetery on College St.

From its founding in 1635, Saybrook has been deeply affected by the sea. Its eastern boundary now is the Connecticut River and its many sandy points of land interspaced by inlets and coves are sites of houses dating from the eighteenth century. Big trade and big ships are gone now, but it is a yachtsman's haven and all summer long sail and power boats move on the waters of the river and the Sound. Summer cottages crowding areas on the Sound and a desire for industrial development are threatening the tranquillity of this community, which, of all shore towns along the Sound, has the site of greatest potential.

Old Saybrook boasts of being the original site of Yale College (called the Collegiate School when it was founded in 1701). And it was the site where first commencements were held. The college moved to New Haven in 1716.

*To See and Do: (1)* Older Bushnell House, Boston Post Rd. The house dates from 1679, when it was first constructed as a cape or $1\frac{1}{2}$-story house. At some later time, the roof was raised and a leanto added, turning it into the traditional form called "saltbox." The house is operated as a museum by its private owner and is furnished in late-seventeenth and early-eighteenth-century style.

*(2)* Summer Sightseeing Cruises aboard a refurbished paddle-wheeler go from Saybrook Point upriver on a regularly scheduled basis.

*(3)* Drive along wide Main St. (Rte. 154) and south of the actual business center the broad avenue is lined with old houses. Follow 154 as it becomes College St. to Saybrook Point and the site of the original fort. Note Cypress Cemetery (see above) and proceed on Rte. 154 across the causeway spanning South Cove. A left turn will take you out to Lynde Point Lighthouse. Continuing on 154 takes you along the beach area and so back to the Boston Post Rd.

*(4)* Duck hunting in season on Ragged Rock Creek (see appendix). Freshwater fishing (river) and saltwater fishing on the Sound.

*(5)* Town beaches. Policy varies regarding nonresident use. Check with the town hall.


ORANGE *(New Haven County. Rtes. into: I–95, Exit 41; U.S. 1; state 15, which is the Wilbur Cross Pkwy., 34, 114, 121, 152; 17.6 sq. mi.; 13,524 pop.)*
Named for William of Orange, the present town was part of the

*Opposite*. Troubadours serenade visitors to the American Shakespeare Festival Theater in Stratford. *Far left*. The entire family enjoys skiing at the Powder Ridge ski area just outside of Middlefield center.

*Below left*. Golfers enjoy a day on the green at the Hopmeadow Country Club, Simsbury.

*Below*. In Essex train buffs can enjoy a leisurely steam train ride to Deep River and along the abandoned tracks of the Connecticut Valley Railroad.

*Above.* Plants scale the sides of an old iron furnace in Lime Rock.

*Above right.* Trout fishing in one of Connecticut's many picturesque streams.

*Left.* Car enthusiasts can visit the Lime Rock Races in northwestern Connecticut and trolley buffs can still catch a ride on a trolley *(opposite)* at the Branford Trolley Museum in East Haven.

Centuries are represented in these three buildings. *Opposite.* The water-wheel of the Old Town Mill in New London dates back to 1650. *Upper left.* A marble and granite kaleidoscope of styles, the State Capitol building in Hartford was completed in 1879. *Above.* The Litchfield Congregational Church was built in 1829.

An imposing town hall greets you when you enter
the riverside hamlet of Washington Depot.

The Christian Science church in Ridgefield *(opposite)*, the Congregational
Church in Hampton *(above left)* and the Congregational church in Farmington *(above right)*, all reflect the plain dignity of New England design.

New Haven colony and today is largely a prosperous residential community with industry concentrated along the Boston Post Rd. (U.S. 1). In the early days, soon-to-be-defeated Indians maintained a fort in the Turkey Hill section, and when whites encroached on their outlying lands, the Indians retreated to the area of their fort and it became a de facto reservation for those who survived.

*To See and Do:* Hunting in the Charles E. Wheeler Wildlife Area (see appendix). Fishing in Cedarcrest Boy Scout Pond (inquire locally). Golfing at the Orange Hills Country Club, on Racebrook Rd.

OXFORD *(New Haven County. Rtes. into: 42, 67, 188; 33.0 sq. mi.; 4,480 pop. Other communities: Quaker Farms.)*
Originally part of Derby, the area now comprising Oxford is believed to have been settled as early as 1680 near what is now the community of Quaker Farms. Who the "Quakers" were who gave it the name is not known. Much of the settlement was Tory at the outbreak of the Revolutionary War but by 1781 the Tories either had left or been converted. Separation from Derby into a distinct town came in 1798 and the name derives from Oxford, England.

Early manufacturing took advantage of water power in Oxford. Woolen cloth, barrels for rum shipment from the West Indies, hats, and matches were among early products. Merino sheep from Spain sparked the woolen industry but when electricity replaced waterwheels as a source of power, industry vanished from the Oxford hills. Today it is a suburban town with a rural atmosphere west of New Haven, with an old-fashioned look to its center, where nineteenth-century churches and homes are still viewable.

*To See and Do:* Southford Falls State Park (Rte. 67) offers fishing, hiking, and picnicking. Part of Kettletown State Park, in the southwest corner of town, on the Housatonic River, offers camping, fishing, hiking, and swimming. Hunters can find game in Seymour Fish and Game Club preserve (see appendix). Lake Zoar (see Southbury) offers fishing and boating, with a launch site.

PLAINFIELD *(Windham County. Rtes. into: Connecticut Turnpike, which is also state 52, 12, 14, 14A, 205; 42.7 sq. mi.; 11,957 pop. Other communities: Almyville, Central Village, Moosup, Wauregan.)*

An early town for an inland location in eastern Connecticut, Plainfield was in existence as Quinebaug Plantation in 1671. In 1699 it was granted township status and in 1700 its plantation name (taken from the river forming the western boundary of the town) was changed to the descriptive one of Plainfield. The river plain made good agricultural land at first, and then industry seeking water power crowded the farmers out. Textile mills produced the towns of Central Village, Wauregan, Moosup, and Plainfield itself. Each was the site of a dominant mill during the nineteenth century. Today more diversified industry supports Plainfield and its several communities. These range from metal furniture to chemicals and machine tools.

One of the few early (1815) stone churches is in the center of Plainfield. It replaced a wooden church which was built in 1784. The wooden church blew down one day—hence the sturdier stone. In the same year that the doomed wooden church was built Plainfield Academy got its start. It was the third incorporated school in Connecticut and its liberal heads frequently took in boys whose families were without funds. Eighteen or twenty Chickasaw Indians from Texas were educated at the academy in the mid-nineteenth century and for many years after the school closed the main building was used as a school district office.

*To See and Do: (1)* The mill community of Wauregan, at the junction of Rtes. 12 and 205, gives a good picture of the economic life of mill towns in the nineteenth century. There is large frame mill housing and a mill store on North Chestnut St. plus the mill itself, built of local stone and with quoined corners and twin towers. It still is in use but now houses a variety of diversified local businesses. The mill is on North Walnut St.

*(2)* Pachaug State Forest lies on Rte. 14A, in the southeast corner of the town. The north end of the Pachaug Trail is on Rte. 14A, just east of the road leading into the state forest. In the forest, visitors may enjoy hunting, picnicking, and hiking. North of Almyville

(Rte. 14) fishing may be enjoyed in Moosup Pond and also in the Quinebaug River, which forms the western border of the town. The Quinebaug shores (see appendix) may be hunted in season.

PLAINVILLE *(Hartford County. Rtes. into: I–84; state 10, 72, 177; 9.9 sq. mi.; 16,773 pop.)*
This small town was first settled as part of Farmington in 1657 but did not gain town status until 1869. Its early history, therefore, is bound up with Farmington's. In 1828 Plainville, along with other towns to the north and south of it, looked for tremendous growth and profits from the ill-fated Farmington-New Haven Canal (see Cheshire). What is now the center of Plainville was the channel of the canal, and warehouses, factories, and taverns lined the banks. When the canal failed, Plainville at least managed to retain some industry and grow as a manufacturing town. Today some eighty diversified industries are found in the town, which has shifted away from its former agricultural dependency.

*To See and Do:* Sunset Rock State Park on Ledge Rd., an undeveloped 15-acre site, offers hiking. A still visible part of the ill-fated canal is now Norton Park, 76 acres in extent between South Washington St. and Redstone Hill St.

PLYMOUTH *(Litchfield County. Rtes. into: U.S. 6, 202; state 72, 262; 22.4 sq. mi; 10,321 pop. Other communities: Greystone, Pequabuck, Terryville.)*
Settled in 1728 and named for Plymouth, Massachusetts, in 1795, this combination rural/industrial town named its largest community, Terryville, after Eli Terry, Jr., who bought a small lockmaking business from the first cabinet lockmaker in America, Englishman Stephen Bucknell. With two partners, Terry built the lock industry into what today is the Eagle Lock Company, in continuous operation since 1835. Eli Terry, Sr., was an earlier clockmaker, who worked with Seth Thomas (see Thomaston). He invented the shelf clock and established clockmaking as a major Plymouth industry.

The village of Plymouth, on a high hill in the western part of town, was also the scene of industrious clockmaking. Streams there provided the essential water power. Early-nineteenth-century homes and the Congregational Church reflect the quiet life its citizens have always known.

*To See and Do: (1)* Lock Museum of America, 114 Main St., Terryville. Hundreds of early locks and keys are on display in this unique museum, plus old-lock catalogues and pictures of early lockmakers.

*(2)* Plymouth Museum, opposite the green in Plymouth village. Local history is displayed with furniture and artifacts of the region.

*(3)* Buttermilk Falls, two miles south of Terryville, on Eagle Rd. A thirteen-acre nature reserve encompasses the 86-foot falls, one of the highest in the state. The stream flows through a bed of rock with pot holes worn two or three feet deep by the force of the water or loosened swirling stones. Picnicking permitted.

*(4)* Mattatuck State Forest reaches into the southwest corner of town and Rte. 262 goes through it. Regulated hunting, hiking, and picnicking are available. The Pequabuck Golf Club is available for golfers in the community of Pequabuck.

POMFRET *(Windham County. Rtes. into: U.S. 44; state 97, 101, 169; 40.6 sq. mi.; 2,529 pop. Other communities: Abington, Pomfret Center, Pomfret Landing.)*
The great legend of General Israel Putnam and the wolf still persists in this old, uphill town in northeastern Connecticut. The story of Putnam and the wolf actually overshadows his Revolutionary War exploits, which made him an outstanding Connecticut patriot. Before the war, as a farmer in Pomfret, Israel Putnam battled drought, insects, and long, cold winters trying to make a living on his farm. When a marauding wolf killed scores of his sheep, however, Putnam's temper was strained. He vowed to track the wolf down, which he and several of his neighbors did. The trail lay half across the state and back as the wolf doubled toward its home ground. The animal finally was cornered in a cave. With a growing crowd as word spread, Putnam and his friends tried to smoke the wolf out. That failed. Next, dogs were sent in but they

came out quickly. Putnam ordered one of his slaves in but the slave declined. So Putnam himself crawled down the cave after his friends tied a rescue rope to his feet. He was hauled out too hastily when the neighbors heard the wolf growl inside—and emerged torn and bleeding. Patching himself together, Putnam entered with a gun and shot the wolf. He was hauled out again, stunned by the blast of his musket. A third time he entered and pulled the wolf out by his ears.

The legend spread, embellished by retelling, and his descendants helped keep the legend alive until it entered the folklore of the entire region. In 1920 the Daughters of the American Revolution erected a bronze tablet near the entrance to the wolf den, making the legend official.

Pomfret's first settler was a Captain John Sabin, who bought one hundred acres of a grant for nine pounds. The year was somewhere between 1691 and 1696. Sabin lived in his fortified house and got on remarkably well with the Indians. Next a Benjamin Sitton settled south of Mashamoquet Brook and created an astonishing feudal domain, completely outside the jurisdiction of either town or the Connecticut colony. For years Mashamoquet Plantation was a law unto itself, paying no taxes, raising no troops for the common defense—and tales of lawlessness and bloodshed surrounded it until 1750, when it was made a parish.

Agriculture languished in the nineteenth century and the era of mills and mill towns turned Pomfret, like so many other villages, into a town of industrial slavery as owners employed men for six days a week. Water power brought the mills and the mills brought the industrial slavery. Next, fortune smiled on Pomfret. It became a fashionable place for summer homes of the very rich. Estates were built after the Civil War, on back roads off Rte. 169, bearing such grandiose names as Glen Elsinore, Wyndlawn, Hamlet Lodge, and Ingleside. The owners traveled from their home cities to get to the open countryside from Philadelphia, New York, and Boston. And it was this influx that gives Pomfret much of its present-day appearance. The Pomfret School (preparatory) was established in 1894 and its picture-book buildings and campus, on the west side of Rte. 169, in the village, form the visual ideal of New England private schools: order, wealth, and Spartan country living.

Also in Pomfret is the Rectory School, a long-established private elementary institution. Old houses cluster in the center and face the older roads, while the nineteenth-century estates can still be seen here and there among Pomfret's hills.

*To See and Do: (1)* Putnam's Wolf Den, south of U.S. 44, just east of Abington. A visit here is worth a short side trip—if for no other reason than to keep legends alive (see above). The den lies within Mashamoquet State Park, where extensive facilities can make a day's outing after visiting the den. There are camping facilities, hiking trails, swimming, picnicking, and fishing—all available in the 781-acre area. Golfing is available at the Pomfret Golf Club, in Pomfret Center.

*(2)* Drives along any of Pomfret's back roads and into Abington will show colonial homes and a variety of upland estates and views that make this one of the most delightful of the northeastern towns in the state.

PORTLAND *(Middlesex County. Rtes. into: state 17, 17A, 66; 23.7 sq. mi.; 8,812 pop.)*
This small town changed the face of New York City. Portland brownstone, quarried in many places within its borders, was barged down the Connecticut River, which forms the town's western border, and wound up providing façades for New York socialites' homes. This soft, brown stone no longer is used and it has not worn well. Now, the quarries are closed. The shipbuilding that flourished for a century along the town shore on the Connecticut River has vanished, and the principal visible business in town is gasoline and oil storage. Deep-water dockage on the river makes marine transport favorable to Portland. Yet there was a time when the ships built in Portland sailed for the Orient, for Europe, and South America. Today it is a residential town and its citizens work in Middletown or Hartford.

Job's Pond lies north of Rte. 66, a short distance from the center of Portland. Situated in a glacial kettle, the pond rises and falls mysteriously as much as fifteen feet over a six-month period. It is unaffected by rainfall and, curiously, will rise during dry spells and sink in wet weather. Not surprisingly, its other name is Mystery Lake.

*To See and Do: (1)* Two nineteenth-century brownstone octagonal houses (privately owned), on Rte. 66, a few hundred yards beyond the point where the highway turns south off Main St.

*(2)* Mineral collecting. Rock hounds will delight in searching the abandoned quarries, ledges, outcroppings, and escarpments in the eastern section of the town, for Portland has beryl, garnet, quartz, feldspar, and mica in quantity (see Chapter 4).

*(3)* Fishing in Great Hill Pond, north of Cobalt, and hunting along Hales Brook, along the Connecticut River shore and east of Rte. 17. Hiking, hunting, and fishing in Meshomasic State Forest (6,603 acres), in the northeastern section of town. Hunting in Wangunk Meadows and in the 2,268-acre Portland Farmers Fish and Game Club (see appendix).

PRESTON *(New London County. Rtes. into: 2, 12, 117, 164, 165; 31.3 sq. mi.; 3,850 pop. Other communities: Hallville, Long Society, Poquetanuck, Preston City.)*
There is no center simply called Preston. From some ancient grandiose dream, the center is named Preston City. It is only a small crossroads hamlet but a delightful one and the antithesis of what we feel when the word "city" is mentioned.

The town's naming is obscure but a leading family in early days came from Preston, England, which may provide a clue. From its beginnings in 1687, Preston has been a small, rural community, where farming is the principal activity. West of its small green stands a Baptist church, built in 1818 and spruced up with Greek Revival ornamentation about two decades later. Across from the church is a large eighteenth-century home, formerly Treat's Tavern. North of the church is a fine example of transitional Federal–Greek Revival dwellings. An early blacksmith shop and a unique early town pound complete the nostalgic scene in the village.

Poquetanuck, located in the southern portion of the town, was an early seafaring village and many of its early homes were built and occupied by men of the sea.

Dotted throughout the town are examples of early Connecticut farmhouses. A short drive in any direction will reveal a number of these early dwellings, and along the brooks and small ponds you may still see evidence of stone work and eroded dams and recognize early mill sites.

*To See and Do:* (1) Long Society Church and Early Burial Ground. First established in 1726, the church is surrounded by an interesting old cemetery. Historical exhibits may be viewed in the gallery.

(2) Preston City Blacksmith Shop. Built in 1871, it is a working museum.

(3) Avery Pond and Amos Lake, east of Rte. 164, offer boating with launch sites, and fishing. Hunting in Rose Hill Management Area's 413 acres (see appendix).

PROSPECT *(New Haven County. Rtes. into: 68, 69; 14.3 sq. mi.; 6,543 pop.)*

The town name is descriptive and stems from the fact that at its center on a hilltop great views of the surrounding countryside can be seen. Eastward are the Hanging Hills of Meriden (see Meriden). Sturdily undistinguished, Prospect had a counterfeiter, a far-out religious sect, and a home industry that characterized the town like so many other "one-industry communities" of the nineteenth century.

The local shoemaker, Peter Golkey, had grandiose schemes for getting rich in the eighteenth century. He tunneled a secret underground room off his cellar, set up a furnace, connecting it to the chimney flue of his house. His plan: make Spanish dollars and sell 'em. A snoopy neighbor heard underground thumpings as Peter worked at completing his counterfeit factory and sent for the sheriff. Peter's house seemed empty and they left. But a searcher noticed smoke coming from the chimney and recalled no fires in the fireplaces. They returned. Peter was caught and jailed. But since Peter never made a single dollar he was soon free.

The Perfectionists of Prospect (part of the Congregational membership) believed in *not* keeping the Sabbath. To them, all days were holy (and who shall say them nay?). They also believed men were easily slipped into three categories: unconverted, converted, and those who had undergone a new birth and were thus saved for all time to come. Guess which category they slipped themselves into.

And in the heyday of specialization, friction matches became Prospect's hallmark. Some thirty people in the town worked diligently producing the matches. From that industrial apogee, Prospect subsided to an agricultural community, which it still is, as well as being a home for workers in nearby Waterbury.

*To See and Do: (1)* Prospect Historical Society Building, Center St. (Prospect Historical Society). First a schoolhouse, then a town hall, now a local museum, which displays historical items on home and farm life prior to 1900.

*(2)* Golf can be played at Highland Greens Golf Course, on Cook Rd.


PUTNAM *(Windham County. Rtes. into: U.S. 44; state 12, 21, 52, 171; 20.1 sq. mi.; 8,598 pop. Other communities: Putnam Heights.)* The area now included in the town of Putnam was first settled in 1693 by men from Massachusetts and was considered part of Killingly until, in 1855, it was incorporated and named after General Israel Putnam of Revolutionary War fame. In 1895, the city of Putnam, which occupies the northwest corner of the town and straddles the Quinebaug River, was incorporated.

Original settlers lived first in what is now Putnam Heights (formerly Killingly Hill) and the few eighteenth-century buildings in the town exist here. From Putnam Heights there are fine views out over the Quinebaug River valley to the west.

Like many eastern Connecticut towns, Putnam depended first on water power furnished by the Quinebaug, and it developed rapidly in the nineteenth century into the industrial center of the northeast part of the state. Textiles was its main business and today much of the economy of Putnam has to do with textiles:

curtains, synthetic yarns, buttons, silk, nylon, cotton thread, and sailcloth. But phonograph needles, safety equipment, and motor pumps lend some diversity to the economy. When the textile boom days struck, most of the population moved to what is now the city of Putnam. Today 85 percent of the population lives in the city, which is crowded with stores and shops along Main St., some new and some with nineteenth-century brick façades. The remainder of the township is rural and agriculture is its business.

*To See and Do:* Keach Pond offers fishing in the northeast tip of town, north of U.S. 44.

REDDING *(Fairfield County. Rtes. into: 53, 58, 107; 32.2 sq. mi.; 5,590 pop. Other communities: Georgetown, Redding Ridge, West Redding.)*
As cosy a New England village as you will find anywhere, quiet, content, off the beaten track. The small green in the center basks in afternoon light and all is tranquil. An early settlement, Redding was part of Fairfield and set apart, as they say, in 1767 and named Reading, which became Redding. Such immortality as small communities can claim comes from three sources for Redding. It was the site of a particularly rigorous winter encampment of American forces during the Revolutionary War (see below); it was the last home of Mark Twain; and in 1877 Redding's Reverend John Dickinson discovered a host of new minerals, one of which he named reddingite.

Today many families that have lived in Redding for more than two hundred years, like the Sanford clan, calmly watch city folk move in and out, for it has long been a favorite of escapees from New York City and the narrow steep roads leading over the ridges of the town attract them by such nomenclature as Umpawaug Rd. and Peacable St. Redding Ridge, as its name implies, offers many views from the road, as do other sections of the town. Georgetown is the location of the town's dominant industry: wire-screen production, and Finnish immigrants long ago moved in to work the factory.

*To See and Do: (1)* Israel Putnam Memorial State Park is the site of New England's Valley Forge. On November 14, 1778, Major General Israel Putnam, who commanded what has been described as the entire right wing (nonpolitical) of the American Army, took up winter quarters in Redding in three locations in the town. There were at least two Connecticut brigades, one from New Hampshire, plus a corps of infantry and cavalry. It was a particularly severe winter and poor food, clothing, and general ennui brought some of the troops close to a mutinous state. Some soldiers raided nearby farms and the entire command might have fallen in disarray save for Putnam's determined leadership. There is a museum on the site and remnants of fireplaces, a bakeshop, and powder magazine. Other facilities in the 183-acre park include hiking, fishing, and picnicking. The park is located at the junction of Rtes. 58 and 107.

*(2)* Mark Twain Memorial Library, Redding Rd., in the center. When Mark Twain settled finally in Redding in 1908 and built Stormfield, a grandiose estate with majestic views, he took up the project of starting a library in this small town that he loved. Cajoling publishers and dunning friends for donations, he got the project started. His home burned in 1925, but the library he founded almost single-handedly survives—with a recently dedicated new wing attached to the older building. Many volumes from Twain's library are on display as are several letters written by him.

RIDGEFIELD *(Fairfield County. Rtes. into: U.S. 7; state 33, 35, 102, 116; 35.0 sq. mi.; 18,188 pop. Other communities: Branchville.)*
Proud of its rurality, historic past, and contemporary charm, Ridgefield is probably the least spoiled town in southwestern Connecticut. It was founded in 1708 and incorporated with its descriptive name one year later. Original settlers came from Norwalk and Milford, twenty-eight families in all, and the original grant cost a hundred pounds, the price paid to the local Ramapoo Indians.

During the Revolutionary War, the British, returning from their raid on Danbury to the north (see Danbury), were met and their way was contested by a hastily gathered militia. A barricade was put across the main street and an exchange of fire delayed the British progress. In the brief skirmish that ranged along the ridge in the center of town (the exact location is not known) the British used artillery and one cannonball buried itself in a corner post of the Keeler Tavern, where it can be seen today (see below). The principal street running north and south through the center of Ridgefield is as handsome a thoroughfare as can be found in the state. The roadway is wide and the old houses are well spaced and set back in dignity from the roadway. Most of the houses are late-eighteenth or nineteenth century but it was along this road that first settlers built their homes. The town lay on a turnpike of the early days and several taverns became well known to travelers between New York and Boston; modern versions of these taverns or inns remain and can be enjoyed today.

As though fearing a loss of integrity, the town has managed better than most to control the inroads of unsightly industry. Ridgefield is zoned for light industry only—and that of the "clean" or nonpolluting variety. And more than 10 percent of the town's acreage is forever protected as open space or conservation land. An accurate impression of affluence comes from drives along the main roads and winding hilly back roads of the town.

*To See and Do:* (1) Keeler Tavern, 132 Main St. (Keeler Tavern Preservation Society). Until recently the old tavern (1760) was a private residence. In one corner post of the old building is a cannonball fired from a British gun in the Battle of Ridgefield in 1777. Handcrafts are the specialty on display and for sale in the tavern.

(2) Ridgefield Historical Society Museum, 151 Main St. Features 75,000 books and documents of historical interest.

(3) Aldrich Art Museum, 258 Main St. A museum of contemporary art with outdoor sculpture displayed behind the museum.

(4) Seth Low Pierrepont State Park, east of Rte. 116 in the north-central part of the town. Three hundred and five acres exclusively for hiking. Mamanasco Lake, off Rte. 116 on Mamanasco Rd., in the central section of the town offers boating, with a launch site, and fishing.

ROCKY HILL *(Hartford County. Rtes, into: I–91, Exits 23, 24; state 99; 13.9 sq. mi.; 11,103 pop.)*
Originally Stepney Parish of Wethersfield, the town name came from a singularly rocky hill in the parish when it was incorporated from Wethersfield in 1843. The first important industry in the town was shipbuilding (it was the principal port of its parent town) but now agriculture and the manufacture of castings, bearings, aircraft parts, and electronics support the community.

Today, the center, cluttered by gas stations and drive-in eateries along Rte. 99, gives way in the western part to gently rolling hills and fields where farms still operate.

*To See and Do: (1)* Dinosaur State Park, West St. About 200,000,000 years ago, dinosaurs walked where today's Rocky Hill citizens tread. Hundreds of preserved footprints were discovered by a bulldozer operator, Edward McCarthy, as he was excavating a site for a state building in 1966. The building was then planned for another site and the geologists and paleontologists took over. In the days of the dinosaurs, Rocky Hill was part of a broad flood plain covering central Connecticut. Streams from a range of eastern hills deposited silt and mud in this plain, making it an ideal stamping ground for dinosaurs that wished to be remembered. Today, the thirty-acre state park displays over five hundred preserved footprints in a large exhibit building and an outdoor area is used by visitors to make plaster-of-Paris impressions of the prints.

*(2)* Academy Hall Museum, Old Main St. (Rocky Hill Historical Society). This old school building contains Indian stone, domestic implements, clothes, farming equipment, and antique furniture.

*(3)* For a drive around Rocky Hill, note the Congregational Church, an excellent example of postcolonial architecture built in 1808; the spire is a late addition (center of Rocky Hill). Thomas Danforth House (private), built in 1783. Danforth established the first chain store in the United States with branches as far south as Atlanta, Ga., prior to 1818 (corner of Main and Ferry Sts.). Duke of Cumberland Inn (private), built in 1767. This is a sophisticated brick building for its place and period. It has the mass and elegance of the successful merchant and sea-captain houses found

in Salem and Portsmouth (262 Old Main St.). There are many other colonial houses on Old Main St. worth a look. An interesting way to enter or leave Rocky Hill is by means of the Rocky Hill–Glastonbury Ferry, which operates back and forth across the Connecticut River. It now consists of a tug strapped firmly to a car-bearing barge.

ROXBURY *(Litchfield County. Rtes. into: 67, 199, 317; 26.4 sq. mi.; 1,238 pop. Other communities: Roxbury Falls, Roxbury Station.)*
Being rockier than its parent town, Woodbury, to the east, Roxbury gained its name and individuality in 1796. The rock has been a source of income, as granite has been quarried here from early times and there was a time when many citizens thought silver was going to make them rich. Iron ore on Mine Hill west of the Shepaug River was found as early as 1724 (and old mine works are visible today, if you hike up from the river north of Roxbury Station), and then a German speculator hinted there might be silver too—and he would be only too glad to sell the citizens stock—which he did. He displayed silver-plated metal bars as a convincer and did well enough until the credibility gap widened and the speculator was ridden out of town. End of silver dream? Not quite. As the German was unceremoniously leaving Roxbury a case dropped, and several genuine silver bars fell out of his hastily assembled luggage. In pensive moments, Roxbury citizens may wonder yet.

Beneath a granite monument on the small, triangular green lie the remains of Roxbury's most famous son: Colonel Seth Warner, a favorite of General Washington and a leader in Ethan Allen's roistering troops in Vermont.

Today the small village is as peaceful as ever. There are a number of eighteenth- and nineteenth-century homes along its quiet roads and only a short walk from any point brings a hiker to undisturbed hills and valleys and streams.

*To See and Do:* The Shepaug River offers fishing, and at the southern end of town Roxbury Falls presides over an impressive spill of water as the Shepaug flows south.

SALEM *(New London County. Rtes. into: 11, 82, 85, 354; 29.9 sq. mi.; 1,453 pop.)*

Orramel Whittlesey comes to mind at the mention of Salem, as well as his Music Vale Seminary of the mid-nineteenth century. Established in 1835, it was the first Normal School in the United States to confer a degree in music, and this brought fame to Salem. Orramel Whittlesey taught singing, piano, and other instruments, while composing and publishing songs with such titles as "Harp of the Wild Wind" and "The Dying Soldier of Buena Vista." Sentimental as all the music was, the program of instruction was rigorous and young ladies from the West Indies, the Southern states, and all the way north to Canada, were up and busy at five in the morning. They could not speak to one another during practice hours. Whittlesey's aging and the advent of the Civil War brought an end to the importance of Salem as a music center and all that remains of the bustling boarding school today is the cellar hole south of the village center on Rte. 85. However, his home and barn still remain.

The center of Salem today consists of the Salem Green, on which is located the Town House (1831), formerly an Episcopal church, with country Gothic windows and Doric columns supported by large granite slabs forming the porch. It is now the headquarters of the Salem Historical Society, which is in the process of restoring it for use as a museum. The 1885 Center School house with the small bell tower is now the Grange Hall; the Hearse House, formerly owned by the Congregational Church, is now on town property between the Town House and the Center School and will be restored by the Salem Historical Society, as will the Congregational Church (1838) with a portico treatment similar to the Town House.

Salem still remains a rural area with several large operating dairy and cattle farms, but with some new housing developments in progress. Over fifty eighteenth- and nineteenth-century homes are still standing in the town.

*To See and Do:* Gardner Lake (east of Rte. 354) plus minuscule Minnie Island State Park offers boating (with a launch site on the southwest shore of the lake) and fishing.

SALISBURY *(Litchfield County. Rtes. into: U.S. 44; state 41, 112; 60.5 sq. mi.; 3,573 pop. Other communities: Amesville, Lakeville, Lime Rock, Taconic.)*

A hill town, a lake town, the town of Salisbury enjoys as much scenic beauty as any Connecticut community. The two centers of population, Lakeville and Salisbury village, have attracted enough residents to leave much of the remaining countryside free of human habitation. Salisbury is in the northwest corner of the state and contains the highest point in Connecticut, 2,355-foot Bear Mountain.

To the possible chagrin of Nutmeggers, the town was first settled by Dutch families from New York State in the second decade of the eighteenth century. Perhaps to save face, some historians point to the fact that Major John Talcott led troops against Indians in the region in 1676 during King Philip's War and killed a great many in a fierce fight. In any event, by 1734 one Thomas Lamb was working an iron furnace near Lime Rock. With the discovery of iron in Salisbury, settlers, including the ubiquitous Ethan Allen, flooded into the area, and soon the town was prospering and the glare of blast furnaces was its hallmark.

When the Revolutionary War broke out, Salisbury became "the arsenal of democracy." Cannon, cannonballs, muskets, swords, sabers, shot, and grenades all came from the busy furnaces of Salisbury and the quality of the steel was ranked higher than that of any other domestic or foreign product.

A natural lake atop Mt. Riga and the surrounding land became the center of a colony of Swiss, Swedish, and Latvian workers during the iron days and other furnaces blazed away at Lime Rock and Salisbury village itself. Ethan Allen held joint ownership in a furnace for a time and then went to Vermont at the outbreak of the Revolutionary War to become famous. Salisbury, in fact, has been called the mother of Vermont, since many notable early Vermonters came from the town. The Salisbury names of Chipman, Allen, and Chittenden are cornerstones of Vermont history.

Iron continued to be the dominant industry and Salisbury citizens believed their town would become the "Birmingham (England) of the United States." Alas, four factors killed the dream: depletion of the ore (and of the formerly wooded slopes that supplied fuel for the furnaces); discovery of larger iron deposits in the western lands; the advent of the railroad; and the invention of the Bessemer processing of iron, which allowed lower-grade ores to be reduced more economically. With the ending of the iron industry, Salisbury returned to agriculture and dairy farming, which are the chief industries today, except for residents and visitors who go there because of its natural beauty. Remnants of furnaces can be found in the town (see below), and well-preserved ones still stand in Lime Rock on the east side of Old Furnace Rd. and on Cemetery Rd., west off Mt. Riga Rd.

The foothills of the Berkshires and the Taconics, which characterize the town, are interrupted by lakes and ponds. Like nearly all hill or mountain towns everywhere, Salisbury is replete with legends and myths of odd recluses. In Salisbury's case, there was, and still is, a group of people known as the Raggies, who keep apart; they live in a colony near Mt. Riga, intermarry, and live in poverty.

Today only about fifteen homes of the earliest settlers remain; most of the old houses are of the Federal and Greek-Revival periods during the first half of the nineteenth century. They are handsome buildings, often set on well-kept, spacious estates, making a leisurely drive through Lakeville and Salisbury village or a walk along one of the country roads a pleasure. Of particular interest is the Congregational Church, relatively unchanged from its original form, which was built in 1799–1800 at the corner of the present Rte. U.S. 44 and Library St. in Salisbury. The Palladian windows in the tower and the open cupola give it unique charm. The Hotchkiss School (preparatory) is at the junction of Rtes. 41 and 112.

*To See and Do:* (1) The town hall in Salisbury displays old maps of the nineteenth century.

(2) Mt. Riga State Park, west of Rte. 41, in the northern part of town. Hiking amid furnace ruins in this undeveloped 276-acre park, and hiking also on the Appalachian Trail, which passes through the town, going from southeast (near Amesville) to northwest and on into Massachusetts. Fishing in Wononscopomuc Lake (boat-launch site available on U.S. 44) in Lakeville. There is

also a boat-launch site at Twin Lakes near Taconic, north of U.S. 44. Golf can be played on the Hotchkiss Golf Course.

*(3)* Lime Rock Raceway. Auto races on a nationally known scale.

SCOTLAND *(Windham County. Rtes. into: 14, 97; 18.3 sq. mi.; 1,022 pop.)*
Settled in 1700 and named in 1706 by a homesick Scotsman named Magoon, this small town among the high hills and ridges of eastern Connecticut has had little to disturb it throughout its history. The only recorded incident hinting at a disturbance came in 1746 when a ruckus between separatists and traditionalists within the church broke out. The separatists were thrown out and started their own meeting house, which lasted sixty-seven years. In 1781, Rochambeau's trudging troops camped in Scotland over-night, causing mild excitement. A portrait painter of note, Samuel Waldo, was born in what is now Scotland (it was part of Windham until 1857). He studied and worked in England, South Carolina, and New York City. His work hangs in the Metropolitan Museum and he is represented in the collection of Yale University.

Today Scotland remains a placid crossroads hamlet with a sprinkling of homes along Rtes. 97 and 14 and a small Catholic church facing Rte. 97 where the highways meet at the center.

*To See and Do:* Views and hiking (in Mohegan State Forest, east of Rte. 97, south of the center), and hunting in the Pudding Hill Management Area (see appendix).

SEYMOUR *(New Haven County. Rtes. into: 8, 34, 67, 188, 313; 14.7 sq. mi.; 12,776 pop.)*
A manufacturing town astride the Naugatuck River, Seymour was at first agriculturally oriented, but as early as any Connecticut town, it turned to industry. In 1806 David Humphreys (see Ansonia) introduced a radical plan that put Seymour into the front rank of growing state towns. In 1802 he had imported Merino sheep and a woolen mill was in operation by 1806. Humphreys' mill was the first successful one to be operated in the United

States. More importantly, Humphreys paid attention to the welfare of his workers. He pushed through labor legislation to protect their health and working conditions. He ran schools for them—and even drilled them as militia himself. Result: a booming early economy for the town. Humphreys, in short, used the incentive system long before it occurred to businessmen elsewhere.

The center of Seymour today is crowded by highway interchanges and new and old store and shop architecture typical of industrial Connecticut towns. If a visitor merely enters and leaves the town on Rte. 8 he can get an erroneous impression of the community. The western section of Seymour (try Rte. 188) offers hills and meadows, sloping down toward the banks of the Housatonic River.

Today, Seymour manufactures brass and copper goods, paper products, textiles, telegraph cables, and small tools. Like other Naugatuck Valley towns, the community is made up of skilled workers who came in the waves of nineteenth-century emigration from Europe.

*To See and Do:* Lake Housatonic—actually impounded water of the Housatonic River (Rte. 34)—offers fishing (see Shelton), and there is golf at the Great Hill Country Club, on Great Hill Rd.

SHARON *(Litchfield County. Rtes. into: U.S. 7; state 4, 41, 343, 361; 60.3 sq. mi.; 2,491 pop. Other communities: Ellsworth.)*
Getting away from it all is what people do who go to this beautiful western Connecticut village. On the plateau of the Taconic Mountains, made up of mild rolling hills and broad meadows, it gives all its residents views of distant mountains—particularly Mt. Riga and Bear Mountain to the north (see Salisbury). Settled in 1739 and incorporated that year, Sharon (from the Hebrew meaning "a plain") was the scene of great industrial activity in earlier days, which peaked out in the production of mousetraps. It was the site, in the mid-nineteenth century, of the plant of Andrew Hotchkiss, whose inventions, a rifled projectile and a Hotchkiss gun, were used widely in the Civil War. By the time that

conflict was upon the nation, the plant had removed to Bridgeport.

Following that period of industry, the town gradually subsided into agriculture, which remains today the chief occupation of its citizens. For many years the town has attracted vacationers and summer homes abound in the village and outlying countryside. During its industrial heyday, however, Sharon citizens were wealthy enough to import Italian stone workers who built substantial homes (using a secret mortar process that makes the mortar harder today than the stones themselves) and several "mansions" (either of brick or stone) are still standing in the town: Some of these can be seen on Rte. 41 and in the center on Main St. Of particular interest is the Congregational Church on the west side of the green. The brick structure dates from 1824 and its three similar doorways in the front with their Adamesque fanlights are particularly attractive. The widespread use of brick in Sharon's eighteenth-century homes is the outcome of brick making in the south end of town, begun by Appollos Gay, a local builder.

During the Revolutionary War, Sharon citizens played their part as more than a hundred formed a company to go to the assistance of fellow patriots in Boston. At least four Sharon men were with Ethan Allen in an abortive attempt to invade Canada early in the war. They, along with Allen, were taken prisoner and sent to England, where one of them, Adonijah Maxam, was so emaciated by sickness he was put on display as a representative example of the "Yahoos" who had the temerity to rise up against the king. All were soon transported to Long Island prisons, from which they escaped and returned to fight again.

*To See and Do: (1)* The Gay-Hoyt House, on the green across from the Congregational Church (Sharon Historical Society). Built by Ebeneezer Gay in 1775, this fine example of center-hall, twin-chimney colonial architecture is made of brick, as are so many other colonial houses in Sharon. Its interior is little changed and the original fireplaces set at an angle in front and rear chambers near the end walls of the house are a regional architectural characteristic.

*(2)* Sharon Audubon Center, Rte. 4. A nature center with books and materials in natural history. There are exhibits, guided tours, and lectures.

*(3)* Sharon Playhouse, Rte. 343. Summer-stock theater is staged here from June through Labor Day. There also is an art gallery in the theater building.

*(4)* Housatonic Meadows State Park, U.S. 7. Nearly 450 acres developed to provide camping, fishing, hiking, and picnicking. Housatonic State Forest, north of the park, offers hiking, hunting, and fishing in the Housatonic River. Fishing also in Indian Pond (Rte. 361) and Mudge Pond (north of the village center), which has a boat-launch site on its eastern edge.


SHELTON *(Fairfield County. Rtes. into: 8, 108, 110; 31.4 sq. mi.; 27,165 pop. Other communities: Huntington.)*
The biggest thing to happen in Shelton since its settlement in 1697 was the building of the dam on the Housatonic River in 1877. The river forms the eastern border of the town and the dam brought industry there for the water power. Today the old manufacturing buildings are still in use (though other industrial areas are now developed). The tide of nineteenth-century manufacturing swept away most evidence of the town's early history.

A hint of that history can still be found in the center of Huntington where, on the green, are St. Paul's Episcopal Church and several eighteenth-century buildings.

Rurality is still evident in the rolling countryside to the north and summer cottages line the banks of the Housatonic upriver from the city's center (Rte. 110). The river above the dam is used by Yale boat crews for practice and racing in the spring of each year.


*To See and Do:* Indian Well State Park (Rte. 110, upriver from the center) has 151 acres, much of which lines the river, offering hiking, boating, fishing, swimming, with concessions and shelters. Hunting in the Bridgeport Hydraulic state-leased area (794 acres).

SHERMAN *(Fairfield County. Rtes. into: 37, 39, 55; 23.5 sq. mi.; 1,459 pop.)*
The town was named for Roger Sherman of New Milford, one of the authors of the U.S. Constitution. The land, which included the town, and more, was bought from the Indians in 1729 for sixty-five pounds and in 1737 the first settlers moved in. The backwater nature of the town has often drawn searchers for the "true Yankee character," whatever that may be. Young people left the town in the first years of this century and the old folks remained, lending more mystery to the Yankee myth. In 1926 power companies created Lake Candlewood, where once had stood more than a hundred houses. The northern part of that artificial lake is in Sherman, and today it is a resort area and country retreat for New Yorkers and escapees from other urban centers. It also has helped the economy of small, rural Sherman, which remains, thankfully, off the beaten path among the hills and meadows. And though fame has passed Sherman by, it *does* have a brook that attracts attention. Its name is Naromiyocknowkusunkatankshunk. The brook flows under Rte. 39, a few yards north of Church Rd., which is a mile north of the center. But don't look for signs. As fast as the highway department puts them up, collectors take them down.

*To See and Do:* Lake Candlewood (see New Fairfield for access) offers boating and fishing and there is plenty of mileage for hiking among what are essentially the beginnings of the Berkshire Mountains to the north—take Rte. 39 north and go west on Rte. 55.

SIMSBURY *(Hartford County. Rtes. into: U.S. 202; state 10, 167, 185, 309, 315; 34.5 sq. mi.; 17,475 pop. Other communities: Tariffville, Weatogue, West Simsbury.)*
Before 1650 the first white men to see what is now Simsbury entered the area in search of pine pitch and turpentine-producing trees. They were representatives of His Majesty's Navy, and they needed that pitch to maintain the wooden hulled ships of the day. Their report of the lush land they found brought men from Windsor and Hartford to settle Simsbury, which was incorporated in 1670, and named after Simondsbury, in England. The earliest

families formed communities that exist today in Weatogue, Hopmeadow (now Simsbury Center), and Terry's Plain. In those days Simsbury was a frontier town, and the settlers were forcibly reminded of it just five years after the town was born. King Philip's War—the last desperate attempt of the Indian tribes to throw off the yoke of white domination—broke out. Understandably terrified, Simsbury families fled to the protection of nearby Windsor. When they returned, their homes and everything except what they had carried with them had been burned. With the end of that war, Simsbury began to grow. Sawmills and gristmills, tar- and pitch-producing shops, soap and candle businesses, bullets, and salt peter were among the seventeenth-century activities that supported the town. With the discovery of copper in northeast Simsbury (now East Granby) and the working of iron into steel, two major industries developed, and by the end of the eighteenth-century Simsbury was an "old town."

The nineteenth century saw more technical industries springing up in the town, and one of the earliest was the manufacture of safety fuses for explosives. They are still manufactured there. Most of the town today is residential. The growth of the Hartford area, the need for homes, and the advent of highways combined to give Simsbury its present look. There are more than a few eighteenth- and nineteenth-century homes, some frame construction and some brick. And the Congregational Church, originally built in 1830, is an excellent example of a transitional Federal to Greek-Revival style church with an intricate three-stage tower. The building was nearly lost to a fire in 1965, but the shell was saved and the tower rebuilt with infinite care to recreate the original work. The church is at the junction of Hopmeadow St. (Rte. 10, 202 here) and Rte. 309.

*To See and Do: (1)* Simsbury Historic Center, 800 Hopmeadow St. This cluster of buildings brought together on one pleasant site makes an impressive grouping.

(A) The gambrel-roofed *Elisha Phelps House and Tavern,* built in 1771, is a large combined house and tavern with a ballroom (and original plastered barrel ceiling) on the second floor. Rooms are furnished in the period of the house. On display are Higley coppers, the first copper coins struck in America (1737). They were made with copper from deposits found in East Granby.

(B) *The Meeting House* (a reproduction). The seventeenth-century architecture gives the feel of the earliest time in Simsbury. Before the original one was built in 1683 there was dissension among the congregation as to where the planned meeting house should be located. No one would give in and so, early records report, "Whereas there has been a difference arising amongst us, concerning ye setling the place of ye meeting house; that a settled peace may be obtained amongst us, to ye Glory of God, and the comfort of ourselves and ours, we . . . do so agree and appoint as soon as may be comfortably obtained a day solemnly to meet together, in a solemn manner to cast lots for ye place where ye meeting-house shall stand."

(C) *Ice House.* Winter ice, cut and stored in straw, lasted through the hot summer months in buildings like this. Tools for cutting and moving slabs of ice are inside.

(D) *Phelps Barn.* Craft shops sometimes are held here and antique farm tools and horse harness are on display.

(E) *The Shed.* Attached to the barn, the small ell contains a peddler's cart with tinware, a sample of the kind of cart Yankee peddlers used that made Connecticut famous.

(F) *The Sleigh Shed.* Also attached to the barn, it contains the winter mode of travel in the early days, complete with sleigh bells.

(G) *The Carriage House.* A Victorian building where carriages of the wealthy were kept and shined and horses groomed for the moment the master or mistress sent word a carriage would be "required."

(H) *Fuse Manufacturing Building.* This sandstone building was an early plant for the manufacture of fuses in Simsbury—still filled with operable wooden machinery of the time. A new building attached to the factory contains, on one level, an exhibition hall sometimes used as a craft shop.

(I) *A Little Red Schoolhouse* occupies a far corner of the site and it is furnished as it was when children of years ago attended their lessons within its walls.

(J) *The Hendricks Cottage,* a story and a half gambrel-roofed eighteenth-century home, is another example of early Simsbury houses furnished in the proper period. The kitchen fireplace, seven feet wide, is exceptionally large for stone lintel construction and is the size of the cottage itself.

*(2)* Stratton Brook State Park. Southwest of the center of Simsbury, on Rte. 167, this 148-acre park offers swimming, fishing, hiking, picnicking, and winter sports. Massacoe State Forest (adjoining the park) offers hiking and there is hunting in the Simsbury Management Area, along the Farmington River east of the center (91 acres). McLean Game Refuge of some 2,500 acres is open for hiking and nature study. Fishing in Simsbury Town Park Pond and the Farmington River.

*(3)* Simsbury Farms, Old Farms Rd. Three hundred acres near the center of the town; has pool swimming, an artificial ice rink, tennis courts, picnic areas, children's play areas, outdoor amphitheater, nature trails, and a golf course.


SOMERS *(Tolland County. Rtes. into: 83, 186, 190; 28.7 sq. mi.; 6,893 pop. Other communities: Somersville, North Somers.)*
Originally part of Enfield to the west and Massachusetts, Somers was named after Lord Somers, and was annexed in 1749 by the Connecticut colony. From Rte. 83 coming into the town from the south there are excellent views to the north and west, since this highway runs along the crest of one of the long, undulating ridges that are characteristic of eastern Connecticut. At the junction of Rtes. 190 and 83, the Somers Inn is an interesting building with its columned first- and second-floor porches. The center of Somers stretches along 190 and Somersville to the west is strung out in the same fashion. Mill houses still line the Main St. (190) of Somersville, attesting to its prominence as a mill town in bygone days.

A Shaker colony set up shop in the town and in this early commune conservationist practices first began. In 1866 Elder Omar Pease of the colony planted the first man-sown forest in the United States. The Shakers left in 1915 for Massachusetts and New York and their settlement is now the site of a state prison north of Somersville off Rte. 190.

*To See and Do:* The more than 6,000-acre Shenipsit State Forest stretches into the southeastern corner of the town, south of Rte. 190, and Shenipsit Trail runs through. It's good hiking country. Soapstone Mountain (in the state forest), rising to just over 1,000 feet, offers tremendous views to the industrious walker. There is regulated hunting in the northern portion of town in the 11,800-acre Tolland Area (see appendix). Fishing in Somersville Mill Pond and Lafayette Pond (inquire locally), and golf at Cedar Knob Golf Course, on Billings Rd.

SOUTHBURY *(New Haven County. Rtes. into: I–84; U.S. 6, 202; state 67, 172, 188; 40.9 sq. mi.; 7,852 pop. Other communities: White Oak, South Britain, Southford.)*
Southbury is regarded by many people as their ideal early Connecticut town and it is one of the most beautiful by any standards. Such light industry as exists (screw machine parts, tacks, steel traps, and electrical switching gear) does not intrude on the broad main street (Rtes. U.S. 6, 202, and state 67 conjoined here), which has excellent examples of eighteenth- and nineteenth-century homes on spacious acreage, well kept and well displayed. The land is alternately wide plains and gentle to rugged hills and there is a sense of elevation, of a lot of sky available in the town.

Settled in the seventeenth century by inland-pushing pioneers from Stratford who came up the Housatonic and Pomperaug rivers, it was not a formal town until 1787. Originally it was part of Woodbury. South Britain on Rte. 172 has solved most of its problems by dozing away the years in peace. The church there, built in 1825, is a fine example of late Federal church treatment with three pedimented doors and a three-stage spire giving it a lot of elegance for a small community. Both Southford and White Oak are small communities too. In Southbury is one of the oldest school buildings in the United States. The Bullet Hill School of worn red brick on the west side of Main St. at the junction of Seymour Rd. and Rte. 67 is supposed to have been built in 1778 but some experts believe it antedates the Revolutionary War, which would make it a bit earlier.

*To See and Do: (1)* The Southbury Playhouse, on Oak Tree Rd., offers summer-stock theater.

*(2)* Drive along the principal street (U.S. 6 and 202) of Southbury center, slowly, and take nearly any back road westward toward the Housatonic and Shepaug rivers, or northeast into the hills. It will be worth it. South of the center, a modern condominium complex, Heritage Village, reaches west of the highway covering hundreds of acres.

*(3)* George C. Waldo State Park, on the banks of the Housatonic River, west of Rte. 172, offers 150 undeveloped acres for tramping about. Kettletown State Park, in the southern tip of town, has camping, fishing, swimming, hiking, and picnicking. Hunting in Woodbury-Southbury Rod and Gun Club (see appendix).

SOUTHINGTON *(Hartford County. Rtes. into: I–84; state 10, 66, 120, 229, 322, 364; 36.9 sq. mi.; 30,946 pop. Other communities: Marion, Milldale, Plantsville.)*

Named from South(Farm)ington in 1726, the town became a separate entity in 1779 and was a manufacturing center from the earliest of manufacturing times. Tinware was an early product (1795) and in the early part of the nineteenth century machine-produced tinware became a flourishing industry. Seth Peck patented the machines and today his name persists in the Southington firm of Peck, Stow, & Wilcox—and sheet-metal products are part of their output.

The community of Marion (named from Marion, Georgia) was the site of a plant that first used bolt-threading machinery and put nuts and bolts on a mass-production basis. Plantsville and Milldale were both created by industry and exist today through industrial manufacturing.

Southington's central area is a minor river valley through which the Quinnipiac and Eight Mile rivers flow. Steep north-south running ridges line the eastern border of the town, while rising hills form the western edge of the valley.

Only a few old houses recall Southington's earliest years. The Congregational Church opposite the narrow green was built in 1828 and either is a copy or a duplication of the Hoadley church in

Milford. Whatever its origin, it is an outstanding example of early, well-handled Greek Revival church architecture.

During World War II, when war production was at its peak, Southington plants drew the attention of *The New York Times* with their excellent production record. *The Times* referred to the town as "A Microcosm of America." The accolade was picked up by the Office of War Information and Southington became known throughout the world through pictures and articles published in an attempt to explain America to such (then) friendly powers as the U.S.S.R.

*To See and Do:* Mount Southington Ski Area, north of Marion, off Rte. 322. Winter sports are offered here with a hiking trail leading north among the Farmington Hills. Golfers can have a heyday on three courses: Patton Brook Country Club, on Pattonwood Dr., Pine Valley Golf Course, on Welch Rd., and Southington Country Club, on Savage Rd.

SOUTH WINDSOR *(Hartford County. Rtes. into: U.S. 5; state 30, 174, 194; 28.5 sq. mi.; 15,553 pop. Other communities: East Windsor Hill, Wapping.)*
The town, on the east bank of the Connecticut River, originally was part of East Windsor—which in turn came from Windsor. It consists of gently rolling hills with many level areas. It is and has been for many years a "tobacco town." Raising tobacco has been a principal industry since the seventeenth century. In that time, raids by the warlike Pequots and Narragansetts of Rhode Island kept all but a few hardy settlers on the west side of the Connecticut River in the larger communities. Not until the end of King Philip's War (1675–76) did permanent settlers move in among the friendly Podunk Indians, who had one of Connecticut's largest Indian communities on the Podunk River (which flows under Rte. 30 and U.S. 5 today). Most of the early homes were fortified against Indian attack.

South Windsor is the birthplace of Jonathan Edwards, a Puritan minister widely known as the man who sparked the "Great Awakening" among American church folk and has been called "the greatest interpreter of eighteenth-century Puritanism of New England." Also born here was Oliver Wolcott, signer of the Declaration of Independence and later governor of the state; John Fitch, who invented a workable steamboat (1787) long before Robert Fulton, was a native of the town. And Eli Terry, who applied mass-production methods to clockmaking, thus getting rich while revolutionizing that industry.

During the Revolutionary War a number of noted British and American Tory prisoners were kept in the town. Among them: Governor Franklin of New Jersey (son of Benjamin Franklin) who remained loyal to the crown. He was quartered—and lived in luxury—at the home of Ebeneezer Grant. That house still stands on the west side of Main St., north of Strong Rd. The house has what has often been described as the most handsome doorway of any Connecticut home. General Prescott (captured in Rhode Island) also spent his days of captivity here.

The industrial zone of South Windsor is spread along U.S. 5 and the railroad running south to north through the town. This fortunately spares Main St. and the lateral roads, where more than two dozen noteworthy early private homes are located. They date from the late seventeenth through the mid-nineteenth century. East Windsor Hill, a small community in the northern part of town, has a number of similarly handsome homes.

*To See and Do:* (1) A walk through South Windsor: It's worthwhile to see these Connecticut River houses that have lasted two and three hundred years. Main St. has the majority of them.

(2) The Old Cemetery, Main St. near East Windsor Hill. The Memorial Gate at the entrance is dedicated to Jonathan Edwards, South Windsor's most illustrious son. In the cemetery are graves of soldiers from many colonial wars: Queen Anne's War (1702–13), King George's War (1744–48), and the French and Indian War (1756–63).

(3) Fishing in the Connecticut River (boat-launch site on west side, in Windsor) and the Scantic River, in the northern part of town, crossing U.S. 5. Hunting in the South Windsor Area (see appendix).

SPRAGUE *(New London County. Rtes. into: 97, 138, 207; 13.4 sq. mi.; 2,912 pop. Other communities: Baltic, Hanover, Versailles.)*
The town was named for Governor William Sprague of, surprisingly, Rhode Island. Not because of sentiment, but because in the 1850s the Rhode Islander bought some 300 acres of land and water rights along the Shetucket River, which runs through the town, and began a mill town that was later named Baltic. It brought nineteenth-century prosperity to Sprague, hence the town name. Baltic and Versailles are still redolent of mill days. Rte. 97, entering Baltic from the south, is lined with identical mill houses, and diversified businesses occupy the large stone mill itself on the east bank of the Shetucket River. The old mill in Versailles stands empty, but a new plant downriver hums with activity.

Hanover is a quiet residential community where trim lawns and white houses give an air of leisure to the hamlet. Agriculture still forms part of the livelihood of Sprague, but paperboard manufacture, boxes, woolens, and engraving are town industries.

*To See and Do:* Fishing in the Shetucket River. Hunting in the Sprague Rod and Gun Club Area (see appendix).

STAFFORD *(Tolland County. Rtes. into: 19, 20, 32, 140, 190; 60.8 sq. mi.; 8,680 pop. Other communities: Orcuttville, Stafford Springs [borough of], Staffordville.)*
Long before white men came, Indians bathed in and drank the supposedly beneficial water coming from springs in the town. When the town was laid out and purchased by the General Assembly in 1718 and named Stafford, its springs were known. In 1771, John Adams came to Stafford for the "cure" of the sulfur and iron-water baths, and by the turn of the century it seemed the town would make its economic way by becoming a health resort. A Stafford Springs hotel was built. Hope was that it would rival such watering places as Saratoga Springs in New York. The idea never caught on widely and the town had to revert to woolen-goods manufacture, pearl-button making, and the mining and processing of iron. Iron deposits had been found early (1734) and

the community was a source of arms during the Revolutionary War. Afterward, iron pots and pans were produced and sold.

Today, Stafford Springs, which is the seat of town government, is a typical nineteenth-century industrial town with elaborate late Victorian homes and red brick buildings to proclaim it. Staffordville, built around the button industry, has nineteenth-century homes in a quiet setting. Stafford itself is a mixture of industry and country village with woolen mills supporting its economic existence.

The essentially rolling meadowed and wooded countryside changes in the southeastern part of town (Rte. 190), where Mt. Ochepetuck rises to over 1,200 feet and affords views of over 100 miles in all directions.

*To See and Do: (1)* As a wealthier-than-average nineteenth-century center, Stafford Springs offers excellent examples of late-Victorian domestic architecture, which can be viewed on Rte. 190, going east from the center of town and north on Rte. 19 off Rte. 190.

*(2)* Shenipsit State Forest, reached by going west from Stafford Springs and north on Rte. 32, offers picnicking, hiking, and hunting. The same is true of Nipmuck State Forest, south of Rte. 190 in the eastern part of town. For hardy hikers, the Shenipsit Trail runs through the western edge of town, crossing Rte. 190 2.4 miles west of West Stafford. Fishing may be enjoyed in Stafford Reservoir, which runs along the west side of Rte. 19 north of Staffordville. Fishing also in Crystal Lake east of Rte. 30, 2.5 miles south of West Stafford. There is a boat-launch site half a mile farther south in the town of Ellington.

STAMFORD *(Fairfield County. Rtes. into: I–95, Exits 6 through 9; U.S. 1; state 15, which is the Merritt Pkwy., 104, 137; 38.5 sq. mi.; 108,798 pop. Other communities: Belltown, Glenbrook, High Ridge, Long Ridge, Springdale, Turn of River.)*

Stamford residents boast they have more large corporate headquarters in their city than exist in any U.S. community outside of New York. Known as "Research City," Stamford today has new architecture in business buildings, research laboratories, high-rise apartments—and more are in the planning stage. In many ways Stamford resembles, on a modest scale, New York City itself, and the building boom that has transformed New York's Park Ave., Third Ave., and Sixth Ave. is reflected in Stamford's recent face lifting. Most of the new architecture is pleasing and worth a drive around the city to examine.

The character of Stamford is avowedly high-class industrial and it always has been an industrial community. Inventors like Simon Ingersoll created the friction clutch, the spring scale, and a steam-driven wagon—which was demonstrated as early as 1858. Linus Yale put the town on the industrial map when he invented the first cylinder lock in 1848, revolutionizing the lock industry and giving his company the most commonly known lock name in the world. With the coming of the railroad in 1848, Yale locks were shipped from Stamford in such quantity that the city became known as the place where locks were made. The list of large concerns headquartered in Stamford today includes such well-known corporations as Pitney-Bowes, American Cyanamid, Olin, Xerox, CBS Research Labs, General Electric Credit, and many others.

Little remains today of the seventeenth-century Stamford. The town was settled in 1641 by unhappy Wethersfield families and in 1642 took the name Stamford from the town in Lincolnshire, England. At the time of the French and Indian War, in 1756, Stamford was a settled and growing community and several Stamford men served in British forces—and so prepared themselves for leading troops when the Revolutionary War came. During that war, Stamford was a focal point for supply, training, and encampment of American forces. And being just across the Sound from the British on Long Island, the town felt the danger of invasion which, however, never came. A fort was manned but the worst Stamford faced was periodic raids from British landing parties in search of cattle for food. Tories in Stamford aided and abetted them. Retaliatory raids were launched across the Sound by patriot troops from time to time to keep British raiders off balance. And men of Stamford formed a whaleboat fleet to harass British warships in Long Island Sound.

As a representative commuter town, Stamford has its morning and evening stampedes to and from the railroad station, which clutter the downtown streets. But there is rurality and country living north of the city in Long Ridge and High Ridge, where estates are well kept and serenity reigns.

*To See and Do:* (1) Hoyt Farmhouse, 713 Bedford St. (Stamford Historical Society). Various dates of origin are ascribed to this simple story-and-a-half farmhouse built by a descendant of one of the early settlers of Stamford, Simon Hoyt. The dates of presumed construction range from 1690 to 1750. In any event such simple buildings were common in that sixty-year period and old clay mortar in the chimney and whitewash made from oyster shells speak of the rurality and want of funds, if not the earliest date. The exhibits include seventeenth- and eighteenth-century Americana with farm implements, china, lace, needlework, quilts, dolls, costumes, and household equipment.

(2) Stamford Museum and Nature Center, 39 Scofieldtown Rd., north of Merritt Pkwy. This multifaceted museum is situated on a 100-acre site in the rolling hills north of the center of town. Painting, sculpture, and graphics are exhibited; a children's farm and botanical exhibits are outside the building. There are entomological, geological, mineralogical, and other scientific exhibits. Indian exhibits make up an important part of the displays and there are an astronomical observatory, a planetarium, a zoo, and a theater on the premises.

(3) Bartlett Arboretum, 151 Brookfield Rd. Sixty-two acres of woodlands, ten under cultivation, can be enjoyed along the nature trails.

(4) Boating and fishing can be enjoyed from several marinas located on the Sound and there is a municipal landing ramp at West Beach. Golf may be played at Hubbard Heights (451 Stillwater Rd.) or Sterling Farms (1349 Newfield Ave.) municipal golf courses.

(5) Town beaches. Policy varies regarding nonresident use. Check with the city hall.

STERLING *(Windham County. Rtes. into: 14, 14A, 49; 27.2 sq. mi.; 1,853 pop. Other communities: Ekonk, Oneco, Sterling Hill.)*
The few scattered communities that make up this rural eastern town do little to intrude on the country atmosphere. The name of the town comes from a Voluntown doctor, John Sterling, and the town itself was formerly part of Voluntown. In Oneco (an Indian name) there are factory workers' houses of granite that tell of former industrial activity. Sterling Hill's principal street has a number of older houses and an impressive late-eighteenth-century church (Baptist) with wooden quoined corners. Ekonk's Congregational Church, built in 1858 and set among evergreens, presents a curious problem. The church is on the town line between Sterling and Voluntown. To avoid confusion, a Mooseup address is used—and Mooseup is in the town of Plainfield. To make matters worse, the town line runs smack up the middle of the central aisle. So does the county line. The result is that bridal couples can't stand in the usual position before the altar—else one would be in one county, the other in another. And it wouldn't be legal.

*To See and Do: (1)* Pachaug State Forest spills into southern Sterling along Rte. 49 (see Voluntown) and there is plenty of hiking, fishing, picnicking, and regulated hunting to be enjoyed. There is hunting also available in the Ross Marsh Management Area (see appendix). The Sterling Fire Tower on Ekonk Hill gives widespread panoramic views into Rhode Island. Rte. 49 follows the crest of the hill along its entire length.

STONINGTON *(New London County. Rtes. into: I–95; U.S. 1 and 1A; state 2, 27, 49, 184, 201; 42.7 sq. mi.; 15,940 pop. Other communities: Mystic, Pawcatuck, Wequetequock.)*
Of all Connecticut communities on the coast of Long Island Sound, Stonington tells us most about the sea and the days when Yankee sailors swarmed over the seven seas. Its earliest days, however, go much further back in time than that, as far back as 1637, when the Pequot War raged in the area. Both Massachusetts and Connecticut men were engaged in that struggle and for many years both colonies claimed jurisdiction over the land that is now

Stonington. Little suited to agriculture, stony and so named, infested with rattlesnakes and wolves, the struggling settlers in this wilderness could not even depend on a quiet rest in their graves when life was done. Wolves marauding from the northern hills dug up the bodies. To prevent this, citizens began topping graves with heavy slabs of stone to keep the wolves away. They are called locally wolf stones and some may still be seen in an old cemetery near Wequetequock. Take Greenhaven Rd. south, off U.S. 1, and the first road right, off Greenhaven. The cemetery is on your left.

Stonington men turned naturally to the sea, since the land was so poor. And their feats and ships are part of the legend of the entire country. Most famous among them is Nat Palmer who, as a young man bent on getting ahead, sailed his small sloop *Hero* south with other sealing vessels in 1821. He sailed to Antarctic waters for a catch. While there, the twenty-year-old Palmer searched fogshrouded uncharted seas and rocky islands for a catch and one day was surprised by a Russian squadron of ships under Admiral Bellingshausen. The Russian commander, on a voyage of exploration, granted Palmer the distinction of being the first to discover the Antarctic continent off the shores of what was later named Palmer Land, a long peninsula reaching north below South America. And Palmer, still looking for seals, shrugged the matter off and sailed on in the icy waters looking for a cargo before sailing back to his small New England hometown.

Then there was Edmund Fanning, sailing casually into the Pacific Ocean and discovering what are named the Fanning Islands (a thousand miles south of Hawaii) at the ripe age of eighteen. His brother, Nathaniel Fanning, served in the navy as midshipman under John Paul Jones on the *Bonhomme Richard* when that ship engaged the *Serapis* in that famous sea battle.

Before the Revolutionary War Stonington was known as widely as any New England port. During the Revolution ships sailed regularly from and to Stonington, and the activity of the port prompted a request from the colony for more military and cannon to defend the town against possible British attack. Militia were raised but cannon remained in short supply. Actually only one British attack occurred, when the *H.M.S. Rose* tried to put a supply party ashore. The party was driven off and that was that. The list of

Stonington men in the army is impressive for so small a town. Incomplete though that list may be, it records over three hundred men who served—among them twenty captains, three colonels, a sergeant, chaplain, and many lesser officers and privates.

The War of 1812 brought a little more action to the town (see below) and, following that, the heyday of Stonington shipping began. Seafaring activity grew to such an extent that in the mid-nineteenth century, the federal government built a protective breakwater at a cost of over $34,000 to ensure the safety of the ships. Only when steam displaced sail did the port stop growing. So it remains a sailors' town without the encroachment of iron ships.

In the town of Stonington, but almost a separate entity, is the village of Mystic—which lies on either side of the Mystic River. This puts half of the Mystic community in Stonington and half in neighboring Groton. The split is a source of confusion to strangers but since Mystic was a very real part of Stonington's seafaring history too, it is included here.

During the Revolutionary War the British referred to Mystic, located up the estuary of the Mystic River, as a hornets' nest since privateers under audacious skippers attacked British merchant shipping vigorously. The community became a major shipbuilding center in the early nineteenth century and there was scarcely a family in the village that was not connected with either the sailing or the building of ships. The shipyards of Mystic produced everything from small coastal sloops to large clipper ships, one of which, the *Andrew Jackson*, beat the record of the *Flying Cloud* around the Horn to San Francisco. Today it is still a seafaring place. The small drawbridge on U.S. 1 linking both parts of Mystic is used frequently as yachts and fishing vessels enter or leave the tucked-away safe harbor of the estuary. Here too is Mystic Seaport, a re-creation of a nineteenth-century port and a storehouse of sea history, lore, and legend (see below).

*To See and Do: (1)* Mystic Seaport (Marine Historical Association, Inc.). On Rte. 27 between I–95 and U.S. 1. To see and enjoy all that this burgeoning re-creation of an old port has to offer requires a full day at least. Marine history buffs will have to spend more time and probably they will come away with the dream of retiring in such a place. Moored at the forty-acre site are *The Charles W. Morgan*, one of the last active whalers sent from U.S. ports, and the square-rigger *Joseph Conrad.* Other small vessels representing early types of sail and steam either lie to at the wharves or are displayed in sheds. All phases and trades of ships' maintenance and operation are in the port. Coopers, sailmakers, and smithies ply their trades, answer questions, and are housed in period buildings along cobblestoned streets that give authenticity to the entire scene. Old homes, inns, taverns, churches, and schools are here too.

In more modern buildings collections are housed: ships' figure-heads, models, wheels, pictures, binnacles—the entire apparatus of the sea. A planetarium and slide lecture hall operate for visitors and the library is open to scholars.

*(2)* The center of Stonington, south of U.S. 1 on U.S. 1A. Where Mystic Seaport brought its ships and buildings together to form a village, the older part of Stonington exists pretty much as it always has. Laid out in 1752, and isolated from too much change by its position on a jut of land, the center is well worth a leisurely walk along its narrow streets. If you start on Water St. at Wadawanuck Park in the northern part of town and proceed down Water St. you pass a mixture of late-eighteenth and early-nineteenth-century homes and shops—including the birthplace of Nat Palmer, the Peleg Brown House, dated 1786.

At Cannon Square are two cannon (18 pounders) that have great bearing on Stonington's history. In August 1814, a British fleet of five warships stood off Stonington and demanded the surrender of the town. The Stonington people decided not to. Militia repulsed landing parties and these two guns with their smaller helpmate replied to the guns of the British fleet, which carried 140 guns in all. Stonington casualties amounted to three wounded men. The British reported more than ninety, and one ship, *H.M.S. Despatch*, was severely damaged.

Below Cannon Square near the seaward end of the town stands an old granite lighthouse abutting a granite building. It is the oldest lighthouse in Connecticut. Its original site was higher up on the point, but when it was moved the granite was hauled to the new site and reerected. It served until 1889 when the Watch Hill (R.I.) light went up. Then an oil light was placed on the breakwater and tended in fair weather or foul for twenty-one years. Today the original lighthouse is a museum (Stonington Historical Society). In the museum are Stonington-made firearms, stoneware, early portraits, ship models, whaling gear, Oriental curios, tools, toys, and Indian relics. Cannon and a unique shot-torn sixteen-stripe, sixteen-star U.S. flag on display in the bank across from Cannon Square are reminders of the War of 1812.

Water St. leads eventually to the Point, the outermost spur of land, from which families waved farewell to departing seamen for over a hundred years. Retracing your steps and passing the lighthouse you can walk east on Omega and Hancox Sts. and north, zigzagging, to Main St. Like Water St. it is lined with buildings that speak of the town's history. Back at Wadawanuck Park is the Stonington Library, and behind its high wall, a short way along the west end of Broad St., is an old burying ground where there are early headstones.

*(3)* Whitehall Mansion, Rte. 27, just north of I-95 (Stonington Historical Society). This 1775 house was built on the foundation of an earlier house (1690) and the kitchen of the present building may be that of the seventeenth-century dwelling. Architecturally handsome and tastefully restored, Whitehall is headquarters of the Stonington Historical Society, which maintains a genealogical and historical library on the second floor.

*(4)* Denison Homestead and Denison-Pequotsepos Nature Center, east of Rte. 27, going left off Mistuxet Ave, on to Pequotsepos Rd. This house has been and still is in the ownership of the Denison family since it was built in 1717. It has a unique display. Memorabilia from successive generations of Denisons was stored until attic and barn were full. And when restoration took place rooms were treated in the taste of various eras of the house and the family's history. Thus the house has a colonial kitchen, a Revolutionary era bedroom, a Federal parlor, a Civil War bedroom, and a 1942 living room, which was the year the Homestead became a museum. Much of the furnishing was used by earlier Denisons and the result is three centuries of authenticity.

The Denison-Pequotsepos Nature Center is across the road from the Denison Homestead. The 120-acre area it occupies was part of the original Denison grant. There are hiking trails here for the nature lover.

(5) Saltwater fishing, of course, is available on the Sound and in Wequetequock Cove, Stonington Harbor, and Mystic River. Freshwater fishing can be tried in Godfrey Pond (inquire locally). Hunting is permitted on Barn Island (see appendix). Golf can be played at the Pequot Golf Course (Wheeler Rd.), Stonington Manor Club (U.S. 1), and, in Pawcatuck, the Elmridge Golf Course, on Elmridge Rd.

(6) Town beaches. Policy varies regarding nonresident use. Check with the town hall.


STRATFORD *(Fairfield County. Rtes. into: I–95, Exits 31, 32, 33; U.S. 1; state 108, 110, 113; 18.7 sq. mi.; 49,775 pop.)*
Today an industrial city in the Bridgeport complex along the shores of Long Island Sound, Stratford has few hints of its early origin in 1639. Efforts have been made to recall the late colonial aspects of the settlement, which was named obviously enough from Stratford-on-Avon. It is the home of the American Shakespeare Theatre (see below). In the burgeoning days of aircraft development and manufacture, Stratford was the home of world-famous Sikorsky Aircraft. The Sikorsky Division of United Aircraft still operates there and parts manufacturers for aircraft are numerous. In the last twenty years the town has grown rapidly, although presently its growth rate is leveling off and, late though it may be, attention is being paid to preserving the wetlands along the shore and the Housatonic River estuary, which are the principal geographic features of the city.

During the French and Indian War, British officers quartered here took potshots at the weather cock atop the Episcopal Church, whiling away their time in target practice. That peppered vane can be seen today on the present Christ Church at Broad and Main Sts., built in 1858.

The Revolutionary War history of Stratford is relatively placid, save for some trafficking with the British by somewhat-less-than-loyal businessmen and Tories (some 1,500 bushels of salt obtained illegally from the British were sold at five dollars a bushel to salt-hungry farmers). The expected quota of supplies and arms was raised in Stratford during that war and the traffickers and profiteers were admonished at a town meeting in 1779; bounties were voted to stop the "wicked tribe of monopolizers," as the declaration read.

*To See and Do:* (1) The Captain David Judson House, 967 Academy Hill (Stratford Historical Society). This handsome colonial house (built in 1723 on an older foundation) has an elegant curved pediment doorway with original iron hinges and latch. For architectural buffs, it is a delight. The curved pediment probably influenced the design of similar doorways later in Connecticut Valley towns, such as Glastonbury. Interior restoration as close to original condition as possible is highly successful and a huge fireplace in the cellar was worked by slaves, of which David Judson's son, Abner, had seven, according to his estate inventory in 1775. The slaves lived in the cellar of the house. Furnishings are nearly all "of the period," with a few items of a later time. Also on hand for study is an 800-volume library, cemetery records, family records, wills, deeds, and account books.

(2) American Shakespeare Festival Theatre and Academy, Stratford Ave. at the easterly end. Justifying the town name of Stratford, the theater is attended by some 350,000 people every year. Repertory theater covers the main season, which runs from June through September. Ballets, concerts, and opera are presented in the off-season months by nonprofit organizations.

(3) Waterfowl hunting in season in the 812-acre Charles E. Wheeler Wildlife Area (see appendix).

(4) Town beaches. Policy varies regarding nonresident use. Check with the city hall.

SUFFIELD *(Hartford County. Rtes. into: 75, 159, 187, 190; 43.1 sq. mi.; 8,634 pop. Other communities: West Suffield.)*
Suffield is a quiet country town on the Massachusetts border. The

Connecticut River forms the eastern boundary of the town, which stretches west from the river plain into mild hills. The village is small and peaceful.

In 1674, when Suffield (a contraction of "South Field") was settled, it was part of Massachusetts, but after lengthy bickering about the border, the town was annexed to Connecticut in 1749. Agriculture is and has been its principal industry, although the business of cigar making in the first half of the nineteenth century provided release from dawn-to-dusk farm chores for a time.

*To See and Do:* (1) The Hatheway House, High St. (Antiquarian and Landmarks Society). The original part of the house dates from prior to 1760, when it was owned by Abraham Burbank, who sold it to Oliver Phelps in 1788. Phelps brought a small eighteenth-century building to the house and hooked it onto the south side to serve as an office. In 1795 he added a north wing—one of the most important parts of the presently viewable structure. There is a signed and dated room (very rare). It contains four original French hand-blocked wallpapers and outstanding Adamesque plaster decoration in the English style of the late-eighteenth century. Interior paneling and furnishing reflect the elegance of wealth in that period. Even by today's standards, the entire building—white clapboarded and gambrel roofed—is a country mansion.

(2) The Dr. Alexander King House, South Main St. (Suffield Historical Society). Built in 1764, the austere colonial home has an original porch on its south side with Dr. King's office in a small ell at the rear. A fine corner cupboard in the house and a panel painting over a fireplace are worth noting. Dr. King, an active patriot before and during the Revolution, worked to draft resolutions relative to the Stamp Act. Among his varied activities, the doctor produced saltpeter for gunpowder and his diary reveals the recipe.

(3) A drive through the quiet streets of the village of Suffield will reveal many other fine colonial and later houses, all privately owned and occupied today.

(4) The Suffield Sportsmen's Association allows hunting on its 2,372-acre preserve (see appendix). Fishing is allowed in Congamond Lakes (South, Middle and North ponds), off Rte. 190 at the

Massachusetts border. The Metacomet Trail passes through the western section of town, crossing Rte. 190 just over 2 miles west of West Suffield.

THOMASTON *(Litchfield County. Rtes. into: U.S. 6, 202; state 8, 109, 222, 254; 12.0 sq. mi.; 6,233 pop.)*
The town was named in 1866 for Seth Thomas, who established the most popular name in clocks. As a young man he worked with Eli Terry, Sr. (see Plymouth) and lived in the area then called Plymouth Hollow, west of the Naugatuck River. As his business genius almost created the community, people began referring to Plymouth Hollow as Thomas Town. Today's industries in Thomaston still include a Seth Thomas Division of General Time Corporation, and electronic parts and metal fabrication of many kinds.

Away from the concentration of industry along the Naugatuck River the small town is still rural, and from the hills west of Humaston Hill Rd. good views of the river valley are plentiful.

*To See and Do: (1)* The Thomaston Opera House, Main St. A restored late-nineteenth-century building with the ornateness expected of an opera house of that period offers locally created programs of light opera in the summer season.

*(2)* Historical Museum, Main St., in the old library building. Local artifacts and memorabilia are on display.

*(3)* Black Rock State Park (439 acres), technically in Watertown, lies on the southern border of Thomaston. It offers camping, fishing, swimming, picnicking, and winter sports. Hiking trails are available in Mattatuck State Forest (Rte. 109), as is hunting; and hunting is also permitted in the preserve of the Thomaston Fish and Game Club.

THOMPSON *(Windham County. Rtes. into: 12, 21, 52, 131, 193, 197; 48.7 sq. mi.; 7,580 pop. Other communities: East Thompson, Fabyan, Grosvenor Dale, North Grosvenor Dale, Mechanicsville, Quaddick, Quinebaug, West Thompson, Wilsonville.)*

The green in Thompson, which is the northeasternmost town in the state, was the meeting place of militia from other eastern Connecticut towns when the call to arms came from Lexington, Massachusetts, in 1775. Today no militia disturb the quiet center where the well-kept houses, mostly of early-nineteenth-century days, make it one of the most attractive villages in the state.

In early days, many taverns in Thompson gave shelter to stagecoach passengers after weary hours of travel over the poor roads en route to and from Boston. One of them was a favorite for eloping couples. It was Vernon Stiles's tavern, and he was justice of the peace who looked with favor on eloping couples, unlike other J.P.'s in the vicinity. Word of Stiles's permissiveness got around—and kept him busy.

During the latter half of the nineteenth century Thompson shared in the textile boom, and since three rivers flow through the town (Quinebaug, Five Mile, and French), a number of communities sprang up around major factories. The only one of consequence today is East Thompson, which is known to stock and sport-car racing buffs from coast to coast for its racetrack.

Fort Hill (1.2 miles east of the village, on Quaddick Rd., left on dirt road) is the location of an Indian fort of many years ago. The Nipmucks protected themselves from the raiding Narragansetts in it. According to ancient reports, the enmity of the tribes stemmed from a reason that would interest Julia Child. Invited for a dinner of eels, the Narragansetts complained about the lack of a sauce. A fight broke out and the visiting Narragansetts were nearly wiped out. Hostilities followed, so the fort was built. On that hilltop today a fine, peaceful view can be had of the countryside, with neither an Indian nor an eel in sight.

*To See and Do: (1)* Quaddick State Park (north of Quaddick on Quaddick Rd.) offers hunting, boating, fishing, picnicking, and swimming. Hiking in Quaddick State Forest (Baker Rd.). Boating (launch site west of Sand Dam Rd.) and fishing at Little Pond, above East Thompson on Rte. 193.

*(2)* East Thompson Raceway. Stock and sports-car racing in season at East Thompson.

TOLLAND *(Tolland County. Rtes. into: I–86, Exits 99, 100; state 30, 31, 74; 40.4 sq. mi.; 7,857 pop.)*
Urban sprawl apparently affected citizens of Windsor as early as 1715, when some of them hiked east into "real country" and bought what is now Tolland from the bewildered Indians for what today amounts to $2,500. The town name is from Tolland, in Somerset, England, whence came one of the chief founders, Roger Wolcott. The principal occupation is and has always been agriculture. The long, narrow green is bordered by many eighteenth-and nineteenth-century homes. The Congregational Church dates from 1838 and Clough's store, across the green, is an attractive, restored building.

*To See and Do:* *(1)* Benton Homestead, Metcalf Rd. (Tolland Historical Society). This very early Cape Cod house, believed to have been built in 1720, has furnishings of the period. Other early homes can be seen on Tolland St.

*(2)* Tolland State Jail, on the green. Built in 1856, the jail now has a small museum with memorabilia of the town and some Indian artifacts. Several of the old cells are intact and can be visited.

*(3)* Hunting in Tolland Shooting Grounds (see appendix) and Nye Holman State Forest (Old Stafford Rd., north from the center), where hiking and fishing can also be enjoyed.

TORRINGTON *(Litchfield County. Rtes. into: 4, 8, 25, 183, 272; 40.0 sq. mi.; 31,952 pop. Other communities: Burrville, Drakeville, Torringford, West Torrington.)*
The largest community in Litchfield County, Torrington is also the industrial center of the region. Situated near the junction of the east and west branches of the Naugatuck River, the town was severely damaged in the flooding of 1955, caused by torrential rains from hurricanes.

First settlers began arriving in 1737. In 1738 the name Torrington (from a town in Devonshire) was approved; incorporation came in 1740. It was chartered as a city in 1923. Much of the terrain of Torrington is flat, being on the river plain, and the region was called Mast Swamp before 1740 because of the tall, straight timber growing there, which was used for ships' masts.

Industry grew with the advent of the nineteenth century and, like many other towns, Torrington became known for a particular business, the business of turning out brass products. Shell casings, brass kettles, and many other items came from the mills in town. Swiss metal workers brought their skills to bear on the industry in the mid-nineteenth century. Among the other industries dairy products have been important, and in 1856 a young man, Gail Borden, developed the process of canning condensed milk. His process, used in the Civil War to provide milk for Union soldiers, grew to become a national industry and his name, a household phrase.

During the Revolutionary War, Torrington's population of 843 supplied two companies totaling 169 men—every able-bodied man over twenty in the town. And in 1800, one man born in Torrington was to have a profound effect on a later war. John Brown, son of Owen and Ruth Brown, began his long and stormy abolitionist career here.

*To See and Do: (1)* Torrington Historical Society, 192 Main St. Displays cover the industrial and social history of Torrington from 1750 to the present.

*(2)* The Turner Museum, Torrington Library, 12 Daycoeton Place. A general museum exhibiting items of local history, antique glass, and dolls.

*(3)* Indian Lookout, off Mountain Rd. in West Torrington, Rte. 4. A sixty-acre display of June-blooming mountain laurel, the state flower.

*(4)* Burr Pond State Park, west of Rte. 8, in the northern part of town. The 436-acre park offers boating, camping, fishing, hiking, picnicking, swimming, and winter sports. Hall Meadow State Park, Rte. 272, in the northwest corner of the town, has 678 acres and offers fishing, hiking, picnicking, swimming, and winter sports. Paugnut State Forest (1,600 acres), just south of Burr Pond Park, offers hiking and hunting. Hunting can also be enjoyed in the 4,600-acre Torrington Fish and Game Club (see appendix). Golf is available at the Eastlawn Country Club, on Torrington West St.

TRUMBULL *(Fairfield County. Rtes. into: Merritt Pkwy., which is also state 15, Exits 49, 50, 51, 52; state 25, 108, 111, 127; 23.5 sq. mi.; 31,394 pop. Other communities: Long Hill.)*
Settled first in the 1670s and called North Stratford, the town was incorporated from Stratford in 1797 and named for Governor Jonathan Trumbull (see Lebanon). Today it is a crowded town which serves as a residential suburb of the Bridgeport-Stratford industrial area to the south—and as might be expected, its principal industry is the buying and selling of homes; in short, real estate.

Trumbull's most famous native son was Benjamin Silliman (1779–1864). A Yale graduate, he made the first geological survey in the United States, taught at Yale, and conceived, produced, and edited the *American Journal of Science.*

*To See and Do:* Hunting in the Bridgeport Hydraulic Shooting Area's 794 acres (see appendix). Less violent recreation is available in Trumbull's Old Mine Park (Old Mine Rd., east off Broadway) and Indian Ledge Park (Whitney Ave., east off Rte. 25).

UNION *(Tolland County. Rtes. into: I–86, Exits 104, 105, 106; state 171, 190, 191; 29.9 sq. mi.; 443 pop.)*
Union has two records to its credit: least densely populated town in the state and smallest number of people. The town is mostly rolling wooded hills where the outdoor life can be enjoyed. It was named from the "union" of land from other towns in 1727.

*To See and Do:* Bigelow Hollow State Park, with 518 acres (Rte. 197), offers boating, fishing, picnicking, and hiking. Regulated hunting is available in Yale Forest (see appendix), in the southern part of town, and hiking and fishing are available in Nipmuck State Forest, on Rte. 190 (7,863 acres).

VERNON *(Tolland County. Rtes. into: I–86, Exits 95 through 98; state 30, 31, 74, 83; 18.6 sq. mi.; 27,237 pop. Other communities: Rockville, Talcottville.)*

The town is thought to derive its name from Washington's home, Mt. Vernon. It was first settled by one Samuel Grant in 1726, when he traded his home and lands in Windsor for five hundred pure wilderness acres. On busy highways, Vernon and its other communities Rockville and Talcottville carry on a good deal of manufacturing, which ranges from military equipment to baseballs. Several nineteenth-century industries remain, one being an envelope factory and others dealing with the production and dyeing of textiles. So far as is known, Vernon's most famous foreign visitor was General Lafayette, who stayed overnight on his tour of the United States in 1824.

*To See and Do:* Hunting is allowed in the 1,800-acre Tolland Area (see appendix). Fishing can be enjoyed in Tankerhoosen Lake, Walker's Reservoir (East), Crystal Lake, and Bolton Lakes (inquire locally).

VOLUNTOWN *(New London County. Rtes. into: 49, 138, 165; 39.7 sq. mi.; 1,452 pop.)*
Named for and granted to volunteers who helped in the war with the Narragansett Indians in 1708, the town today has proportionately more state forest land than any in the state. It had a brief spurt of industry in the manufacture of cotton thread, but with the collapse of the New England textile industry, it sank into rural quietude, where it now remains.

*To See and Do:* Pachaug State Forest, some 22,000 acres of it, offers hiking on the Pachaug Trail, which crosses Rte. 49 north of the village center, and elsewhere, as well as hunting, camping, picnicking, and fishing. Fishing is also available in Beach Pond (north of Rte. 165 at the R.I. line), Beachdale Pond (on the west side of Rte. 49 at Rte. 165), Green Falls Reservoir (south of Rte. 138 on R.I. border)—all with launch sites—and Hodge Pond, which is just 3 miles south of the center, on Rte. 49.

WALLINGFORD *(New Haven County. Rtes. into: I-91, Exits 13, 14, 15; U.S. 5; state 15, which is the Wilbur Cross Pkwy. here, 68, 71,*

150; 39.8 sq. mi.; 35,714 pop. Other communities: East Wallingford, Quinnipiac, Yalesville.)

Like Meriden, its larger neighbor town to the north, Wallingford is known for the production of silverware. The communities of Quinnipiac and Yalesville in the town have many old companies working in the semiprecious metal. It all began with a Robert Wallace in 1835, who set up a Britannia ware shop. There are, of course, other industries in the town. Steel, plastics, and hardware are produced here, and the eastern farms, up on the eastern slopes of the Quinnipiac River valley, produce, as they have for years, fruit, flowers, shrubs, and garden crops.

Originally part of New Haven, the land that is now Wallingford was the "second purchase" by the founders of the parent colony. It was named a separate town in 1670 and its early inhabitants have passed on their feelings about that wilderness in a quotation now inscribed on a plaque on the Nehemiah Royce House (1672) on North Main St. Part of the inscription reads, "The rest of the state was wilderness. The enemies were the Indians, the wolves and bears, and the French, the Dutch and the Devil."

In 1675, when King Philip's War disturbed the settlers, several Wallingford homes were fortified for protection and the inhabitants of the town had fair reason to be fearful. During the Revolutionary War, Wallingford was a staunch supporter of the patriots. Tories were tongue-lashed in resolutions while goods, bounties, and supplies were raised for the patriot soldiers and the town gave serious consideration to the Articles of Confederation as a form of national government when the war was over.

*To See and Do: (1)* The Parsons House, 180 South Main St. (Wallingford Historical Society). Built in 1759, this twin-chimney gambrel-roofed house displays antique furniture in two rooms devoted respectively to the eighteenth and nineteenth centuries. One room is filled with Civil War relics, one with small farm tools, and another with firearms. Also on display are costumes, silver, pewter, musical instruments, and old school books. There is also a 200-volume library of old publications and documents.

The house was built for Samuel Parsons and was once a tavern on a post route for coaches jolting between New York and Boston.

*(2)* Choate School. The large campus "begins" at the corner of

Elm and Christian Sts. It is a large preparatory school and among its many illustrious graduates was the late President John F. Kennedy. A walk about the campus is worthwhile as there are a number of distinguished buildings ranging from colonial houses to the Andrew Mellon Library. The extent of the campus gives it the air of a small college.

(3) North Farms Reservoir has a boat-launching site and fishing is available there just north of Rte. 68 (take Exit 15, I–91). Wharton Brook State Park (Exit 13, I–91) offers fishing, hiking, picnicking, swimming, and winter sports. Trimountain State Park, between Rtes. 17 and 68 on the eastern border of town, offers hiking. It contains the Blue Trail Shooting Range, where rifle and pistol may be exercised. Hunting on 1,712 acres in the Wallingford Rod and Gun Club's preserve (see appendix).

(4) Oakdale Musical Theater. Summer stock in theater-in-the-round.


WARREN (Litchfield County. Rtes. into: 45, 341; 28.0 sq. mi.; 827 pop.)
Settled well before the Revolutionary War, in 1737, as part of Kent, Warren was first called East Greenwich. When it was incorporated in 1786 it was renamed Warren in honor of a Revolutionary War hero, General Joseph Warren. Set high in hills, which are the foothills of the Berkshires, in western Connecticut, the town is rural, and holds something of a Puritan frugality in its houses and farms. The Congregational Church, completed in 1820, has seen changes but its sturdy country form remains.

For its size and its air of prudent restraint, Warren has produced more than a few notables. Six natives were officers in the Revolutionary War and some fifteen ministers came from the town. Many went west in the early years of the nineteenth century and rose to become presidents of colleges. One, Charles G. Finney, was president of Oberlin College from 1851 to 1866—after serving as professor of theology there for sixteen years.

Warren, in its quietude, was the scene of a rebirth of the custom of bell ringing on the Fourth of July. In 1963 two residents of the town reinstituted the custom that heralded the birth of the country with the ringing of the Liberty Bell in Philadelphia. Since then it has spread and is becoming more and more common in celebrating our independence.

*To See and Do: (1)* Old Brick Schoolhouse, Brick School Rd., off Rte. 45 (Warren Historical Society). As a producer of ministers and college educators, Warren may hold the record on a per capita basis. And the source of this scholarship may well have started in this schoolhouse, which dates, some say, from 1784. It was in operation until 1940. Closed then, it stood disused until 1962, when Mr. Frank Reinhold bought the school and began renovation at his own expense. He then gave it to the town and the historical society. Furnished with antiques, the old schoolhouse still serves to educate those who stop by.

*(2)* Above All State Park, off Rte. 45, has thirty-one acres atop a hill where the views and sense of height produced the name. The hike to those views is worthwhile. Kent Falls State Park, which is partially in Warren (275 acres), lies west of Rte. 45, in the northern section of town, and offers camping, hiking, fishing, and picnicking. Lake Waramaug, on the southern edge of town and on Rte. 45, has swimming, boating, and fishing in Waramaug State Park, at the northwestern end of the lake.


WASHINGTON *(Litchfield County. Rtes. into: 25, 45, 47, 109, 199; 38.7 sq. mi.; 3,121 pop. Other communities: Marble Dale, New Preston, Washington Depot, Woodville.)*
When you get to Washington, just north of the junction of Rtes. 47 and 199, you will come upon a village center as clean and white and green and crisp as any in Connecticut. Around such greens, legends that created the mythical New England were born. And at least half the United States today moons over that heritage. The first meeting house of Congregationalists was built in 1742—a rude log structure. A more elaborate (vanity of vanities?) meeting house was built in 1754 and it burned (all is vanity) in 1799. In 1801, on Thanksgiving Day, the first service was held in the present Federal-style church. Fluted pilasters flanking the main entrance, quoined corners, a delicate Palladian window, and the modillions

ornamenting both the portico and main pediments lend period elaboration to the country meeting house. The rather heavy porch was a Greek influence of a few decades later.

The houses at the center all are well kept and trim so that an air of affluence gives the green a storybook atmosphere. Mingling with private homes are the excellently maintained buildings of The Gunnery School—a name not derived from firearms, but from Frederick W. Gunn, who founded the school in 1830. A rather bizarre educator, he believed that physical, social, and moral development was as important as intellectual skill. It is today a well-known preparatory school where emphasis still is placed on more than the intellectual accomplishment.

Washington Depot and Marble Dale are descriptive names for two of the town's other communities. The railroad and depot are gone, but Washington Depot today is the shopping hub of the affluent town. Marble Dale, where marble was quarried, is a small community stretching along Rte. 25 in the southern part of town.

During the Revolutionary War citizens of the town (then a part of Woodbury) were zealous patriots, many of whom met in a house of the town to discuss how to rid the community of hated Tories. One result of this patriotism was the petition to become a separate town named after General Washington in 1779. Thus it became the first town in the United States to be named for the general.

New Preston was named by the first settler there, who was William Cogswell of the eastern town named Preston. Large landowner, and ardent patriot during the Revolution, he became a major and left his supremely efficient wife, Anna, to raise the children, manage the two thousand acres, and run the home as a tavern while he was away fighting the redcoats. On one reported occasion, Anna Cogswell served breakfast in the tavern to three hundred Continental soldiers.

*To See and Do: (1)* Gunn Memorial Library Historical Museum, Wykeham Rd. (The Gunnery School). Housed in a 1780 structure, the museum has letters of General George Washington and of Thomas Jefferson, plus artifacts of the Revolutionary and Civil wars, and World War I. From the Far West there came a gift of artifacts from the Oglala Sioux of the Dakotas. There also are Connecticut Indian materials, a doll collection, and portraits.

*(2)* Lake Waramaug. Located on the northwestern border of the town, this resort lake has many private homes and cottages surrounding it, and many boats, fishermen, and swimmers in and on it. The 114-acre Mt. Bushnell State Park offers hiking to the west of the lake shore. Lake Waramaug State Park, on the northwest edge of the lake, offers camping, hiking, and swimming, while Mt. Tom State Park, south of Rte. 25, east of Woodville, (223 acres) offers boating, with a launch site, fishing, picnicking, swimming, and hiking.

WATERBURY *(New Haven County. Rtes. into: I–84, Exits 18 through 21; state 8, 64, 69, 73, 262; 28.8 sq. mi.; 108,033 pop.)*
Steep, hilly, rocky ground on either side of the Naugatuck River made the earliest settlers in 1674 wary of overpopulating the community. Wresting a living from the inhospitable soil prompted the first pioneers to limit their group to thirty families. Its original name was Mattatuck, which means badly wooded place—so even the Indians were aware of the problems. For at least three decades there was no growth in the town and as early as 1750 the citizens turned to manufacture to support themselves.

Not until 1840 did the character of the town as an industrial center begin to emerge. The production and development of brass products became that character. Today Waterbury produces brass products known throughout the world. Many nonferrous metallurgical discoveries were made here as the infant industry grew to gianthood. Everything from buttons to shell casings are part of Waterbury's output.

Clock and watch making also got an early start here. Robert H. Ingersoll's famous dollar watch made a fortune for him and took watches from gentlemen's vests and put them in everyone's overall pockets. It is reported that Ingersoll marketed as many as five million watches a year for many years.

Architecturally, Waterbury is noted for several monumental works by Cass Gilbert, an early-twentieth-century architect of note. His trademark, so to speak, was a combination of white marble and red brick. The Municipal Building (Grand and Field Sts.) is an outstanding example. Others by Gilbert's architectural firm are the Chase Building, facing the Municipal Building, and the Waterbury National Bank, on the southeast corner of Grand and Field Sts.

St. Margaret's School for Girls on Chase Pkwy. offers a campus of tree-shaded quiet in the busy city.

The first settlers built homes in what is now the center of the city and no evidence, save the green, remains of those times as industrial development pushed the artifacts of history into oblivion.

*To See and Do:* *(1)* Mattatuck Museum, 119 West Main St., on the south side of the green (Mattatuck Historical Society). A building dedicated to history of the town and region includes Indian artifacts, furnished period rooms, paintings by Connecticut artists, and an industrial section. A Junior museum in the building displays sculpture and jewelry from many countries and has also a small apothecary shop and post office of olden times.

*(2)* Holy Land—U.S.A., Pine Hill. A miniature replica of Bethlehem with nearly two hundred model buildings faithfully reproducing Christ's birthplace. A lighted cross marks the village the year round.

*(3)* Hamilton Park, East Main St. Rose gardens flourish here during the seasonal months.

*(4)* Fishing is allowed in the Hancock Brook Flood Control Pool (inquire locally) and golfers can swing at the East Mountain Golf Course, on East Mountain Rd., or the Western Hills Golf Course on Park Rd.


WATERFORD *(New London County. Rtes. into: I–95, Exit 77; U.S. 1, which is coincident with I–95, U.S. 1A; Connecticut Turnpike, which is state 52, also 32, 85, 156, 213; 36.7 sq. mi.; 17,227 pop. Other communities: Pleasure Beach, Quaker Hill.)*
Ranging from seaside resort in character along part of its Sound frontage to open meadows and woods in the north, Waterford was originally part of New London and became a separate town in

1801. Its history, however, goes back to the seventeenth century, when first settlers came to the area now included in the town. Fishing, trade, and agriculture were its mainstays and at what today (as yesterday) is called Millstone Point (south of Rte. 156, on the edge of Niantic Bay) is a granite quarry. Formerly owned by a Gardiner of Plum Island, N.Y., across Long Island Sound, it produced millstones exclusively for many years, then it was leased and large granite chunks from this quarry became a part of many forts built in the United States.

The town today is largely a suburb of New London. There is little industry except for catering to summer people and the generating of electricity in one of Connecticut's atomic generating plants.

*To See and Do:* (1) Harkness Memorial State Park, Rte. 213. Fully half of this 231-acre park is dedicated to the care of handicapped children as was the wish of Edward S. and Mary Stillman Harkness, whose summer estate this was. Their 42-room Italianate mansion is set amid extensive gardens that can be enjoyed by the public. Inside the mansion are displays of the remarkable work of Rex Brasher, Brooklyn-born artist, who lived and worked most of his life in Kent, Connecticut. His aim was to paint as many species of birds found in North America as he could. He released none of the paintings until he was 51. His 874 watercolors containing "portraits" of more than 1,000 species were exhibited then and nine years later a twelve-volume work titled *Birds and Trees of North America* was issued in a limited edition. The state of Connecticut bought the entire collection and they are on exhibition in the Harkness Mansion. Limited space for display restricts the watercolors on view to 180 at a time. These are changed periodically.

(2) The Eugene O'Neil Memorial Theatre, at the town beach, Rte. 213. The theater, which is an important showcase for new playwrights, seasonally has performances that can be attended.

(3) Waterford Shooting Grounds offers hunting on 1,125 acres (see appendix).

(4) Town beaches. Policy varies regarding nonresident use. Check with the town hall.

WATERTOWN *(Litchfield County. Rtes. into: U.S. 6, 202; state 8, 63, 73, 132; 29.8 sq. mi.; 18,610 pop. Other communties: Oakville.)* This industrial town, fortunately, has a center that doesn't reflect that fact. The green has several late-eighteenth-century buildings, dozing tranquilly, and the Ivy League Taft School's brick buildings on Woodbury Rd. add dignity to the scene. Yet Watertown exists on industry. Plastics, synthetic fabrics, ferrous and nonferrous metal products, and watchmaking are the backbone today. In earlier times hat making and stock breeding, plus agriculture and early clock manufacture, were key industries.

Watertown was the home of the legendary James Bishop, a farmer and tavern owner who rivals P. T. Barnum, at least on the farm circuit. He'd swear to cut his 50-acre hayfield in one day, hire several score of mowers, hand out scythes, and when the sun showed over the eastern hills, he'd blow the horn that started the show. Almost continuous meals, cider and rum drinking, and exhortation did the job. By sundown the entire field was mown with haycocks stacked neatly. On another occasion he swore to take his entire hay crop in one wagonload to New Haven. Bridges were strengthened, a building moved, and trees were cut down for the enormous wagon he built. Twenty-four oxen were hitched to the huge vehicle and, with streamers flying and a band playing on the top of the enormous load, he made his way to New Haven where, of course, he was greeted by a cheering crowd. He's probably the only man who had fun farming in those days.

Out from the town's center and industrial area, country still quickly takes over and the ponds and hills give no hint of urban problems.

*To See and Do:* (1) Watertown Museum, 22 DeForest St. (Watertown Historical Society). A general museum with artifacts and exhibits pertinent to the region and the state.

(2) Black Rock State Park, west of U.S. 6, 202 north of center. There are 439 acres including Black Rock Pond that offer camping, hiking, picnicking, swimming, fishing, and winter sports. Fishing is also available in Winnemaug Lake, out Hamilton Ave., southwest of the center, and in the Black Rock Flood Control Pool (inquire

locally). Mattatuck State Forest offers hunting and hiking. Going north on U.S. 6 and 202 you go through the forest.

**WESTBROOK** *(Middlesex County. Rtes. into: I–95, Exits 64, 65; U.S. 1; state 145, 153, 166; 16.2 sq. mi.; 3,820 pop.)*
This shore town was originally part of Old Saybrook. Boats and beaches are its chief attractions. The shore plain slopes gradually to mild hills in the northern part of town. U.S. 1 (the Boston Post Rd.) clutters the small business and shopping center where Rte. 153 joins U.S. 1. Here also is the Congregational Church and a newly renovated town hall in the New England tradition.

Westbrook's most distinguished citizen, David Bushnell, was a prophet without honor in his home town. Despite criticism and ridicule, he invented the submarine and devised a method of exploding gunpowder under water (where its force produced tremendous and potentially destructive water pressures). He built a small one-man powered submarine, the *Turtle,* and was invited to try his contraption out during the Revolutionary War, but an attempt to sink the British flagship *Eagle* in New York harbor failed. So also did similar attempts in Boston Harbor and the Delaware River. Discouraged, David Bushnell migrated to Georgia and under the name of Dr. Bush spent the remainder of his life there.

*To See and Do: (1)* Fishing and boating (rentals on U.S. 1.) on Long Island Sound can be enjoyed from Westbrook.
*(2)* Town beaches. Policy varies regarding nonresident use. Check with the town hall.

**WEST HARTFORD** *(Hartford County. Rtes. into: I–84, Exits 40 through 44; U.S. 6, which is concurrent with I–84 here, U.S. 44; state 4, 71, 173, 176, 185, 189, 218; 22.2 sq. mi.; 68,031 pop. Other communities: Elmwood.)*
Historically and currently West Hartford is associated with its parent town of Hartford. Known in the seventeenth century as the

West Division, the town had its share of early settlers, and originally was an agricultural community. Gristmills, sawmills, and pottery works in the eighteenth century began to industrialize the town. Today it is a much-sought-after residence, with industry confined to the southeastern corner. The eastern town line separating West Hartford from Hartford is blurred and a visitor driving to the town from the center of the capital city would have difficulty knowing just when he entered West Hartford. Farmington Avenue, Asylum Avenue, and Albany Avenue are principal east-west thoroughfares, and beyond the large business buildings, the streets become all residential, with, here and there, apartment buildings rising among the houses. West Hartford is the location of St. Joseph's College, Hartford College (two-year women's), the University of Hartford, the University of Connecticut Law School, and the School of Social Work. All of the above colleges are on Asylum Ave. except the University of Hartford, which is on Bloomfield Ave.

The crowded impression of the eastern edge of town gives way in the west to rapidly rising highlands that culminate in Avon Mountain and many acres of unoccupied land.

The history of the town during the Revolutionary War coincides with that of Hartford, since West Hartford was not a separate entity until 1854. British prisoners from the capture of Fort Ticonderoga were quartered in West Hartford for a time, and the legend of Moses Goodman lingers. In the winter of 1777, when General Washington was suffering through Valley Forge with his troops and the war was at a low ebb, patriots in and around West Hartford donated $30,000 in cash, which Goodman put in his saddlebags and rode south. He arrived safely across the hundreds of miles of wilderness and delivered the cash to the government— a substantial help to the patriot cause.

*To See and Do: (1)* The Noah Webster House, 222 South Main St. (Noah Webster Foundation). This simple farmhouse was built in 1676 and it is the birthplace of the man who has been called "the father of his country's language." The small building was at first a two-room, central-chimney home. When more space was needed, the traditional lean-to was added, turning the house into what we call a saltbox. An eighteenth-century ell and some paneling were later "improvements." Noah Webster's father and brother worked an eighty-acre farm around the house when Noah was at Yale. Important as the house is as an example of early architecture, it is secondary to the achievement of the man born in it. In 1789 Noah Webster began his work on American textbooks and the dictionary that still bears his name. "*Now* is the time," he wrote, "and *this* is the country, in which we may expect success, in attempting changes favorable to language, science, and government. . . . Let us then seize the present moment, and establish a *national language,* as well as a national government." Noah Webster ended once and for all America's dependence on England for school texts and the style and usage of language. Millions of Americans studied his grammar texts and consulted his dictionary. His work has had as profound an effect on America as that of any other individual.

*(2)* Children's Museum of Hartford, 950 Trout Brook Dr. This is a combined museum and educational training institution affiliated with the University of Hartford. There is a planetarium and permanent exhibits of fossils, shells, insects, birds, and mammals. There also is Indian material and colonial Americana as well as displays of Oriental and Pacific Island cultures. A 2,000-volume library, summer science academy, workshops, and education programs help children and teachers of children to understand their subject areas.

*(3)* A visit to West Hartford ought to include North Main St., where a number of eighteenth-century homes can be seen. There also is an ancient cemetery on the east side of North Main, one street above Farmington Ave., where headstones dating from 1725 are well preserved.

*(4)* Elizabeth Park, 915 Prospect Ave. Flowers, particularly roses, bloom in their appropriate seasons in this delightful park several acres in extent.

*(5)* The Metacomet Trail (crossing U.S. 44) offers hiking in the highlands of the western section of town west of the reservoirs in what is called the Metropolitan District. Golfing is offered at the Buena Vista Golf Course, on Buena Vista Rd., and the Rockledge Country Club, on South Main St.

WEST HAVEN *(New Haven County. Rtes. into: I–95, Exits 42, 43, 44; U.S. 1; state 34, 162; 10.6 sq. mi.; 52,851 pop. Other communities: Allingtown.)*
Although West Haven did not attain city status until 1921, the history of these few square miles dates back to the early seventeenth century when Dutch traders landed and made contact with the Indians. When New Haven colony was settled in 1638 only a few years elapsed before farmers began to work the land along the western shores of New Haven harbor. That area became known as West Farms and following King Philip's War (1675–76) the region was divided into farm lots, which were allocated by public drawing. Veterans of the war were given preference.

About all that remains of those days is the large green and a very few old houses. The growth of the region encompassing West Haven and the invasion of industry have wiped out all else. Many of the eighteenth-century homes were burned in the Revolutionary War when General Tryon put 1,500 men ashore from a fleet of 48 British warships at what is now called Savin Rock on the Sound. The alarm was given and hastily mustered militia forced the British to abandon the quick route of entry to New Haven and march a longer way around. In that battle a British officer, William Campbell, was shot. He had acted gallantly in restraining his men from looting and burning and had saved the life of a local clergyman. Adjutant Campbell was buried in West Haven and today Campbell Ave., a main thoroughfare, commemorates his humanity. On his gravestone is the inscription "Blessed are the merciful."

WESTON *(Fairfield County. Rtes. into: 53, 57; 20.8 sq. mi.; 7,417 pop. Other communities: Lyon Plains.)*
Named in 1787 as the "West Town" of earlier settled Fairfield, the community is largely residential with homes set amid lawns and shade trees. The topography varies but generally rises from south to north and there are some rocky hills and ledge outcroppings along Rte. 57 north of the center of town. Good views to the south and Long Island Sound can be had from some of the roads. Largely

a New York–oriented town, it is the home of artists, writers, and admen.

*To See and Do: (1)* Old Barn Museum, Weston Rd., Rte. 57 (Weston Historical Society). Built in 1835, the old barn houses Indian relics and old farm tools on permanent exhibition.

*(2)* Fishing in the Saugatuck River along Lyons Plains Rd., the West Branch of the Saugatuck River, north of the center on Rte. 57, and by permit from the shores only (no boating) of Saugatuck Reservoir, in the northeastern part of town (Rte. 53).

WESTPORT *(Fairfield County. Rtes. into: I–95, which is the Connecticut Turnpike here, Exits 17, 18; U.S. 1; state 15, which is the Merritt Pkwy., 33, 136; 22.4 sq. mi.; 27,414 pop. Other communities: Greens Farms, Saugatuck.)*
Although Westport was not incorporated until 1835 from Norwalk, Fairfield, and Weston, it was early settled. In 1637, during the Pequot War (see Chapter 3), an English sea captain, John Gallup, sailed his ships along what is now the town's active and affluent shore. A few years later five farmers moved into what is now the Greens Farms shore community and that area became a parish of Fairfield to the east. Today the town is as well known as any community its size in the entire country. It is the prototype of an author–artist–advertising–public relations community that has figured in many stories and movies. Westport began developing this character in the late 1920s and early 30s as a hinterland town where New York families could "get away from it all." And the adman's adage, "Put it on the train and see if it gets off at Westport," was, for a tiresome time, hurled at every new ad campaign idea developed in the leading Madison Avenue firms.

Actually, Westport has settled into a new maturity and the colonial homes in Greens Farms set on well-trimmed estates give it dignity beyond its rather raucous beginnings. And it still is the home of many important writers, publishers, and ad-agency executives whose families have at last found and shaped a village to their satisfaction: a blend of New England high-cost homespun and sophistication. Yet it remains a New York-oriented town.

On April 25, 1777, Westport citizens were alarmed to see 26 British ships, clustered at the mouth of the Saugatuck River, from which some 2,000 British troops disembarked. They marched away to raid Danbury (see Danbury) and before their return, patriot troops were hastily assembled. Efforts to trap the returning British failed and, their mission accomplished, the king's troops sailed away. Later, when General Tryon burned New Haven and Fairfield, his Hessians continued their burning right along into Westport.

*To See and Do:* (1) Mid Fairfield County Youth Museum, 10 Woodside Lane. A children's museum featuring geology, entomology, ornithology, herpetology, mineralogy, and astronomy in exhibits. A fulsome 2,500-volume science library is available on the premises.

(2) Westport Country Playhouse, 25 Powers Court. Summer stock program, in season, and at the White Barn Theatre, Newtown Ave.

(3) Sherwood Island State Park. One of three state saltwater beaches on a 233-acre island connected by road to the mainland, the park offers fishing, picnicking and swimming.

(4) Town beaches. Policy varies regarding nonresident use. Check with the town hall.

WETHERSFIELD *(Hartford County. Rtes. into: I–91; U.S. 5; state 3, 99, 175, 314; 13.0 sq. mi; 26,662 pop.)*
Settled in 1634, Wethersfield lays claim to being the oldest settled Connecticut community. Windsor has disputed that claim for many years—and everyone has conveniently forgotten the Dutch, who were the first white settlers of Connecticut. In any event, Wethersfield *is* a very old town, being settled in September of 1634 by one Captain John Oldham, formerly of the Massachusetts Bay colony. He and seven companions arrived by boat and built huts near or on the shores of Wethersfield Cove, which then was open to the Connecticut River. According to records, they also planted grain that first fall to ensure a crop as early as possible the following spring, at which time they expected to be joined by more settlers from Massachusetts.

Originally the town was much larger geographically, and Wethersfield is the parent town of all or part of Berlin, Glastonbury, New Britain, and Rocky Hill. In addition, some of its restless citizens left the town only a few years after its founding to begin other Connecticut towns: Milford, Branford, and Stamford, to name three. Situated where it is on the Connecticut River, Wethersfield was in an ideal location for trade and for attack. The Pequot Indians were closer to Wethersfield than to Hartford or Windsor and they did attack in 1637, killing, by some reports, six men, three women, and a number of cows. They also took two young girls captive. This attack is known as the Wethersfield Massacre, and it prompted the commissioning of Captain Mason of Windsor (see Windsor) to lead a group in reprisal to wipe out the Pequot stronghold near Norwich.

The fortunate aspect of Wethersfield's location is that it led to early industry: shipbuilding; and a business: trading with the West Indies. One of the first oceangoing ships built in Connecticut, the *Tryall*, was launched in Wethersfield in 1649 and from that early time the town engaged in trade with the West Indies. The cargo shipped from Wethersfield, and that received, demanded warehouses (see below) and wharves and ships. All of these soon crowded Wethersfield Cove and its shores. For an outgoing cargo Wethersfield supplied bricks, hides, salt beef, fish, and onions—millions and millions of onions. For someone had discovered that the soil around Wethersfield would grow onions beautifully. In fact, for a long time the dignified old town was known as Onion Town, and the smell of onions anywhere along the Atlantic coast would prompt some joke about a Wethersfield tradesman or ship approaching, upwind.

In touch, as Wethersfield was, with all the history of the Connecticut River valley, it is not surprising that its men served in all the military engagements that have affected the state: the Pequot War in 1637; battles with the Dutch in 1653; the Indians in King Philip's War in 1675–76—and all the "later ones" up to and including the Revolutionary War. During the fight for independence, Wethersfield men served aboard raiding vessels (the brig *Minerva*, owned by a Wethersfield man, was armed and sailed from Wethersfield). Men of the town joined companies that went through the war from Charlestown to Yorktown. On two occasions General Washington visited Wethersfield, and on one of them important conferences and plans were made that affected the outcome of the war (see below).

The importance of Wethersfield as a shipping center declined along with that of the other Connecticut River towns when shipping became concentrated in the saltwater ports of New London, New Haven, and other cities on the Sound. Gradually, and fortunately for historic Wethersfield, industry moved to outlying towns like Berlin and New Britain. As Hartford grew, Wethersfield became more and more a residential community with development of new living areas in the low hills to the west of the old center. Left behind, so to speak, and happily so, are the seventeenth- and eighteenth-century homes of the early residents. Taken as a Historic District, it is as well preserved an area as can be found in the state.

*To See and Do:* (1) The Webb House, 211 Main St. (Connecticut Society of Colonial Dames). Built in 1752 (with a rear ell dating from 1678) this handsome twin-chimney gambrel-roofed house (mansion, really) is of national historic importance, since it housed General Washington when he was in Wethersfield in 1781. For several days he conferred with Count De Rochambeau and others here, and within the walls of this house they planned the Yorktown campaign. Carefully preserved is the bed chamber General Washington used during those days of fateful planning. The antiques furnishing that room and the rest of the house are of the finest.

(2) Silas Deane House, 203 Main St. (Connecticut Society of Colonial Dames). On his first visit to Wethersfield in June of 1775 General Washington stayed in this handsome house built by Silas Deane in 1764. Deane was a wealthy merchant who later served as emissary to France. While there he was charged with embezzlement, and was not cleared until after his death—which came as a direct result of the charges. He died while still away from his home. It is furnished in the period, and has several unique interior features, a corner hallway, and an elaborate staircase.

*(3)* Buttolph-Williams House, 249 Broad St. (Antiquarian and Landmarks Society). This seventeenth-century gem was considered a mansion in its day and, though life then was more primitive than in the days of the Webb and Silas Dean houses, it *was* a mansion of its time. David Buttolph, son of Lt. John Buttolph, either used an older frame for this home or designed one just like his father's house and erected it. In 1947 the changes wrought over the years were removed and the house returned to its original state. It is correctly furnished to give a picture of the first century of this country's settlement. Pilgrim Century chairs and tables, pewter and delft, fabrics, and all implements of that time are tastefully displayed. The kitchen is regarded as perhaps the most completely furnished one in New England, with its wrought iron, wooden ware, curved settee, high chairs, and other accessories.

*(4)* Isaac Stevens House, 213 Main St. (Connecticut Society of Colonial Dames). This house, next to the Webb House, is one of three owned and operated by the Colonial Dames. It is the plainest of the group—a twin-chimney, central-hall type (with an unusually wide hall). Paneling is evident in this house, as in the Silas Deane House, and it is the latest of the three, having been built in 1788. The clapboards are fastened with original hand-wrought nails and some of the panes of the windows are original or at least very early, being still of hand-pressed glass. Its plain exterior indicates not a lapse of taste or elegance, but rather a combination of economy and application of a later "less is more" philosophy. There are family furnishings correct for the period and in addition displays of antique toys and ladies' bonnets. In the rear of the house is an early herb garden, a feature of all houses of that day.

*(5)* Old Academy Museum, 150 Main St. (Town of Wethersfield and Wethersfield Historical Society). Built in 1801–04, this former school building of brick on sandstone foundation is an excellent example of early, almost tentative, Federal treatment. It was built by the First School Society and served Wethersfield for many years, latterly as a town hall. Now it is the headquarters of the Wethersfield Historical Society and a museum. Exhibits include Indian artifacts, household equipment, farm and trade tools, and

maritime items. There is also an extensive genealogical library of Wethersfield families.

*(6)* A drive or walk through the Historic District will prove worthwhile. The district includes Main St., Broad St., State and Garden Sts., Elm St. to its junction with Maple St., south along Middletown Ave., Marsh and Hart Sts., north along Hartford Ave., and Wethersfield Cove. There are many eighteenth-century homes in this area, and of particular interest is the Congregational Church on the northeast corner of Marsh and Main Sts. The church or meeting house was built in 1761 and is the earliest brick church in the state. Recent restoration has taken the dignified building back as nearly to its original appearance as possible. Behind the church is the Ancient Burial Ground. First an Indian burial place, it was used by the earliest settlers of Wethersfield. The headstone of Leonard Chester is still in place, dated 1648. On Wethersfield Cove, at the northern end of Main St., is what must be the oldest warehouse in the United States. It dates from 1661 and was one of six built then to hold goods bound for the West Indies. Doubtless onions were often stored in it.


WILLINGTON *(Tolland County. Rtes. into: I–86; U.S. 44, 44A; state 32, 320; 34.8 sq. mi.; 3,755 pop. Other communities: East, South, and West Willington.)*
High, rugged countryside with many extensive views is the character of Willington. Named Wellington from the Somerset-shire town in England, it was incorporated as Willington in 1727. From earliest days, industry mingled with agriculture and in the nineteenth century South Willington was practically created by the Hall family. Gardiner Hall, Jr., laid out the tidy mill town and produced thread there. A glass factory, and later a pearl-button factory, helped keep the town's economy going. Today's indus-tries sound more natural to us: machined metal parts, electroplat-ing, and tire recapping.

Men of Willington went to fight in the Revolutionary War and patriotism ran deep—all the way to a fourteen-year-old boy who served as a drummer and an eleven-year-old who marched off as a fifer.

*To See and Do:* Fishing in Fenton River, in the eastern section, and in the Willimantic River, which forms the western border of town. Nye Holman State Forest, along the Willimantic River, offers hiking, and the Nipmuck Trail passes through the southwest corner, off Rte. 44A.

WILTON *(Fairfield County. Rtes. into: U.S. 7; state 33, 53, 106; 30.6 sq. mi.; 56,487 pop. Other communities: Cannondale, North Wilton, South Wilton.)*
Settled early, in 1639, named as a "society" in 1726 for Wiltshire, England, the town was not incorporated until 1802. Today it is a well-to-do town in the commuting range of New York and the daily trek of professional people is a hallmark of the community. Spread on either side of U.S. 7, it has open uplands to the north and west and a hill-and-valley character to the east. Some industry and newer buildings in the center obscure the colonial character of the town but some of it remains in older houses along U.S. 7 and in the outer fringes. One pre-Revolutionary home, the Scott Homestead (privately owned), passes the years serenely with a Revolutionary War cannonball embedded in one wall. In Cannondale, a small community on U.S. 7, north of Wilton's center, is Sharps Hill Burying Ground. Here many veterans of the Revolutionary War are buried, including one Azur Belden, who fought the war through from Bunker Hill to Yorktown.

*To See and Do: (1)* Craft Center Museum, 78 Danbury Rd. (U.S. 7). A metal-work museum with everything from armor to metal spinning, including work in copper, lead, silver, and brass. Its metallic character is somewhat lightened with exhibits of wood-work and leatherwork.

*(2)* Lambert House, 150 Danbury Rd. (Wilton Historical Society). The gambrel-roofed, 1726 house today, with some porches and dormers added, looks like a peaceful residence. But it reportedly was fired on in the Revolutionary War by the British and later served as a hiding place for slaves fleeing the South—a legend supported by the discovery of a secret tunnel connecting it to another house, and rusted manacles found in the tunnel.

*(3)* Sloan/Raymond/Fitch House (Wilton Historical Society).

Built in 1760, this house has exhibits of the colonial period and memorabilia of the community.

*(4)* Wilton Playshop, Lovers' Lane. The 150-seat theater gives dramatic performances in the summer season.

*(5)* Fishing in the state-stocked Saugatuck River, which runs beneath Rte. 53 en route to the center of Weston; fishing also in the Norwalk River, which runs beside U.S. 7 north of the center of Wilton.

WINCHESTER *(Litchfield County. Rtes. into: U.S. 44; state 8, 20, 183, 263, 272, 800; 34.0 sq. mi.; 11,016 pop. Other communities: City of Winsted, Winchester Center.)*
The wooded, hilly character of the town kept its first "proprietors" or owners from moving in rapidly. They met to talk things over in 1744 but not until 1771 was the town incorporated. The small but bustling city of Winsted is the place where most of the population live—which leaves the other parts of town in a rural and semiwilderness condition. Winsted was a clockmaking center early in the nineteenth century and has gone on in typical Connecticut town fashion to be a manufacturing center of diversified products ranging from dog collars to Waring blenders. It was hard hit in the floods of 1955, which inundated the industrial river valleys in Connecticut (see Naugatuck).

During the Revolutionary War, Winchester had a population of less than 350 people but managed to send its able-bodied men to fight. As a result, a great many women, children, and old people underwent privation during that time of turmoil.

*To See and Do: (1)* Solomon Rockwell House, Prospect and Lake Sts., Winsted (Winchester Historical Society). This mansion in Winsted was built in 1813 and has a Greek Revival architectural treatment which, in certain ways, is more reminiscent of a Southern plantation house than a Yankee iron manufacturer's home—which is what it was. Portraits, local memorabilia, and the house itself are the interest here.

*(2)* Highland Lake, Rte. 263. Boating with a launch site and fishing in this large lake, the shores of which in olden days saw

many summer Indian encampments. Quantities of Indian artifacts have been found here. Boat-launch sites and fishing are also in Winchester Lake, north of Rte. 263. Mad River Flood Control Pool and Park Pond (inquire locally) also offer fishing. Hall Meadow State Park (Rte. 272) covers the southwest corner of the town and offers fishing, swimming, hiking, picnicking, and winter sports. Hunting is available in East Branch Naugatuck Preserve and in the Torrington Fish and Game Preserve (see appendix). Golf in Greenwoods Country Club in Winsted, on Rte. 183.

WINDHAM *(Windham County. Rtes. into: U.S. 6, state 14, 32, 195, 203, 289; 27.9 sq. mi.; 19,626 pop. Other communities: City of Willimantic, North Windham, South Windham.)*
Don't mention frogs in Windham. The Battle of the Frogs lingers in memories far and near. During the French and Indian War, a farmer there decided to drain his pond. As night came, the high and dry frogs began a chorus of complaint so thunderous that Windham citizens believed Indians were whooping up a war dance outside the village. Alarms were given, women and children hidden, and the men, armed and trembling, stood ready to defend their families. And it was only a chorus of bullfrogs. The tale spread far and wide and lasted for a long, long time. One writer reported 125 years later, "Let a son of Windham penetrate to the uttermost part of the earth, he will find that the story of the frogfight preceded him."

Frog Pond is still there just east of the village of Windham, to the north of Rte. 14. And today the green and village center is much as it was then with great green trees and eighteenth-century houses making as pleasant a village scene as is to be found in Connecticut.

The city of Willimantic lies in the town of Windham and is known as Thread City. Like many other Connecticut towns, the community became known for one dominent industry—thread making. The American Thread Co., in existence since 1854, researched and produced the first spool-wound cotton thread in the United States. It is still going strong and provides major employment for people of the city and surrounding country. A fair percentage of the workers are either Puerto Rican or French Canadian in origin and it is not uncommon to hear Spanish or a dialect of French Canadian spoken.

Interstate I–84 will eventually go through North Windham, a small industrial village on present U.S. 6. The community grew there because of water power available on the Natchaug River, which passes through.

*To See and Do:* Fishing, boating, and picnicking are available in Beaver Brook State Park (401 acres) with a boat-launch site on Beaver Brook Pond. Go southeast off Rte. 203, at the junction with U.S. 6.

WINDSOR *(Hartford County. Rtes. into: I–91; state 20, 75, 159, 178, 305; 31.2 sq. mi.; 22,502 pop. Other communities: Poquonock, Rainbow, Wilson, Windsor Center.)*
Credited with being the first settled community in the state, the town of Windsor occupies a unique position in the history of Connecticut. In September of 1633 an English company from Massachusetts Bay Colony sailed up the Connecticut River, past the Dutch fort and trading post at Hartford, and landed at what is now the center of Windsor at the junction of the Farmington and Connecticut Rivers. And they landed with, of all things, a prefab house. It had been built in Massachusetts, dismantled, and stowed aboard the ship to give them instant shelter when they arrived.

The location they chose was a popular Indian location too, and several tribes made it and the surrounding country their homes. The Englishmen, in fact, brought a number of Indian sachems of those local tribes upriver with them and were welcomed by the Indians, since they lived in fear of the Pequot tribe to the east. The sachems (or warrior chiefs) hoped the English would discourage Pequot raids and had asked the English to settle among them.

Other parties of English in Massachusetts Bay Colony heard of the new settlement in what has to be described as raw wilderness, and soon arrived. After some dissension and jockeying for position, the town of Windsor began to thrive. Land along the river was fertile and by 1640 tobacco had become a crop for the settlement to trade with. It is still a principal product of Windsor today.

Although the local Indians were friends and allies, the raiding Pequots were not, and they attacked Wethersfield in 1637 (see Wethersfield). Fearing an attack on Windsor, the settlers built a palizado or palisade, fortifying a small area north of the Little (Farmington) River and providing sanctuary for families on outlying farms in case of attack. The Fyler House (see below) and Palisado Ave. to Pierson with adjoining house lots were enclosed by the original fortification.

A more fearful enemy than Indians nearly wiped out the little colony during the first year. That winter the rivers froze in November (nearly entrapping a ship sent with supplies from Massachusetts). Snow was deep and came early. It stayed, too, on the shivering colony all that long, dreadful winter. The friendly Indians did what they could to help, but the unusual weather, coupled with smallpox among the susceptible Indians, brought Windsor to the edge of disaster.

The Palisado Green (and Avenue) exist today and the green was the hub of the village early in the seventeenth century. Along Palisado Ave. and around the green are some of the earliest surviving homes in the town. Many of them are brick houses, for the brick industry began early in the eighteenth century in Windsor. In fact, below Windsor, on the shores of the Connecticut River, many early houses have brick fireplaces and chimneys, which are a direct result of the Windsor brick-making industry.

Like other early towns in the state (Wethersfield, Guilford, Old Saybrook, for example) Windsor was a settled and thriving community when the eighteenth century arrived. Many areas in the state were still wilderness then, and Windsor men and women supplied many of the towns in the western part of the state with *their* earliest settlers.

In the more than three centuries of its existence, Windsor quite naturally has produced men who were important in the formation of the state and national government. Some, like Captain John Mason (an early settler from England), gained military fame in the first years of Windsor's history. For it was he who was sent by Windsor citizens to defeat the Pequot Indians in the region of

Norwich and so end the threat of Indian raids. And his son, Major John Mason carried on, fighting and dying in King Philip's War in 1675. Daniel Bissell is another name counted as valorous in military affairs. As a sergeant in the Revolutionary War, he was ordered by General Washington to infiltrate the British stronghold in New York City. This he did and he enlisted in the traitor Benedict Arnold's command and served over a year, all the while storing up information that he later carried to Washington.

The list, over those long early years, of distinguished men from Windsor is long. Joseph Loomis, on whose original land the famed Loomis School stands today, came to Windsor in 1640. Roger Ludlow, from England, served early in the crude government and removed to Fairfield (see Fairfield) to help found that town. Oliver Phelps, who lived from 1749 to 1809, was a land speculator who would put today's real estate developers to shame. With a partner, he bought six million acres of land in New York State and began selling home sites. Later he joined a syndicate, and in 1795 it bought over three million acres from the state of Connecticut. The land, known as the Western Reserve, was in Ohio. Yet, of all the first families of Windsor (the Haydens, the Loomises, and the Masons among them), the dominant family was the Ellsworths, and of that family, Oliver Ellsworth is Windsor's most notable son (see below).

When the Revolutionary War came, Windsor was well over a hundred years old. Twenty-eight men marched off to help the Massachusetts troops after the Battle of Lexington. By 1780 every able-bodied man (and some boys) had left for the fighting, and the women and children worked the farms and kept the town going. Legend has it that there were no clocks workable in Windsor during the war. The weights had all been melted down for bullets.

With the coming of the nineteenth century, Windsor, like many Connecticut towns, entered the industrial age with enthusiasm. Its position on the Connecticut River made it a natural trading point and shipbuilding was among the industries that flourished. And through it all, the carefully grown and harvested tobacco plants made a crop that never failed. Today, machine tools, iron castings, turbines, and other machinery are made in Windsor. Along with

Hartford and the neighboring towns, Windsor has become a part of the Hartford industrial region and its subsequent suburbanization, with the clutter such growth always brings. There are many houses standing that date from the eighteenth century—but Windsor is the victim of suburban growth and it is becoming more difficult to preserve its colonial heritage.

*To See and Do: (1)* The Oliver Ellsworth House, "Elmwood," 778 Palisado Ave. (Daughters of the American Revolution). Built by Captain David Ellsworth in 1740 on land bought by Josias Ellsworth in 1665, the present house is one of the most important structures historically in the state. David Ellsworth's sons were all outstanding, but Oliver Ellsworth, who was born in the house and who later owned it, was Windsor's leading citizen. He helped draft the Constitution of the United States, served as a delegate from Connecticut to the Continental Congress, and was Senator from Connecticut in the first meeting of the Congress. He was described by John Adams as "the firmest pillar of Washington's administration." He eventually became Chief Justice of the United States Supreme Court. Prior to that, Ellsworth wrote the Judiciary Act, the foundation of our present court system. He later was sent as envoy to France, where Napoleon, on meeting him said, "We must make a treaty with this man."

The house today is furnished with articles from the Ellsworth family, including several brought by Oliver Ellsworth when he returned from France. The envoy also added the colonnaded wing upon his return and included in the furnishings is a tapestry presented to him by Napoleon. The building, as well as the furnishings, is well worth attention. It is a center-hall, twin-chimney colonial of a style not common in Connecticut at the time of its building. The paneling, doors, and windows are all outstanding, making Elmwood a showplace not to be missed.

*(2)* The Fyler House and Wilson Museum, 96 Palisado Ave. (Windsor Historical Society). The earliest portion of this complex house is believed to have been built in the seventeenth century. It is situated on land awarded Lieutenant Walter Fyler for his services in the Pequot War in 1637. The small, original house remained in the Fyler family until 1763 when a sea captain, Nathaniel Howard,

who added the gambrel-roof section after one of his voyages, bought the place. He brought silks and other Eastern goods and opened a store in the house—and since it was near the center of the community, the building became Windsor's first post office. Today, furnished as a Windsor home in the early days, it is a fine example of the way people lived more than two hundred years ago.

Attached to the house is the relatively new Wilson Museum, made of brick and built in Georgian style. Within it are Indian relics and early Americana on display, and a fine historical and genealogical library and many ancient maps.

*(3)* A walk through Windsor should include Broad St. and Palisado Ave. Here many fine houses, brick and frame, give the feel of old Windsor. Batchelder Road (off Broad St.) has at its end the campus of the Loomis and Chaffee School. On the campus is the old Loomis Homestead, a saltbox house dating from the seventeenth century (not open to the public). On the campus, which is located at the junction of the Farmington and Connecticut Rivers, is a large rock inscribed to commemorate the first English settlement in Connecticut (1633).

*(4)* Fishing and boating (with launch sites) on the Farmington River and in Rainbow Reservoir (inquire locally). Golf at the Millbrook Golf Course, on Pigeon Hill Rd., and the Pine Hill Golf Club, on Matianuck Ave.


WINDSOR LOCKS *(Hartford County. Rtes. into: I–91; state 20, 75, 140, 159; 9.2 sq. mi.; 15,080 pop.)*
Dutch traders from New Amsterdam probably were the first Europeans to see the area now forming the town of Windsor Locks. In 1614 they sailed up the Connecticut River to this point, where they were stopped by impassable shallow rapids. Twenty years later men from Windsor to the south bought the land (called Pine Meadow) from the Indians. Not until 1663, however, did a family venture to settle that wilderness. Then the Denslow family staked out a homestead and began to farm. In 1675, King Philip's War brought Indian raids and the Denslows sought safety in the settlement of Windsor. The next spring, Henry Denslow set out to

cultivate his land and was never seen again. At war's end, the Denslows, led by Henry's seventeen-year-old son, returned to Pine Meadow and settled permanently on their land. Today, a flint boulder surrounded by an iron fence and inscribed to the first-family Denslows can be seen in the north access loop to I–91 from Rte. 159.

For many years the rapids that had stopped the Dutch traders brought all northbound shipping to a halt. Hartford entrepreneurs decided to build a canal complete with locks to bypass the falls and so open the northern settlements (not to mention western Massachusetts) to trade. Upon completion in November 1829, the canal drew crowds of watchers as the first attempt was made to steam around the river barrier through the locks. It failed. But a few days later a second attempt in the steamer *Barnet* succeeded, and the boat, laden with officials, went as far north as Brattleboro, Vermont. Soon sternwheelers and sidewheelers were regularly steaming between Hartford and Springfield, carrying passengers and freight. Enthused by the success of the canal and the growing importance of the town, its citizens voted to rename their community Windsor Locks. Today the canal and locks remain in place and are visible from Rte. 159, the main street of the town, as you drive or walk through the center.

Today, Bradley International Airport is a dominant facet of Windsor Locks. The former World War II field serves all of Connecticut and western Massachusetts and provides employment for many town workers. Paper manufacture (begun in the nineteenth century), metal products, aircraft-parts manufacture, processing tobacco, and food servicing are the town's principal industries.

*To See and Do:* Bradley Air Museum, Bradley Field. A collection of aircraft includes twenty-six airplanes, three balloons, eleven helicopters, one missile, and one rocket.

WOLCOTT *(New Haven County. Rtes. into: 69, 322; 20.6 sq. mi.; 12,495 pop.)*
Indian trails and horse trails, well marked in the mid 1700s, later

became main roads and helped define the area that is now Wolcott. An outgrowth of Waterbury to the west of town, the community petitioned to become a separate town several times, and when the petition was finally granted, the deciding vote in the matter came from then Lieutenant Governor Oliver Wolcott. Hence the town name. Many hills and steep slopes characterize the topography of the town and Mad River, a principal feature of the town, has been dammed to produce reservoirs that supply water to larger nearby communities.

Wolcott's most interesting first citizen has to be Amos Bronson Alcott. An unsuccessful peddler (all the way to Virginia), he left commerce and went into schooling. His first teaching job was in Bristol but he soon removed to Boston and opened his own school. There he caused such an uproar with innovative techniques that his school failed. His radical ideas produced a positive reaction in England, however, and an institution known as Alcott House was opened there. He visited there in 1842 and returned with enough fervid followers to found an idealistic colony at Harvard, Massachusetts. It failed too. Reduced to near penury, he put himself and his wife and children to work to support the family. One of them, Louisa May Alcott, obliged by writing *Little Women*. Alcott represents that peculiar strain of New England eccentricity that made such reputations as those of Henry James, Sr., and, not surprisingly, Emerson and Thoreau. Of Alcott, Thomas Carlyle was reported to have said he was "all bent on saving the world by a return to acorns and the golden age."

*To See and Do:* Cedar Lake, west of Rte. 69 in the northern part of town, offers fishing.

WOODBRIDGE *(New Haven County. Rtes. into: 15, which is the Wilbur Cross Pkwy., 63, 67, 69, 114, 243, 313; 19.3 sq. mi.; 7,673 pop.)*
During the heyday of Connecticut inventing and tinkering, the town had one citizen who chalked up a monumental failure. Thomas Sanford, formerly of Beacon Falls, built a huge waterwheel, which took all of his capital. It was so huge that the water

power available at the site wouldn't turn it. To recoup, Sanford sold rights for ten dollars to another product of his imagination: friction matches—which were snapped up and later produced by the Diamond Match Co. Each Connecticut town, it seemed, finally settled on one item and everyone fell to work turning it out. Woodbridge opted for iron candlesticks and produced five-hundred dozen in one year.

Today the town is a pleasant, spacious residential community where New Haven professional people live. Its name came from one of its early pastors, Benjamin Woodbridge, and like other towns surrounding present-day New Haven, it was once part of the New Haven colony.

WOODBURY *(Litchfield County. Rtes. into: U.S. 6, 202; state 47, 61, 64, 132, 317; 36.8 sq. mi.; 5,869 pop. Other communities: Hotchkissville, Minortown, North Woodbury, Pomperaug.)*
The town is one of the oldest in the inland section of the west part of Connecticut. Dissidents (or colonizers, depending on your view) from Stratford received permission to set up a community on the land belonging to Pomperaug, a Potatuck (or Pootatuck) chief. Fifteen families did so, laying out the present Main St. along an old Indian trail. Chief Pomperaug, in fact, lies buried along Main St. and a marker commemorates his life.

Woodbury originally was a much larger town than it is today. Parts of it over the years were chipped off to help found Washington, Roxbury, Southbury, Bethlehem, and Middlebury. The original large town (with a population of over 5,000 in 1776) contributed many men—some 1,500—to the Revolutionary War effort and many of the young men assisting Ethan Allen in the capture of Fort Ticonderoga (N. Y.) came from Woodbury. Stores and ammunition were supplied by the patriots of the town but it was not all an outpouring of riches. Jabez Bacon, a leading merchant of Woodbury, saw the war conclude while eyeing a $500,000 fortune made during that period. And Jabez could afford a whim we all wish were more widespread today. At his store a fulsome buffet meal was available free to his shoppers, some of whom came a distance for supplies. After buying, they were often served a solid meal in his home on Hollow Rd. before heading toward their own homes.

Main St. of Woodbury is almost a tour through architectural history as sturdy eighteenth, prim nineteenth-century houses, and churches of the early nineteenth-century grace that thoroughfare. This section is now a Historic District, preserved from any encroachment or defacing change. In North Woodbury, the Second Congregational Church, built in 1814, is as unspoiled an example of delicate church architecture as one can find.

*To See and Do: (1)* Glebe House, Hollow Rd. (Seabury Society for the Preservation of the Glebe House). As it exists presently, the Glebe House is mid-eighteenth-century architecture and it was brought to this elaboration in 1750. Part of it, however, has been attributed to the earlier year of 1690. Its importance lies in the fact that in 1783 ten of fourteen Anglican clergymen in Connecticut met here and elected Dr. Samuel Seabury (of Groton, Ledyard, and New London) the first Episcopal bishop in the United States. The Glebe House was then the home of Rev. John Rodgers Marshall. It was called a "glebe," since it was surrounded by farm land belonging to the Anglican church (in a village the house and grounds would be called a rectory). All the Anglican clergy during the Revolutionary War were harassed as Tories and Rev. Marshall was no exception. The house today contains a sliding secret panel through which he made his way to the basement and from there through a tunnel to a neighbor's house. It is said he appeared only on the Sabbath, when even ardent patriots stayed their hands. Then he'd vanish for the week via the secret door and tunnel.

Furnished today as in the heyday of its history, with elegant paneling and articles, it is both an outstanding example architecturally and a shrine for Episcopal Church members.

*(2)* The Hurd House, situated in The Hollow, one hundred yards east of the Glebe House (Old Woodbury Historic Society). Around 1680 John Hurd, formerly of Stratford, built a one-room two-story end-chimney house in The Hollow near his corn mill. Around 1720 a similar house belonging to Joseph Hurd, his son, was moved from its location near the mill site and joined with the original house. These two houses—now one—are the only surviving

examples of this house type in Connecticut. The house is in the process of restoration.

*(3)* Orenaug Rocks and Bethel Rocks (now a town park), in the highlands east of U.S. 6 and 202, on Orenaug Park Rd., offer views of surrounding towns. Bethel Rock was where first settlers in the seventeenth century met and worshiped until they could build a meeting house.

*(4)* Drives through any part of Woodbury at a leisurely pace will prove rewarding both as to countryside, meadows along the Pomperaug River, and hilly terrain to the east, as well as architecturally. There are many eighteenth-century farmhouses in this ancient town.

*(5)* Flanders Nature Center, Van Vleck Sanctuary, off Flanders Road, and Whittemore Sanctuary, off Route 64, are two areas totaling about eight hundred acres set aside as wilderness land for the many species of birds and animals that make these havens their home. They are open to the public during daylight hours; the Marsh and Botany Trails at Van Vleck's and the Bog Walk at Whittemore's are especially recommended for bird watchers and wild-life enthusiasts.

*(6)* The Tapawingo ski area, in the northwest part of town (Rte. 47) above Hotchkissville, attracts many winter visitors and there is hunting in the 3,500-acre Woodbury-Southbury Rod and Gun Club Area in the southwest corner of town (see appendix). Quassapaug Lake, north of Rte. 64 on the eastern edge of town, with a boat-launch site, offers boating and fishing.


WOODSTOCK *(Windham County. Rtes. into: 169, 171, 197, 198; 61.6 sq. mi.; 4,311 pop. Other communities: Harrisville, Kenyonville, Woodstock Valley, and North, East, South, and West Woodstock.)*
Originally part of Massachusetts, the town was named New Roxbury by the thirteen founding families from the Bay State town who came to Woodstock in 1686. Four years later it got its present name from a town in Oxfordshire, England. Connecticut annexed the town in 1749.

The green in Woodstock is completely unspoiled by any

commercial structures. A large estate with extensive gardens flanks it on one side (see below) and the Woodstock Academy, in operation since 1801, lies at the north end. It still serves the community as a school. The buildings on the green are well-preserved examples of nineteenth-century architecture.

The entire town lies in rugged topography, with hills, valleys, and streams giving it character. The highest elevations are in the west and northwest part of the town and nearly any back-road driving will reveal views of the surrounding countryside. A tableted erratic (see Chapter 4) west of the village center is notable, for it served as a pulpit long ago for John Eliot, New England missionary extraordinary to the "heathen" Indians. He preached from atop the rock in 1674 in the Indians' own language. For years he had worked to learn it and by 1663 had translated the Bible and a catechism into their tongue.

Textile manufacture came to Woodstock in the nineteenth century but faded as it did in so many Connecticut towns bypassed by railroad development. Today the town is largely residential with a few light industries.

*To See and Do: (1)* Roseland, west side of the green (Society for the Preservation of New England Antiquities). It is the former estate of a native son, Henry C. Bowen, who became rich and gave extensive parties and had gardeners plant large rose gardens. His feverish patriotism exploded every Fourth of July at a gala including fireworks and the entertainment of notables from all over, such as Presidents Grant, Hayes, Harrison, and McKinley; Oliver Wendell Holmes; and Harriet Beecher Stowe.

*(2)* Hunting in Woodstock Landowners Preserve (see appendix). Boating (launch site) in Roseland Lake and fishing (north of South Woodstock). Fishing and boating (launch site) in Black Pond (north of West Woodstock). Fishing in Muddy Pond and Golf at the Harrisville Golf Club, on Harrisville Rd.

# 3

## Appendices and Reference Works

# INDEX TO OTHER NAMED COMMUNITIES

Many of the 169 towns in Connecticut have other communities within their borders. The following index lists those mentioned in the town descriptions whose location might prove confusing to the visitor. For instance, Middle Haddam is not in Haddam or East Haddam, but in East Hampton, and included in that town's description.

| Community | Town |
|---|---|
| Bashan | East Haddam |
| Beardsley | Bridgeport |
| Belltown | Stamford |
| Bishop's Corner | West Hartford |
| Black Hall | Old Lyme |
| Black Point | East Lyme |
| Blue Hills | Bloomfield |
| Boardman's Bridge | New Milford |
| Botsford | Newtown |
| Branchville | Ridgefield |
| Broad Brook | East Windsor |
| Buckingham | Glastonbury |
| Buckland | Manchester |
| Bull's Bridge | Kent |
| Burnetts Corner | Groton |
| Burnside | East Hartford |
| Burrville | Torrington |
| Byram | Greenwich |
| Cannondale | Wilton |
| Centerbrook | Essex |
| Centerville | Hamden |
| Central Village | Plainfield |
| Chesterfield | Montville |
| Chestnut Hill | Lebanon |
| Clark's Corner | Hampton |
| Clarks Falls | North Stonington |
| Cobalt | East Hampton |
| Collinsville | Canton |
| Cos Cob | Greenwich |
| Crescent Beach | East Lyme |
| Crystal Lake | Ellington |
| Danielson | Killingly |
| Dayville | Killingly |
| Devon | Milford |
| Doaneville | Griswold |
| Dodgingtown | Newtown |

| Community | Town |
|---|---|
| Drakeville | Torrington |
| Eagleville | Mansfield |
| E. Windsor Hill | South Windsor |
| Ekonk | Sterling |
| Ellsworth | Sharon |
| Elmville | Killingly |
| Elmwood | West Hartford |
| Exeter | Lebanon |
| Fair Haven | New Haven |
| Falls Village | Canaan |
| Fenwick | Old Saybrook |
| Fitchville | Bozrah |
| Flanders | East Lyme |
| Flanders | Kent |
| Forestville | Bristol |
| Foxon | East Haven |
| Gales Ferry | Ledyard |
| Gaylordsville | New Milford |
| Georgetown | Redding |
| Germantown | Danbury |
| Gilead | Hebron |
| Gilman | Bozrah |
| Glasgo | Griswold |
| Glenbrook | Stamford |
| Glenville | Greenwich |
| Goshen Hill | Lebanon |
| Greens Farms | Westport |
| Greenville | Norwich |
| Greystone | Plymouth |
| Grosvenor Dale | Thompson |
| Gurleyville | Mansfield |
| Hadlyme | Lyme |
| Hallville | Preston |
| Hamburg | Lyme |
| Hanover | Sprague |
| Harrisville | Woodstock |
| Hattertown | Newtown |

| Community | Town |
|---|---|
| Hawleyville | Newtown |
| Hazardville | Enfield |
| Higganum | Haddam |
| Highland Park | Manchester |
| High Ridge | Stamford |
| Highwood | Hamden |
| Hillstown | East Hartford |
| Hockanum | East Hartford |
| Hopeville | Griswold |
| Hotchkissville | Woodbury |
| Huntington | Shelton |
| Huntingtown | Newtown |
| Huntsville | Canaan |
| Indian Neck | Branford |
| Ivoryton | Essex |
| Jewett City | Griswold |
| Kensington | Berlin |
| Kenyonville | Woodstock |
| Lakeside | Morris |
| Lakeville | Salisbury |
| Laurel Glen | N. Stonington |
| Laysville | Old Lyme |
| Liberty Hill | Lebanon |
| Lime Rock | Salisbury |
| Lime Rock Sta. | Canaan |
| Long Hill | Trumbull |
| Long Ridge | Stamford |
| Long Society | Preston |
| Lower City | Canaan |
| Lower Merryall | New Milford |
| Lyon Plain | Weston |
| Macedonia | Kent |
| Marble Dale | Washington |
| Marion | Southington |
| Massapeag | Montville |
| Mechanicsville | Thompson |
| Melrose | East Windsor |

| Community | Town |
|-----------|------|
| Pawcatuck | Stonington |
| Pequabuck | Plymouth |
| Perkins Corner | Mansfield |
| Phoenixville | Eastford |
| Pine Meadow | New Hartford |
| Pine Orchard | Branford |
| Plantsville | Southington |
| Pleasant Valley | Barkhamsted |
| Pleasure Beach | Waterford |
| Pomperaug | Woodbury |
| Poquetanuck | Preston |
| Poquonock | Windsor |
| Poquonock Bridge | Groton |
| Quaddick | Thompson |
| Quinnipiac | Wallingford |
| Rainbow | Windsor |
| Rivercliff | Milford |
| Riverside | Greenwich |
| Riverton | Barkhamsted |
| Robertsville | Colebrook |
| Rockfall | Middlefield |
| Rockland | Madison |
| Rockville | Vernon |
| Rogers | Killingly |
| Rowayton | Norwalk |
| Sadds Mill | Ellington |
| Sandy Hook | Newtown |
| Saugatuck | Westport |
| Scantic | East Windsor |
| Scitico | Enfield |
| Short Beach | Branford |
| Sodom | N. Canaan |
| Sound View | Old Lyme |
| South Britain | Southbury |
| Southford | Southbury |
| Southport | Fairfield |

| Community | Town |
|---|---|
| Springdale | Stamford |
| Spring Glen | Hamden |
| Spring Hill | Mansfield |
| Stepney | Monroe |
| Stevenson | Monroe |
| Stony Creek | Branford |
| Storrs | Mansfield |
| Straitsville | Naugatuck |
| Taconic | Salisbury |
| Taftville | Norwich |
| Talcottville | Vernon |
| Tariffville | Simsbury |
| Thompsonville | Enfield |
| Torringford | Torrington |
| Turn of River | Stamford |
| Uncasville | Montville |
| Union City | Naugatuck |
| Unionville | Farmington |
| Upper Merryall | New Milford |
| Upper Stepney | Monroe |
| Versailles | Sprague |
| Wapping | South Windsor |
| Warehouse Point | East Windsor |
| Warrenville | Ashford |
| Wauregan | Plainfield |
| Weatogue | Simsbury |
| Wequetequock | Stonington |
| Westchester | Colchester |
| Westford | Ashford |
| Westminster | Canterbury |
| West Mystic | Groton |
| Westville | New Haven |
| Whigville | Burlington |
| White Oak | Southbury |
| Whitneyville | Hamden |
| Willimantic | Windham |
| Wilson | Windsor |

| Community | Town |
|---|---|
| Wilsonville | Thompson |
| Windermere | Ellington |
| Windsorville | East Windsor |
| Winsted | Winchester |
| Winthrop | Deep River |
| Woodmont | Milford |
| Yalesville | Wallingford |
| Yantic | Norwich |

# CULTURAL CONNECTICUT

**Historic Houses and Historical Museums**

Ansonia  *David Humphreys House,* Elm St. For hours, inquire locally.
*Rev. Richard Mansfield House,* 22 Jewett St. Shown by appointment.

Barkhamsted  *John Tarrant Kenney Hitchcock Museum,* Rte. 20, Riverton. May–Nov. 30, Tues.–Sat. 10–5. Dec.–Apr. 30, Sat. 10–5. No charge.

Branford  *Academy Building,* Branford Green. In process of restoration.
*Blackstone Memorial Library Museum,* West Main St. Mon.–Fri. 9–8; Sat. 9–5. No charge.

Bridgewater  *Captain's House, Elijah Peck House,* Main St. May–Sept., Sat. 2–5. No charge.

Canaan  *Beebe Hill School,* Rte. 7 and Beebe Hill Rd. May–Oct. For hours, inquire locally.
*Falls Village–Canaan Historical Society Museum,* Main St., Falls Village. Fri. 10–12, 2–5. Dec.–Mar., closed morning hours. Also open by appointment. No charge.

Canton  *Canton Historical Museum,* 11 Front St., Collinsville. Wed., Thurs., Fri. 12–4; Sun. 2–5. Closed Dec. 15–Feb. 15. Guided tour $3.50.

Clinton   *Adam Stanton House*, 63 E. Main St., U.S. 1. Tues.–Sun., May–Nov. 2–5; July–Aug. 11–5. No charge.

Colebrook   *Underwood House or Seymour Inn*, Village Center. May 30–Oct. 12, weekends and holidays, 2–4. No charge.

Cornwall   *Cornwall Historical Society Museum.* Open in summer, closed Nov.–May 1. No charge.

Coventry   *Nathan Hale Homestead*, South St. Daily, May 15–Oct. 15, 1–5. $1.00

Danbury   *Danbury Scott-Fanton Museum*, 43 Main St. Wed.–Fri., 2–5; Sat. 10–5; Sun. 1–5.

Darien   *Bates Scofield Homestead*, 45 Old Kings Highway. Wed. 10–4, Sun. 2:30–4:30. No charge.
*Milestone Village Museum*, 1844 Boston Post Rd. Open only by request.

Deep River   *The Stone House*, S. Main St. Tues., Thurs. 2–5. No charge.

East Granby   *Old Newgate Prison and Copper Mine*, Newgate Rd. Memorial Day–Oct. 31, Tues.–Sun. 10–4:30. Adults $1.00, children 50¢.

East Haddam   *Amasa Day House*, Main St., Moodus. May 15–Oct. 15, 1–5. Adults 50¢, children 25¢.
*Nathan Hale Schoolhouse*, Rte. 149. For admission, inquire at the Chamber of Commerce Information Booth.
*Goodspeed Opera House.* For tours inquire at the Opera House or the Chamber of Commerce Information Booth.

East Lyme   *Thomas Lee House*, Rte. 156, Niantic. Memorial Day–Columbus Day, Mon., Wed.–Sun., 10–5. 75¢, which includes admission to the Little Boston School House.
*Little Boston School House*, Rte. 156. See above.

Essex   *Lieutenant William Pratt House*, 20 West Ave. Open by appointment. 50¢.

Fairfield  *Historical Museum,* 636 Old Post Rd. Mon.–Fri. 9:30–4:30. No charge.

Farmington  *Farmington Museum, Stanley-Whitman House,* 37 High St. Apr.–Dec. 1, Sun. 2–5, weekdays except Mon. 10–12, 2–5; Dec.–Apr. 1, Fri., Sat. 10–12, 2–5, Sun. 2–5. Adults 50¢, children 25¢.

*Hill-Stead Museum,* 671 Farmington Ave. Wed., Thurs., Sat., Sun. 2–5. Other times by appointment. Adults 50¢, children 25¢.

Glastonbury  *Old Town Hall Museum,* Main and Hubbard Sts. Sun. 2–4, Apr. 15–Sept. 27. No charge.

*Welles-Shipman-Ward House,* 972 Main St., S. Glastonbury. Open by appointment. 50¢.

Goshen  *Goshen Historical Museum,* Old Middle Rd. July–Sept., Fri. 2–5. Oct.–June, by appointment. No charge.

Granby  *Abijah Rowe House,* 208 Salmon Brook St. Open first Sun. of each month, May–Nov., and by appointment. $1.00 per family.

Greenwich  *Bruce Museum,* Steamboat Rd. Mon.–Fri. 10–5, Sun. 2–5. Closed national holidays. No charge.

*Bush-Holley House,* 39 Strickland Rd., Cos Cob. Tues.–Sat. 10–12, 2–5. Sun. 2–4.

*Putnam Cottage.* 243 E. Putnam Ave. (Rte. 1). Mon., Thurs.–Sat. 10–5. Closed national holidays. Adults 50¢.

Groton  *Indian Museum,* Old Mystic, north of I–95 on Rte. 27. Mon.–Wed., Sat. 2–4. No charge.

*Monument House Museum,* Park Ave., Fort Griswold State Park. Tues.–Sat. 1–4, Sun., holidays, 1–5. No charge.

*Noank Museum,* 17 Sylvan St., Noank. July–Aug., Sat., Sun. 2–5; Sept.–June, Wed. 2–5. Other times by appointment. No charge.

Guilford  *Thomas Griswold House,* Boston St. Apr.–Nov., Wed.–Sun. 11–5. Adults 50¢, children under 12 no charge.

*The Hyland House,* Boston St. June 15–Sept. 29, daily except Mon. 10:30–4:30. Adults 50¢, children under 12 no charge.

*Henry Whitfield Museum,* Old Whitfield St. Apr.–Nov., Wed.–Sun. 11–5; Nov.–Apr., 11–4. Closed Dec. 15–Jan. 15. Adults 50¢, children under 12 no charge.

Haddam    *Thankful Arnold House,* Rte. 9 and Walkley Hill. July–Sept., weekends, 1–5. No charge.

Hamden    *Jonathan Dickerman House,* Mt. Carmel Ave. Mid-May–mid-Oct., Sat., Sun. 2–5 and by appointment. No charge.

Hartford    *Antiquarian and Landmarks Society,* 394 Main St. May 15–Oct. 15, Mon.–Sun., holidays, 1–5. Adults 50¢, children 25¢.

*Conn. Historical Society,* 1 Elizabeth St. Museum 1–5, Library 9:30–5:30. Closed Sun., holidays, Sat. afternoons in summer. No charge.

*Conn. State Library,* 231 Capitol Ave. Mon.–Fri. 8:30–5; Sat. 9–1 except holiday weekends. Closed Sun. and holidays. No charge.

*Nook Farm* (Twain-Stowe houses.) Combined tour $2.00.

*Harriet Beecher Stowe House,* 77 Forest Rd. Sept. 15–June 15, afternoons 2–5, closed Mon. June 15–Sept. 15 weekdays, except Mon. 10–5. Sun. 2–5. $1.00; 18 and under 50¢; preschool no charge.

*Mark Twain House,* 351 Farmington Ave. Same schedule as Stowe House (above). Adults $1.25; 18 and under 50¢; preschool no charge.

*Old State House,* 800 Main St. Tues.–Sat. 12–4. Closed some holidays. Adults 50¢, children under 15 10¢.

*The State Capitol,* Capitol Hill.

Kent    *Sloane–Stanley Museum,* U.S. 7, Kent Furnace.

Memorial Day–Oct. 31, Wed.–Sun. 10–4:30.
Adults 50¢, children 25¢.

Lebanon   *Jonathan Trumbull House,* Main St. and Colchester Rd. May–Nov., Tues.–Sat. 1–5. 50¢.
*War Office,* W. Town St. May–Labor Day, Sat. 2–5 and by appointment. 25¢.

Ledyard   *Nathan Lester House,* off Rte. 12. Tues., Thurs. 2–5; Sat., Sun. 1–5. No charge.

Litchfield   *Heritance House,* Sawmill Rd. By appointment only. Limited to groups of four. Closed Jan.–May.
*Litchfield Historical Society Museum,* East St. May 15–Labor Day, Tues.–Sat. 11–5, Sun. 2–5. Labor Day–May 14, Tues.–Sat. 2–4. No charge.
*Tapping Reeve House and First Law School,* South St. May 15–Labor Day, Tues.–Sat. 11–5, Sun. 2–5. Labor Day–May 14, Tues.–Sat. 2–4. Adults 50¢, children 25¢.

Lyme   *Gillette Castle,* Gillette Castle State Park. Memorial Day–Columbus Day 11–5. 50¢.

Madison   *Nathaniel Allis House,* Post Rd. June 15–Sept. 15, Tues.–Sat. 10–5. Adults 50¢, children 25¢, children under 12 no charge.

Manchester   *Cheney Homestead,* 106 Hartford Rd. Thurs., Sun. 1–5. Adults 50¢, children under 16 no charge.
*Lutz Jr. Museum,* 132 Cedar St. Tues.–Sun. 2–5. No charge.

Mansfield   *Old Eagleville School.* Rte. 32 and S. Eagleville Rd., Storrs. June–Aug., Thurs. 2–5. No charge.

Meriden   *Andrews Homestead,* 424 W. Main St. Sun., Wed. 2–5, and by appointment. Adults $1.00, children 16 and under no charge.

Middletown   *General Mansfield House,* 151 Main St. Wed. 3–5. 35¢.

Milford   *Eells-Stow House,* 34 High St. May 30–Labor Day, Wed. 1–5, Sun. 2–5. Donation.

Monroe    *Barn-Hill-East Village Schoolhouse,* Monroe Center. By appointment. No charge.

Montville    *Tantaquidgeon Indian Museum,* Rte. 32. May–Oct., Mon.–Sun., holidays, 10–6. Donation.

Morris    *James Morris Reading Room,* Morris Academy. Tues.–Sat. 1–4. No charge.

New Britain    *Children's Museum,* 28 High St. (Hawley Memorial Library) Mon.–Fri. 9–2, Sat. 10–4. Closed holidays and Sat. July–Aug. No charge.

New Canaan    *Hanford-Silliman House, Town House, John Rogers Studio, Cody Drugstore,* 13 Oenoke Ridge. Tues.–Sat. 9:30–12:30, 2–4:30. No charge, except 50¢ admission to costume museum.

New Haven    *Pardee Morris House,* 325 Lighthouse Rd. May–Oct., Mon.–Fri. 10–5, Sun. 2–5, closed holidays. No charge.
*New Haven Colony Historical Society,* 114 Whitney Ave. Tues.–Fri. 9–5; Sat., Sun. 2–5. No charge.

New London    *Hempstead House,* 11 Hempstead St. May 15–Oct. 15, daily 1–5, Sun. 2–5. Adults 50¢, children 25¢.
*Lyman Allyn Museum,* 100 Mohegan Ave. Tues.–Sat., holidays, 1–5; Sun. 2–5. No charge.
*Nathan Hale Schoolhouse,* Mill St. For hours, inquire locally.
*New London County Court House,* Huntington St. For hours, inquire locally.
*Old Town Mill,* Mill St. June–Sept. 15 daily except Mon. 12:30–5. No charge.
*Shaw Mansion,* 11 Blinman St. Tues.–Sat. 1–4. Adults 50¢, children 25¢.

New Milford    *New Milford Historical Museum,* 6 Aspetuck Ave. Wed., Sat. 2–5, closed legal holidays. No charge.

Norfolk    *Norfolk Historical Society Museum,* Village

| | |
|---|---|
| | Green. June 16–Sept. 14, Sat. 10–12, Sun. 2–5. No charge. |
| North Branford | *Red School House,* Old Post Rd. Open by request. |
| Norwalk | *Lockwood-Mathews Mansion,* 295 West Ave. In process of restoration. For hours, inquire locally. |
| Norwich | *Backus House, Rockwell House,* 42 Rockwell St. July–Aug., Wed. 2–5. No charge. *Leffingwell Inn,* 345 Washington St. May 16–May 31, daily except Mon. 2–4; June–Labor Day, 10–12:30, 2–4; Labor Day–Oct. 15, 2–4; Oct. 16–May 15, Sat., Sun. 2–4 or by appointment. Adults 50¢, children no charge. |
| Old Lyme | *Florence Griswold House,* Lyme St. Tues.–Sun. and holidays 1–5. Closed Sept. 10–June 15. Adults 50¢, children 25¢. |
| Old Saybrook | *Older Bushnell House,* Boston Post Rd. Tues.–Sun. 12–5, summer. Adults $1.00, children 25¢. |
| Plymouth | *Plymouth Museum,* opposite the green. By appointment. No charge. |
| Preston | *Preston City Blacksmith Shop,* Preston City. By appointment. Contact town clerk. No charge. |
| Prospect | *Prospect Historical Society Building,* Center St. By appointment. |
| Redding | *Colonial Museum,* Israel Putnam Memorial State Park, Rte. 58. Memorial Day–Labor Day, 12–4. No charge. *Mark Twain Memorial Library,* Redding Rd., in the Center. Mon., Fri. 10–5; Tues., Wed. 1–5; Thurs. 1–8:30; Sat. 10–1. No charge. |
| Ridgefield | *Keeler Tavern,* Main St. Wed., Sat., Sun. 2–5. Adults $1.00, children 25¢. *Ridgefield Historical Society Museum,* 151 Main St. Mon.–Sat. 10–6. Closed holidays. No charge. |

Rocky Hill    *Academy Hall Museum,* Old Main St. May–Nov., Sun. 3–5. No charge.

Salisbury    *Town Hall.* Mon.–Fri. 9–5. No charge.

Sharon    *Gay-Hoyt House,* Main St. May–Nov., Tues.–Sat. 12–5.

Simsbury    *Simsbury Historic Center,* 800 Hopmeadow St. May–Oct., Tues.–Sat. 1–4. Adults $1.25, no charge to children under 12.

Stamford    *Hoyt Farmhouse,* 713 Bedford St. By appointment only. Donation.

*Stamford Museum and Nature Center,* 39 Scofieldtown Rd. Mon.–Sat. 9–5; Sun., holidays, 2–6. No charge.

Stonington    *Denison Homestead,* Pequotsepos Rd., Mystic. May 15–Oct. 31, Sat., Sun. 1–5. Other hours by appointment. Adults 75¢, children 25¢.

*Mystic Seaport,* Rte. 27. March 27–Nov. 1, Mon.–Sun., holidays, 9–5; Nov. 2–March 26, Mon.–Sun., holidays, 9–4. Admission: Mar. 27–Nov. 1, Adults $3.00, children $1.25; Nov. 2–Mar. 26, Adults $2.50, children $1.00.

*Old Lighthouse Museum,* Water St. July 1–Labor Day 12:30–4:30 daily except Mon. Adults 75¢, children 6–12 25¢, children under six no charge.

*Whitehall Mansion,* Rte. 27. Daily except Sat. 1–4. Adults 75¢, children 6–12 25¢.

Stratford    *Captain David Judson House,* 967 Academy Hill. May 1–Labor Day, Wed., Sat., Sun. 11–5. Adults $1.00, children 50¢.

Suffield    *Hatheway House,* High St. May 15–Oct. 15, daily, 1–5. $1.00.

*Dr. Alexander King House,* 234 S. Main St. For hours, inquire locally.

Thomaston    *Thomaston Opera House,* Main St. For hours, inquire locally.

*Historical Museum,* Main St. For hours, inquire locally.

| | |
|---|---|
| Tolland | *Benton Homestead,* Metcalf Rd. Sun. 1–4. 50¢. *Tolland State Jail,* Tolland Green. For hours, inquire locally. |
| Torrington | *Torrington Historical Society Hotchkiss Fyler House,* 192 Main St. By appointment. *Turner Museum,* Torrington Library, 12 Daycoeton Pl. Sat. 9:30–12, 1:30–5 or by appointment. No charge. |
| Wallingford | *The Parsons House,* 180 S. Main St. Sun. 2–5 and July 4. No charge. |
| Warren | *Old Brick Schoolhouse.* Brick School Rd. July, Aug. Sun. 2–5. No charge. |
| Washington | *Gunn Memorial Library Historical Museum,* Wykeham Rd. Tues., Thurs. 2–5; Sat. 1–4. No charge. |
| Waterbury | *Mattatuck Museum,* 119 W. Main St. Tues.–Sat. 12–5, Sun. 2–5. Closed weekends July, Aug. No charge. |
| Waterford | *Harkness Mansion,* Rte. 213. May 30–Oct. 12, weekdays 10–5, weekends and holidays 10–6. Park admission: adults 50¢, children under 12, no charge. |
| Watertown | *Watertown Museum,* 22 DeForest St. Wed. 2–4, Thurs. 7–9, and by appointment. No charge. |
| West Hartford | *Central Conn. Museum,* 2783 Albany Ave. For hours, inquire locally. *Noah Webster House,* 222 S. Main St. Thurs. 10–4, Sun. 2–4. Adults 50¢, children 6–12 25¢. |
| Weston | *Old Barn Museum,* Weston Rd., Rte. 57. By appointment. No charge. |
| Wethersfield | *Buttolph-Williams House,* 249 Broad St. May 15–Oct. 15, daily 1–5. 50¢. *Cove Warehouse,* Wethersfield Cove. By appointment only. *Silas Deane House,* 203 Main St. Tues.–Sat. 10–4; Sun. 1–4, mid-May–Sept. Adults $1.00, children 25¢. |

*Old Academy Museum,* 150 Main St. Tues., Thurs., Sat. 1–4. Adults 75¢, children 25¢.

*Isaac Stevens House,* 213 Main St. Tues.–Sat. 10–4; May 15–Nov. 1, Sun. 1–4. Adults $1.00, children 25¢.

*The Webb House,* 211 Main St. Tues.–Sat. 10–4, Sun. 1–4 May 15–Nov. 1. Adults $1.00, children 25¢.

Wilton    *Craft Center Museum,* 78 Danbury Rd., U.S. 7. Mon.–Fri. 10–4. Closed Jan., Feb., all national holidays. No charge.

*Sloan/Raymond Fitch House, Lambert House,* 150 Danbury Rd. Wed.–Fri., Sun. 2–5. No charge.

Winchester    *Solomon Rockwell House,* Prospect and Lake Sts., Winsted. For hours, inquire locally.

Windsor    *Oliver Ellsworth House.* 778 Palisado Ave. May–Nov., Tues.–Sat. 1–6. Adults 50¢, children under 16 no charge.

Woodbury    *Glebe House,* Hollow Rd. Tues.–Sat. 11–5, Sun. 2–5. No charge.

*Hurd House,* Hollow Rd. In process of restoration. For hours, inquire locally.

Woodstock    *Roseland* (Henry C. Bowen House), Rte. 169. June–Oct., Tues., Thurs., Sat. 1–5. Conn. residents $1.00, others $2.00.

## Art Museums, Galleries, and Centers

Bridgeport    *Housatonic Museum of Contemporary Art,* 510 Barnum Ave. For hours, inquire locally.

*Museum of Art, Science and Industry,* 4450 Park Ave. Tues.–Sun. 2–5. Closed national holidays. Adults $1.00, children 50¢.

Danbury    *Danbury Scott–Fanton Museum,* 43 Main St. Wed.–Fri. 2–5; Sat. 10–5; Sun. 1–5. No charge.

Farmington    *Hill-Stead Museum,* 671 Farmington Ave.

Wed., Thurs., Sat., Sun. 2–5, and by appointment. Adults 50¢, children 25¢.

Greenwich  *Bruce Museum,* Steamboat Rd. Mon.–Fri. 10–5, Sun. 2–5. Closed national holidays. No charge.

Groton  *Indian Museum,* Old Mystic, north of I–95 on Rte. 27. Mon.–Wed., Sat. 2–4. No charge.

*Mystic Art Gallery,* Water St., Mystic. For hours, inquire locally.

Hartford  *Austen Arts Center,* Trinity College. For hours, inquire locally.

*Conn. Historical Society,* 1 Elizabeth St. Museum hours 1–5, Library 9:30–5:30. Closed Sundays, holidays, Sat. afternoons in summer. No charge.

*Wadsworth Atheneum,* 600 Main St. Tues.–Sat. 10–5, Sun. 1–6. Closed Mon., major holidays. No charge.

Manchester  *Antique Auto Museum,* Slater St. Daily, 11–5. Adults $1.00, children under 12, 50¢.

*Lutz Jr. Museum,* 132 Cedar St. Tues.–Sun. 2–5. No charge.

Mansfield  *William Benton Museum of Art,* University of Connecticut. For hours, inquire locally.

Middletown  *Davison Art Center,* Wesleyan University, 301 High St. Mon.–Fri. 9–5, Sat. 9–12, Sun. 2–5. June–Aug., Mon.–Fri. 9–4. No charge.

Montville  *Tantaquidgeon Indian Museum,* Rte. 32. May–Oct., Mon.–Sun., holidays, 10–6. Contribution.

New Britain  *Central Conn. State College Museum.* For hours, inquire locally.

*Children's Museum,* 28 High St. (Hawley Mem. Library) Mon.–Fri. 9–2, Sat. 10–4. Closed holidays and Sat., July and Aug. No charge.

*New Britain Museum of American Art,* 56 Lexington St. Daily, except Mon. and holidays, 1–5. No charge.

New Canaan    *Silvermine Guild of Artists Museum,* Silvermine Rd. Daily. No charge.

New Haven    *New Haven Colony Historical Society,* 114 Whitney Ave. Tues.–Fri. 9–5; Sat., Sun. 2–5. No charge.

*Yale University Art Gallery,* 1111 Chapel St. Tues., Wed., Fri., Sat. 10–5; Thurs. 10–5, 6–9; Sun. 2–5. No charge.

New London    *Lyman Allyn Museum,* 100 Mohegan Ave. Tues.–Sat., holidays, 1–5; Sun. 2–5. No charge.

Norfolk    *Yale Summer School.* Weekly exhibits. For hours, inquire locally.

Norwalk    *Karamuseum,* 133 Lexington Ave. Tues.–Sat. 10–5. No charge.

Norwich    *Slater Museum* (Converse Art Gallery), 108 Crescent St. Sept.–May, Mon.–Fri. 9–4; Sat., Sun. 2–5. June–Aug., Tues.–Sun. 1–4. No charge.

Old Lyme    *Lyme Art Gallery,* Lyme St. For hours, inquire locally.

Ridgefield    *Aldrich Museum of Contemporary Art,* Main St. Apr. 22–Dec. 16, Sat. and Sun. 2–5. Adults $1.00, children 50¢.

Sharon    *Sharon Playhouse Gallery of Art.* Late June–Labor Day.

Stamford    *Stamford Museum and Nature Center,* 39 Scofieldtown Rd. Mon.–Sat. 9–5; Sun., holidays, 2–6. No charge.

Stonington    *Mystic Seaport.* See "Historical Museums" for schedules and rates.

Washington    *Gunn Memorial Library Historical Museum,* Wykeham Rd. Tues., Thurs. 2–5; Sat. 1–4. No charge.

Waterbury    *Mattatuck Museum,* 119 West Main St. Tues.–Sat. 12–5; Sun. 2–5. Closed weekdays, July, Aug. No charge.

Waterford    *Harkness Mansion* (Brasher Collection), Rte. 213. May 30–Oct. 12, weekdays 10–5, week-

ends and holidays 10–6. Park admission: adults
50¢, children under 12, no charge.
West Hartford    *St. Joseph College Museum,* 1678 Asylum Ave.
For hours, inquire locally.

Many communities also have seasonal, informal outdoor art and
craft shows, often on the town greens. For these schedules,
consult the local newspapers.


**Theaters, Auditoriums, and Stadiums**

The major theaters, auditoriums, and stadiums are indicated in the
town descriptions. Colleges have the usual campus performances,
lectures, theatrical productions, concerts, and athletic events—and
for details of these you should consult college information offices.
There are also 150 community theater groups throughout Connecticut. New ones come into existence; unsuccessful ones
disband. At any given time, therefore, it is not possible to compile
a list of those that will be performing when you may wish to
attend. You should consult the town clerk's office and local papers
for information.

The list below contains many of the major permanent theaters,
auditoriums, and stadiums where entertainment is available.

Bridgeport    Bernhard Center, University of Bridgeport
University Ave.
Klein Memorial Auditorium
910 Fairfield Ave.
Sacred Heart University Auditorium
Park Ave.
Polka Dot Playhouse
Pleasure Beach
Wonderland of Ice
Glenwood Park
Canaan    Magic Mountain
Falls Village
Clinton    William Stanton Andrews Town Hall
Rte. 1

|  |  |
|---|---|
| Danbury | Berkshire Auditorium |
|  | Western Conn. State College |
| East Haddam | Goodspeed Opera House |
|  | The Plaza (east end of bridge at Conn. River) |
| Essex | Ivoryton Playhouse |
|  | Main St., Ivoryton |
| Fairfield | Fairfield University Playhouse |
|  | North Benson Rd. |
|  | Fairfield University Shell |
|  | Fairfield University |
| Farmington | Triangle Playhouse |
|  | Farmington Ave. |
| Hartford | Bushnell Memorial Hall |
|  | 166 Capitol Ave. |
|  | Trinity College Austin Arts Center |
|  | Summit St. |
|  | Dillon Stadium |
|  | Colt Park |
|  | Hartford Stage Company |
|  | 65 Kinsley St. |
| Manchester | Manchester Community College Auditorium |
|  | Hartford Rd. |
| Mansfield | Jorgensen Auditorium |
|  | University of Conn., Storrs |
|  | Fine Arts Center |
|  | University of Conn., Storrs |
| Middletown | The Big Barn |
|  | Wesleyan Hills |
|  | Wesleyan University Rich Hall |
|  | Wesleyan University |
| New Britain | Welte Auditorium |
|  | Central Conn. College |
|  | Darius Miller Music Shell |
|  | Walnut Hill Park, W. Main St. |
| New Fairfield | Candlewood Theatre |
|  | Rte. 39 |
| New Haven | Long Wharf Theatre |
|  | 222 Sargent Dr. |

Shubert Theatre
247 College St.
Lyman Auditorium
Southern Conn. State College
Yale University School of Drama
222 York St.
Yale Repertory Theatre
1120 Chapel St.
Woolsey Hall
254 College St.
Sprague Hall
470 College St.
New Haven Veterans Memorial Coliseum
275 S. Orange St.
Payne Whitney Gymnasium
Tower Pkwy.
Yale Bowl
Derby Ave.

New London    Palmer Auditorium
Connecticut College
Dana Concert Hall
Connecticut College

Norfolk    Yale Summer School of Music and Art

Sharon    Sharon Playhouse
Main St.

Simsbury    Simsbury Farms Amphitheatre
Simsbury Farms
Old Farms Rd.

Southbury    Southbury Playhouse
Oak Tree Rd.

Stamford    Stamford Museum
39 Scofieldtown Rd.

Stratford    American Shakespeare Festival Theatre
and Museum
1850 Elm St.

Thomaston    Thomaston Opera House
Main St.

| | |
|---|---|
| Wallingford | Oakdale Theatre |
| | Old Hartford Turnpike |
| Waterford | Eugene O'Neill Memorial Theatre |
| | Waterford Beach Park |
| West Hartford | Millard Auditorium, Auerbach Auditorium |
| | University of Hartford |
| Westport | Westport Country Playhouse |
| | 25 Powers Court |
| | White Barn Theatre |
| | Newtown Ave. |
| Wilton | Wilton Playshop Theatre |
| | 15 Lovers Lane |

## Science and Industry Museums

Barkhamsted    *John Tarrant Kenney Hitchcock Museum,* Rte. 20, Riverton. May–Nov. 30, Tues.–Sat. 10–5. Dec.–Apr. 30, Sat. 10–5. No charge.

Bridgeport    *Museum of Art, Science & Industry,* 4450 Park Ave. Tues.–Sun. 2–5. Closed national holidays. No charge.

Bristol    *American Clock and Watch Museum,* 100 Maple St. Apr.–Oct. 31, Tues.–Sat. 1–5. Adults $1.00, children 50¢, children under 8 no charge.

East Haven    *Branford Trolley Museum.* See "Excursions—Trains and Trolleys" for hours and rates.

East Windsor    *Conn. Electric Railway Assoc.* See "Excursion—Trains and Trolleys" for hours and rates.
*Scantic Academy Museum,* Rte. 191, Warehouse Point. Sun., May–June, Sept.–Oct., 2–5. Other days by appointment. No charge.

Greenwich    *Bruce Museum,* Steamboat Rd. Mon.–Fri. 10–5, Sun. 2–5. Closed national holidays. No charge.

Groton    *U.S. Naval Submarine Base.* Weekends only, by prearrangement—Base Public Affairs Office.

Haddam    *Conn. Yankee Atomic Power Plant,* Rte. 151.

| | |
|---|---|
| Manchester | *Lutz Jr. Museum,* 132 Cedar St. Tues.–Sun. 2–5. No charge. |
| Middletown | *Submarine Library & Museum,* 440 Washington St. Weekdays 10–1, weekends 10–5. No charge. |
| New Britain | *Central Conn. State College Museum,* 1615 Stanley St. For hours, inquire locally. |
| | *Children's Museum,* 28 High St. (Hawley Mem. Library) Mon.–Fri. 9–2, Sat. 10–4. Closed holidays, Sat. in July and Aug. No charge. |
| New Haven | *Southern N. E. Telephone Co. Exhibit,* 227 Church St. Mon.–Fri. 8:30–4:30. No charge. |
| | *Winchester Gun Museum,* 275 Winchester Ave. Mon.–Sat. 9–4. Closed national holidays. No charge. |
| Newington | *American Radio Relay League Museum of Amateur Radio,* 225 N. Main St. Mon.–Fri. 8–4, Sat.–Sun. by appointment. No charge. |
| New London | *Thames Science Center,* Gallows Lane. Mon.–Fri. 9–5, Sat. 1–5. No charge. |
| | *U.S. Coast Guard Academy.* Grounds open daily until sundown. |
| Norwalk | *Karamuseum,* 133 Lexington Ave., S. Norwalk. Tues.–Sat. 10–5. No charge. |
| Plymouth | *Lock Museum of America,* 114 Main St., Terryville. May–Oct., daily except Mon. 1:30–4:30. Adults 50¢, children under 12 no charge. |
| Stonington | *Mystic Seaport.* See "Historic Houses and Historic Museums" for hours and rates. |
| West Hartford | *Children's Museum,* 950 Trout Brook Dr. Daily 9–5, Sun. 1–5. No charge. |
| Wethersfield | *Wethersfield Cove Warehouse.* By appointment. |
| Wilton | *Wilton Craft Center Museum,* 78 Danbury Rd. (U.S. 7) Mon.–Fri. 10–4. Closed Jan.–Feb., all national holidays. No charge. |
| Windsor Locks | *Bradley Air Museum,* Bradley Field. Sat., Sun., Memorial Day, Fourth of July, Labor Day, 12–6. |

Closed during inclement weather. Adults 75¢, children 5–16, 25¢.

## Natural History Museums, Zoos and Nature Centers, and Sanctuaries

Bridgeport  *Beardsley Park Zoo,* Noble Avenue. Daily 6–6. Bird and Mammal Building: 11–4. Closed Thanksgiving, Christmas, and New Year's days. No charge.

Canton  *Roaring Brook Nature Center,* Gracey Rd. Tues.–Sat. 10–5; Sun. 2–5. No charge.

Fairfield  *Birdcraft Museum,* 314 Unquowa Rd. Tues., Thurs. 2–5; Sat. 10–5; Sun. 12–5. No charge.
*Natural History Museum and Larsen Sanctuary,* 2325 Burr St. Tues.–Sat. 9–5, Sun. 12–5. $1.00 per car.

Greenwich  *Audubon Nature Center,* Riversville Rd., Quaker Ridge. For hours, inquire locally.
*Bruce Museum,* Steamboat Rd. Mon.–Fri. 10–5, Sun. 2–5. Closed national holidays. No charge.

Hartford  *Keeney Park Children's Zoo.* For hours, inquire locally.

Litchfield  *Nature Center and Museum,* south of Rte. 25. Mid-June–Labor Day, Tues.–Sat. 10–4:30, Sun. 2–5; mid-Apr.–mid-June, Labor Day–Oct., Sat., Sun. 2–5. No charge.

Manchester  *Lutz Jr. Museum,* 132 Cedar St. Tues.–Sun. 2–5. No charge.

New Britain  *Children's Museum,* 28 High St. (Hawley Mem. Library) Mon.–Fri. 9–2, Sat. 10–4. Closed holidays and Sat., July and Aug. No charge.

New Canaan  *New Canaan Nature Center.* Tues.–Sat. 10–5, Sun. 1–5. Closed major holidays and weekday mornings in July and Aug. No charge.

New Fairfield  *Hidden Valley Nature Center,* Gillotti Rd. Weekdays by appointment, Sun. 2–5. Closed in winter and inclement weather. No charge.

New Haven  *Peabody Museum of Natural History,* 170

Whitney Ave. Mon.–Sat. 9–5; Sun., holidays, 1–5. Adults 50¢, children 25¢.

*West Rock Nature Center,* West Rock Park. Daily, holidays, 9–one hour after sunset. Zoo: 9–4:30. No charge.

New London   *Herbert F. Moran Nature Center and Zoo,* Chester St. Summer, daily 10–8:30, holidays 10–8:30; winter, daily and holidays 10–4:30. No charge.

*Thames Science Center,* Gallows Lane. Mon.–Fri. 9–5, Sat. 1–5. No charge.

North Canaan   *Douglas Library, C. H. Pease Nature Museum.* Library hours.

Norwalk   *Karamuseum,* 133 Lexington Ave. Tues.–Sat. 10–5. No charge.

*Old MacDonald Farm,* 768 Conn. Ave. Daily, holidays, 11–6, summer. $2.25.

Rocky Hill   *Dinosaur State Park,* West St. Daily, 10–5, Apr.–Nov. No charge.

Sharon   *Sharon Audubon Center,* Rte. 4. Tues.–Sat. 9–12, 1–5; Sun. 1–5. No charge.

Simsbury   *McLean Game Refuge.* For hours, inquire locally.

Stamford   *Stamford Museum and Nature Center,* 39 Scofieldtown Rd. Mon.–Sat. 9–5; Sun. and holidays, 2–6. No charge.

Stonington   *Denison Pequotsepos Wildlife Sanctuary,* Pequotsepos Rd., Mystic. Daily 9–5, Sun. 1–5. Adults 50¢, children 25¢.

Waterford   *Harkness Mansion* (Brasher bird studies), Rte. 213. May 30–Oct. 12, weekdays 10–5, weekends and holidays 10–6. Park admission, adults 50¢, children under 12, no charge.

West Hartford   *Children's Museum of Hartford,* 950 Trout Brook Dr. Daily 9–5, Sun. 1–5. No charge.

Westport   *Mid-Fairfield County Youth Museum,* 10 Woodside Lane. Mon.–Sat. 9–5, Sun. and holidays, 2–5. No charge.

Woodbury    *Flanders Nature Center-Van Vleck Sanctuary,* off Flanders Rd. Open daylight hours. *Whittemore Sanctuary,* off Rte. 64. Open daylight hours.

## Arboretums and Gardens

| | |
|---|---|
| Bristol | Bristol Nurseries<br>Pinehurst Rd. |
| East Hartford | Oriental Garden<br>Wickham Park |
| Hartford | Rose Gardens<br>Elizabeth Park, West Hartford |
| New London | Connecticut Arboretum<br>Williams St., Conn. College |
| Norwich | Memorial Rose Garden<br>Mohegan Park |
| Stamford | Stamford Museum and Nature Center<br>39 Scofieldtown Rd.<br>Bartlett Arboretum<br>151 Brookdale Rd. |
| Waterbury | Hamilton Park Rose Garden<br>East Main St. |
| Waterford | Harkness Memorial State Park<br>Rte. 213 |
| West Hartford | Elizabeth Park<br>915 Prospect Ave. |
| Woodstock | Roseland<br>West side of town green |

## Churches and Cemeteries

Most Connecticut towns and many of their communities have a green, on or near which are older church buildings, cemeteries, and monuments. The town descriptions contain many references to churches of particular historic and architectural interest. We suggest that you inquire locally about those open to the public. Cemeteries and burial grounds are usually open during daylight hours, or their schedules will be posted. A listing of those mentioned in the town descriptions follows:

| | |
|---|---|
| Andover | Townsend Cemetery |
| | Center Cemetery |
| Ansonia | Old Town Burying Ground |
| Burlington | Burlington Cemetery |
| Derby | Colonial Cemetery |
| East Haddam | Old Cove Burying Ground |
| Hartford | Ancient Burial Ground |
| Lebanon | Old Burial Ground |
| Milford | Old Burying Ground |
| Montville | Indian Burial Ground |
| New Haven | Center Church Crypt |
| | Grove St. Cemetery |
| New London | Ye Ancientist Burial Ground |
| Norwich | Royal Mohegan Burial Ground |
| Old Saybrook | Cypress Cemetery |
| Preston | Long Society Early Burial Ground |
| South Windsor | The Old Cemetery |
| Stonington | Old Burial Ground |
| West Hartford | Old Burial Ground |
| Wethersfield | Ancient Burial Ground |

## Other Places of Interest

(For explanation, see individual towns and cities.)

| | |
|---|---|
| Bethlehem | *Regina Laudis Priory Creche,* Flanders Rd. |
| Bridgeport | *Barnum Museum,* 820 Main St. Tues.–Sat., 2–5 Closed major holidays. No charge. |
| Colchester | *Comstock Covered Bridge,* junction Rtes. 16 and 149. |
| Cornwall | *Covered Bridge,* Rtes. 7 and 128. |
| Greenwich | *Greenwich Garden Center,* Bible St., Cos Cob. 9–4, except July, 9–12; closed August. No charge. |
| Kent | *Covered Bridge,* U.S. 7. |
| New Haven | *Yale Collection of Musical Instruments,* 15 |

Hillhouse Ave. Tues., Thurs. 2–4, Sun. 2–5. No charge.

North Stonington    *Grist Mill,* Clarks Falls.
Salisbury    *Lime Rock Race Track.*
Stonington    *Cannon Square.*
Thompson    *East Thompson Raceway.*
Torrington    *Indian Lookout.*
Waterbury    *Holy Land U.S.A.,* Pine Hill. Apr.–Dec. 1, 1:30–4:30, Sat. and Sun. 11–6. No charge for admission, 50¢ donation for parking.

# RECREATIONAL CONNECTICUT

### Boating

A digest of Connecticut Boating Laws and Regulations is available from the Boating Commission of the State of Connecticut, Department of Agriculture and Natural Resources, Hartford, as is the *Connecticut Boatman's Manual.*

The boatman should be familiar with and follow all regulations. In addition, in federal waters under Connecticut jurisdiction, U.S. Coast Guard regulations apply.

### Boat-Launch Sites

The Connecticut Board of Fisheries and Game, Hartford, makes available a listing of sites of "Public Access to Connecticut Fishing Waters." These waters are listed below by towns. For directions, see individual towns and cities.

*Fresh water*

| | |
|---|---|
| Barkhamsted | Compensating Reservoir |
| Berlin | Silver Lake |
| Bolton | Bolton Lakes |
| Bridgewater | Lake Lillinonah |
| Chester | Cedar Lake |
| | Pataconk Lake |
| Colchester | Pickerel Pond |

| | |
|---|---|
| Colebrook | Colebrook River Flood Control Impoundment |
| Cornwall | Mohawk Pond |
| Coventry | Bolton Lakes |
| | Waumgumbaug Lake |
| Danbury | Lake Kenosia |
| Eastford | Halls Pond |
| East Haddam | Bashan Lake |
| | Hayward Lake |
| | Moodus Reservoir |
| | Salmon River off Rte. 149, at river mouth |
| East Lyme | Dodge Pond |
| | Gortons Pond |
| | Patagansett Lake |
| | Powers Lake |
| Ellington | Crystal Lake |
| Enfield | Connecticut River |
| Farmington | Batterson Park Pond |
| Goshen | Dog Pond |
| | Mohawk Pond |
| | Tyler Pond |
| | West Side Pond |
| Griswold | Glasgo Pond |
| | Hopeville Pond |
| Guilford | Quonnipaug Lake |
| Haddam | Connecticut River |
| Hartland | Howells Pond |
| Hebron | Holbrook Pond |
| Kent | Waramaug Lake |
| Killingly | Wauregan Reservoir |
| Ledyard | Lantern Hill Pond |
| | Stoddard Hill, Thames River |
| Lyme | Norwich Pond |
| | Rogers Lake |
| | Uncas Lake |
| Mansfield | Naubesatuck Lake |
| Meriden | Silver Lake |
| Middlefield | Beseck Lake |
| | Black Pond |

| | |
|---|---|
| Middletown | Connecticut River |
| | Crystal Lake |
| | Dooley Pond |
| Montville | Gardner Lake |
| New Britain | Batterson Park Pond |
| New Fairfield | Ball Pond |
| | Candlewood Lake |
| | Squantz Pond |
| New Hartford | West Hill Pond |
| New London | Thames River |
| Newtown | Pond Brook |
| Norfolk | Wood Creek Pond |
| North Stonington | Andersons Pond |
| | Billings Lake |
| | Lake of Isles |
| | Long Pond |
| | Wyassup Lake |
| Old Lyme | Rogers Lake |
| Old Saybrook | Connecticut River |
| Preston | Amos Lake |
| | Avery Pond |
| Ridgefield | Mamanasco Lake |
| Salem | Gardner Lake |
| Salisbury | East Twin Lake |
| | Wononscopomuc Lake |
| Sharon | Mudge Pond |
| Shelton | Lake Housatonic |
| Southbury | Lake Zoar |
| Thompson | Little Pond |
| | Quaddick Reservoir |
| Torrington | Burr Pond |
| Union | Bigelow Pond |
| | Mashapaug Lake |
| | Morey Pond |
| Vernon | Bolton Lakes |
| Voluntown | Beach Pond |
| | Beachdale Pond |
| | Green Falls Reservoir |

|              |                        |
|--------------|------------------------|
| Wallingford  | North Farms Reservoir  |
| Winchester   | Highland Lake          |
|              | Park Pond              |
|              | Winchester Lake        |
| Windham      | Beaver Brook Pond      |
| Windsor      | Connecticut River      |
|              | Farmington River       |
|              | Rainbow Reservoir      |
| Woodstock    | Black Pond             |

*Saltwater*

|              |                          |
|--------------|--------------------------|
| Branford     | Branford River           |
| Bridgeport   | Seaside Park             |
| Groton       | Bayberry Lane            |
| Guilford     | East River               |
| Madison      | Hammonasset State Park   |
| New Haven    | Fort Hale                |
|              | Lighthouse Point         |
| Old Lyme     | Blackhall River          |
|              | Great Island             |
| Stonington   | Barn Island              |
| Waterford    | Dock Road                |
|              | Niantic River            |

## Camping

### State Campgrounds

There are over fifteen hundred campsites administered by the State of Connecticut, Department of Environmental Protection, Parks and Recreation, Hartford. Five of the campgrounds do not accept reservations, the rest of the sites must be reserved by mail. For facility, regulation, and reservation information, contact the Department.

|                |                                                          |
|----------------|----------------------------------------------------------|
| Canaan         | Housatonic Meadows State Park (Cornwall Bridge), 100 sites. |
| East Haddam    | Devils Hopyard State Park, 27 sites.                     |
| East Hampton   | Hurd State Park, 6 sites (no reservations).              |

| | |
|---|---|
| East Lyme | Rocky Neck State Park (Niantic). |
| Griswold | Hopeville Pond State Park (Jewett City), 80 sites. |
| Haddam | Cockaponset State Forest, 12 sites (no reservations). |
| Hamden | Sleeping Giant State Park (Mt. Carmel), 6 sites (no reservations). |
| Kent | Kent Falls State Park, 12 sites (no reservations). Macedonia Brook State Park, 80 sites. |
| Madison | Hammonasset Beach State Park, 460 sites. |
| Pomfret | Mashamoquet Brook State Park (Pomfret Center), 80 sites. |
| Southbury | Kettletown State Park, 80 sites. |
| Thomaston | Black Rock State Park, 90 sites. |
| Torrington | American Legion State Forest, Austin F. Hawes Memorial Campground, 30 sites. Taylor Brook Campground, Burr Pond State Park, 46 sites. |
| Voluntown | Pachaug State Forest, Mt. Misery Area, 20 sites (no reservations). |
| Washington | Lake Waramaug State Park (New Preston), 100 sites. |

**Privately Operated Camp and Mobile Equipment Sites**

There are varied camping sites available on privately operated grounds. A partial listing (with no attempt made to check facilities) follows:

| | |
|---|---|
| Bozrah | Acorn Acres Campsites Rte. 9, Fitchville |
| Branford | Paved Lane Motor Court 19 Leetes Rd. Shore Line Trailer Park 525 East Main St. (Rte. 1) |
| Brooklyn | Big Valley Family Campground One mile east off Rte. 6 |
| Canaan | Lone Oak Campsites Rte. 44 |

| | |
|---|---|
| Chaplin | Natchaug Valley Campground |
| | Between Rtes. 44 and 6 |
| Clinton | Riverdale Farm Campsites |
| | River Rd. |
| | River Road Campsites |
| | 13 River Rd. |
| Colchester | Zagerwood Family Camping |
| | Bush Rock Rd. |
| Eastford | The Pines Family Camping |
| | Rte. 171 |
| | Bobs Campground |
| | Rte. 198, Phoenixville |
| | Charlie Brown's Campground |
| | Rte. 198 |
| East Haddam | Wolf's Den Family Campsite |
| | Rte. 82 |
| East Hampton | Nelson's Family Campground |
| | Mott Hill Rd. |
| Griswold | High Hopes Campground |
| | Rte. 201, Jewett City |
| Groton | Arlington Acres Mobile Home Park |
| | Rte. 201 |
| | Dolphin Mobile Home Park |
| | Rte. 117 |
| | Travel Trailer Haven |
| | 88 Pleasant Valley Rd. |
| Killingly | Rockin D. Campground |
| | Snake Meadow Road, Danielson |
| | Hide A Way Cave |
| | East Killingly |
| Lisbon | Ross Hill Park |
| | Off Rte. 138 |
| Middlefield | North Powder Hill Ski/Resort Area |
| | Powder Hill Rd. |
| Milford | Riders Mobile Homes |
| | Rte. 1 |
| North Branford | Pleasant Acres Trailer Park |
| | Rte. 80 |

| | |
|---|---|
| North Stonington | Mobile Home Gardens |
| | Rte. 184 |
| Norwich | Hidden Acres Family Campground |
| | Off Rte. 165 |
| Pomfret | Laurel Heights |
| | Rte. 44, Abington |
| | This-is-it Camping |
| | Fay Road, Abington |
| | Whispering Winds |
| | Rte. 97, Abington |
| Putnam | Quaddick Lake |
| | North of Quaddick State Park |
| Salem | Witch Meadow Lake Campsites |
| | Witch Meadow Rd. |
| Sprague | Salt Rock Family Camping |
| | Rte. 97, Baltic |
| Stafford | Roaring Brook Campgrounds |
| | South Rd., Stafford Springs |
| Sterling | Sterling Highlands Family Camping |
| | Calvin French Dr. |
| | Sterling Park |
| | Gibson Hill Rd. |
| | River Bend |
| | Rte. 14A, Oneco |
| Torrington | Laurel Crest Campsites |
| | Highland Lake Rd. |
| Voluntown | Purola Farm Campground |
| | Rte. 49 |
| Wallingford | Gopian's Trailer Park |
| | Rte. 150, Yalesville |
| Westbrook | Green Acres Park |
| | Rte. 1 |
| Willington | KOA Moose Meadow Campgrounds |
| | Moose Meadow Rd. |
| Winchester | Laurel Crest Campground |
| | Highland Lake Rd., Winsted |

**Excursions—Boats and Ferries**

### Boats

*River Queen,* Saybrook Point, Old Saybrook. This paddlewheeler offers cruises of varied lengths weekends and holidays, spring and fall; and every day during summer: a ½-hour "Lighthouse Cruise," a 1½-hour "Lower River Cruise," and a 3-hour "Historic River Cruise." For fares and schedules contact the Connecticut Steamboat Line, 263 Main St., Old Saybrook (388-4664).

*See Submarines by Boat,* 86 Fairview Ave., Groton. Three 48-passenger tour boats operate April–September from the permanently moored ferry, Jamestown. One-hour, 7-mile tours. For fares and schedules contact the Whaling City Dredge and Dock Corp., 86 Fairview Ave., Groton (445-7401).

*Thimble Island Boat Tours,* Town Dock, Thimble Island Rd., Stony Creek, Branford. Seasonal operation. For fares and schedules contact Capt. Richard Howd (488-9978).

*Yankee Clipper,* Goodspeed Landing, East Haddam. A 400-passenger vessel, which cruises the lower Connecticut River spring and fall weekends, and daily through the summer. There are 3-hour cruises on either the upper or lower Connecticut River and a Sunday 5-hour cruise into Long Island Sound. The afternoon cruise on the lower river connects with the "Steam Train" at Deep River (see "Excursions, Trains"). For fares and schedules, contact the Connecticut Steamboat Line, 263 Main St., Old Saybrook (388-4664).

### Ferries

*Block Island—New London Ferry,* foot of State St., New London. Offers the 2½-hour trip to Block Island from early June to September. Car accommodations. For fares and schedules contact Block Island Ferry, Shaw's Cove, New London (442-9553).

*Bridgeport-Port Jefferson Ferry,* Union Square Dock, Bridgeport. One-way and round-trip passenger excursions available in addition to the usual car accommodations for crossing. Operates May–Oct. For fares and schedules contact the Bridgeport and Port Jefferson Steamboat Company (367-8571 or 334-5993).

*Chester-Hadlyme Ferry*, Rte. 148. Seasonal operation of small, car-ferry crossing the Connecticut River.

*Fishers Island—New London Ferry*, foot of State St., New London. A 45-minute trip to Fishers Island, operated year-round, with car accommodation. For fares and schedules contact Fishers Island Ferry District (443-6851).

*Orient Point-New London Ferry*, 112 Pequot Avenue, New London. A 1½-hour crossing of Long Island Sound. Cars accommodated. Round-trip crossings available. Operates March to January. For fares and schedules contact the ferry office at 112 Pequot Ave., New London (443-5281).

*Rocky Hill-Glastonbury Ferry*, Rte. 160. Seasonal operation of small, car-ferry crossing the Connecticut River.

### Excursions—Trains and Trolleys

**Trains**
*The Valley Railroad*, Company of Connecticut, Essex Station, Exit 3, Conn. Rte. 9, Essex. Fifty-minute steam-train rides offered spring and fall weekends, daily in summer, from the old Essex railway depot to Deep River and return. In the summer and fall schedules one trip daily connects with the excursion boat *Yankee Clipper* of the Conn. Steamboat Line (see "Excursions—Boats"). The equipment of the company includes three steam engines, coaches from four different railroads, two diners, three cabooses, a crane, and other equipment. The lines are being extended and will eventually run between Chester Ferry and Haddam to Old Saybrook. For fares and schedules contact the Valley Railroad Company, Essex (767-0103).

## Trolleys

*The Branford Electric Railroad* Association and Trolley Museum, 17 River St., East Haven. Open Sundays 1–5 early spring and late fall; weekends 1–5 during June and Sept.; daily through summer, 10–5 on weekdays, 11–6 on weekends. Adults 75¢, children 6–14 30¢. Rides on operating electric cars; with permanent exhibitions of electric street railway, interurban and rapid-transit railway cars and equipment, and models.

*Connecticut Electric Railway* Association, North Rd., Warehouse Point. Open May 30–Oct. 30; Sat., 1–5; Mar. 1–Dec. 31, Sun., 1–dusk. Adults 50¢, children 25¢, children under 5 no charge. Rides on operating equipment; with permanent exhibitions of electric streetcars from 1880–1947, railway equipment, and historical documents.

### Chronological Listing of Connecticut Fairs

The following is a listing of fairs arranged by the time periods in which they are usually held. As the specific dates change yearly, local papers and notices will be a good source of information for the actual dates. A *Handbook of Connecticut Fairs* is also available from the Department of Agriculture, State Office Building, Hartford, Connecticut 06115.

| *Time Period* | *Name* | *Location* |
|---|---|---|
| Late June | New London County 4-H | Norwichtown |
| Mid July | North Stonington Fair | North Stonington |
| Late July | Marlborough Grange Fair | Marlborough |
| Late July | Pachaug Community Fair | Griswold |
| Late July | Conn. State Grange Fair | Durham |
| | | |
| Early Aug. | New Haven County 4-H Fair | North Haven |
| Early Aug. | Lebanon Country Fair | Lebanon |
| Mid Aug. | Fairfield County 4-H Fair | Bethel |
| Mid Aug. | Coventry Town 4-H Fair | Coventry |
| Mid Aug. | Winchester Grange Fair | Winchester Center |

| | | |
|---|---|---|
| Mid Aug. | Litchfield County 4-H Fair | Goshen |
| Mid Aug. | Hamburg Fair | Hamburg |
| Mid Aug. | Preston City Fair | Preston |
| Mid Aug. | New London County 4-H Fair | Lebanon |
| Mid Aug. | Bridgewater Country Fair | Bridgewater |
| | | |
| Mid Aug. | Tolland County 4-H Fair | Rockville |
| Mid Aug. | Windham County 4-H Fair | South Woodstock |
| Mid Aug. | Middlesex County 4-H Fair | Durham |
| Late Aug. | Fairfield Old Fashion Fair | Fairfield |
| Late Aug. | Brooklyn Fair | Brooklyn |
| | | |
| Late Aug. | Chester Fair | Chester |
| Late Aug. | Hartford County 4-H Fair | Windsor Locks |
| Late Aug. | Southington Grange Fair | Southington |
| Early Sept. | Cheshire Fair | Cheshire |
| Early Sept. | Goshen Fair | Goshen |
| | | |
| Early Sept. | Woodstock Fair | South Woodstock |
| Early Sept. | Haddam Neck Fair | Haddam Neck |
| Early Sept. | Ledyard Fair | Ledyard |
| Early Sept. | North Haven Fair | North Haven |
| Early Sept. | Portland Agricultural Fair | Portland |
| | | |
| Early Sept. | Wapping Fair | South Windsor |
| Early Sept. | Cherry Brook Grange Fair | North Canton |
| Early Sept. | Echo Grange Fair | Mansfield Center |
| Early Sept. | Wethersfield Grange Fair | Wethersfield |
| Early Sept. | Bethlehem Fair | Bethlehem |
| | | |
| Mid Sept. | Meriden Grange Fair | Meriden |
| Mid Sept. | The Guilford Fair | Guilford |
| Mid Sept. | Hebron Harvest Fair | Hebron |
| Mid Sept. | Union Agricultural Society (Four Town Fair) | Somers |
| Mid–late Sept. | Eastern States Exposition | W. Springfield, Mass. |

| | | |
|---|---|---|
| Mid Sept. | Granby Grange Fair | Granby |
| Mid Sept. | Norwich Grange Fair | Norwichtown |
| Mid Sept. | Prospect Grange Fair | Prospect |
| Mid Sept. | Rocky Hill Grange Fair | Rocky Hill |
| Mid Sept. | Wallingford Grange Fair | Wallingford |
| | | |
| Mid Sept. | Terryville Country Fair | Terryville |
| Mid Sept. | Norfield Grange Fair | Weston |
| Late Sept. | Durham Agricultural Fair | Durham |
| Late Sept. | Mad River Fair | Waterbury |
| Late Sept. | Beacon Grange Fair | Northfield |
| | | |
| Late Sept. | Berlin Fair | Berlin |
| Late Sept.–early Oct. | Danbury State Fair | Danbury |
| Early Oct. | Harwinton Fair | Harwinton |
| Early–mid Oct. | Glastonbury Grange Fair | South Glastonbury |
| Mid Oct. | Riverton Fair | Riverton |

## Golf Courses Open to the Public

| Town | Name; Telephone | No. of Holes |
|---|---|---|
| Berlin | Timberlin Golf Club, Southington Rd., Kensington; *828-3228* | 18 |
| Bethel | Terre Haute Golf Course, Rte. 53; *no phone* | 9 |
| Bristol | Red Stone Hill Golf Club, Red Stone Hill Rd., Forestville; *583-6400* | 9 |
| Brookfield | Brookfield Golf Course, Brookfield Center; *775-2464* | 9 |
| Canaan | Canaan Country Club, South Canaan Rd.; *824-7683* | 9 |
| Canton | Canton Public Golf Course, Rte. 44; *693-8305* | 9 |
| Cromwell | Edgewood Golf Club, Golf Rd.; *346-9782* | 18 |

| | | |
|---|---|---|
| East Granby | Copper Hill Country Club, Newgate Rd.; *653-7087* | 9 |
| East Haddam | Banner Lodge Golf Course, Banner Rd., Moodus; *873-8652* | 18 |
| East Hartford | East Hartford Golf Club, Long Hill St.; *528-5082* | 18 |
| East Windsor | Tobacco Valley Country Club, Rte. 5, Warehouse Point; *623-7405* | 9 |
| Fairfield | Fairchild-Wheeler Golf Course, Eastern Turnpike; *374-6355* | |
| | Black Course | 18 |
| | Red Course | 18 |
| Farmington | Tunxis Plantation Country Club, Town Farm Rd.; *677-1367* | |
| | Tattagan | 9 |
| | Poquanoc | 9 |
| | Tokone | 9 |
| | Westwoods Country Club, Plainville Ave.; *677-9192* | 18 |
| Glastonbury | Minnechaug Golf Course, Manchester Rd.; *643-9914* | 18 |
| Groton | Shennecossett Golf Course, Plant St.; *445-0262* | 18 |
| Hamden | Laurel View Golf Course, West Shepard Ave.; *288-9625* | 18 |
| | Meadowbrook Golf Course, Dixwell Ave.; *248-9464* | 18 |
| Hartford | Goodwin Golf Course, Maple Ave.; *566-6535* | |
| | Front Nine | 9 |
| | Back Nine | 9 |
| | Flat Nine | 9 |
| | Keney Golf Course, Windsor Ave.; *566-6537* | 18 |
| Hebron | Blackledge Country Club, West St.; *228-9483* | 18 |
| | Tallwood Country Club, Rte. 85; *646-1151* | 18 |

| | | |
|---|---|---|
| Killingly | Woodlawn Country Club, South St., Danielson; *774-9438* | 9 |
| Lisbon | Lisbon Country Club, Kendall Rd.; *376-4325* | 9 |
| Litchfield | Stonybrook Golf Course, Milton Rd.; *567-9977* | 9 |
| Madison | Madison Country Club, Rte. 1; *245-2336* (May 15–Sept. 15 only) | 18 |
| Manchester | Manchester Country Club, South Main St.; *646-0103* | 18 |
| | Red Rock Golf Course, Slater St.; *649-8083* | 9 |
| Meriden | Pleasant View Golf Course, Paddock Ave.; *235-2953* | 9 |
| | Hunter Memorial Golf Course, Westfield Rd.; *634-9573* | 18 |
| Middlefield | Indian Spring Golf Course, Mack Rd.; *349-8109* | 9 |
| | Lyman Meadow Golf Club, Rte. 157; *349-8055* | 18 |
| Naugatuck | Hop Brook Golf Course, North Church St.; *729-8013* | 9 |
| New Britain | Stanley Golf Course, Hartford Rd.; *225-7312* | |
| | Blue Course | 9 |
| | Red Course | 9 |
| | White Course | 9 |
| New Haven | Alling Memorial Golf Course, Eastern St.; *562-0151 Ext. 598* | 18 |
| New Milford | Candlewood Valley Country Club, Danbury Rd.; *354-6250* | 18 |
| North Branford | Rolling Acres Golf Club, Rte. 80; *484-0631* | 9 |
| Norwalk | Oak Hills Park Golf Course, Fillow St.; *838-0303* | 18 |
| Norwich | Norwich Golf Club, West Thames St.; *889-1303* | 18 |

| | | |
|---|---|---|
| Orange | Orange Hills Country Club, Racebrook Rd.; *795-4161* | 18 |
| Plymouth | Pequabuck Golf Club, Pequabuck; *583-9661* | 9 |
| Pomfret | Pomfret Golf Club, Pomfret Center; *928-4159* | 9 |
| Prospect | Highland Greens Golf Course, Cook Rd.; *758-4022* | 9 |
| Salisbury | Hotchkiss Golf Course, Hotchkiss School; *435-9033* | 9 |
| Seymour | Great Hill Country Club, Great Hill Rd.; *888-3250* | 9 |
| Simsbury | Simsbury Farms Golf Course, Old Farms Rd.; *658-2512* | 18 |
| Somers | Cedar Knob Golf Course, Billings Rd.; *749-3550* (Reservations required for weekend play) | 18 |
| Southington | Patton Brook Country Club, Pattonwood Dr.; *628-0985* | 18 |
| | Pine Valley Golf Course, Welch Rd.; *628-0879* | 18 |
| | Southington Country Club, Savage Rd.; *628-7032* | 18 |
| Stonington | Pequot Golf Course, Wheeler Rd.; *535-1898* | 18 |
| | Elmridge Golf Course, Elmridge Rd., Pawcatuck; *599-4648* | 18 |
| | Stonington Manor Club, Rte. 1; *535-9336* | 9 |
| Torrington | Eastlawn Country Club, Torringford West St.; *489-9102* | 9 |
| Waterbury | East Mountain Golf Course, East Mountain Rd.; *753-1425* | 18 |
| | Western Hills Golf Course, Park Rd.; *756-1211* | 18 |
| West Hartford | Buena Vista Golf Course, Buena Vista Rd.; *523-1133* (13–14-year- |

|  | olds permitted if accompanied by an adult) | 9 |
|  | Rockledge Country Club, South Main St.; *521-3156* (no one under 14 permitted) | 18 |
| Winchester | Greenwoods Country Club, Rte. 183, Winsted; *379-8051* | 9 |
| Windsor | Millbrook Golf Course, Pigeon Hill Rd.; *688-2575* | 18 |
|  | Pine Hill Golf Club, Matianuck Ave.; *688-9796* | 9 |
| Woodstock | Harrisville Golf Club, Harrisville Rd.; *928-6098* | 9 |

**Hiking Trails in Connecticut**

Connecticut has an elaborate system of trails for hikers. It includes the nationally known Appalachian Trail (which goes from Georgia to Maine), a system of trails laid out and maintained by the Connecticut Forest and Park Association, Inc. (a private group), trails developed and maintained by the state within the state parks and forests, and community-developed trails.

Regulations governing the use of state trails are available from the Department of Environmental Protection, State Office Building, Hartford, 06115. The Forest and Park Association trails are, for the most part, on private land and they exist through the courtesy of the various property owners. Experienced hikers know their social obligations under conditions of this sort. Beginning hikers should learn the rules and when in doubt take the most prudent course of action. Obviously, the hiking privilege across private land, if abused, can be withdrawn at any time by the owners of the land.

The complete rules and trail directions exist in *The Connecticut Walk Book*, published by the Connecticut Forest and Park Association, Inc., 1010 Main Street, East Hartford. Good manners alone will suffice but thoughtlessness and ignorance may cause the uninitiated to commit some breach of trail etiquette. Gates and fences, for example, must be left closed. No litter should be left at all on the trails. If a trail is obstructed by a fallen tree limb, take a few moments to clear it. Fires are permitted *only* in official fireplaces. And no fires *at all* are allowed from mid-October to the first of December. The same prohibition applies between the first of March and mid-May. Seasonal conditions during those periods make fires prohibitively dangerous.

The trails maintained by the Association are blazed blue. Some side and loop trails are blue blazed with different-colored center dots. Trails in state parks and forests have a varying system of blazes and this information can be obtained from forest and park rangers. The Appalachian Trail has white blazes.

State trails are in the following state parks and forests: American Legion (Barkhamsted); Cockaponset (Haddam, Killingworth, Durham, Deep River); Gay City (Hebron); Macedonia Brook (Kent); Old Furnace (Killingly); Pachaug (Voluntown, Plainfield, Sterling, Griswold, North Stonington); People's (Barkhamsted, Hartland); Sleeping Giant (Hamden); Tunxis (Hartland, Colebrook, Barkhamsted, Granby). Other state forests and parks offer hiking but do not have formal trail systems.

The city of Waterbury maintains a five-trail system that offers short hikes. Guilford has nearly two thousand acres laced with trails of varying length and difficulty in what is called Westwoods. And the McLean Game Refuge in the towns of Granby and Simsbury also has a trail system.

The trails of the Connecticut Forest and Park Association often pass through state parks and forests (as does the Appalachian Trail) and many times trails coincide. The trails described below are indicated as beginning from the southern end if it is a north-south trail, or from the eastern end if the trail runs east-west. Several of the Association trails continue into Massachusetts or Rhode Island, where they may be part of trail systems in those states.

*Appalachian Trail.* Length: 56 miles. Begins: in New York on Rte. 55 at Webatuck Bridge, about $2\frac{1}{2}$ miles west of Gaylordsville in New Milford. The trail goes through Kent, Cornwall, Sharon, and Salisbury. Ends: west of Rte. 41 in Salisbury, at the Massachusetts border. For detailed instructions and information about the

Appalachian Trail write: Appalachian Trail Conference, Inc., 1718 N Street, N.W., Washington, D.C. 20036.

*Housatonic Range Trail.* Length: 8 miles. Begins: west side, U.S. 7, about 1½ miles north of the center of New Milford. Ends: U.S. 7, just south of Gaylordsville, in New Milford.

*Mattabasett Trail.* Length: 30 miles. Begins: Brainard Hill Rd. just east of Oxbow Rd. in Haddam. Goes through Durham, Killingworth, North Guilford, Wallingford, Middlefield, Middletown, and Berlin. Ends: east of Wilbur Cross Highway on Spruce Brook Rd. in Berlin.

*Mattatuck Trail.* Length: 35 miles. Begins: Mad River Rd. just off Rte. 69 in Wolcott. It runs through Wolcott, Plymouth, Watertown, Morris, Litchfield, Warren, Goshen, and Cornwall. Ends: junction of Appalachian Trail west of Rte. 4 in Cornwall.

*Metacomet Trail.* Length: (to Massachusetts state line) 45 miles. Begins: on U.S. 5, in Berlin, at Orchard Rd. It goes through Berlin, Meriden, New Britain, Southington, Plainville, Farmington, Bloomfield, Simsbury, East Granby, and Suffield. Ends: on Massachusetts state border, South Longyard Rd., in Suffield. The trail continues into Massachusetts and goes to Mt. Monadnock in New Hampshire.

*Natchaug Trail.* Length: 9.5 miles. Begins: north of U.S. 5 on Potter Rd. Goes through Hampton, Chaplin, and Eastford. Ends: east of Rte. 198 on Pilfershire Rd. in Eastford.

*Narragansett Trail.* Length: 16 miles (in Connecticut). Begins: on state border of Rhode Island on Green Fall Rd. in Voluntown. Goes through Voluntown and North Stonington. Ends: south of Rte. 2 on Winterhog Hill Rd. in North Stonington.

*Nehantic Trail.* Length: 14 miles. Begins: north end of Green Fall Pond north of Green Fall Rd. in Voluntown. The trail goes through

Voluntown and Griswold. Ends: Park Rd. in Hopeville Pond State Park in Griswold.

*Nipmuck Trail.* Length: 15 miles. Begins: (eastern branch) on Bassetts Bridge Rd. in Mansfield; (western branch) Puddin Lane in Mansfield. The two southern branches of the trail join just west of Chaffeeville Rd. in Mansfield. The trail then goes north into Willington and Ashford. Ends: on Westford Hill Rd. west of Rte. 89 in Ashford.

*Pachaug Trail.* Length: 15 miles. Begins: at the Rhode Island border in Voluntown, where it is an extension of the Tippecansett Trail, which starts at Beach Pond Park just inside Rhode Island north of Rte. 165. The trail goes through Voluntown and into Griswold. Ends: where Rte. 138 crosses the Pachaug River just east of the village of Pachaug.

*Paugusett Trail.* Length: about 4½ miles. Begins: Indian Wells State Park in Monroe. The short trail joins the Pomperaug Trail at Rte. 34, where it crosses Stevenson Dam on the Housatonic River.

*Pequot Trail.* Length: 10 miles. Begins: at Lantern Hill south of Rte. 2 in North Stonington. Goes through Ledyard and into Preston. Ends: on Rte. 165 just east of the village of Long Society in Preston.

*Pomperaug Trail.* Length: just under 10 miles. Begins: on East Village Road to the east of Rte. 111 in Monroe. It goes across the Housatonic at Stevenson Dam into Oxford. Ends: in Kettletown State Park in Oxford.

*Quinebaug Trail.* Length: about 7½ miles. Begins: at Lowden Brook in Voluntown, where it briefly coincides with the Pachaug Trail. The trail goes into Plainfield. Ends: at junction of Spaulding Road and Rte. 14A west of the Connecticut Turnpike.

*Quinnipiac Trail:* Length: 21 miles. Begins: just south of the end of Barton St. in North Haven. The trail goes from North Haven through Hamden into Cheshire. Ends: on Rte. 68 just north of the Cheshire Reservoir in Cheshire.

*Regicides Trail.* Length: 6 miles. Begins: at Judges Cave in West Rock Park in New Haven. The trail goes into Hamden and joins the Quinnipiac Trail just north of West Shepard St. in Hamden.

*Shenipsit Trail.* Length: 30 miles. Begins: on Great Hill Rd. north of Cobalt in East Hampton. The trail (while it has some gaps) goes through Portland, Glastonbury, Manchester, and Bolton, this section ending at Bolton Center Rd. (Rte. 85). The next section begins on Rte. 140 in Ellington near its junction with Hopkins Road. This part of the completed trail goes through Ellington into Somers. Ends: at Stafford Rd. in Somers, a short distance south of the Massachusetts border.

*Tunxis Trail.* Length: nearly 57 miles. Begins: in Southington at the intersection of Mt. Vernon Rd. and Whitman Rd. The trail has a gap of several miles in Bristol. There also are numerous looping side trails for short, return-to-starting-point hikes. The main trail goes from Southington, through Wolcott, and into Bristol. This southern section ends just south of Rte. 72 west of Lake Ave. in Bristol. The trail begins again in Plymouth on March Rd. west of a reservoir dam. With no more breaks in it, the trail goes from Plymouth through Burlington, New Hartford, Canton, Barkhamsted, and Hartland to the Massachusetts border at Pell Rd. in Hartland.

### Fishing and Hunting

An abstract of Connecticut laws and regulations covering hunting, trapping, and sport fishing is available from the State Department of Environmental Protection, Hartford, and may also be available in some town clerks' offices. Ordinances affecting the use of boats are contained in the *Connecticut Boating Manual* (see "Boating").

State hunting and fishing areas are posted.

Licenses are required of persons sixteen years of age or over, and must be displayed on outer clothing at all times while hunting, trapping or fishing.

No license to trap will be offered a nonresident.

A nonresident, three-day fishing license is available for any three consecutive days between July 1 and December 31. Licenses are also required to fish in tidal waters within the inland district.

Fishing and hunting seasons, hours, creel and bag limits, and taking are established by state regulation. Waterfowl seasons, hours, limits, and taking are governed by federal regulations.

The Connecticut Department of the Environment stocks over 250 trout streams, which are open to public fishing. The state controls the fishing rights on all or parts of many streams through cooperative agreement with the owners, by lease or by outright ownership; these streams are so posted.

**Regional listing of stocked streams**

**(A)** = Largest and most heavily stocked.

**(B)** = Other good small stream trout fishing.

**Litchfield–Hartford Area** **(A)** *Bantam River* (outlet) from Bantam to West Morris Station. Restricted to fly fishing as indicated by posters.

*Blackberry River,* from Norfolk to Canaan.

*Farmington River,* Pleasant Valley to New Hartford, intermittent stretches at Satan's Kingdom, New Hartford; Cherry Brook, Canton; Winchell Smith, Farmington; Polychoke, Simsbury; Spoonville Bridge, East Granby; Collinsville Dam to Rte. 4 Bridge at Unionville.

*Farmington River, West Branch,* intermittent stretches in Colebrook, Hartland, and Barkhamsted.

*Furnace Brook,* from the bridge on Rte. 4 upstream approximately 1½ miles as indicated by posters.

*Housatonic River,* intermittent stretches. Restricted to fly fishing in Francis L. Sheane Memorial Area (Housatonic Meadows State Park) as indicated by posters.

*Nepaug River,* New Hartford from Niles Rd. to Rte. 25 bridge.

*Salmon Brook* and *Salmon Brook East Branch,* Granby and East

Granby, from Rte. 189, North Granby below Goddards Pond to mouth.

*Salmon Brook West Branch,* intermittent stretches in North Granby and below Rte. 10, Granby.

*Sandy Brook,* from Sandy Brook Rd., Colebrook to mouth.

**Litchfield–Hartford Area     (B)**     *Bakersville Brook,* New Hartford; *Bantam River* (tributary to Bantam Lake), Litchfield; *Beaver Brook,* Barkhamsted; *Belcher Brook,* Berlin; *Branch Brook,* Thomaston, Watertown; *Bunnell Brook,* Burlington; *Butternut Brook,* Litchfield; *Cannons Brook,* Suffield, Granby; *Carsh Brook,* Sharon; *Cherry Brook,* Canton; *Coppermine Brook,* Bristol; *Eight Mile River,* Southington; *Furnace Brook,* Cornwall; *Hall Meadow Brook,* Torrington, Goshen; *Hancock Brook,* Plymouth, Waterbury; *Hatchery Brook,* Berlin; *Howell Pond Brook,* Hartland; *Iron Ore Brook,* Bloomfield; *Ivy Mountain Brook,* Goshen; *Kent Falls Brook,* Kent, Warren; *Lake Waramaug Brook,* Warren; *Lead Mine Brook and West Branch,* Thomaston, Harwinton; *Macedonia Brook,* Kent; *Mad River,* Norfolk; *Mad River,* Wolcott; *Marshepaug River,* Goshen; *Mill Brook,* Windsor, Bloomfield; *Mohawk Brook,* Cornwall; *Morgan Brook,* Barkhamsted; *Muddy Brook,* Suffield; *Naugatuck River,* east branch, Torrington, Winchester; *Northfield Brook,* Thomaston, Litchfield; *Potter Brook,* Cornwall; *Quinnipiac River,* Meriden; *Riga Brook,* Salisbury; *Shepaug River East Branch,* Goshen, Cornwall; *State Line Brook,* Suffield, *Stony Brook,* Suffield; *Stratton Brook,* Simsbury; *Taylor Brook,* Winchester; *Ten Mile River,* Cheshire, Southington; *Torringford Brook,* New Hartford; *Unionville Brook,* Farmington; *Wash Brook,* Bloomfield; *Wickwire Brook,* Canaan, Cornwall; *Whiting River,* North Canaan, Norfolk.

**Fairfield–New Haven Area     (A)**     *Aspetuck River,* east branch, intermittent stretches from New Preston down through Wellesville, New Milford.

*Farmill River,* intermittent stretches from Huntington Center downstream to junction with Housatonic River as indicated by posters; upstream from Waverly Rd. approximately $\frac{3}{4}$ mile as indicated by posters.

*Mill River,* Hamden, intermittent stretches from Tuttle Ave. south to Skiff St.

*Muddy River,* Wallingford and North Haven, intermittent stretches from below McKenzie Res. to Spring St., North Haven.

*Norwalk River,* from Rte. 35, Ridgefield, to Riverside Ave. Park, Norwalk.

*Pequonnock River,* from Stepney Depot to Beardsley Park, Bridgeport.

*Pequonnock River,* west branch, Monroe.

*Pomperaug River,* from North Woodbury to South Britain.

*Rippowam River,* Stamford.

*Saugatuck River,* intermittent stretches as indicated by posters from Rte. 7, Danbury, south to 1 mile north of Mark Twain Library on Rte. 53, Redding. Also intermittent stretches from Saugatuck Reservoir Dam downstream to salt water. Restricted to fly fishing below Dorr's Mill Dam to Merritt Pkwy. as indicated by posters.

*Shepaug River,* scattered sections in Roxbury Station, Woodville.

**Fairfield–New Haven Area (B)** *Aspetuck River,* Fairfield, Weston; *Ball Pond Brook,* New Fairfield; *Beacon Hill Brook,* Bethany, Naugatuck; *Bladens Brook,* Woodbridge, Seymour; *Bronson Brook,* Beacon Falls; *Byram River,* east branch, Greenwich; *East Swamp Brook,* Danbury, Bethel; *Eight Mile Brook,* Southbury; *Five Mile River,* New Canaan, Darien; *Fulling Mill Brook,* Prospect, Naugatuck; *Hop Brook,* Middlebury, Naugatuck, Waterbury; *Hopp Brook,* Bethany; *Indian River,* Milford; *Indian Hole Brook,* Shelton; *Kettletown Brook,* Southbury; *Little River,* Oxford; *Long Meadow Pond Brook,* Middlebury; *Long Swamp Brook,* Middlebury; *Mianus River,* Greenwich, Stamford; *Mill River,* Fairfield, Easton; *Mopus Brook,* Ridgefield; *Morrissey Brook,* New Milford; *Nonewaug River,* Bethlehem, Woodbury; *Pequonnock River,* west branch, Monroe; *Pond Brook,* Newtown; *Pootatuck River,* Newtown; *Race Brook,* Orange; *Ridgefield Brook,* Ridgefield; *Saugatuck River,* west branch, Weston, Westport; *Sawmill Brook,* Sherman; *Silvermine Brook,* New Canaan, Norwalk, Wilton; *Sprain Brook,* Washington, Woodbury; *Titicus Brook,* Ridgefield; *Town Farm Brook,* New Haven; *Transylvania Brook,* Southbury; *Two Mile Brook,*

Orange; *Weekeepeenee Brook,* Bethlehem, Woodbury; *Wepawaug River,* Orange; *West River,* Woodbridge, New Haven.

### Tolland-Middlesex Area    (A)    *Blackledge River,* intermittent state-owned stretches from a point 1½ miles north of Rte. 6A southerly to junction with Salmon River.

*Branford River,* Branford and North Branford, from cement bridge on Rte. 139 downstream to Wards Mill Pond. Section from Rte. 139 upstream to about 1 mile above the Valley Rd. Bridge restricted to women only.

*Chatfield Hollow Brook,* Cockaponset State Forest, Killingworth, above Schreeders Pond.

*Coginchaug River,* Durham-Middlefield, intermittent stretches along Rte. 17, from Durham to Wadsworth Falls State Park.

*Dickinson Creek,* from Rte. 6A to junction with Salmon River.

*Eight Mile River,* Devil's Hop Yard State Park, East Haddam.

*Farm River,* East Haven, intermittent stretches from rifle range, East Haven, north to Bush Shop Pond, Northford.

*Fenton River,* intermittent stretches from Daleville, E. Willington, south to Rte. 89.

*Hammonasset River,* Madison, Killingworth, and Clinton, intermittent stretches, mouth to Fields Bridge.

*Hop River,* Bolton, Columbia, Coventry, Andover.

*Jeremys River,* Colchester, intermittent stretches from old U.S. 2 to junction with Blackledge River.

*Latimer Brook,* East Lyme.

*Mt. Hope River,* from its junction with the Fenton River north to Rte. 44.

*Roaring Brook,* intermittent stretches, Nipmuck State Forest, Stratford, to Willimantic River.

*Salmon River,* intermittent stretches from junction with Blackledge River to Power House at Leesville. Restricted to fly fishing from Day Pond Bridge to Browns Dam as indicated by posters.

*Scantic River,* intermittent stretches as indicated by posters from state line to head of Somerville Mill Pond as indicated by stream-pond demarcation line poster and from 100 yds. below the dam, approximately 1 mile downstream.

*Skungamaug River,* intermittent stretches from bridge at Rte. 74 downstream as indicated by posters.

**Tolland–Middlesex Area (B)** *Abbey Brook,* Somers; *Alden Brook,* Stafford; *Allyn's Brook,* Durham; *Asman's Brook,* Durham; *Beaver Meadow Brook,* Haddam; *Bible Rock Brook,* Middletown, Haddam; *Blackledge River,* Bolton; *Boones Brook,* Westbrook; *Broad Brook,* Ellington, East Windsor; *Buck Brook,* Portland; *Buckhorn Brook,* Enfield; *Butternut Brook,* East Windsor; *Candlewood Hill Brook,* Haddam; *Cattle Lot Brook,* East Hampton; *Cedar Swamp Brook,* Mansfield; *Cedar Swamp Brook,* Stafford; *Charter Brook,* Ellington, Somers; *Conant Brook,* Wellington; *Cox Brook,* Portland; *Crystal Lake Brook,* Stafford; *Dark Hollow Brook,* Glastonbury; *Deep River,* Deep River; *Delphi Brook,* Stafford; *East River,* Guilford; *Falls River,* Essex; *Fawn Brook,* Hebron; *Fawn Brook,* Marlborough; *Flat Brook,* East Hampton; *Fraser Brook,* Salem; *Fresh Water Brook,* Enfield; *Furnace Brook,* Stafford; *Gifford Brook,* Columbia; *Ginger Brook,* Stafford; *Great Brook,* Chester, Haddam; *Green River,* East Hampton; *Gulf Stream,* Somers; *Harris Brook,* Salem; *Hemlock Valley Brook,* East Haddam; *Hope Valley Brook,* Hebron; *Huzzle Guzzle Brook,* Madison; *Indian River,* Clinton, Killingworth; *Jawbuck Brook,* Enfield; *Johnson's Brook,* South Windsor; *Laurel Brook,* Middletown, Middlefield; *Long Hill Brook,* Middletown; *Meadow Brook,* Colchester; *Menunketesuck Brook,* Killingworth, Westbrook; *Middle River,* Stafford; *Mine Brook,* East Hampton; *Muddy Gutter Brook,* East Hampton; *Neck River,* Madison; *Parmelee Brook,* Durham; *Pataconk Lake,* Chester; *Pine Brook,* East Hampton; *Podunk River,* South Windsor; *Ponset Brook,* Haddam; *Raymond Brook,* Hebron; *Reservoir Brook,* Portland; *Roaring Brook,* Glastonbury; *Roaring Brook,* Haddam; *Salmon Brook,* Glastonbury; *Soestrom Brook,* East Hampton; *Sumner Brook,* Middletown; *Tankerhoosen River,* Vernon; *Thrasher Brook,* Somers; *Trout Brook,* Westbrook; *Wadsworth Brook,* Durham; *Watchaug Brook,* Somers; *Weaver Brook,* Mansfield; *West River,* Guilford; *Willeys Brook,* East Hampton; *Woods Stream,* Somers.

**Windham–New London Area    (A)**    *Beaver Brook,* from highway bridge above Donahue's Pond, Baltic to 1 mile below Bailey's Ravine.

*Bigelow Brook,* junction with Natchaug River about 7 miles northerly to G. H. Meyer's land in Yale Forest, Union.

*Blackwell's Brook,* intermittent stretches, from 1 mile above U.S. 6 to junction with Quinebaug River.

*Broad Brook,* Preston, from junction with Quinebaug River to ¼ mile above cement bridge on Rte. 164.

*Five Mile River,* Killingly, Putnam, Rte. 44 downstream to Rte. 12, Killingly.

*Great Meadow Brook,* Pachaug State Forest, Voluntown.

*Hunt's Brook,* Waterford, intermittent stretches from ¼ mile west of Smith's Cove to dam on Miller's Road.

*Indiantown Brook,* Preston, Ledyard, intermittent stretches from Hallville Pond to Rte. 2.

*Little River,* Canterbury, south of Rte. 14 as indicated by posters.

*Mashamoquet Brook,* Pomfret, intermittent stretches from Mashamoquet State Park downstream.

*Moosup River,* Plainfield, Sterling, intermittent stretches from Sterling Pond to the Rhode Island line.

*Mt. Misery Brook,* Pachaug State Forest, Voluntown.

*Myron Kinnie Brook,* Pachaug State Forest, Voluntown.

*Natchaug River,* from Phoenixville to Kirby's Mills, Mansfield Hollow.

*Pachaug River,* Pachaug State Forest, Voluntown. (Demarcation line between Pachaug River and Beachdale Pond the west side of the bridge on Rte. 49.)

*Quanduck Brook,* intermittent stretches from Potter Mill Section to junction with Moosup River.

*Quinebaug River,* Canterbury, Plainfield, Griswold from Rte. 205 bridge at Wauregan to Aspinook Pond and stretches below Jewett City.

*Shetucket River,* Sprague, from Scotland Dam downstream to the highway bridge at Baltic.

*Shunock Brook,* North Stonington, intermittent stretches from Hewitts Pond to the Rhode Island line.

*Snake Meadow Brook,* intermittent stretches from its source to Moosup River, as indicated by posters.

*Still River,* Eastford, intermittent stretches along Rte. 198.

*Susquetonscut Brook,* Franklin, Lebanon, intermittent stretches from Rte. 207 to Yantic River.

*Yantic River,* from Fitchville Pond upstream as indicated by posters to section posted by East Glastonbury Fish & Game Club above Barstow Bridge. Restricted to fly fishing in sections above Johnson's Bridge.

**Windham–New London Area    (B)**    *Anquilla Brook,* Stonington; *Backwater Brook,* Thompson; *Blissville Brook,* Lisbon; *Buttonball Brook,* Chaplin; *Carson Brook,* Sterling; *Copps Brook,* Stonington; *Corry Brook,* Canterbury; *Crooked Brook, East Branch,* Sterling; *Denison Brook,* Voluntown; *English Neighborhood Brook,* Woodstock; *Five Mile Brook,* Thompson; *Gardner Brook,* Bozrah; *Green Falls River,* North Stonington, Voluntown; *Herridean Brook,* Woodstock; *Horse Brook,* Plainfield; *Jordan Brook,* Waterford; *Kitt Brook,* Canterbury; *Knowlton Brook,* Ashford; *Lantern Hill Brook,* North Stonington; *Long Branch Brook,* Thompson; *Lowden Brook,* Voluntown; *Mary Brown Brook,* Putnam; *Mashentuck Brook,* Killingly; *McCarthy's Brook,* Franklin; *McGuire Brook,* Groton; *Merrick Brook,* Scotland; *Mill Brook,* Plainfield; *Mill Brook,* Woodstock; *Mountain Brook,* Franklin; *Muddy Brook,* Woodstock; *Oxoboxo Brook,* Montville; *Pease Brook,* Lebanon; *Pendleton Hill Brook,* North Stonington; *Quaker Meeting House Brook,* Pomfret; *Seth Williams Brook,* Ledyard; *Shunway Brook,* Thompson; *Stony Brook,* Montville; *Taylor Brook,* Woodstock; *Trading Cove Brook,* Bozrah, Montville, Norwich; *Whetstone Brook,* Killingly; *Whitfords Brook,* Ledyard, Stonington; *Wood River,* Voluntown; *Wyassup Brook,* North Stonington.

*Saltwater Fishing* is available in Lond Island Sound throughout the year. There are eighteen varieties of fish available, with the big season running from mid-April to mid-November.

*Seasons* for the fish varieties are:

| | |
|---|---|
| Blackfish | May–October |
| Bluefish | Mid-June–October |
| Bonita | July–mid-September |

| Cod | All year |
|---|---|
| Dolphin | August |
| Flounder | April–October |
| Fluke | June–September |
| Mackerel | May–October |
| Marlin | July–mid-September |
| Pollock | All year |
| Porgies | June–September |
| Sea Bass | June–October |
| Shark | July–September |
| Snapper Blues | August–October |
| Striped Bass | All year |
| Swordfish | Mid-June–mid-September |
| Tuna | July–mid-September |
| Weakfish | June–October |

**Regulated Hunting Areas**

Areas are marked with posters. Following is a list of major sections; inquire locally regarding smaller sections; and see the places listed for permits.

**(A)** = License and permit required.

**(B)** = State-owned or leased areas. License required, permit not required.

**Litchfield–Hartford Area    (A)**    *Bristol Fish and Game Club:* Terryville, Harwinton, and Bristol. North of Rte. 6/Bristol Hardware Co., 430 Middle St.; S and M Fly Tying, 95 Union St., Bristol.

*Goshen Rod & Gun Club:* Goshen. South of Rte. 4 and west of Rte. 63/West Goshen Store, West Goshen.

*Harwinton Rod & Gun Club:* Harwinton and New Hartford. Scattered areas along Harmony Hill Rd., Woodchuck Lane, County Line Rd. and Hill Rd/Harwinton Pharmacy, Litchfield Rd., Harwinton.

*Suffield Sportsmen's Association:* Suffield. From North St., Windsor Locks north to Massachusetts state line, east to the Connecticut River and south to Russell Road, East Granby/Town Clerk, Suffield.

*Torrington Fish & Game Club:* Torrington, Goshen, Winchester,

Harwinton, and Litchfield/Sportsmen's Paradise, 182 Water St., Torrington.

**Litchfield–Hartford Area   (B)**   *Cromwell Meadows Management Area:* Cromwell, Middletown. North of Sebethe River, west of railroad tracks. Enter area by turning west from Rte. 9 on South St., Cromwell. Entrance is approximately ½ mile from Rte. 9. *Farmington (state-leased):* Farmington. In southwestern section north of Rte. 6. Turn north off Rte. 6 on Rte. 117. *Metropolitan District (state-leased):* Colebrook and Hartland—Hogback Dam Section. New Hartford—Greenwood Dam Section. *Simsbury Management Area:* Simsbury.

**Fairfield–New Haven Area   (A)**   *Brookfield Sportsmen's Club:* Brookfield Joe's Barber Shop, Rte. 7, Brookfield.

*Hamden Fish & Game Prot. Assoc.:* Hamden. West and northwest section/Tac's Service Station, 878 Dixwell Ave., Hamden; Ardmore Office Supply, 2582 Whitney Ave., Hamden.

*Meriden Rod and Gun Club and Meriden Farmers:* Meriden and Cheshire—Broadbrook area/Ed's Sporting Arms, 237 West Main St., Meriden; The Tackle Box, West Main St., Meriden.

*New Milford Sportsmen's Association:* New Milford. Scattered areas in Merryall and Second Hill sections/Village Hardware, 12 Main St., New Milford.

*Seymour Fish and Game Club:* Oxford. East and northeast sections/Duke's Service Station, 163 West St., Seymour.

*Wallingford Rod & Gun Club:* Wallingford/Wallingford Rod & Gun Club, 411 North Branford Rd., Wallingford.

*Woodbury-Southbury Rod & Gun Club:* Woodbury and Southbury/C. L. Adams & Co., Woodbury and Southbury.

**Fairfield–New Haven Area   (B)**   *Bethel (East Swamp) Management Area:* Bethel. *Bridgeport Hydraulic (state-leased):* Monroe, Shelton, and Trumbull. *Charles E. Wheeler Wildlife Area:* (waterfowl) Stratford, Milford, and Orange (Housatonic River).

**Tolland–Middlesex Area   (A)**   *Belltown Sportsmen's Club:* East Hampton. Chestnut Hill and Hog Hill sections south of Rte. 16

and Flanders section/Clark's Corner Store, 73 Main St., and Paul's Home and Garden Supply, Rte. 66, East Hampton.

*Bolton Area:* Bolton. ½ mile north of Bolton-Hebron town line, and west of Rte. 85/Rose & Bill's Store, Rte. 85, Bolton.

*Bradford Rod & Gun Club:* Branford/Page's Sport Shop, 1000 Main St., Branford.

*East Windsor-Enfield Farmers:* East Windsor and Enfield. From junction of Rte. 5 and Trombly Rd. east to Rte. 140, along Rte. 5 to Weymouth Rd., Enfield, east on Rte. 140 to Scantic River; from junction of Rtes. 5 and 140 to Rte. 191 east of Melrose, north to Hazardville, along Rte. 191/Enfield town clerk and landowners.

*Glastonbury Sportsmen's Assoc.:* Glastonbury. Along Rte. 17 from East Hartford town line to Portland town line and along Rte. 2 from East Glastonbury to junction of Rtes. 2 and 17/Glastonbury Sports Center, 361 New London Turnpike, Glastonbury.

*Guilford Sportsmen's Assoc.:* Guilford/Shoreline T.V., 13 Water St., Guilford.

*Higganum-Haddam Rod & Gun Club:* Haddam. Little City and Candlewood Hill section/Town and Country T.V., Main St., Higganum.

*Middlefield Fish & Game Club:* Middlefield. East of Rte. 157 and along Rte. 145/John Jagoda, 577 Ross Rd., Rockfall.

*Middletown Sportsmen's Club, Inc.:* Middletown/Dreher-Smith, South Main St., Middletown.

*Nathan Hale State Forest Management Area:* Andover and Coventry/Coventry Police Station.

*Pataconk Fish & Game Assoc.:* Chester. Vicinity Rtes. 9 and 148/Carini's Hardware, Main St., Chester.

*Portland Farmers Fish & Game Club:* Portland. Great Hill, both sides Great Hill Rd., and Wangunk Meadow area, Gildersleeve/Western Auto, Rte. 66, Portland.

*Suburban Sportsmen's Assoc.:* North Branford and Northford. South of Northford Center between Rte. 17 and 22/Village Gun Shop, Rtes. 17 and 22, Northford.

*Westfield Sportsmen's Club:* Middletown. Westfield section west of Ridgewood Rd. from Sebethe River or Little River to Westfield St. and west of Middle St/ J. McCoid, Westfield Store, East Street, Westfield.

**Tolland–Middlesex Area** **(B)** *Durham Meadows:* Durham. North of Rte. 17, 1 mile south of village. *Great Harbor:* (waterfowl) Guilford. Reached by leaving southwest corner of Guilford Green and going west on Water St. (Rte. 146) for 1.7 mile. Area is north and south of road. *Great Island:* (waterfowl) Old Lyme. Mouth of Connecticut River; can be reached by boat only. Take Rte. 156 from Old Lyme, turn right at four corners, after railroad underpass known as Smith's Neck Rd. Continue on hard surface to state boat-launch site. *Haddam Neck:* Haddam and East Haddam. *Higganum Meadows:* Haddam. *Holbrook Pond:* Hebron. North on Rte. 85 out of Hebron Center; second paved road to the right. *Larson Lot Management Area:* Westchester. Shalor Hill Road west of Rte. 149. *Lord's Cove and Nott Island:* (waterfowl) Lyme. First town landing approximately ½ mile on Rte. 156 from Rte. 1. *Mansfield (state-leased):* Mansfield, Chaplin, and Windham. *Dr. John E. Flaherty Field Trial Area (Pelton's Pasture):* East Windsor. East from Rte. 5 opposite E. Windsor H.S. No hunting permitted on authorized field trial days. *Ragged Rock Creek:* (waterfowl) Old Saybrook. Off Connecticut River north of Ragged Rock Creek. Boat landing on North Cove Rd. Boats may also put in north of steamboat dock. *South Windsor (state-leased):* South and East Windsor. Between Main St. and the Connecticut River near east end of Bissell Bridge. Access by dirt road at King St. extension. Scattered sections at Barber Hill, South Windsor, and East Road, East Windsor. *Selden's Island:* (waterfowl only) Lyme. *Tolland (state-leased):* Tolland, Vernon, Ellington, East Windsor, Somers, and Enfield. From junction of Rtes. 15 and 83, south of Rte. 15 to Tankerhoosen Brook; along Rte. 83 from junction with Rte. 15 north to Massachusetts state line; along Rte. 140 from Rte. 83 to East Windsor town line; along Rte. 15 from Tolland Center to Nye Holman State Forest and Mile Hill Rd., Tolland. *Wangunk Meadows:* Portland. Off Rte. 17A. *Wopowog Management Area:* East Hampton, Haddam & East Haddam. East of Rte. 196; ¼ mile north of junction of Rtes. 151 and 196.

**Windham–New London Area** **(A)** *Eastern Connecticut Sportsmen's Assoc.:* Ashford. South of Warrenville on Rte. 89; east of Ashford-Willington line on Rte. 44A/Ashford Shopping Center, Warrenville.

*Norwich Fish & Game Assoc. and Wawecus Hill Farmers:* Norwich and Bozrah. North of Rte. 82 and along Rte. 2/See posters for permit agents.

*Sprague Rod & Gun Club:* Franklin and Sprague. Along Pautipaug Hill Road, north of Rte. 297, along Church Hill Rd., Baltic/Town Clerk; Allen Hardware, Baltic.

*Woodstock Landowners:* Woodstock. Rte. 171 from West to South Woodstock and Rte. 169 from South to North Woodstock/ Woodstock Variety Store, South Woodstock.

*Yale Forest:* Eastford, Union, and Ashford/Harold Barrett's Store, Eastford; Hall's Annteaks, Union.

**Windham–New London Area    (B)**    *Assekonk Swamp:* North Stonington. South of village and Rte. 2.    *Barn Island:* Stonington. Six miles from Mystic Center on Rte. 1 toward Westerly, R.I., turn at head of Wequetequock Cove, bear right to sound.    *Bartlett Brook Management Area:* Lebanon and Franklin. Along Rtes. 207, 87, and 32.    *Brooklyn (state-leased):* Brooklyn. South of Rte. 6 along Rte. 169, North Brooklyn.    *Franklin Swamp:* North Franklin. East of Rte. 32 halfway to Yantic.    *Lebanon-Franklin (state-leased):* Lebanon and Franklin. Along Rtes. 207, 87, and 32.    *Pease Brook:* Lebanon. Reached via East Hebron Turnpike Rd.    *Pudding Hill Management Area:* Scotland. .Along Rte. 97 north of Rte. 14.    *Quinebaug River:* Canterbury and Plainfield. From Rte. 14 upstream for about 3 miles, both sides of river, including land along Blackwell Brook where it enters the Quinebaug.    *Rose Hill Management Area:* Preston and Ledyard. East of Rte. 117, south of Rte. 2 to Thomas Road.    *Ross Marsh Management Area:* Killingly and Sterling. On Quanduck Brook, south of Rte. 6.    *Tetreault Pond:* Killingly.

## Connecticut Highway Picnic Areas

Many state and U.S. highways in Connecticut have picnic areas for travelers. Although camping is prohibited at these sites, most have fireplaces (F) available, many have rest rooms (R), and some have water (W).

| Route | Location | Name | Facilities |
|-------|----------|------|------------|
| U.S. 1 | Milford | Liberty Grove | F, R, W |
| U.S. 1A | Waterford | Oswegatchie Rest | F |
| Conn. 2 | Colchester | The Old Bank | F |
| Conn. 2 | N. Stonington | Indiantown Rest | F |
| Conn. 2 | N. Stonington | Lantern Hill Rest | F, R |
| | | | |
| Conn. 4 | Burlington | Woodruff Hill | F, R |
| Conn. 4 | Cornwall | Furnace Brook | F, R |
| Conn. 4 | Cornwall | Fishing Area # 1 | F |
| Conn. 4 | Cornwall | Fishing Area # 2 | F |
| Conn. 4 | Harwinton | Birge Park | None |
| | | | |
| Conn. 4 | Harwinton | Cooks Dam | F |
| Conn. 4 | Sharon | Grist Mill | F, R |
| U.S. 6 | Bolton | Bolton Pines | F, R, W |
| U.S. 6 | Bristol | Carrington Park | F |
| U.S. 6 | Brooklyn | Blackwell's View | F, R |
| | | | |
| U.S. 6 | Chaplin | Button Ball Brook | F, R, W |
| U.S. 6 | Columbia | Riverside Elms | F, R |
| U.S. 6 | Danbury | Mill Plain Rest | F |
| U.S. 6 | Farmington | Shade Swamp | F, R |
| U.S. 6 | Newtown | Pleasant Valley Rest | F, R |
| | | | |
| U.S. 6 | Southbury | Maple Shade | None |
| U.S. 6 | Windham | Mansfield Hollow Dam | F, R, W |
| U.S. 7 | Canaan | Housatonic Rest | F, R |
| U.S. 7 | Danbury | Kiss'n Brook | F |
| U.S. 7 | New Milford | Housatonic River | None |
| | | | |
| U.S. 7 | Redding | Riverside | F |
| U.S. 7 | Redding | The Oaks | F |
| U.S. 7 | Wilton | Zion Hill | F |
| Conn. 8 | Beacon Falls | High Rock | F |
| Conn. 9A | Haddam | Seven Falls | F, R, W |
| | | | |
| Conn. 10 | Simsbury | Picnic Area | R |
| Conn. 12 | Lisbon | Quinebaug River View | F |

| Route | Location | Name | Facilities |
|-------|----------|------|------------|
| Conn. 12 | Plainfield | Hilltop View | F |
| Conn. 12 | Putnam | Valley View | None |
| Conn. 12 | Thompson | French River | F |
| | | | |
| Conn. 14 | Sterling | Pitch Pine Grove | F, R |
| Conn. 14 | Sterling | Ye Olde Voluntown Pound | F |
| Conn. 15 | Orange | Wilbur L. Cross | F, R |
| Conn. 15 | Union | Martin Fenn | F, R |
| Conn. 15 | Union | Union Lands | F, R |
| | | | |
| Conn. 15 | Wallingford | The Glen | F, R, W |
| Conn. 15 | Willington | Rest Area | F, R |
| Conn. 15 | Woodbridge | Woodbridge Rest | F |
| Conn. 16 | Colchester | Babcock Pond | F, R |
| Conn. 17 | North Haven | Harten's Pond | None |
| | | | |
| Conn. 17A | Portland | Wangunk Meadows | F |
| Conn. 20 | Barkhamsted | Hitchcock Chair | F, R |
| Conn. 20 | East Granby | Turkey Hills | F, R |
| Conn. 20 | Granby | E. Branch, Salmon Brook | F, R |
| Conn. 25 | Litchfield | Mt. Tom | None |
| | | | |
| Conn. 25 | New Milford | Hickory Haven | None |
| Conn. 25 | Newtown | Newton Rest | F |
| Conn. 25 | Newtown | Twin Bridges | None |
| Conn. 25 | Washington | East Aspetuck | F |
| Conn. 30 | Tolland | Crystal Springs | F, R, W |
| | | | |
| Conn. 33 | Ridgefield | Twin Maples | F |
| Conn. 34 | Newtown | The Berkshires | F |
| Conn. 39 | Danbury | Clapboard Ridge | F |
| Conn. 41 | Salisbury | Gateway Rest | F |
| Conn. 43 | Cornwall | General Sedgewick | F, R |
| | | | |
| U.S. 44 | Ashford | Nott Memorial | F |
| U.S. 44 | Avon | MacDonald Memorial | F, R |

| Route | Location | Name | Facilities |
|-------|----------|------|------------|
| U.S. 44 | Eastford | Frog Rock | F, R |
| U.S. 44 | New Hartford | Satan's Kingdom | F, R |
| U.S. 44 | Norfolk | Albany Turnpike | F, R |
| U.S. 44 | North Canaan | Garden Shadows | F, R |
| U.S. 44 | Putnam | Five Mile River | F, R |
| U.S. 44A | Coventry | Middle Turnpike Rest | None |
| Conn. 47 | Washington | Bee Brook | F |
| Conn. 47 | Woodbury | Toll Gate | F |
| Conn. 49 | Voluntown | Roadside Oaks | F |
| Conn. 63 | Goshen | Robert's Hill | F |
| Conn. 63 | Goshen | Wadham's Grove | F, R, W |
| Conn. 63 | Litchfield | Schermerhorn Grove | F |
| U.S. 64 | Middlebury | Shepardson Haven | F R, W |
| U.S. 64 | Middlebury | Wm. H. Bristol | None |
| U.S. 66 | Marlborough | Marlborough Rest | F |
| Conn. 67 | Bridgewater | Lili-No-Nah | F |
| Conn. 67 | Oxford | John Griffin Wayside | F, R |
| Conn. 67 | Roxbury | Hodge Park | F |
| Conn. 79 | Madison | Madison Pines | F, R |
| Conn. 80 | Deep River | Lake View | F, R |
| Conn. 80 | Deep River | Post Hill | F |
| Conn. 81 | Clinton | Old Toll House | F, R |
| Conn. 82 | Bozrah | By The Rock | F |
| Conn. 82 | Lyme | Roaring Brook | F, R |
| Conn. 82 | Salem | Music Vale Road | F |
| I–84 | Danbury | Rest Area | F, R, W |
| I–84 | Southington Area | Rest Area | F, R, W |
| Conn. 85 | Hebron | Raymond Hill | F |
| Conn. 85 | Salem | Brookside | F, R |
| Conn. 85 | Salem | Shady Brook | F, R |

| Route | Location | Name | Facilities |
|-------|----------|------|------------|
| Conn. 87 | Lebanon | Lebanon Rest | F |
| I-91 | Meriden (South) | Rest Area | F, R, W |
| I-95 | East Lyme | Blue Star Memorial | F, R, W |
| I-95 | N. Stonington | Rest Area | F, R, W |
| I-95 | Westbrook | No Name | R,   W |
| Conn. 97 | Pomfret | Ye Windham Rest | F |
| Conn. 128 | Cornwall | Cobblestone | F |
| Conn. 131 | Thompson | Knollwood | F, R |
| Conn. 133 | Brookfield | Obtuse Hill | None |
| Conn. 149 | East Haddam | Sipple Hill | F |
| Conn. 151 | East Hampton | Sexton Hill | None |
| Conn. 156 | East Lyme | Apple Tree Rest | F, R |
| Conn. 156 | Old Lyme | Shore Road Rest | F, R, W |
| Conn. 161 | Montville | Roadside Birches | F |
| Conn. 163 | Bozrah | Gay Hill | F, R |
| Conn. 165 | Griswold | Pachaug Pond | F, R |
| Conn. 165 | Preston | Folly Works Brook | F, R, W |
| Conn. 179 | Barkhamsted | Washington Hill | F, R |
| Conn. 184 | Groton | Gray Rock | F, R |
| Conn. 184 | N. Stonington | Picnic Area | None |
| Conn. 188 | Oxford | Marion's Grove | F |
| Conn. 190 | Stafford | Towne Grove | F |
| Conn. 197 | Thompson | Quinnebaug Rest | F |
| Conn. 207 | Lebanon | Lebanon Town Pound | F |
| S.R. 800 | Torrington | Still River | F |
| S.R. 816 | Newtown | Pootatuck | F |

## Ski Areas

Brooklyn    *Brooklyn Ski Area,* telephone 774–5937 Church
St., north of U.S. 6, 2 miles east of town.

Cornwall    *Mohawk Mt. Ski Area,* telephone 672–6100 Off

Conn. 4, 4 miles east of U.S. 7, privately operated within Mohawk Mt. State Park.

Middlefield    *Powder Ridge,* telephone 349–3454 Powder Hill Rd. off Conn. 147.

New Hartford    *Ski Sundown,* telephone 379–0610 Conn. 219, two miles north of New Hartford.

Southington    *Mt. Southington Area,* telephone 628–0954 One mile from Int. 84, via Exit 30 (Marion Ave.).

Woodbury    *Tapawingo Ski Area,* telephone 263–2203 Conn. 47, 4 miles north of Woodbury.

## Snowmobile Areas

### State Forests

| | |
|---|---|
| Barkhamsted | *Peoples* State Forest, Rte. 482 |
| Cornwall | *Mohawk* State Forest, Rte. 4 |
| Eastford | *Natchaug* State Forest, Rte. 198 |
| Sharon | *Housatonic* State Forest, Rte. 7 |
| Stafford | *Shenipset* State Forest, Rte. 190 |

### Private Grounds

| | |
|---|---|
| Litchfield | *Cozy Hills,* Rte. 25 |
| | *White Memorial,* Rte. 25 |
| North Canaan | *Lone Oak,* Rte. 44, East Canaan |
| Sterling | *River Bend,* off Rte. 14A, Oneco |
| North Stonington | *Purola Farm,* Rte. 49 |
| Tolland | *Del-Aire,* Shenipsit Lake Rd. |
| Willington | *Moose Meadow,* Moosemeadow Rd., West Willington |

# REFERENCE WORKS

Babbitt, Lewis Hall, *The Amphibia of Conn.* State Geological and Natural History Survey. Bulletin No. 57.

Bradstreet, Howard, *The Story of the War with the Pequots.* Pamphlet 5, Connecticut Tercentenary Commission, Yale U. Press, 1933.

Collins, Henry Hill, Jr., *Complete Field Guide to American Wildlife East, Central and North.* Harper and Bros., N. Y., 1959.

————. *Complete Field Guide to American Wildlife.* Harper and Bros., N. Y., 1959.

*Connecticut: A Guide to Its Roads, Lore and People.* Written by Workers of the Federal Writers' Project, Houghton Mifflin Co., Boston, 1938.

*Connecticut Walk Book.* Conn. Forest & Park Association, 9th Edition, 1972.

*Connecticut Forest Facts.* Conn. Forest Industries Committee, 1963.

*Connecticut Geological and Natural History Survey,* vol. 9, Bulletins 43–48, 1928–30.

Cook, Thomas A. *Geology of Connecticut.* Bond Press, Hartford, 1933.

Crofut, Florence S. M. *Guide to the History and Historic Sites of Conn.* 2 vols. Yale U. Press, 1937.

DeForest, John W. *History of the Indians of Connecticut.* 1852.

Egler, Frank E. and Niering, W. A. *Vegetation of Connecticut*

*Natural Areas,* no. 1, Yale Natural Preserve, New Haven. State Geological and Natural History Survey, 1965.

*Encyclopedia Britannica,* vol. 6, 1964 ed.

Goodwin, George Gilbert, *The Mammals of Conn.* State Geological and Natural History Survey Bulletin. No. 53.

Klimas, John E., Jr. *Wild Flowers of Connecticut.* Walker and Co., N. Y., 1968.

Lee, Storrs, W. *The Yankees of Connecticut.* Henry Holt and Co., N. Y., 1957.

Mason, Randolph, H. F. *Historic Houses of Connecticut.* Pequot Press, 1966.

Rice, William N. and Gregory, Herbert E. *Manual of the Geology of Connecticut.* Hartford Press, Hartford, Conn.

Rickett, H. W., ed. *Wild Flowers of America.* Crown Publishers, Inc., N. Y., 1968.

Roberts, Mervin F. *Tidal Marshes of Conn.* Connecticut Arboretum, Conn. College, New London, Conn., 1971.

Ryerson, Kathleen H. *Rock Hound's Guide to Connecticut.* Pequot Press, Chester, Conn., 1972.

Silverstein, Samuel, *Fifty Common Birds of Connecticut.* Shiver Mountain Press, Washington Depot, Conn., 1972.

Spiess, Mathias, *The Indians of Connecticut.* Pamphlet 19, Connecticut Tercentenary Commission, Yale U. Press, 1933.

Trumbull, Benjamin, *A Complete History of Connecticut.* Maltby, Goldsmith and Co., and Samuel Wadsworth, New Haven, 1818.

Upham, Alan W., *The Flora of Windham County, A Check List.* State Geological and Natural History Survey, 1959.

Van Dusen, Albert E., *Connecticut.* Random House, N. Y., 1961.

Whipple, Chandler, *The Indian in Connecticut.* Berkshire Traveler Press, 1972.

# INDEX

379